# CONTEMPORARY SPORT MANAGEMENT

Janet B. Parks, DA
Beverly R.K. Zanger, MEd
Jerome Quarterman, PhD

Bowling Green State University

Editors

Human Kinetics

**Library of Congress Cataloging-in-Publication Data**

Contemporary sport management / Janet B. Parks, Beverly R.K. Zanger,
   Jerome Quarterman, editors.
      p.  cm.
    Includes bibliographical references and index.
    ISBN 0-87322-836-7
    1. Sports administration.   2. Physical education and training-
-Administration.  I. Parks, Janet B., 1942-   . II. Zanger,
Beverly K.  III. Quarterman, Jerome, 1944-    .
GV713.C66   1998
796'.06'9--dc21                  97-35194
                              CIP

ISBN: 0-87322-836-7

Copyright © 1998 by Janet B. Parks, Beverly R.K. Zanger, and Jerome Quarterman

All rights reserved. Except for use in a review, the reproduction or utilization of this work in any form or by any electronic, mechanical, or other means, now known or hereafter invented, including xerography, photocopying, and recording, and in any information storage and retrieval system, is forbidden without the written permission of the publisher.

**Developmental Editors**: Andrew Smith and Holly Gilly; **Assistant Editors**: John Wentworth, Cassandra Mitchell, and Phil Natividad; **Editorial Assistant**: Laura Seversen; **Copyeditor**: Denelle Eknes; **Proofreader**: Mandolin Slicer Editorial Services; **Indexer**: Tom Brown; **Production Manager**: Judy Rademaker; **Graphic Designer**: Nancy Rasmus; **Graphic Artist**: Sandra Meier; **Photo Editor**: Boyd Lafoon; **Cover Designer**: Jack Davis; **Mac Illustrator**: Sara Wolfsmith; **Printer**: Braun-Brumfield

Human Kinetics books are available at special discounts for bulk purchase. Special editions or book excerpts can also be created to specification. For details, contact the Special Sales Manager at Human Kinetics.

Printed in the United States of America     10  9  8  7  6  5  4  3  2

**Human Kinetics**
Web site: http://www.humankinetics.com/

*United States:* Human Kinetics, P.O. Box 5076, Champaign, IL 61825-5076
1-800-747-4457
e-mail: humank@hkusa.com

*Canada:* Human Kinetics, 475 Devonshire Road, Unit 100, Windsor, ON N8Y 2L5
1-800-465-7301 (in Canada only)
e-mail: humank@hkcanada.com

*Europe:* Human Kinetics, P.O. Box IW14, Leeds LS16 6TR, United Kingdom
(44) 1132 781708
e-mail: humank@hkeurope.com

*Australia:* Human Kinetics, 57A Price Avenue, Lower Mitcham, South Australia 5062
(088) 277 1555
e-mail: humank@hkaustralia.com

*New Zealand:* Human Kinetics, P.O. Box 105-231, Auckland 1
(09) 523 3462
e-mail: humank@hknewz.com

796.06
A1012233
PAR

*To all the undergraduate and graduate sport management students
at Bowling Green State University.
Thank you for being a source of inspiration for all these years!*

Janet B. Parks

*To my son and daughter, Jack and Polly Jo Zanger.
Enjoy the legacy of laughter, love, and loyalty.*

Beverly R.K. Zanger

*To Terrance, my son, and Michele, my daughter.
I wish LMH, my aunt/mother, were still living to see this document.
She would be so proud of me.*

Jerome Quarterman

# ■ Contents

# ■ Preface

In 1985, when we conceived the idea for *Sport & Fitness Management* (Parks & Zanger, 1990), resources that addressed managing sport enterprises were limited. Professors of sport management orientation courses typically used self-prepared materials gleaned from an assortment of articles, books, and personal experiences. Journals such as the *Journal of Sport Management (JSM)*, the *Journal of Legal Aspects of Sport (JLAS)*, and the *Sport Marketing Quarterly (SMQ)* had not yet been published; consequently, articles about managing sport were rare. The North American Society for Sport Management (NASSM) was in its early stages of development; therefore, there was no forum providing opportunities for sport management professors and students to present their research and share their ideas. The Joint Task Force of the National Association for Sport and Physical Education (NASPE) and NASSM had not established curriculum standards, so program content varied widely.

Since 1985, the academic field of sport management has flourished. Several new journals have emerged, many books devoted to sport, fitness, and management have been published, NASSM has become well established as a scholarly association, and the NASPE-NASSM program approval standards have been implemented. These developments and the wealth of additional information currently available about sport management mandated the publication of this new book designed to orient aspiring sport managers to this exciting and rapidly expanding field of study.

## About This Book

*Contemporary Sport Management* is an edited book containing 21 chapters contributed by 26 authors. This diversity of authorship means that readers will benefit from the knowledge and experience of a variety of experts. This diversity is reflected in the operational definitions you will find in the book. For example, individual authors might define the terms skill or classifications in different ways. Such differences are common, not only in sport management literature but in all fields of study. A flexible approach to terminology and an understanding that terms used in different contexts take on different shades of meaning should eliminate any problems you might encounter with definitions.

In this book, we use the broad definition of sport provided by Pitts, Fielding, and Miller (1994), who suggested that sport is any activity, experience, or business enterprise focused on fitness, recreation, athletics, or leisure. According to this definition, the term sport implies a wide spectrum of physical and recreational activities and is not limited to competitive athletics events. This definition of sport allows readers to incorporate fitness, recreation, and other activities into the term, eliminating the need to use sport and fitness management or sport and recreation management repeatedly throughout the book.

This book is designed to orient beginning students to the academic and professional field of sport management. It provides an overview of sport management rather than detailed instructions about how to manage sport enterprises. This distinction is important because the book must meet the needs of the two types of students who typically enroll in sport management orientation classes. Some students are currently majoring in fields such as sport management, exercise specialist, fitness management, or athletic training. These students usually want to learn more about the professional opportunities that await them. Other students are only contemplating majoring in one of these fields, and they want to gain general knowledge about them before making a final decision. The information in this book will be useful to both groups. For some, it will affirm their choice of major. These students will then pursue the remainder of their curriculum with enhanced understanding, insight, and maturity of purpose. After studying this book, other students will discover that sport management isn't really their cup of tea, and they will choose a different major. In either case, the book and the course will have served a valuable purpose.

# Scope and Organization of the Book

The content of this book is based on the philosophy that individuals who are embarking on the study of sport management should begin to understand four primary aspects of the field: disciplinary foundations of sport and physical activity, theoretical and applied foundations of organization and management, opportunities available in various segments of the sport industry, and professional preparation and development. Each section of the book is dedicated to one of these aspects.

## Section I: Disciplinary Foundations of Sport Management

The three chapters in this section constitute the sport studies portion of the book. They introduce students to basic knowledge about sport as an influential entity that permeates our culture and affects people in a variety of ways. This is the first section of the book because we believe that understanding and appreciating historical, psychosocial, and philosophical aspects of sport are critical elements in becoming effective sport managers.

## Section II: Theoretical and Applied Foundations of Management and Organization

The first two chapters of section II are History of Management Thought and Organizational Behavior. These chapters provide critical information about the evolution of contemporary management theories and how we can use theoretical constructs to analyze the structure and behavior of organizations. The third chapter, The Business of Sport, synthesizes the information in the two preceding chapters, discussing organization and management theories as they are applied in the sport industry.

## Section III: Segments of the Sport Industry

The first chapter of this section provides information about applying traditional management skills in sport organizations. Using this information as a foundation, each of the 11 chapters in this section addresses a segment of the sport industry. In developing the framework for this section, we drew on the work of several authors who have studied the sport industry and have examined various approaches to sport management curricular content (DeSensi, Kelley, Blanton, & Beitel, 1990; Parks, Chopra, Quain, & Alguindigue, 1988; Pitts, Fielding, & Miller, 1994). Although each researcher conceptualized sport management differently, we were able to use aspects of each of their interpretations in formulating the content of this section.

## Section IV: Professional Development in Sport Management

The two chapters in this section address professional style and professional preparation. Chapter 20 presents information about individual image, style, and communication. Chapter 21 provides students with necessary information to prepare for success in the sport industry.

# Features of the Book

Following are the key features of *Contemporary Sport Management.*

■ Readers should assume that each chapter is inclusive of diverse populations, such as people of different ages, genders, abilities, social classes, sexual orientations, races, ethnicities, and cultures. There are no separate chapters dedicated to select groups, such as opportunities for women, or sport for the disabled or the Black athlete. The inclusive nature of this text fosters understanding and appreciation of the coexistence of a variety of consumers and opportunities in the sport industry.

■ The unbiased language used throughout the book is a conscious attempt to reflect and embrace this diversity.

■ Although each chapter addresses a particular aspect of sport management, many chapters share important similarities. For example, most chapters include information about publications, governing bodies, and professional associations unique to the topic covered. In many chapters there are references to the economic impact of sport, developments in the international arena, and predictions for the future. Several chapters address ethical, legal, and communication concerns and opportunities for consulting and entrepreneurship.

• All chapters begin with learning objectives, have a summary, learning activities, and guides providing sources for more information. Some chapters contain real-life scenarios, case studies, profiles of sport managers, or news stories that illustrate a point. We hope these features contribute to the user-friendliness of the book.

## Benefits to the Reader

If students conscientiously study the material in this book, they should be able to (a) define sport management and discuss the scope of opportunities the sport industry presents; (b) discuss major challenges confronting various segments of the industry; (c) demonstrate an understanding of historical, psychological, sociological, and philosophical foundations of sport; (d) demonstrate an understanding of management and organizational behavior and how they are applied in sport enterprises; (e) apply information about sport management to diverse populations in an unbiased fashion; (f) demonstrate critical professional skills; and (g) become members of the profession who will have a positive impact on how sport is managed in the future.

## Coeditors and Contributing Authors

Jerome Quarterman, a faculty colleague at Bowling Green State University, joined Janet Parks and Beverly Zanger as a coeditor of *Contemporary Sport Management*. The 23 other authors who contributed chapters to this book are scholars and leaders in their respective fields. The biographical sketches presented on pages 345-349 testify to these authors' credibility and expertise.

## Acknowledgments

Anyone who has attempted a project such as this knows that it could not be done without the assistance of many other people. We are, therefore, eager to acknowledge those individuals and groups whose collective contributions made this book a reality.

First and foremost, we express our sincere gratitude to the 23 contributing authors who enthusiastically and diligently shared their expertise with us. They not only provided up-to-the-minute information, but they also responded to our every request (and there were lots of requests) with courtesy and professionalism. We appreciate their concern for the quality of this book and for dedicating countless hours and untold energy to the education of the sport managers of the future.

We are grateful to Bowling Green State University and the School of Human Movement, Sport, and Leisure Studies for providing the resources that facilitated the completion of this book. We are privileged to be university professors, and we are fortunate to work in an environment that supports such efforts.

We are especially appreciative of the support of Mary Ann Roberton, Director of the School of HMSLS at BGSU. Mary Ann's continual reassurance that our energy was being well-spent and that this book was destined to make an important contribution to sport management was often the stimulus we needed to keep going.

We are proud to acknowledge several BGSU sport administration graduate students who made valuable contributions to the book. Chris Kennedy, Jill Lawson, Duarte Morais, and Brent Ridenour read drafts of the manuscript and offered insightful suggestions. L.J. Archambeau conducted valuable library research. James Hartsook drew the figures in chapter 8. Carla Costa spent countless hours in tedious and exacting proofreading. Our sincere thanks to all of you!

Many thanks to Judy Maxey and Sherry Haskins, College of Education and Human Development Word Processing Center, for their valuable assistance with manuscript preparation. Appreciation is also extended to Margaret Bobb, secretary of the Sport Management, Recreation, and Tourism Division, for typing parts of the manuscript. Additionally, we are grateful to Kim Sebert, Lee Floro-Thompson, and Kevin Work, of BGSU Instructional Media Services, whose talent contributed to the visual appeal of the book.

To Andy Smith and Holly Gilly, our developmental editors, Rick Frey and Becky Lane, our acquisitions editors, and all the other personnel at Human Kinetics Publishers who were associated with this project—thanks for a great collaborative effort!

Finally, Janet extends special thanks to Dolores Black for her patience and encouragement.

# Chapter 1

# Introduction to Sport Management

**Janet B. Parks, Beverly R.K. Zanger, and Jerome Quarterman**
Bowling Green State University

## Learning Objectives

After studying this chapter, you will be able to

1. explain the definition of sport suggested by Pitts, Fielding, and Miller (1994) and list examples of activities that we can consider sport;

2. differentiate between sport and sports;

3. discuss sport management as a profession and as a major area of study;

4. explain the three task clusters that distinguish sport management career groups;

5. discuss the four unique aspects of sport management;

6. explain differences between public and private organizations;

7. give examples of sport organizations within each of the three product segments of the sport industry; and

8. discuss issues of social responsibility within sport management.

---

Sport management has existed for a long time. Sport promoters, event organizers, and athletics directors have been managing sporting events for more years than most people have ever imagined. Consider the following description from the first issue of the *Journal of Sport Management* (Parks & Olafson, 1987, p. 1):

Lest we be deluded by the notion that contemporary sport management is markedly different from the ancient art of staging athletic spectacles, let us consider for a moment the following description of the Games sponsored in 11 B.C. by Herod the Great, King of Judea and Honorary President of the Olympics:

The games began with a magnificent dedication ceremony. Then there were athletic and musical competitions, in which large prizes were given not only to the winners but also—an unusual feature—to those who took second and third place. Bloody spectacles were also presented, with gladiators and wild beasts fighting in various combinations, and there were also horse races.

Large prizes attracted contenders from all areas and this in turn drew great numbers of spectators. Cities favored by Herod sent delegations, and these he entertained and lodged at his own expense. What comes through most clearly . . . is that gigantic sums of money were spent. (Frank, 1984, p. 158)

Herod's Games must have been staged by the counterparts of today's sport managers. Surely, there was a general manager, a business manager, marketing and promotions specialists, communication experts, and crowd-control personnel, all of whom must have had assistants. Obviously, sport management is an ancient practice, and there are many parallels between Herod's Games and ours. It must be noted, however, that sport and management have changed dramatically since ancient times. Today's students who wish to pursue careers as sport managers can learn about this complex field through formal professional preparation programs, such as the one in which you are enrolled.

This chapter is the first step on your journey toward becoming a sport manager. We hope it will provide you with valuable information, setting the stage for you to study subsequent chapters with greater insight. We have included definitions of basic terms, our operational definition of sport management, a discussion of sport management as a practice, and an overview of sport management as an academic major. Additionally, you will read about the responsibilities of sport managers in various settings, the scope of sport management, types of sport organizations, the need for sport managers, examples of jobs obtained by graduates of sport management programs, and what the future might have in store.

# Defining Sport and Sport Management

Most people know through experience and intuition what the word "sport" means. For most of us, sport implies having fun, but it can also be work (professional athlete), a means of employment (sport tourism), or a business (sport marketing agency). Sport takes many forms. It might include many participants, as in team sports such as soccer and volleyball; two participants, as in dual sports such as tennis and badminton; or one person, as in individual sports such as golf and surfing. Sport includes a combination of these configurations when it involves team competitions, tournaments, or matches in dual sports (wrestling) or individual sports (in-line skating). What criteria qualify games or activities to be classified as sport? Is horse racing a sport? What about cycling, waterskiing, pocket billiards, or chess and other table games? We know that football, basketball, ice and field hockey, tennis, golf, baseball, and softball are sports. Are they different from sailing, dog racing, marathoning, and scuba diving?

Snyder and Spreitzer (1989) defined sport as competitive human physical activity that is governed by institutional rules. VanderZwaag (1988) was more definitive: "Sport is a competitive physical activity, utilizing specialized equipment and facilities, with unique dimensions of time and space, in which the quest for records is of high significance" (p. 3). Loy (1968) provided another perspective with his suggestion that sport should (a) be playlike in nature; (b) involve some element of competition; (c) be based on physical prowess; (d) involve elements of skill, strategy, and chance; and (e) have an uncertain outcome. Clearly, we can conceptualize sport in a variety of ways.

## Operational Definition of Sport

Pitts, Fielding, and Miller (1994) broadened previous definitions of sport considerably by stating that sport is any activity, experience, or business enterprise focused on fitness, recreation, athletics, or leisure. In their view, sport does not have to be competitive, nor does it always require specialized equipment or rules; sport includes activities such as working out, running, and dancing. This is how we will use the word sport in this book—as a term that includes an expansive variety of physical activities and associated business endeavors. If your academic major is exercise specialist, athletic training, fitness management, health

## Learning Activity

Find the sport-related businesses listed in the business pages of your local telephone directory. How many different sport businesses are listed?

promotion, or another sport science area, please understand that our definitions of sport and sport management also encompass those fields.

## What Is Sport Management?

Sport management exists in two forms. First, it is an area of professional endeavor in which a variety of sport-related managerial careers exist. It is also an area of academic professional preparation—a major—in many institutions of higher education.

### Area of Professional Endeavor

DeSensi, Kelley, Blanton, and Beitel (1990) defined sport management as "any combination of skills related to planning, organizing, directing, controlling, budgeting, leading, and evaluating within the context of an organization or department whose primary product or service is related to sport and/ or physical activity" (p. 33). VanderZwaag (1988) identified a variety of sport settings, such as community recreation sport programs, industrial sport programs, military sport programs, corporate sponsors (e.g., LPGA Jamie Farr Kroger Classic, Volvo International Tennis Tournament), the sporting goods industry, developmental sport programs (e.g., Athletic Institute, National Golf Foundation, Women's Sports Foundation), social agencies (e.g., Catholic Youth Organization, Jewish Community Centers, Young Men's Christian Association, Young Women's Christian Association), the sport news media (e.g., print and broadcast), and academic programs in sport management.

### Area of Professional Preparation

In the United States, the inspiration for sport management curricula began in 1957, when Walter O'Malley, owner of the Los Angeles Dodgers, wrote a letter to James Mason at Ohio University in which he asked the following question:

> Where would one go to find a person who by virtue of education had been trained to administer a marina, race track, ski resort, auditorium, stadium, theater, convention or exhibition hall, a public camp complex, or a person to fill an executive position at a team or league level in junior athletics such as Little League baseball, football, scouting, CYO, and youth activities, etc.? (Mason, Higgins, & Wilkinson, 1981, p. 44)

As a result of that inquiry, Ohio University started a master's level sport administration pro-

gram in 1966. This program was the first applied sport management program in the United States. Although several universities had been offering professional preparation programs in athletics administration for many years, the Ohio University program was the first recorded attempt to study sport management in the private sector emphasizing practica and internships as well as academic course work. By the early 1990s, there were more than 200 graduate and undergraduate sport management programs in the United States and Canada (NASPE-NASSM Joint Task Force, 1993).

## The Term Sport Versus Sports

You might have noticed that many professional preparation programs are titled *sport* management whereas others are called *sports* management. In our view, people prefer one or the other based on their connotations of the words sports and sport. To many academics, ourselves included, sports implies a collection of separate activities such as golf, soccer, hockey, volleyball, softball, and gymnastics—items in a series that we can count. Sport, however, is an all-encompassing concept. It is a collective noun that includes all sporting activities, not just those that we can place on a list. We have found that students in our classes relate well to the parallel with the different connotations of the words religions and religion. The word religions typically connotes several specific faiths or belief systems— different denominations or sects that we can quantify. Religion, on the other hand, is a broad term that we can interpret as a general reverence or faith held by any number of people and churches.

Adding to the confusion is the fact that many professional preparation programs are titled sport(s) management, and others are called sport(s) administration. In the past, there seemed to be a clear distinction between administration and management, with administrators working primarily in the public sector and managers working in the private sector. Currently, however, the line between administration and management has become blurred, making it counterproductive to debate which term is more appropriate. You will find excellent academic programs by either name. Remember—the quality of the curriculum is more important than the title of the program.

## What Do Sport Managers Do?

As shown in figure 1.1, we can classify the responsibilities of sport managers into four clusters of

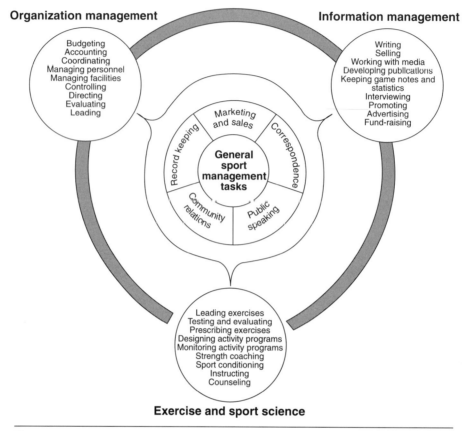

Exercise and sport science

**Figure 1.1**  Sport management task clusters.

activities: general management tasks, organization management, information management, and
exercise and sport science (Parks, Chopra, Quain,
& Alguindigue, 1988). The tasks in the middle of
figure 1.1 are general management tasks, those
that all sport managers must understand and, to
varying degrees, perform on the job. For example,
regardless of whether you work in a sport club, a
fitness spa, a sports medicine clinic, or an intercollegiate athletics department, you need to know
something about marketing, sales, public speaking, and the other tasks shown in the figure. These
competencies are transferable skills, which means
that you would be able to perform these tasks in
a variety of settings, not just in sport organizations.

Sometimes, individuals preparing for careers in
health-related industries are unconvinced of the
need to understand and practice management.
Health care professionals who work in the industry for several years soon learn that management
skills are required. B.J. Mullin, currently Director
of Marketing for the University of Denver Department of Athletics, offers sound advice in this regard:

Individuals who aspire to careers in the health
industry must be aware that management
and marketing skills are *also* important in
that area. Many health and fitness enterprises are quite small, and entry-level employees invariably are assigned management
and marketing responsibilities. Knowing only
the scientific base to the exclusion of the
business aspect is insufficient for success in
the fitness industry. (Personal communication, February 28, 1989)

Along the same lines, a contemporary trend is
for athletic trainers to work in commercial enterprises such as sports medicine clinics, hospitals,
professional sport teams, and industrial fitness
programs. For athletic trainers who work in these
settings, proficiency in management skills is as
important as proficiency in athletic training (Moss
& Parks, 1991). Moreover, skill in management
functions will be valuable to athletic trainers and
other health care professionals if they receive
opportunities to manage the settings where they
work. Additional information about the impor-

tance of management skills for students preparing to work in the health industries is presented in chapters 8, 14, and 15.

## Learning Activity

Conduct an informational interview with someone who has been employed in a commercial health-related setting for 5 years or longer. Ask about the use of management skills. See chapter 21 for suggestions about informational interviews.

In figure 1.1, the tasks within each of the three clusters that branch out from the general task cluster reflect distinctions among sport career groups. For instance, leadership and management skills are necessary for performing tasks in the organization management cluster. Good organizational skills are needed to direct and supervise subordinates in settings such as sport clubs, municipal recreation programs, or sport associations for specific populations, such as seniors or people with differing abilities; in intercollegiate athletics and professional sport; and in the business aspect of any sport- or fitness-related enterprise.

In the information management cluster, writing and communication skills are of paramount importance. Practitioners in this area acquire, organize, analyze, synthesize, store, retrieve, and disseminate information regarding sport (Meltzer, 1967). They are increasingly expected to be highly skilled in computer technology related to data storage and retrieval. Examples of positions in this area are sport marketing director, sports information director, and sport journalist.

The tasks presented in the exercise and sport science cluster require an extensive base of scientific knowledge. You can find careers in this area in exercise leadership, cardiac rehabilitation, sport conditioning, athletic training, aquatics programs (camps, resorts, agencies, municipal recreation),

campus recreation programs, and the physical fitness industry.

## Unique Aspects of Sport Management

Mullin (1980) provided insight into three unique aspects of sport management: sport marketing, sport enterprise financial structures, and sport industry career paths. These three aspects of sport management make sport different from other business enterprises and justify sport management as a distinct area of professional preparation. A fourth unique aspect of sport that we would add to Mullin's list is the enormous power and influence of sport as a social institution.

### Marketing

Sport marketing is unique because sport services are unlike other products purchased by consumers. Individuals providing the sport or fitness experience can not predict the outcome due to the spontaneous nature of the activity, the inconsistency of events, and the uncertainty surrounding the results. Sport marketers, therefore, face unique challenges dictated by the nature of the enterprise.

### Financing

Most sport businesses and, to a great extent, fitness businesses are financed differently than the typical business. Typically, the sale of a product or service such as clothing, food, automobiles, or home cleaning finances the business. However, with the exception of sporting goods stores, sport enterprises earn a highly significant portion of revenue not from the sale of a service (e.g., game, workout, or 10K run) but from extraneous sources (e.g., television rights, concessions, road game guarantees, parking, and merchandise). Intercollegiate athletics and municipal recreation sport programs might generate revenue from student or user fees, private donations, taxes, rentals, or licensing fees. Sport mangers continually compete for the discretionary funds of consumers through the sale of items that may or may not be

## The Bottom Line

In 1990, sport was a $63.1 billion a year business, ranking 22nd among 400 plus industries in the United States (Comte & Stogel, 1990). This figure is expected to increase to $121 bil- lion a year by the year 2000 (Rosner, 1989). The economic impact of the sport industry and the proliferation of sporting opportunities mandate the services of skilled managers.

related to the apparent primary focus of the enterprise. One unique aspect of sport is that it invariably attracts consumers who spend more money outside the sporting arena than they spend on the sport itself (e.g., travel, entertainment, souvenirs, and equipment). This unique financial base requires different practices within the sport setting.

## Career Paths

Career paths in sport management are not as well defined as in other vocational areas. Traditionally, many sport management practitioners have been hired from visible groups, such as intercollegiate athletics or professional sport. An example of this phenomenon is the basketball star who becomes a basketball coach and eventually an athletics director. We can find similar career advancement patterns within municipal recreation programs, sport clubs, and professional sports teams.

In some situations, sport is still a closed society in which obtaining employment might depend less on *what* the applicant knows than on *whom* the applicant knows (Clay, 1995). Additionally, the attitude that members of **underrepresented**

**groups** don't have the requisite skills for sport management positions still exists in some organizations, and this attitude creates an obstacle for aspiring sport managers. Arthur Triche, public relations director for the Atlanta Hawks and the first Black public relations director in the NBA, credits volunteering and making contacts in the sport industry as important steps he took toward overcoming this obstacle (Clay, 1995).

Growing evidence suggests that as success in the sporting enterprise depends more on knowing finance, marketing, and management, contemporary sport organizations are abandoning traditional employment practices and attitudes. The current level of economic competition within sport enterprises mandates that employers recognize and appreciate sound business expertise and that their hiring practices reflect these values. Jay Abraham, president of Sports Careers, states, "Companies are saying, 'What can you do for me? Can you sell? Can you do accounting?' They don't want people coming in saying, 'I want to work here because I've always liked football'" (Clay, 1995, p. 160).

Many future sport managers can currently be found on the basketball court, the football field, or the baseball diamond.

## Understanding Sport as a Social Institution

Sport is a distinctive social activity that is frequently the basis of an individual's social identity (McPherson, Curtis, & Loy, 1989). As such, it is a social institution of almost unbelievable magnitude and influence. What other social pursuit is allotted several pages in the daily newspaper, has its own slot on every television and radio news program, has its own cable channel, and creates what appears to be a national withdrawal crisis when members of its workforce go on strike? The sheer power of sport mandates that people who wish to manage it acquire a sound understanding of its historical, psychological, sociological, and philosophical dimensions. Understanding sport marketing and management is essential for prospective managers; so too is understanding and appreciating the social and cultural implications of the activity itself.

### Learning Activity

In small groups, read and discuss one or more books about sport as a social and cultural phenomenon. Your professor can direct you to books you will find interesting.

## The Need for Well-Prepared Sport Managers

Opportunities for sport managers abound as they never have before. Pitts and Stotlar (1996) identified several new sports and physical activities that have emerged in recent years. Among them are various forms of aerobics and new sports such as in-line skating (rollerblading), boogie boarding, snow kayaking, hang gliding, parasailing, windsurfing, ice surfing, knee boarding, sand volleyball, and indoor soccer. In addition, there have been increasing opportunities to engage in tradi-

tional sports and activities, numbers and variety of sport-related magazines, leisure time, mass media exposure of sporting activities, public awareness of fitness, numbers and types of sport facilities and events, and sport-related goods and services for a variety of market segments. New professional sports have emerged, sport opportunities are being offered to a more diverse population, endorsements and sponsorship are on the rise, sport education is becoming more prevalent, profits are up, technological advances are occurring daily, sport as a consumer product is being enhanced, marketing and promotion orientation is growing in the sport industry, sport managers are becoming more competent, and the globalization of the sport industry is progressing rapidly (Pitts & Stotlar, 1996).

### Learning Activity

Speaking of globalization, you could investigate sport management opportunities in countries other than your own. What qualifications are required for these opportunities? Information in chapter 19 will be helpful to you.

Most of these innovations in sport bring with them a need for managers, the individuals responsible for all operational aspects of an organization or unit. In chapter 8, you will learn about the myriad roles of managers. Of all these tasks, decision making is the most important one. In discussing the role of decision making, Boucher (1996) stated, "Those of us in the field of sport management should give greater credence to 'decision making' in our curricula as we prepare potential managers and assist practicing managers in making better decisions about sport." In sport enterprises, wise decisions are based on a solid grounding in management principles *and* an in-depth understanding of the unique aspects of sport. Managers' decisions are also based on their principles, their values, and their beliefs (see chapter 20). Sport

### The Bottom Line

"Sports is not simply another big business. It is one of the fastest-growing industries in the U.S., and it is intertwined with virtually every aspect of the economy—from the media and apparel to food and advertising . . . sports is everywhere, accompanied by the sound of a cash register ringing incessantly" (Ozanian, 1995, p. 30).

enterprises need well-prepared managers who have learned how to make sound management decisions in the context of sport as a powerful social institution.

# Types of Sport Organizations

There are at least two ways to classify entities within the sport industry. One way is to view each organization as either private or public, with several discrete classifications within each group. Another way is to classify the sport industry into segments based on product characteristics (Pitts, Fielding, & Miller, 1994).

## Private Organizations

There are two types of **proprietary** sport organizations: those that operate for a profit and those that provide a service to members or the public (nonprofit).

### Private, For-Profit

Private, for-profit organizations are owned and controlled by individual or group investors. The primary goal of these organizations is to make a profit for the owners through the sale of sport-related goods and services. Profit is the amount of money remaining after an organization's total expenses have been subtracted from its total revenues (Cohen, 1995). We can classify these business organizations according to three types of ownership: (a) sole proprietorship, (b) partnership, and (c) corporate ownership (Skinner & Ivancevich, 1992).

A sole proprietorship business is owned by one individual who is totally responsible for its operation. An example of a *sole proprietor* is Art Modell, the owner of the former Cleveland Browns football team who moved the Browns (now the Ravens) to Baltimore. The Cincinnati Reds Baseball Team, however, is owned by several individuals who constitute a *partnership*. Each partner owns the business with shared financial and managerial responsibilities. A *corporation* is a "legal entity separate from its owners" (Skinner & Ivancevich, 1992). Examples of corporate-owned sport businesses are the Mighty Ducks of Anaheim (Disney Corporation) and Russell Corporation, a manufacturer of athletics apparel.

The survival of private, for-profit organizations is based on profit. The concept of profit is frequently referred to as the bottom line, and sometimes enterprises have to take drastic action to ensure a healthy bottom line. For example, in recent years, several professional sport franchises (e.g., Denver Nuggets, Seattle Mariners, Milwaukee Brewers) have sought new playing facilities or renovations to existing ones to maximize revenues. Without such changes, the teams threatened to relocate so their owners could realize a profit (Dodd, 1995).

Other examples of private, for-profit organizations (also known as commercial clubs) are Gold's Gyms, 24 Hour Nautilus Fitness Centers, Canadian Health and Squash Club (Kanata, Ontario), and Central Fitness Clubs (Japan).

### Private, Nonprofit

Member-owned or investor-owned clubs such as yacht clubs, tennis clubs, swim clubs, country clubs, and university clubs, are examples of nonprofit organizations. These private clubs are created by an individual or group interested in making activities available to its members. Most midsized and large cities have at least one such club, and they usually offer some sport opportunity to their members.

## Public Organizations

Public organizations exist for a variety of purposes. They might foster social interaction, provide cultural activities, facilitate political activities, or accomplish other purposes. In public organizations, there are no ownership shares to sell as with private organizations. Excess revenues beyond expenses do not go to owners or investors but instead function to improve the service capabilities of such organizations.

Although making a profit is not a goal of public organizations, being nonprofit does not mean that such organizations are unconcerned about financial solvency. They need revenue for expansion and continued growth, for meeting the demands of inflation, and for repaying money borrowed for resources such as buildings, equipment, and supplies. We can classify public organizations as either official, voluntary, or quasi-public.

### Public, Official

These organizations are tax supported and are financially managed by federal, state, or local governments. Some widely known examples of federally controlled organizations are the national parks in the United States. Some of the more than 30 national parks are Yellowstone National Park (Wyoming), Everglades National Park (Florida),

Grand Canyon National Park (Arizona), Niagara Falls National Park (New York), and Great Smoky Mountains National Park (Tennessee and North Carolina). Other federal sport organizations provide services for military personnel.

State-regulated sport organizations are funded primarily by the state; however, they can also receive supplemental funds through federal grants. Examples of state-sponsored sport are state sport festivals and state parks systems. Local sport organizations are city recreation departments, county park systems, and service clubs. These enterprises are controlled by elected officials, who are expected to act in the best interests of the people in the community. Although locally sponsored organizations are primarily supported by local taxes, they can also receive state and federal funding.

The Addison Athletic Club North is an example of an innovative approach to sport in a local community. In the late 1980s, Addison, Texas, had fewer than 10,000 residents. Its citizens expressed the desire for an athletic club because Addison offered no recreation programs. Through a full community effort, a $3.25-million facility was built. The facility was originally funded with a $4-million voter approved municipal bond and is maintained through the town's general fund. All Addison residents can become lifetime members of the club for a one-time fee of $10.00. This is an example in which an entire community united behind the effort to build a tax-supported facility that would provide opportunities to develop and maintain health-related fitness (Dorman, 1988).

### Public, Voluntary

These organizations are not affiliated with the government and do not receive any tax support. They are controlled and managed by an individual or group interested in having available a service, such as health-related fitness, competitive sports, and so on. There are literally hundreds of these organizations, such as YW and YMCAs, JCCs, and wellness centers located in hospitals.

### Quasi-Public

These organizations are sponsored or affiliated with government; however, they do not receive any direct tax support. Campus recreation programs at public institutions such as the University of California at Santa Barbara, the University of Minnesota, and Miami University (Ohio) are examples of quasi-public sport organizations (Archibald, 1996).

## Learning Activity

Classify the sport-related businesses in the business pages of your phone book by public or private status (i.e., private, for-profit; private, nonprofit; public, official; public, voluntary; and quasi-public).

## Segments of the Sport Industry

Another way to conceptualize the components of the sport industry is to classify them according to the type of products associated with them (Pitts, Fielding, & Miller, 1994). As shown in figure 1.2, there are three product segments of the industry: sport performance, sport production, and sport promotion. The sport performance segment includes such varied products as school-sponsored athletics, fitness clubs, sport camps, professional sport, and municipal parks sport programs. Examples of products in the sport production segment are basketballs, fencing foils, jogging shoes, sports medicine clinics, swimming pools, and college athletics conferences. The sport promotion segment includes products such as T-shirts, **giveaways,** print and broadcast media, and celebrity endorsements. Within each of the three segments, there are private and public organizations, as well as for-profit and nonprofit sport organizations. In the following chapters, you will learn about career opportunities that exist for you in these segments.

## Learning Activity

Read the Pitts, Fielding, and Miller (1994) article on sport industry segmentation.

## Life After College— What Will You Do?

You might be wondering what types of jobs you will be qualified for when you graduate from college. There is no hard and fast answer to that question. However, to give you a better idea of what might lie in store for you, we have listed below some positions obtained by graduates of baccalaureate degree sport management programs. We classified the positions into the three industry segments according to the primary sport product of the business or organization in which these graduates were employed.

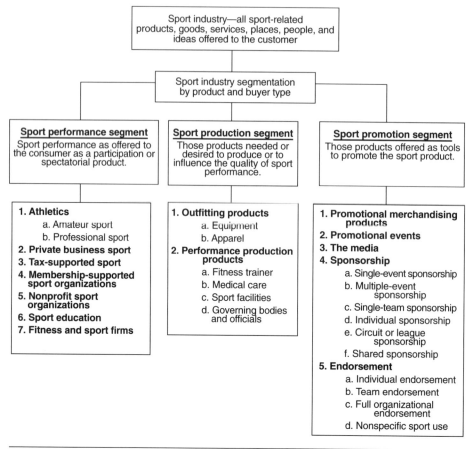

**Figure 1.2**  The sport industry segment model.

Reprinted, by permission, from B.G. Pitts, L.W. Fielding, and L.K. Miller, 1994, "Industry segmentation theory and the sport industry. Developing a sport industry segment model," *Sport Marketing Quarterly*, 3 (Morgantown, WV: Fitness Information Technology, Inc.).

## Sport Performance Segment

Sport management graduates have found employment in many facets of the performance segment of the sport industry including, but not limited to, those listed below.

■ Athletics. (a) Intercollegiate athletics departments—administrative assistant, sports information director, assistant sports information director, facility manager, equipment manager, sports promotion and marketing director, ticket sales manager; (b) campus recreation—intramural director, director of recreational sports and facilities; (c) professional sport—account executive, assistant director of scouting, assistant director of player development, corporate sales manager, marketing assistant, media and public relations assistant, vice president and general manager (minor league baseball), public relations assistant, pro athlete.

■ Tax-supported sport. Municipal recreation departments—assistant athletics supervisor, coach and instructor, assistant general manager, special events director, maintenance coordinator.

■ Nonprofit sport organizations. Marketing representative for International Special Olympics.

■ Fitness and sport firms. Health club owner, golf course manager, director of a nonprofit soccer association, franchise consultant for a franchiser of baseball and softball family entertainment centers, recreation director at a resort.

## Sport Production Segment

The sport production segment of the industry provides many interesting and challenging jobs for graduates of baccalaureate sport management programs. Among them are:

■ Outfitting products. Sales representative for sporting goods manufacturer, sales representative for a sports equipment company, manager of a retail sporting goods and apparel store, account executive for a sporting goods retailer and wholesaler.

■ Performance production products. (a) Fitness trainer—collegiate strength and conditioning coach, exercise specialist in a corporate fitness and sport program; (b) medical care—athletic trainer in a sports medicine clinic, professional sport athletic trainer, health promotion specialist; (c) sport facilities—sales representative for a sport surfacing manufacturer and supplier; (d) governing bodies and officials—assistant media director in a collegiate athletics conference.

## Sport Promotion Segment

Sport promotion is a popular area for sport management degree holders. They have been employed in a wide variety of positions, including:

■ Promotional merchandising products and events. Coordinator of sport marketing for a rental car agency, marketing director for a racetrack, special events marketing (e.g., ski series, sand volleyball tours, tennis tournaments), account executive for a collegiate licensing company.

■ The media. Newspaper sports writer, salesperson for a TV sports channel.

■ Endorsement. Account executive for a sport management and marketing company.

### Learning Activity

Find out what the graduates of your sport management program are doing now. Invite some of them back to speak to your class or your major student organization.

## Your Professional Development

At this point in your academic journey, your attention might be sharply focused on obtaining a position with an organization in the sport industry. There is another group of organizations, however, of which you should be aware. Professional and scholarly associations are an excellent way for you to learn more about your field while you are still a student. After you obtain that coveted job, these associations will help you keep up with advances in your field.

A list of relevant associations and publications is included in most chapters in section III: Segments of the Sport Industry. Membership in one or more of these associations will offer you opportunities to attend conferences and receive publications. Some have student sections, providing you with the additional opportunity to gain experience in governance. Memberships in professional associations are an integral component of your portfolio, but because most sport-related career fields sponsor professional associations, it is sometimes difficult to know which ones to join. You might consider seeking the advice of your professor as to those that would be more helpful to you, both now and in the future.

### Learning Activity

Join the sport management majors club at your university. Run for an office or volunteer to work on a project.

## Future Opportunities and Challenges for Sport Managers

As we move into the future, it would be interesting to reflect on what we will find there. As Zanger (1984) stated, "And then there is Tomorrow and Tomorrow will Bring??? . . . Weightlessness Activities and Space Vacations and . . ." (p. 109). Examples of future possibilities include in-home gyms and spas, a proliferation of personal trainers, a stronger emphasis on preventive medicine, preprogrammed computer software to help people acquire physical skills, using robots as sport partners, major advances in communication technology, and opportunities for nongravity activities (Clement, 1990). All these developments will bring challenges, some of which we are confronting today and others that we can't yet envision. There will be many developments, some of which have begun to emerge and others of which we have only dreamed. You will read about specific challenges in each remaining chapter. For this chapter, therefore, we have chosen to address only three opportunities and challenges that all sport managers will face—challenges associated with technology, ethics, and social responsibility.

## Technology

The technology explosion of the past several decades has been mind-boggling, and this is only the beginning! It is important to remember, however, that technology is not an end unto itself; it is a means to an end—an innovation that facilitates progress and helps us reach other accomplishments. In the future, scientific advances in areas such as computers and communication technology will play an increasingly significant role in our society and in sport management. This progress will be accompanied by acknowledging the human need for "high touch" activities, many of which the sport experience can provide. The challenge, therefore, is to become proficient in using technology while maintaining awareness of the need for human interaction in people's lives and understanding how sport can facilitate such interaction.

## Ethics

A direct outgrowth of advanced technology will be confusion about how to use it ethically. For example, "Just because we can do something as a result of science and technology, should we?" (Rintala, 1995, p. 62). Rintala asks if athletes think of themselves as machines whose movements can be digitized and analyzed, will they overestimate their capabilities, push themselves too far, and incur injuries? If we think of athletes as machines, will we ultimately dehumanize sport? How will genetic engineering (i.e., the ability to create elite athletes) affect sport? Who will be the decision makers about how we use the new technology?

Other ethical questions that sport managers must deal with include the following: How can we best achieve gender, race, and class equity in sport? Does a professional team owner owe primary

---

# For More Information

Use the following sources to learn more about the field of sport management.

### Sport Management Professional and Scholarly Associations, Past and Present

- Sport Management Art and Science Society (SMARTS), 1979 to 1982, included members from United States and Canada.

- Administration Special Interest Group of the Canadian Association for Health, Physical Education and Recreation.

- Sport Management Curriculum Symposium, held at Bowling Green State University in 1983; proceedings were published in a volume titled *Sport Management Curriculum: The Business and Education Nexus*.

- North American Society for Sport Management (NASSM), 1986 to present, annual conference since 1986, E-mail: <NASSM@UNB.CA>.

- National Association for Sport and Physical Education (NASPE) established a curriculum task force in 1986; this task force subsequently formed a joint task force with NASSM representatives and established sport management curriculum guidelines (see chapter 21), <NASPE@AAHPERD.ORG>.

### Other Associations

Sport Management Association of Australia and New Zealand (SMAANZ), China Sport Management, European Association of Sport Management (EASM), Japanese Society of Management for Physical Education and Sports, International Sport Management Alliance (in development).

### Communication Resources

- *Journal of Sport Management (JSM)*—official scholarly journal of NASSM, published four times per year by Human Kinetics, Champaign, IL, E-mail: http://www.humankinetics.com/infok/journals/jsm/intro.htm

- *Global Sport Management News*—newsletter published by James Thoma, Mount Union College (OH), ThomaJE@MUC.edu

- Sport Management, http://www.unb.ca/web/SportManagement

- Sport Management Listserv, SPORTMGT@hermes.csd.unb.ca

### Web Site

- Online Sports Career Center: http://www.onlinesports.com/pages/CareerCenter.html

allegiance to him or herself or to the communities that support the team? Should sports teams appropriate the rituals and symbols of Native Americans? How can we balance academic integrity with the demands of intercollegiate competition? Should gymnasts and wrestlers sacrifice their youth and health for victory? Is winning really the bottom line of sport? The list is endless, and no doubt you could add your concerns to it. Now is the time to begin reflecting on these concerns because you surely will face them in the years to come.

## Social Responsibility

In the future, enlightened sport managers will become more aware of their social responsibilities and will deliver their services in ways that reflect this understanding. For example, professional child care services will become routine in sport facilities, something we have already begun to see. Sport managers will become more conscious of environmental concerns and will incorporate this understanding into their business practices. Sport managers of the future will use previously untapped and undertapped target markets, such as women and people of differing ages, abilities, and sexual orientations. They will also recognize the importance of keeping the sport experience accessible to all socioeconomic groups.

> ## Learning Activity
>
> Write a report on an article that addresses one or more of the myriad challenges facing sport managers. Suggest solutions to these challenges. What new challenges do you think will emerge?

## Summary

Sport is any activity, experience, or business enterprise focused on fitness, recreation, athletics, or leisure. Sport management is both an area of professional endeavor and an academic program of study. Sport managers' tasks might be associated with organization management, information management, or exercise and sport science. The four unique aspects of sport management are sport marketing, the sport enterprise financial structure, sport career paths, and the power of sport as a social institution. Well-prepared sport managers are needed because of the proliferation of sport enterprises and their economic impact. We can classify sport organizations as private (for-profit, nonprofit) or public (official, voluntary, quasi-public). The three product segments of the sport industry are sport performance, sport production, and sport promotion. Professional and scholarly associations are helpful for students as well as for professionals. Three challenges facing the next generation of sport managers will be associated with technology, ethics, and social responsibility. Enlightened sport managers of the future will be agents of change.

> ## Learning Activity
>
> Write a letter to your parents or a friend explaining sport management, why you are majoring in it, and what you want to do after college. Make a presentation about sport management in your speech class. Before writing the speech, you might interview one of your professors to get his or her insights about the field.

## Down the Road

The future will most assuredly bring change, something that can be frightening and is frequently resisted. Progressive sport managers who can anticipate and embrace change will have opportunities to be agents of change who will transform the way sport is managed. We hope you will be those managers!

# Section I

# Disciplinary Foundations of Sport Management

**U**nderstanding sport as a significant entity in society is a critical first step in becoming an effective manager of sport enterprises. In the three chapters in this section, you will learn about historical, psychological, sociological, and philosophical aspects of sport. You will study the history of sport because managers who know about the past are more likely to understand the present and plan for the future. You will find out why fitness activities, sport participation, and spectator sports are important in our society; what motivates people to engage in these pursuits; and what problems exist in sport. Managers who understand the social significance of sport and why people get involved and stay involved are likely to be successful. Finally, you will discover how the study of philosophy will help you become a socially responsible sport manager.

# Chapter 2

# A Brief History of Sport in the United States

**Angela Lumpkin**
State University of West Georgia

## Learning Objectives

After studying this chapter, you will be able to

1. interpret the influence of socioeconomic factors and ethnicity on sport participation in the United States;

2. describe how the major sports associations organized and developed recreational and competitive sport opportunities for various skill levels, ages, and genders;

3. explain the origin, growth, and status of the leading professional sports in the United States;

4. analyze the historical relationships between the print and electronic media and sport; and

5. understand how important historical events contributed to the status of sport in the United States today.

Sport, which pervades so many aspects of American society, has grown into a multibillion dollar industry. This phenomenal explosion in the popularity of sports for all ages and skill levels occurred because of increased leisure time; economic affluence; and using sports for entertainment, fitness, and fun. A historical analysis reveals that sporting pastimes have withstood political bans, societal influences, and economic constraints to attain a status that entices corporations to invest billions of dollars marketing their products to a sport-crazed nation. Sports are no longer just child's play or for the gentleman amateur sportsman. Sport, probably the most discussed, read about, and viewed aspect of society, did not attain this level of popularity rapidly or easily.

Given sport's preeminent place in American society, the purpose of this chapter is to describe the most significant events and factors in the history of sport, emphasizing the 20th century. This chapter focuses on (a) sport participation relative to socioeconomic and ethnic status; (b) recreational and competitive amateur sports; (c) professional sports for entertainment and profit;

and (d) the symbiotic relationship between sport and the media. For ease of reading, this chapter omits citations. However, you can verify historical facts and obtain additional information from the references listed at the end of this book.

# Sport Participation Relative to Social Status

When the first settlers arrived in North America, they found the native people engaged in various sports. Besides the popular game of lacrosse, males, and to a lesser extent females, ran foot races, played ball games, fished, hunted, and swam. Competitive games of chance were especially widespread.

Despite challenges to their survival, laws restricting frivolous activities on the Sabbath, and other religious constraints prohibiting sports, particularly in the New England states, American colonists persisted in their recreational pastimes of hunting, fishing, horse racing, bowling, and swimming. As the new nation spread westward, frontiersmen wrestled, boxed, and raced on foot. As primarily an agrarian country, sports in rural settings remained recreational, individualistic, and primitive.

## Upper-Class Sports

Although we can find various examples of upper-class sports throughout the colonies during the 1700s, a leading example of their importance occurred in Virginia. Many settlers sought to emulate English country gentlemen, whose affluence permitted them to engage in sporting pastimes. They enjoyed fox hunting; hunting with hawks and falcons; **cock fighting**; and tavern games like dice, card playing, and billiards, but the most popular sport was horse racing. Virginians raced and gambled on the outcomes with great regularity and fervor.

The newly acquired or inherited wealth of the 1800s gave rise to a desire to engage in sports as a statement of one's economic and social status. The term conspicuous consumption aptly describes how the rich flaunted their wealth through participation in myriad sports as they enjoyed their bountiful leisure hours. Yachting dramatized how the upper class viewed sports as they sailed their huge crafts from New York City to Newport, Rhode Island, for their summer holidays. The New York Yacht Club, founded by John Cox Stevens in

1844, sought to prove its superiority by commissioning the building of *America* and challenging the Royal Yacht Club of Great Britain to a race. After easily defeating 18 British yachts in 1851, *America* gave its name to the cup that would be presented to the best international yacht, in this the consummate exclusive sport.

The upper class in the United States formed elite **country clubs** starting in the 1880s and built elaborate social and sporting facilities. There males and females played golf, tennis, croquet, and shot archery. Wealthy men raced their horses at Saratoga (opened in 1864) and Churchill Downs (home of the Kentucky Derby since 1875) and their carriages on city streets.

Track and field in the late 1800s epitomized the struggles between **amateurism** and **professionalism.** Initially, members of exclusive athletic clubs, led by the New York Athletic Club founded in 1866, competed against each other. Soon, though, the lure of winning resulted in the surreptitious hiring of excellent athletes, who were not wealthy enough to become members, to represent these clubs. The Amateur Athletic Union (AAU), established in 1888, sought to curb the spread of professionalism in track and field.

## Lower- and Middle-Class Sports

In America, often called the melting pot for the array of immigrants who flocked to its shores seeking a better life, schools provided an important arena for **assimilation.** Luther Gulick, who established the Public Schools Athletic League in New York City in 1903, stated that through after-school track and field events, basketball, and marksmanship activities, the sons of immigrants could learn American values, such as obedience, patriotism, sportsmanship, and teamwork. Gulick and others worked through the Playground Association of America (started in 1906) to provide

## Learning Activity

Select two athletes each from an individual sport, a team sport, and your favorite sport who have reached the top levels in their respective sports. Read at least one biographical article about each of these six athletes. Prepare a two-page paper or a 5-minute class presentation comparing how socioeconomic and ethnic factors influenced these athletes in their early sporting experiences.

playgrounds and recreational programs for immigrant children. Settlement houses, like Jane Addams' Hull House in Chicago, also used play and sports as socializing agents for youth and adults.

Most sports played by Americans have ethnic origins. Table 2.1 shows that most popular sports in the United States were borrowed or evolved from those played by people of other nationalities.

## Table 2.1
### The Country of Origin for the Most Popular American Sports

| Sports | Nations of origin |
| --- | --- |
| Baseball | England (evolved from cricket and rounders) |
| Football | England (evolved from soccer and rugby) |
| Golf | Scotland |
| Gymnastics | Greece; Germany; Sweden |
| Ice Hockey | Canada |
| Tennis | England, France |
| Track and field | Greece; England; Scotland; Germany |

# Recreational and Competitive Amateur Sports

Participation opportunities in sport for males have dramatically exceeded those for females, as have organized competitions. Inside and outside the colleges, men have organized sports as masculine domains and commercialized many of them. Youth sports mimic professional and college teams, whereas sports for the masses emphasize fitness, fun, and entertainment.

## Amateur Sports for Women and Men

Horse racing became a popular recreational and competitive sport, primarily because it provided the opportunity for gambling. Allegedly for improving the breed, upper-class men staged impromptu races and wagered on the outcomes during colonial times. The Union Course on Long Island staged the first sporting contest to attract thousands of spectators when it matched American Eclipse against Sir Henry in 1823.

The common man in the 1800s, unable to own race horses or even to attend races, turned to **harness racing,** or **trotting.** At country fairs and other gatherings, horses used in pulling wagons or daily work were pitted against each other to test for superior speed. The New York Trotting Club (established in 1825) helped this city become the center for trotting contests and launched harness racing into the preeminent spot in sports in the 1830s. The utilitarian characteristics of this thoroughly American sport and its pervasiveness throughout all levels of society added to its appeal, as did friendly wagers.

For more than a century, track and field represented the consummate ideal in amateur sport. When the United States' team entered the first modern Olympic Games in 1896, only amateur athletes from elite colleges or sport clubs were selected. Interestingly, two of the most acclaimed of the Olympic champions, Jim Thorpe and Jesse Owens, were not wealthy or Caucasian. Thorpe, a

Jesse Owens in Berlin for the 1936 Olympic Games. Though United States representatives in the Games were mainly athletes from elite colleges or affluent sport clubs, Owens broke barriers and dominated the Games as few Americans have since.

Native American, won gold medals in the pentathlon and decathlon in the 1912 Stockholm Games. Owens, an African American, won four gold medals, in the long jump, 100 meters, 200 meters, and 400-meter relay in the 1936 Berlin Games.

Women's opportunities in track and field have been restricted because of perceptions that they should not compete in physically strenuous sports. Not until the 1928 Amsterdam Olympic Games were women permitted to participate in five events in this sport. Many U.S. track stars, like Wilma Rudolph, received their training at historically Black colleges and universities (HBCUs), such as Tennessee State College. In 1984 at the Los Angeles Olympic Games, women were allowed to run the marathon and 3000 meters for the first time.

Tennis exemplified the elitism and adherence to the myth of amateurism from its origins in this country in 1874 until the initiation of the open, or professional, era starting in 1968. This sport excluded the less affluent because it was played on the lush grass lawns of private country clubs in the East and because only the upper class enjoyed the leisure time for developing their skills. Even when a few middle-class Californians in the early 1900s learned the game on public courts, they competed for prizes, like silver cups, not for money. Starting with the first national championships in 1881 (held initially for men at the exclusive Newport Casino Club), the United States Lawn Tennis Association (USLTA) permitted only amateurs to compete in its events. Although a few champions like Bill Tilden and Jack Kramer tried to capitalize on their popularity by setting up exhibition tours, most leading players, such as Don Budge (in 1938) and Maureen Connolly (in 1953), who were the first winners of the Australian, English, French, and U.S. singles championships in one year (the Grand Slam in tennis), simply accepted the status quo in amateur tennis.

Golf also began as an upper-class sport played at exclusive country clubs. Bobby Jones was the consummate golfing celebrity, though, because he remained an amateur while winning the U.S. Open, U.S. Amateur, British Open, and British Amateur (the Grand Slam in golf) in 1930. Expensive equipment and the time required to play perpetuated golf's association with the wealthy, at least until former caddie Francis Ouimet won the U.S. Open in 1913.

Despite societal constraints based on conservative religious beliefs, **Victorian** ideals of femininity, and physiological differences from men, some women have persistently participated in sport. In the early 1900s, for example, Eleonora Sears, a wealthy Bostonian, ignored all barriers and, through her numerous sporting achievements and prowess, highlighted how infrequently women were accepted as serious sportswomen. Sears won tennis and squash national championships, and she engaged in distance walks when mostly men competed in endurance walking races for lucrative prizes.

Many daughters and wives played tennis and croquet, shot archery, and skated alongside their wealthy fathers and husbands. Frequently, country clubs set aside ladies' days so females could play golf; some formed women's clubs to participate in these sports. National championships first were conducted for these amateur sportswomen in 1879, 1887, and 1895 in archery, tennis, and golf, respectively. Interestingly, all of these sports were engaged in by women during the late 1800s in long dresses, yards of petticoats, linen stockings, high-heeled shoes, corsets and tight-fitted bodices, and hats.

Swimming, like golf and tennis, increased in number of participants among those affluent enough to afford private instruction and club memberships. The most dominant organization was the Women's Swimming Association (WSA), whose members between 1920 and 1940 captured 25 Olympic team berths and 9 AAU championships. Most notable of the WSA swimmers was Gertrude Ederle. After winning three medals in the 1924 Paris Olympic Games, she amazed the world in 1926 by becoming the first woman to swim the English Channel; plus, she swam it faster than had any man. Swimming (in 1916) was the first sport in which the AAU conducted a national tournament for females, followed by track and field in 1924, basketball in 1926, and gymnastics in 1931.

## Men's Collegiate Sports

The initial intercollegiate competition matched Harvard versus Yale in a **regatta** in 1852. Held in New Hampshire as a promotional activity sponsored by a railroad, this commercialized competition foreshadowed the emergence of college athletics, at least in the larger universities.

Football, the unique American version of the sport in which the ball is carried as well as kicked, traces its origins to interclass play at elite men's colleges. Rutgers defeated Princeton six goals to four goals in 1869 in the first intercollegiate football game. When collegians decided to extend bragging rights beyond the campus walls, they met with resistance from faculties because of missed classes, injuries, financial problems, and rowdy behavior. Although some faculties attempted to exert oversight, for example, through the Intercollegiate Conference of Faculty Representatives (today's Big Ten Conference) starting in 1895, others allowed alumni to administer college athletics. The outward issues in these power struggles allegedly were proper fiscal management and adherence to eligibility and playing rules. However, the underlying factor increasingly was gaining control of the huge revenues and public relations potential of football.

For several decades, Walter Camp of Yale University helped revise the rules of football, such as adding the line of scrimmage and tackling below the waist. Deaths and brutality in football, especially during the 1905 season, however, caused some colleges to drop football, resulting in significant rule changes. Following a meeting of more than 60 college representatives that led in 1906 to establishing the Intercollegiate Athletic Associa-

tion of the United States (which became the National Collegiate Athletic Association or NCAA in 1910), the focus was on rule changes in football, like banning mass plays, requiring a team to make 10 rather than 5 yards in three plays, and legalizing the forward pass. Later, the rule was changed again to require 10 yards in 4 plays.

For the first 30 years of its existence the NCAA remained a weak organization because colleges insisted on retaining local autonomy, or **home rule,** of their athletic programs. The NCAA's major functions were to establish rules of competition and to conduct national championships in a variety of sports for men. Not until the NCAA began to regulate teams' television appearances in 1951 did it begin to exert greater control over football.

The loss of revenue from not appearing on television provided a sufficient penalty to influence most institutions to adhere to NCAA rules. In 1984, the Supreme Court found the NCAA in violation of the Sherman Antitrust Act for acting as a monopoly by restricting television appearances of football powerhouses. A glut of televised football

By the early 1900s, football had become the leading college sport. This 1924 photo shows players from the University of Santa Clara in California.

games resulted, followed by conference realignments as universities sought to maximize their revenues from television.

Although intercollegiate baseball predated the first intercollegiate football game by a decade when Amherst defeated Williams 73 to 32 in 1859, baseball quickly fell behind in popularity. Probably this was due to the existence of and competition from professional baseball, whereas there was no professional football. One major issue facing the NCAA in its early years was trying to keep college baseball an amateur sport because many collegians (under assumed names) played baseball in the major, minor, or semipro leagues in the summers.

Basketball, which was developed in Springfield, Massachusetts, in 1891, initially was viewed as too slow paced and low scoring to appeal to huge audiences. In the 1930s, sportswriter Ned Irish began to stage doubleheader games between local colleges and nationally prominent teams before large crowds in Madison Square Garden. Capitalizing on an increasing popularity of college basketball, the Metropolitan Basketball Writers Association of New York organized the National Invitational Tournament (NIT) in 1938. The University of California at Los Angeles Bruins, coached by John Wooden, helped promote basketball's status on campuses nationwide by winning 10 out of 12 NCAA basketball titles between 1964 and 1975. The NCAA's 10-year, $1-billion television contract for the men's Division I Basketball Tournament starting in 1995 dramatically illustrates the level of popularity to which **March Madness** has grown.

## Women's Collegiate Sports

Women attending primarily single-gender colleges in the 1800s frequently participated in sporting pastimes. They rowed, skated, shot archery, played tennis, and even occasionally engaged in games of baseball. After 1891, they participated in basketball, and it quickly became their most popular sport. Attired in the favorite gymnasium costume of the day, bloomers, these collegians played enthusiastically, despite restrictions on their movement (the court was divided into three sections) and in the rules, such as no grabbing the ball and a two-dribble limit. Constrained by clothing, societal attitudes based on the Victorian ideals regarding femininity, and perceived physiological limitations, women, nonetheless, played interclass basketball games and sometimes even contests against other colleges. Although a few institutions

continued to compete, by the 1940s most had eliminated basketball and other sports teams, although occasionally these collegians traveled to nearby colleges for **play days** or **sport days.**

In an attempt to address the competitive sports needs of highly skilled females, the Commission on Intercollegiate Athletics for Women (CIAW) was established in 1966 to set standards by which to conduct these events. In 1971, the CIAW was replaced by the Association for Intercollegiate Athletics for Women (AIAW), which continued and expanded the number of national championships for college women. Aided by Title IX of the Education Amendments Act of 1972, which required equal opportunity in all programs, including sports, conducted by educational institutions receiving federal funds, opportunities for female athletes in schools and colleges to compete and receive funding expanded dramatically. In 1976, the National Junior College Athletic Association (NJCAA) began to offer championships for women; the National Association of Intercollegiate Athletics (NAIA) conducted its first women's national tournaments in 1980. After the NCAA began offering national championships for women in 1981, the AIAW could not retain its members because the NCAA paid the expenses of teams in its national championships, which the AIAW could not afford to do. Within a year, the female-led AIAW ceased to exist, leaving the control of women's athletics in the hands of the almost exclusively male NCAA.

### Learning Activity

Interview two or three people who can provide you with information about the organization and development of any recreational or competitive sports program. This program could be a college team, a youth or seniors' competition, a professional franchise, or another one of your choice. Write an article about the information you learned and submit it to a local newspaper for possible publication.

## Youth Sports

Play is a child's right. The Puritans in the 1600s may have attempted to suppress these natural tendencies and child labor practices in the 1800s may have squelched youthful vigor, but children seemingly possess a natural inclination to play.

Americans have long espoused a belief that sport teaches values. Parents want their children

Courtesy of Purdue University

Basketball at Purdue in 1992. The 90s showed a steady increase in funding and enthusiasm for major women's collegiate sports, but the vast majority of the teams remained overseen by male athletic directors.

to learn teamwork, sporting behavior, cooperation, discipline, and self-confidence, desired outcomes of sport. Although ideally instilling these values, youth sports are also lauded for helping prevent delinquent behaviors. Sport has been praised for being a great assimilator; that is, through sport young people of different genders, races, and nationalities learn to accept and respect each other.

Following the lead of the colleges, boys in public schools in the late 1800s and early 1900s began to organize baseball, football, and basketball teams. Although boys initiated early school sports, girls did not. Men typically organized and coached the girls' high school basketball teams that were formed in the 1920s and 1930s. Most of these teams lasted only a few years due to societal opposition to competitive sports for females.

Besides school sport, starting in the 1920s, many businesspeople in towns and cities began to organize competitive sports for elementary-aged boys with a primary goal of using sport to deter juvenile delinquency. Pop Warner Football (begun in 1930), Little League Baseball (started in 1939), and national and local organizations like the American Legion and the Young Men's Christian Association expanded to offer national qualifying and elimination events. The past few decades have witnessed massive expansions in sport competitions for youth, sponsored by public recreation departments and private national organizations.

## Sports for Individuals Who Are Physically and Mentally Challenged

For decades children and adults who were different physically or mentally were inevitably excluded from sport and the mainstream of society. Their rights were too often ignored and their needs unfulfilled because most people lacked knowledge and understanding about how to help them achieve within their unique circumstances.

The 1990 Americans with Disabilities Act and other federal legislation require that recreational programs and facilities provide for individuals with limitations. Every person who is physically or mentally challenged must not only have access to courts, fields, and showers, but also have participation opportunities commensurate with their abilities.

## Growth of Professional Sports

Professional sports exist to entertain fans and to make profits. One has to look no further than the 1994 Major League Baseball (MLB) strike to realize that labor (the players) and management (the owners) seemingly prioritize making money over providing enjoyable spectator sports. Significant drops in attendance at MLB games the following year suggested that owners and players may have

been perceived as greedy and self-serving rather than customer oriented.

## Political Factors

The popularity of horse racing and boxing was sporadically reduced by governmental bans on these sports, primarily due to their association with gambling. Each time both sports regained the right to stage competitions, gambling contributed to increased attendance and higher stakes. The transition of boxing from bare knuckle fights to the Marquis of Queensbury rules in the 1890s, highlighted by using gloves, helped boxing become more acceptable to political leaders. Promoter Tex Rickard probably did the most to help boxing gain respectability by scheduling matches in Madison Square Garden and getting socially elite men and women to attend. Most significant were the multimillion dollar matches staged between Jack Dempsey and Gene Tunney in 1926 and 1927.

© Daily Illini

As many physically challenged athletes are proving, the term "disabled" hardly applies in physical activity today.

Gambling and politics also impacted baseball. In 1919, gamblers allegedly succeeded in getting several members of the Chicago White Sox to intentionally lose the World Series. Although acquitted legally, these men were banned from baseball by the newly appointed Commissioner of Baseball, Kenesaw Mountain Landis, who was empowered to control or eliminate anything detrimental to the best interests of the game. Not until the 1980s, when Pete Rose was banned for betting on baseball games, did gambling again threaten the integrity of the sport.

The legal system has helped resolve conflicts between owners and players. Baseball's recent confrontations between owners and players serve as reminders of the many struggles for control and money that occurred between these two groups. After the formation of the National League of Professional Base Ball Clubs in 1876, this **cartel** of owners successfully rejected repeated players' claims for higher salaries, greater benefits, and the freedom to play for teams of their choice. The American Association, Players' League, Federal League, and Brotherhood of Professional Base Ball Players could not wrest control from the owners. The American League, started in 1901, managed to gain equal status with the National League, resulting in strengthening the **reserve clause** and the first World Series in 1903. The Major League Players Association, established in 1953, remained largely ineffective until Marvin Miller was hired as executive director in 1966. He negotiated an increase in minimum salaries, a larger pension fund, and a grievance procedure using an outside arbitrator. Not until 1975 when Andy Messersmith and Dave McNally through arbitration became free agents was the reserve clause changed, resulting in dramatic increases in salaries. See chapter 17 for a discussion of economic issues in Major League Baseball.

## Societal Factors

Socioeconomic status and ethnicity significantly influenced the development of sport in this country. Historically, sports such as golf and tennis have been regarded as elitist. First played almost exclusively at private country clubs, these sports attracted individuals who could afford club memberships, expensive equipment, and private lessons. When the Professional Golf Association (PGA) was founded for men in 1916, most players did not rely on their meager winnings. Even Arnold Palmer in the 1960s and Jack Nicklaus in the 1970s earned more money from commercial endorsements than they received by winning golf tournaments.

Those sports most associated with ethnic groups have been boxing, baseball, basketball, and football. Boxing has consistently attracted athletes from the lower socioeconomic classes, among whom have been Irish, Jewish, and Italian immigrants and African Americans. Jack Johnson, who captured the title in 1908, became the first African American heavyweight champion. His victory stunned most Americans, threatening their perception of white supremacy and physical domination. Johnson's lifestyle of flaunting his riches and marrying and consorting with white women eventually led to a federal conviction and jail term. Joe Louis personified the antithesis of Johnson. Louis remained within the boundaries set by white Americans while holding the heavyweight title for 12 years through 25 title defenses. His 1938 defeat of German Max Schmelling after losing to him in 1936 thrust Louis into the role of national hero for Blacks and Whites.

Baseball, Americans' first national sport, appealed to immigrants who adopted this sport as a way to gain acceptance into society. Although called a pastoral sport and spread throughout the United States in the years after the Civil War, baseball's origins and dispersion began primarily in the cities. Gentlemen amateurs in 1845, led by Alexander Cartwright and the New York Knickerbockers Baseball Club, helped formalize the rules and organize the first leagues. The Cincinnati Red Stockings hired the first professional players and helped popularize the game through its 1869 national tour. This team may have ignited the spark for professional baseball, but A.G. Spalding, player, manager, and entrepreneur, did the most to promote baseball through his equipment company, publications, and tours.

The exclusion and inclusion of African Americans in baseball provides an insight into ethnicity in sport. Although Moses "Fleetwood" Walker and his brother Welday Walker played in the major leagues in 1884, the owners soon officially excluded African Americans through a **gentlemen's agreement**. One contributing factor to this practice was that a large percentage of the players were southerners, who were raised in segregated, and sometimes racist, environments. Another reason was that baseball reflected existing societal views, which seemed to prefer racial segregation.

Despite occasional exhibition games between Major League Baseball (MLB) all-stars and teams from the Negro Leagues, no African American

© UPI/Corbis-Bettmann

Prior to 1947, African Americans, banned from Major League Baseball, played in the "Negro Leagues." This 1942 photo shows, from left, Tex Burnett (manager), Harry Williams, Tom Parker, and Dan Wilson, all members of the Black Yankees.

again played in the major leagues until 1947. Yet, in the 1920s to 1950s the Negro Leagues included dozens of outstanding players, such as Josh Gibson and Satchel Paige, who demonstrated skills comparable to MLB stars like Lou Gehrig and Ty Cobb.

Branch Rickey, general manager of the Brooklyn Dodgers, selected Jackie Robinson to break the racial barrier in modern baseball, not because he was the best player in the Negro Leagues, but because Robinson had proven his ability to exist and even thrive at the University of California at Los Angeles as a three-sport athlete. Robinson withstood death threats, physical abuse, verbal taunts, prejudice, and exclusion to become the National League's Rookie of the Year (1947) and Most Valuable Player (1949). Rickey's experiment, which was attempted because he thought it would lead to winning more games and to greater financial profits, was a resounding success. It resulted in signing other African American players, who comprised about 20% of MLB players in the 1990s.

In basketball the New York Original Celtics (all White) in the 1920s and the New York Renaissance (all Black) in the 1930s were the best professional teams, although most pro teams were located in small towns in the Midwest. The Harlem Globetrotters, organized by Abe Saperstein in 1927, featured talented African Americans who displayed excellent basketball skills and dramatic flair. The

## Learning Activity

View the PBS documentary *Baseball* by Ken Burns. Discuss how baseball reflected or led society. (These videos—Inning 1 Our Game, Inning 2 Something Like War, Inning 3 Faith of 50 Million, Inning 4 National Heirloom, Inning 5 Shadow Ball, Inning 6 National Pastime, Inning 7 Capital of Baseball, Inning 8 Whole New Ballgame, Inning 9 Home—can be obtained from Turner Home Entertainment.)

Boston Celtics signed the first African American, Charles Cooper, in 1950; today, more than 75% of the players in the National Basketball Association (NBA) are African Americans.

Socioeconomic status, rather than race, influenced the early years of professional football, as teams developed primarily in the Midwest using players drawn mostly from working-class, Catholic, and ethnic groups. Aside from attracting a few collegians and high school boys, who played under aliases, football outside the college ranks remained regional and lower class, lacking status and newspaper appeal until long after the American Professional Football Association (today's National Football League or NFL) was established in 1920.

The integration of professional football happened quietly in 1946, one year before Jackie Robinson played for the Dodgers. Kenny Washington and Woody Strode joined the Los Angeles Rams, to become the first African Americans to play in the NFL. One reason for the lack of notice of the integration of the NFL was that professional football remained a regional, middle-class sport with a small fan base. A second factor was that few football players were from the South.

African Americans Althea Gibson in the 1950s and Arthur Ashe in the 1960s became the first of their race to win the USLTA singles championships, even though they had to endure racial prejudice, such as exclusion from many private tennis clubs and competitions. Tennis gradually began to change when recreation departments added public courts and hired instructors to teach the basic skills. Many have cited the Billie Jean King versus Bobby Riggs match in 1973, viewed by the largest audience ever to watch a tennis match, as the pivotal stimulus for this increase in participation.

The All-American Girls' Softball League was created by Philip K. Wrigley in 1942 as a substitute form of entertainment to MLB during the war years. Within the first year, the game began to move closer to baseball, becoming the All-American Girls' Baseball League (AAGBBL) in 1945. Several factors contributed to the popularity of this league during its 12 years of existence. The promotional and organizational efforts of Arthur Meyerhoff and his advertising agency provided a solid foundation, as did almost unlimited financing from supportive communities. Initially, the league office contracted with and allocated players to the teams to equalize the distribution of talent, who were highly skilled softball players. The league promoted and publicized the teams, such as the four original ones located in Racine and Kenosha,

Wisconsin; Rockford, Illinois; and South Bend, Indiana. Mostly, ex-MLB players served as managers, thus contributing to a professional aura. Chaperons ensured that the players dressed and behaved in a feminine manner; plus, to reinforce this image, the athletes played in short skirts.

## Learning Activity

View the video *A League of Their Own* and discuss the historical and current role of women in sport. (You can obtain this video from Columbia Tristar Home FFC.)

## Economic Factors

Auto racing, from dragsters to endurance races, traces its beginnings to dirt tracks in rural areas of this country. Today, hundreds of thousands attend events in the NASCAR, Indy Car, and Formula One series and revel in the high speed and high risk of automobile racing. Corporate sponsorships, as a glance at any race car verifies, is critical to the existence of this sport.

Babe Ruth became a folk hero during the Golden Age of Sports in the 1920s. Christy Walsh, who might be called the first **sports agent** because he skillfully managed Babe Ruth's commercial ventures, helped earn the Sultan of Swat approximately the same amount off the field as he received as baseball's preeminent star.

The location of franchises and the expansion of MLB illustrates the integral relationship between profits and entertainment and baseball's popular status. MLB clubs initially located in the major metropolitan areas in the East. In the late 1800s and early 1900s, owners negotiated alliances with political leaders to obtain prime real estate for stadia and to secure the building of mass transportation lines to ballparks at public expense. Cities that failed to accommodate these demands often lost their teams.

This sports-related blackmail, as some would categorize it, continues apace today. Dozens of MLB, NFL, and NBA owners have convinced voters and city leaders to provide at taxpayers' expense either a new stadium or major renovations to the existing park. The threatened alternative was the team's departure. In many cases, cities provide millionaire team owners with leases that cost the club little, while the owners retain ticket, concession, parking, merchandise, and advertising revenues.

Perhaps the greatest college football player ever, Red Grange in 1924 as a halfback for the University of Illinois, and in 1963.

Hoping to build on the popularity of college football, the Chicago Bears initially attracted the first prominent college star to the league. Following his amazing 1925 season at the University of Illinois, Harold "Red" Grange continued his outstanding running during 10 games over the next 17 days with the Bears. Then, in an exhibition tour organized by Charles Pyle, Grange earned 60% of the gate receipts and endorsements on 14 games played within the next 35 days. His success in the NFL enticed more college athletes into the league, especially after the NFL began its draft in 1936.

Professional football grew up alongside television, but it took Commissioner Pete Rozelle to negotiate the lucrative deals that made the NFL a financial success. Television may have introduced the masses to the entertaining nature of the sport, but football needed celebrities like "Broadway" Joe Namath. His flamboyant prediction that he would quarterback his Jets past the powerful Baltimore Colts in Super Bowl III in 1969 seemed foolhardy at best. When he successfully fulfilled his prediction, he helped legitimize the American Football League, which began in 1959. Namath's success opened the way for even higher salaries for college draftees.

The Super Bowl and Monday Night Football (since 1970) illustrate the almost revered stature of professional football. Corporate sponsors pay millions of dollars to advertise during these games because millions of fans watch. The money gambled, legally and illegally, on these games is astounding. Just as the Super Bowl has become the reason to have a party to watch the game, Monday Night Football has become one of the leading attractions at sports bars.

In 1949 the NBA grew out of a merger of the National Basketball League (small town teams) and the Basketball Association of America (big city teams). Like college basketball at the time, the pros played a slow, deliberate game dominated by set shots until a 24-second clock was added in 1954. The duels under the basket by Wilt Chamberlain and Bill Russell in the 1960s and the nine NBA titles won by the Boston Celtics, coached by Arnold "Red" Auerbach in 1957 to 1966, helped build the stability of the NBA.

The development of a rival league, the American Basketball Association (ABA) in 1967, challenged the NBA for the top collegiate players and fan support. Competition for players between the NBA and ABA escalated salaries dramatically and eventually led to the two associations merging in 1976. Commissioner David Stern is credited for his marketing savvy and stabilizing labor management relations in the NBA, especially through the use of the **salary cap**. You can find a discussion of salary caps in chapter 17.

## Symbiotic Relationship Between Sport and the Media

Since the late 1800s, Americans have read newspapers to learn about sporting achievements. To-day, daily newspapers allocate a high percentage of their pages to sports news; in some cases, more coverage is provided for sporting events than for politics, the economy, or any other single event. Rather than adversely affecting attendance at sporting events, radio and television in the long run have attracted more new fans.

## Newspapers and Magazines

Early Americans looked to England for publications describing sporting pastimes. In the 1800s, this changed dramatically as several magazines in the

News about their heroes—from both on and off the court or field—has reached the point of insatiability for many sports fans.

United States devoted to baseball, boxing, harness racing, horse racing, and other sports became popular. The *Spirit of the Times*, started in 1831, the *New York Clipper*, founded in 1853, and the *National Police Gazette*, begun in 1845, were among the periodicals that helped popularize sports. The *Sporting News*, a weekly newsprint publication since 1886, has focused on professional baseball.

During the Golden Age of Sports in the 1920s, sportswriters like Grantland Rice, Paul Gallico, Ring Lardner, and Allison Danzig glorified sports and its heroes with their emphasis on entertaining readers. In baseball, for example, these men often traveled with the professional teams and knew the players personally. Journalistic protocol at the time did not permit exposés about the unseemly behaviors of the stars, even though many episodes and individual foibles would have made sensational stories. Rather, reporters featured athletes' talents and achievements. Not until players received huge salaries, television created headlines through investigative reports, and a few players exposed what really occurred in the inner sanctum of the clubhouse and locker room did the print media change.

Founded in 1954, *Sports Illustrated* has helped promote and popularize commercialized sports. Although most articles report results of competitions in baseball, football, basketball, and ice hockey and feature the lives and accomplishments of their stars, the reader regularly will find stories about other men's sports and sportswomen and their achievements.

The recent publication of specialty magazines, such as those dedicated to college football or basketball, speak to Americans' nearly insatiable appetite for information about sports. Additionally, almost every imaginable sport has at least one magazine that describes its championships and champions. Many periodicals also provide instruction that helps the fan-participant improve his or her skills.

## Electronic Media

When radio transmission of sporting events increased exponentially in the 1920s, many sport managers feared that some fans would stop buying tickets and listen to games at home. Others predicted that games broadcast on radio would attract new fans. College and professional teams initially did experience drops in attendance. Soon, however, attending sporting events became more popular. Another major change occurred as radio stations began to pay for the right to broadcast

sports, whereas originally the colleges or professional leagues had paid radio stations to broadcast their games.

Concerns about the potential detrimental impact of television on attendance also were expressed. After Major League Baseball began to be televised, attendance at minor league baseball games dropped precipitously, contributing to the closure of more than half of these leagues, especially in the 1950s. In the same vein, because college basketball can be viewed almost every night on television, attendance at high school games has dropped.

Television also has influenced rules in some professional and college sports. Examples include the length of NFL halftimes, the number of time-outs in college basketball games, the change to medal play from match play in golf, the use of tiebreakers in tennis, and the broadcast times for the World Series and Super Bowl.

Today's multibillion dollar sport, fitness, and recreation industry reflects how Americans value their leisure hours. Integral to this explosion in popularity of sports has been television. The answer to the questions, does televised sport reflect society's interest in sport, or does televised sport generate fans and participants, is probably yes. The relationship is symbiotic. The popularity of televised sports has resulted in the cultural phenomena of the "couch potato" and the "armchair quarterback." Both are associated with the passive consumption of sports. The sports fanatic often is characterized as a "channel surfer" who pushes the remote control to catch the action of several sports being televised simultaneously. Another passive way that sports fans get involved with sports is through gambling. Fans annually gamble millions of dollars on sports. When not watching sports, the avid enthusiast often plays sports video games.

The print and electronic media have benefited greatly from sport. Many sporting events are telecast for several reasons: (a) to increase ratings (the number of viewers), which in turn results in charging higher prices for advertising time; (b) to provide an opportunity for networks to promote other programs; (c) to add to a network's status as a leader in sports programming (e.g., for bragging rights); and (d) to make money when the rights fees paid for broadcasts do not exceed the revenues received from advertisers.

Sport has received untold millions of words and years of free publicity for its competitions and stars from the print and electronic media. Certainly, sport sells—newspapers, magazines, radio

## Learning Activity

Watch on television at least four different professional sporting events. Analyze each based on these criteria: (a) information provided about the history of this sport, (b) quality and quantity of the data and information provided about the athletes, (c) amount of violence and incidences of sporting behavior observed, (d) roles played by the coaches or managers, (e) impact of the broadcasters on your understanding and enjoyment of the competition, and (f) your analysis of the importance of this event. In class, compare and contrast your perceptions about the sports you watched with the perceptions of your classmates. Compile a notebook containing at least 20 examples accompanied by your explanations of how sport sells or is sold by the media.

advertisements, and television commercials. These media forms promote sport by influencing fans to attend more games. Sport could not afford to purchase the publicity it gets free. Many of the sports publications and electronic broadcasts would not exist without commercialized sports.

## Summary

Prospective sport managers can more effectively guide the development of their programs if they understand how and why sport has evolved into one of the most pervasive influences in American society today. Sport participation from colonial times until the present has been influenced by socioeconomic and ethnic factors. For example, although golf and tennis have remained associated primarily with the upper class, football, basketball, and baseball have retained their egalitarianism by providing competitive opportunities for individuals from all socioeconomic and ethnic groups. Males historically have been provided more recreational and competitive teams in noncollege, college, and professional sports than have females. Changing societal attitudes and federal legislation contribute to expanding and enhancing equity within sports for females, minorities, senior citizens, and the physically or mentally challenged. The symbiotic relationships between the print and electronic media and sports have helped launch sport into a preeminent status that is likely to continue expanding. Because sport is firmly entrenched into the fabric of American society, sports leaders face the challenge of managing their programs to meet the needs of all involved.

## Learning Activity

Visit a state museum of history. Make a list of the sports equipment displayed in the exhibits. Compare with classmates what you found relative to the history of sport described in this chapter.

# Chapter 3 | Psychosocial Aspects of Sport and Exercise

**Vikki Krane**
Bowling Green State University

**Mary Jo Kane**
University of Minnesota

## Learning Objectives

After studying this chapter, you will be able to

1. define sport and exercise psychology;

2. analyze the distinction and interrelationship between research and applied sport and exercise psychology;

3. differentiate among the various perspectives in sport and exercise psychology;

4. understand the importance of sport and exercise psychology for sport managers;

5. define sport sociology;

6. analyze the significance of sport in our society;

7. identify positive and negative effects of sport on society; and

8. understand the importance of sport sociology for sport managers.

To be a top-notch sport manager, you will need to understand the psychological and sociological contexts in which sport and exercise occur. This understanding will contribute to your appreciation of the roles of sport and exercise in people's lives and in society. With this knowledge, you will be able to approach your management functions from a more informed perspective, and your business decisions can be based on the big picture of what occurs with individuals and groups in sport and exercise settings. Your vision, therefore, will be more enlightened than one focused solely on the bottom line of the business enterprise.

This chapter is presented in two parts. First, you will learn about sport and exercise psychology, the study of the individual in sport and exercise. Some examples of psychological concerns in sport and exercise are performance enhancement, exercise adherence, motivation, and eating disorders. In the second part of the chapter you will learn about sport sociology, the study of cultural and societal aspects of sport. Examples of the sociological impact of sport include the importance of sport as a social institution, the role of sport as a socializing agent and unifier of people, and the power of sport to effect change in society. Although we present separate discussions of psychology and sociology of sport and exercise, it is important to remember that there is a symbiotic (i.e., mutually beneficial) relationship between the individual and social spheres of sport. Although the individual is affected by social and cultural influences, the cultural and social environment is, in turn, affected by the individual. Therefore, overlap between sport psychology and sport sociology is common.

## Sport and Exercise Psychology

Research in sport and exercise psychology examines interactions between psychological variables and other aspects of sport and physical activity. We know, for example, that certain psychological variables will affect an athlete's performance (e.g., excessive anxiety can lead to "choking"). Participation in exercise or sport also might affect an individual's psychological makeup (e.g., exercise participation could reduce stress; sport and exercise success might increase self-confidence). Common areas of study addressed by sport and exercise psychology researchers include (a) characteristics of the participants (e.g., motivation, anxiety, aggression, and confidence), (b) group processes (e.g., leadership and cohesion), (c) performance enhancement, (d) enhancement of health and well-being, and (e) facilitation of psychological growth and development (Kremer & Scully, 1994; Weinberg & Gould, 1995).

### Misconceptions

There are many misconceptions about the content and purposes of sport and exercise psychology. Among them are the following:

- Sport and exercise psychology is concerned only with teaching athletes how to be better athletes.
- Only athletes with severe psychological problems need a sport psychologist.
- Sport psychologists work with athletes who have mental problems.
- Sport psychologists fix athletes who choke.
- Sport and exercise psychology is helpful only for elite athletes.

- Sport and exercise psychology concepts are applicable only to coaching.

Each statement contains an element of truth. Taken individually, however, each notion also misrepresents the field as a whole. Even taken collectively, they address only a small segment of sport and exercise psychology.

Although some people might relate sport and exercise psychology only to elite or highly competitive athletes, the field actually addresses a broad spectrum of individuals and physical activity environments. A wide range of people participate in sport and exercise—novice to elite, youth to elderly. Moreover, sport and exercise take place in a variety of contexts, from recreational to highly competitive. All these domains are of interest to sport and exercise psychologists. Thus, sport and exercise psychology is far more expansive and diverse than most people realize.

## Research and Applied Sport and Exercise Psychology

Research sport and exercise psychology is concerned with theory development, refinement, and testing. The goal is enhancing our knowledge about psychological phenomena in sport and exercise. For example, in the area of exercise adherence, psychologists have been testing several theories to determine the best explanation for why individuals do not adhere to long-term exercise programs. One such theory is self-efficacy theory, which suggests an individual's expectations of successfully completing an exercise will predict whether he or she will continue to participate in exercise. The higher the expectation of achieving exercise goals (e.g., being able to run 20 minutes without stopping), the more likely that they will persist in the effort needed to obtain that goal. This area of sport and exercise psychology also has been referred to as academic sport and exercise psychology (Martens, 1986) or pure sport and exercise psychology (Kremer & Scully, 1994).

"Applied sport and exercise psychology focuses on identifying and understanding psychological theories and techniques that can be applied to sport and exercise to enhance the performance and personal growth of athletes and physical activity participants" (Straub & Williams, 1993, p. 1). This approach to sport and exercise psychology focuses on developing solutions for common questions or problems that arise in sport. For example, following up on the previous example about self-efficacy, an applied sport psychologist might focus on how to increase individuals' performance expectations so they will continue to pursue their goals. Other areas within applied sport and exercise psychology include performance enhancement, increasing participation in exercise, creating positive youth sport environments, and assisting injured athletes during rehabilitation. Enhancing the social atmosphere of a team or exercise setting is another focus of applied sport psychology. This may include increasing group cohesion, reducing negative communication such as complaining and blaming, enhancing the ability of leaders to motivate exercisers and athletes, or increasing adherence to exercise programs. Applied sport psychologists might consult with coaches, athletes, administrators, athletic trainers, parents, and other people involved in sport and exercise environments. They also might work with individuals or groups addressing psychological issues in sport or exercise. Examples of questions in which an applied sport psychologist might be interested include the following:

- What is the best method to reduce anxiety in athletes?
- What is the best leadership style to motivate athletes?
- How can we develop a positive environment for youth sport?
- How can we develop a cohesive sport environment?
- How can we improve exercise adherence?
- What can we do to minimize eating disorders in sport?
- How can we motivate injured participants in rehabilitation?
- Why do some athletes or exercisers seem to give up?

### Learning Activity

What are the similarities and differences between research and applied sport and exercise psychology?

## Areas of Specialization

Research and applied sport and exercise psychology are not antithetical (i.e., diametrically opposed) to one another, nor are they hierarchical

(i.e., arranged in ranked order); there is continuous interplay between them. For example, practical interventions with athletes and exercisers can, and should, be guided by theory. Hence, research sport psychology provides a strong foundation for applied interventions with athletes and exercisers. Likewise, applied sport and exercise psychology informs and guides the research sport and exercise psychologist and identifies important questions for them. This overlapping of research and applied sport psychology enables researchers interested in either approach to examine sport and exercise through six common areas of specialization: cognitive, developmental, health, performance enhancement, psychophysiology, and social. These are areas that have been described in the sport psychology literature. However, this categorization of sport and exercise psychology content is somewhat arbitrary and these areas of focus may overlap.

### Cognitive Sport and Exercise Psychology

Cognitive sport and exercise psychology focuses on individuals' perceptions of the environment and their own behaviors. Sport and exercise participants actively "search, filter, selectively act on, reorganize, and create information" (Straub & Williams, 1984, p. 7). It is assumed that athletes and exercisers constantly interpret their environment and behavior and then act based on those perceptions. Areas of interest to a cognitive sport psychologist include attention and concentration, motivation, **imagery**, self-efficacy, and perceptions and emotions in sport and exercise. For example, applied cognitive sport and exercise psychologists may study imagery as a technique for performance enhancement. They also are interested in understanding how an individual defines success (e.g., based on winning or personal improvement) and the impact of self-efficacy, or one's expectations of success, on athletic performances (Feltz, 1988) and exercise behaviors (McAuley, 1992).

### Developmental Sport and Exercise Psychology

Developmental sport and exercise psychology attempts to describe and explain differences and similarities among groups of individuals at differing developmental, or maturational, stages. Although typically associated with youth sports, developmental sport and exercise psychology actually is concerned with issues related to sport and exercise participants throughout the life span. This includes addressing concerns of seniors as well as youths, and everyone in between. As the life span continues to increase in our society, and the importance of fitness and physical activity are emphasized, more elderly people are becoming and remaining involved in exercise and sport. Thus, it is just as important to understand how to keep them involved in healthy activity as it is to maintain a positive youth sport environment. Examples of other topics of interest to developmental sport and exercise psychologists include enhancing moral development through sport (i.e., understanding the difference between right and wrong), enhancing athletes' self-esteem in youth sport programs, increasing exercise adherence in older adults and children, and explaining the impact of exercise on the psychological well-being of older adults.

---

## Learning Activity

Give two examples, not mentioned in the text, of research questions a developmental sport and exercise psychologist might pursue.

---

### Health Psychology

Health psychology addresses issues such as promoting and maintaining health, assisting sport and exercise participants in benefiting from exercise and sport participation, helping athletes and exercisers maintain a high level of psychological health, supporting injury recovery, and using exercise to increase mental and physical health (Rejeski & Brawley, 1988). The primary premise of health psychology is that participation in exercise and sport can lead to healthy psychological outcomes. This involves a holistic approach to health that emphasizes the interconnection between physical and psychological health. Aspects of health psychology have sometimes been referred to as exercise psychology or rehabilitation psychology.

Health psychologists may be interested in psychological knowledge applied to reduce physical disability and enhance the therapeutic environment (Rejeski & Brawley, 1988). The relationship between injury and psychological states is an area receiving much attention from health psychologists. For example, they may help an injured athlete cope with the psychological trauma of being injured and separated from the team, develop pain-management strategies, or implement psychological strategies to enhance motivation and confidence during rehabilitation. Goal setting and imagery have been effective in assisting injured

exercisers and athletes as they recover (Heil, 1993). Research focused on the role of stress in sport and exercise injury has revealed that athletes and exercisers who have more stressful lives are more likely to become injured (Andersen & Williams, 1988). An important implication of this research is that if health psychologists can help people reduce stress in their lives, they may minimize the likelihood of athletic injury.

Health psychologists also are interested in the psychological benefits of sport and exercise participation. For example, research has shown that participation in exercise is associated with enhanced mood, decreased depression, decreased anxiety, decreased stress, increased self-esteem, and positive psychological well-being (Berger & McInman, 1993; Willis & Campbell, 1992). There is evidence that regular participation in exercise may have a buffering effect on stress. That is, individuals who regularly exercise will not be as adversely affected by stressors as individuals who do not exercise (Berger & McInman, 1993). Additional areas of interest to health psychologists are psychological health problems found in sport and exercise environments, such as burnout, substance abuse, and eating disorders.

### Performance Enhancement

Performance enhancement specialists are concerned with applied issues in sport and exercise psychology. This often includes helping athletes, exercisers, and coaches develop psychological skills that will enable them to perform up to their potential and to perform consistently. For example, consider the athlete who plays well in practice, yet chokes in game situations. This athlete does not suddenly lose physical skills, yet mental mistakes lead to poor performance (Harris & Harris, 1984).

Performance enhancement specialists often employ psychological skills training (PST) as the modality for assisting people in sport and exercise settings. PST may involve learning to manage anxiety, enhance confidence, increase concentration, focus attention appropriately, and enhance communication and cohesion (Martens, 1986). Commonly employed skills in PST include imagery, relaxation, goal setting, and positive thinking. These skills are helpful to competitive athletes and to recreational exercisers. For example, imagery may help a competitive or recreational basketball player improve her free throw ability. Positive thinking skills will help a jogger push himself further as well as help competitive racers maintain their poise when being passed in a race.

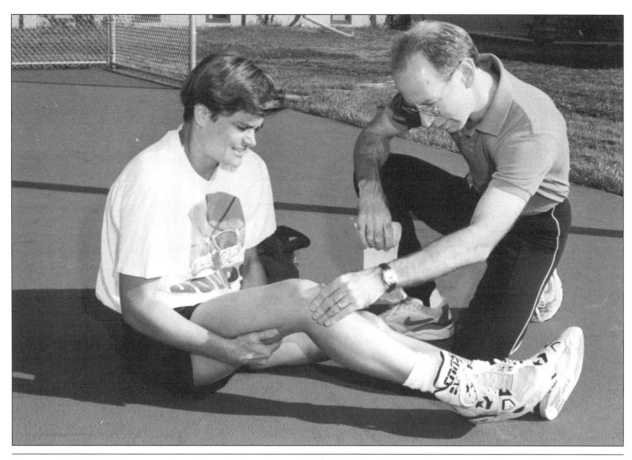

Chance of athletic injury can be reduced through psychological strategies such as goal setting and imagery.

## Psychophysiology of Sport and Exercise

This area of specialization examines interrelationships between psychological and physiological variables (Hatfield & Landers, 1983). Commonly examined physiological processes include heart rate, blood pressure, and muscular tension. These physiological indices are thought to impact psychological states, such as confidence, attentional focus, anxiety, and motivation (Kremer & Scully, 1994).

Physiological states also reflect psychological processes and emotional states. For example, increased heart rate is an indication of anxiety. Psychophysiological psychology embodies the interconnection between the mind and body. It highlights the interactions between psychological and physiological processes and their joint relationship to sport and exercise participation. An example of psychophysiology in sport and exercise is examining muscular responses associated with the process of mental imagery. Jowdy and Harris (1990) showed that when an individual engages in imagery, physical muscular contractions occur, demonstrating the interconnectedness of mind and body.

## Social Sport and Exercise Psychology

**Group dynamics** are within the realm of social sport and exercise psychology. Social sport and exercise psychology addresses psychological processes that affect or are affected by interactions among members of a group. This includes striving to facilitate positive social interactions in sport and exercise settings. Areas of interest within social sport and exercise psychology are team cohesion, leadership behaviors, group productivity, and communication. More recently, social sport and exercise psychologists have focused on the context of the sport environment and examined issues related to gender, race, and sexual orientation in sport and exercise settings (Krane, 1995).

## Learning Activity

Describe each of the following areas of sport and exercise psychology (a) cognitive, (b) developmental, (c) health, (d) performance enhancement, (e) psychophysiology, and (f) social.

## Implications of Sport and Exercise Psychology for Sport Managers

Understanding sport and exercise psychology can benefit sport managers in several ways. For example, managers will be more effective if they have insights into how participants and spectators behave in sport and exercise environments. This knowledge allows managers to create appropriate programming to meet the needs of their diverse clientele. Another important benefit of understanding sport and exercise psychology is the ability to develop positive environments in which sport and exercise can occur. Achieving this goal requires a collective effort from all individuals involved in the environment. Wise leadership from knowledgeable sport managers is an essential ingredient.

On the business side of the ledger, understanding the clientele is essential to successfully promote and market sport and exercise products. As Betty van der Smissen (1987) stated, "Markets are created by making individuals believe they need some sport product for performance or social reasons" (p. 104). Whether you are selling professional sport tickets, memberships in health clubs, or letter jackets to high schools, you will need to know your potential customers—their goals, what motivates them, what excites them, and what they consider socially important. Only then can you

gain their attention and entice them to purchase your product.

## Sociology of Sport

A critical step in becoming a successful sport manager is understanding sport as an important activity that permeates our society and influences individuals in many ways. To understand how and why people participate, you must not only know about individual behavior (i.e., psychology) but also know the social context in which that behavior occurs. During the last three decades, the scientific study of the social context of sport has been at the center of an academic discipline called sport sociology. In the remainder of this chapter we define sport sociology, delineate the nature and significance of sport, and highlight several areas of scholarly inquiry within sport sociology, emphasizing those areas most relevant to sport management. Finally, we outline the direct connection between sport sociology and sport management.

According to Snyder (1990), most people agree that activities such as basketball, football, baseball, tennis, and golf are sports. However, Snyder points out that a wide range of other physical activities are also considered sports. Such activities include walking, fishing, and hiking. What is clear from these examples is that there exists a continuum of physical activity ranging from informal, playlike activity in a leisure setting to the highly competitive, pressure cooker world of professional sports. Figure 3.1 depicts this continuum and includes some characteristics typically associated with such activity.

### Learning Activity

Explain why it is important for sport managers to understand sport and exercise psychology.

## For More Information

The Sport and Exercise Psychology Web site can be found at http://spot.colorado.edu/~collinsj/. Here are some more sources of information.

### Professional Associations

- American Alliance for Health, Physical Education, Recreation and Dance (Sport Psychology Academy)
- American College of Sports Medicine
- American Psychological Association, Division 47

- Association for the Advancement of Applied Sport Psychology
- North American Society for the Psychology of Sport and Physical Activity

### Scholarly Journals

- *Journal of Sport and Exercise Psychology*
- *The Sport Psychologist*
- *International Journal of Sport Psychology*

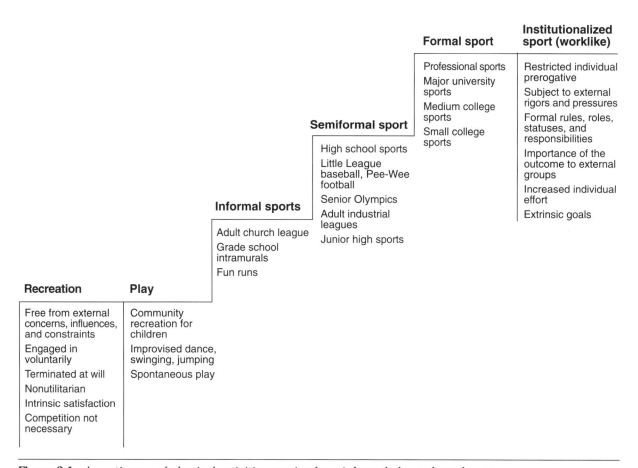

**Figure 3.1**   A continuum of physical activities ranging from informal play to formal sport.

Beginning in the mid-1960s, researchers from academic fields such as sociology and kinesiology tried to do more than define sport—they began to develop a scientific body of knowledge related to its nature and significance. This effort led to the emergence of a new academic discipline called sport sociology. Sport sociologists examine social organizations (i.e., hierarchies), social groupings (i.e., subcultures), and social processes (i.e., **socialization**) within a sport context (Siedentop, 1990). As part of this analysis, they do not typically focus on the behavior of specific individuals but examine instead the social patterns, structures, and organizations of groups actively engaged in sport (McPherson, Curtis, & Loy, 1989). This examination can include a microsystem (e.g., a women's basketball team), a sport subculture (e.g., gamblers), or a multifaceted sport organization (e.g., the National Collegiate Athletic Association).

An underlying assumption of sport sociology is that sport is a highly significant social institution of the same magnitude as the economy, the family, the educational system, and the political structure. A fundamental goal of sport sociology is to describe the complex dynamics surrounding par-

ticipation patterns (e.g., the number of young girls and boys involved in youth sport organizations) and social concerns (e.g., an overemphasis on winning) that make up this important social institution (Nixon & Frey, 1996). It is important to keep in mind, however, that sport sociologists do far more than describe sport involvement by gathering data on how many people participate. Sport sociologists ultimately are concerned with understanding the social context in which this participation occurs, as well as the meaning of sport as a highly influential social, political, and economic institution (Siedentop, 1990).

## Social Significance of Sport

Sport is an all-pervasive entity that influences almost every aspect of our daily lives. For example, the sport and fitness industry has an enormous economic impact on American society. With respect to discretionary spending alone, billions of dollars are spent annually on the sale of licensed sport products, such as baseball caps. In 1992, retail sales of all licensed sport merchandise totaled $12.2 billion (Gorman & Calhoun, 1994). In the early 1990s, the top four men's professional sport leagues (football, basketball, baseball, and ice hockey) generated almost $4 billion in revenues (Baldo, 1993). Anheuser Busch signed a $40-million contract to be the official beer sponsor of the 1996 Olympic Games held in Atlanta, Georgia (New York Times, 1993).

Sport holds a place of eminence in our society, and it has both positive and negative aspects. We can see positive outcomes of sport through its role as a socializing agent and a unifier of people. We see the negative side of sport through its reflection of some ills that exist in society at large, such as sexism, racism, **homophobia**, and violence. An important fact to remember, however, is that regardless of the negatives, sport has incredible power to serve as a vehicle for social change. All these aspects of sport are areas of inquiry for sport sociologists.

Sport can help to shape and perpetuate many social values held in high regard. Such values include hard work, self-sacrifice, fair play, loyalty, commitment, dependability, and self-discipline. Sport can contribute to the stability of individuals and to society as a whole.

## Sport as a Socializing Agent

A major consequence of the socialization process is role learning, where young children learn the social roles available to them (Greendorfer, 1993). Because many of us are socialized into play, sport, and physical activity at an early age, these activities become an important incubator for mastering such roles as good citizen, responsible neighbor, student, coworker, friend, and companion.

A variety of research studies have provided empirical evidence to support this claim. These studies investigated the effects of play, games, and sport and found that involvement in such activities enabled children to learn about relationships both inside and outside of sport (Coakley, 1993; McPherson et al., 1989). Coakley argued that the socialization aspects of sport can be so far reaching they even affect individuals who do not actively participate; spectators also learn about the values and attitudes this culture has toward authority and organizational competence. With this in mind, it is easy to see how involvement in sport—either as participants or as spectators—can influence individuals to think and behave in ways that enable them to contribute to the larger social agenda.

## Sport as a Unifier of People

Sport can bring people together by giving them a sense of personal identity, social identification, and feelings of group membership (Coakley, 1990). There are many ways that sport accomplishes this, from an individual level (e.g., "I feel good about myself because I helped my team win"), to a region of the country uniting behind a team (e.g., University of Connecticut, 1995 NCAA women's basketball champions), to an entire nation rooting for an Olympic athlete (e.g., U.S.'s Jackie Joyner-Kersee or Bonnie Blair). We believe that few, if any, institutions in this society have the ability to bring people together the way that sport can. This is because the popularity of sports cuts across social class, gender, race, and age barriers. Because of its enormous visibility and appeal, sport also creates linkages among people that may transcend tension and conflict. In an era of unprecedented hostility and violence among Americans, it is critical that we not forget, nor fail to use, sport as a means to bring together individuals as team members of a family, a neighborhood, a city, a nation. Examples of this in sport and exercise management include developing midnight basketball leagues, sponsoring busses to take local fans to championship high school basketball games, and having a bike ride or fun run to generate funds for cancer research.

## The Dark Side of Sport

We have just discussed ways in which sport involvement produces beneficial outcomes, not just for individuals, but for society as a whole. This is not meant to suggest that sport participation results only in good things. There is a darker side to such involvement. For example, when individuals are denied the opportunity to experience feelings of competence and self-worth by achieving success in sports, the consequences can be damaging. The abuses of youth sport programs, in which the standards of excellence are often impossible to achieve given the physical, social, and psychological maturation levels of young children, are well documented. We also know that the pressure-filled world of big-time athletics can distort and undermine fundamental values such as honesty and integrity because of its winning at all costs mentality.

Four areas of sport that reflect and contribute to some of the most troubling aspects of our society are sexism, racism, homophobia and

**heterosexism,** and violence. In the following section, we will highlight research findings from sport sociology as we explore each area.

## Sexism in Sport

In the wake of the modern feminist movement begun in the early 1970s, a number of women's roles expanded into areas traditionally occupied by men. The world of sport was no exception. In 1972, Title IX of the Education Amendments Act was passed. Title IX prohibited sex discrimination in educational programs and activities that received federal financial assistance. This legislation made it possible for millions of girls and women to enjoy the benefits of school-sponsored sport. In 1984, however, Grove City College (Pennsylvania) challenged Title IX, claiming that programs not receiving direct federal funding (e.g., athletics) should be exempt from its mandates. The Supreme Court ruled in Grove City's favor, finding that Title IX's specific reference to "programs and activities" excused athletics programs from its provisions. Four years later, however, Congress passed the Civil Rights Restoration Act of 1988, making it crystal clear that the intent of Title IX was to hold the entire institution, including athletics, responsible for nondiscriminatory practices (Carpenter, 1993).

Enormous changes have taken place since 1972. There have been substantial gains for women in participation rates, access to athletic scholarships and facilities, athletic budgets, and media coverage. Participation rates have exploded with more than two million females currently involved in interscholastic sports, compared with only 300,000 before Title IX. At the intercollegiate level, more than 30% of all participants are female, compared with only 15% who participated in the early 1970s (Kane & Greendorfer, 1994). Millions of girls and women participate in physical fitness activities and recreational pursuits. Change is also reflected in an ever-increasing acceptance of women's involvement in sport: In the late 1980s, a nationwide survey found that most parents and children believed that sports are no longer just for boys (The Wilson Report, 1988).

Although women have made enormous strides in sport, it would be a mistake to assume that equality has been attained. For example, almost 25 years after the passage of Title IX, women received approximately one third of athletic scholarships at the intercollegiate level (Kane & Greendorfer, 1994). Athletic budgets and access to facilities and equipment are nowhere near a 50-50 ratio in interscholastic and intercollegiate sports. Finally, sportswomen lag far behind their male counterparts in leadership roles (Acosta & Carpenter, 1992) and in mass media coverage of women's sporting events (Kane, 1996).

### Leadership Positions

In terms of leadership positions in women's athletics, females have lost more than they have gained since Title IX. Before 1972, more than 90% of the coaches and administrators (such as athletics directors) in women's intercollegiate sport nationwide were female; in the early 1990s, however, approximately 43% of head coaches and 15% of administrators in women's athletics were female (Acosta & Carpenter, 1992). In 1996, the proportion of women coaches and administrators in women's intercollegiate sport had declined to 47.7% and 18.5%, respectively (Acosta & Carpenter, 1996). Some people have suggested that this imbalance has occurred because men are better qualified than women. This belief is not supported by empirical evidence. Research studies have indicated that women are often as qualified or more so than their male counterparts. In a nationwide study, Acosta and Carpenter (1988) asked athletics directors—the individuals most responsible for recruiting and hiring college head coaches—to list the reasons for the dramatic decline in the number of women coaches since the passage of Title IX. The findings indicated that male athletics directors perceived the four most important reasons to be (a) lack of qualified female coaches, (b) failure of women to apply for job openings, (c) lack of qualified female administrators, and (d) time constraints on women due to family obligations. Researchers empirically tested two such beliefs—that women are less qualified than men and that women are more restricted than men because of family obligations (Hasbrook, Hart, Mathes, & True, 1990). Interestingly, these researchers discovered that female coaches were more qualified in terms of coaching experience with female teams, professional training, and professional experience. They further found that male coaches were more restricted due to family responsibilities than were female coaches. These findings suggest that harmful stereotypes can disadvantage females who want to become coaches because "the beliefs expressed by male athletic directors appear to be based more on a gender-stereotypic bias about female competence than on any objective data" (Stangl & Kane, 1991, p. 49).

## Media Coverage of Female Athletes

There are many female athletes who have become household names as a result of sport media coverage during the last two decades. Martina Navratilova, Monica Seles, Steffi Graf, Sheryl Swoopes, Rebecca Lobo, and Jackie Joyner-Kersee immediately come to mind. In spite of this, many research studies have demonstrated that sportswomen and men are treated differently by the media. Sport sociologists have discovered two themes regarding the media portrayal of female and male athletes. First, although there has been a tremendous participation increase for a variety of women across an array of activities, sportswomen continue to be grossly underrepresented in amount of coverage (Kane & Greendorfer, 1994). A study conducted by the Amateur Athletic Foundation of Los Angeles illustrates this trend: Examining sport coverage on three local network affiliates (ABC, CBS, and NBC) in Los Angeles, researchers reported that women received only 5% of the overall coverage (Duncan, Messner, & Jensen, 1994).

The second theme involves type of coverage. Males are portrayed in ways that emphasize their athletic strength and competence, whereas females are presented in ways that highlight their femininity and physical attractiveness (Kane & Parks, 1992). For example, female athletes are significantly more likely than male athletes to be portrayed off the court, out of uniform, and in highly passive and sexualized poses.

The amount and type of media coverage that sportswomen receive is not a trivial matter. By creating the impression that females are largely absent from the sporting scene, and by treating the female athletes we do see, read, and hear about in ways that denigrate them and their athletic endeavors, the media marginalize women's sport involvement. This in turn denies them the status, power, and prestige that is given to male athletes (Duncan & Hasbrook, 1988).

### Learning Activity

Why do you think females and males are treated differently by the mass media? Can you think of specific examples where you have noticed such a difference? How would you as a sport manager (e.g., sports editor or sports information director) change such practices?

## Racism in Sport

Since Jackie Robinson broke the color barrier in baseball in the 1940s, minorities have made important progress in all levels of sport. Despite this, racism remains deeply entrenched throughout the sport world. A number of research studies have revealed a phenomenon called *stacking*, whereby minority groups are steered into or away from certain player positions that are directly linked to status, prestige, and power (Johnson & Johnson, 1995; Phillips, 1991). For example, anecdotal evidence suggests that many African American football players who were quarterbacks on their college teams are encouraged to become wide receivers or defensive backs in the pros. Theoretically, the latter positions are less central to the action and more distant from the head coach than is the position of quarterback. Data from the 1995 NFL season support this claim. Even though approximately 68% of all NFL players in 1995 were African Americans, only three starting quarterbacks were Black—Warren Moon of the Minnesota Vikings, Jeff Blake of the Cincinnati Bengals, and Rodney Peete of the Philadelphia Eagles.

Minorities are also underrepresented at all levels of sport leadership positions. In 1996, Dennis Green (Minnesota Vikings) and Ray Rhodes (Philadelphia Eagles) were the only Black head coaches in the NFL. Lapchick and Benedict (1993) pointed out that in the early 1990s, there were no Black general managers in the NFL nor in Major League Baseball; heading into the 1996 season the NFL had only two general managers of color, while MLB had one. The NBA has shown the greatest progress: In 1996, 6 out of 29 general managers were African American. Lapchick and Benedict also found that as of the early 1990s, the highest management positions in professional sports—chair of the board and president or CEO—were overwhelmingly dominated by White males.

The lack of minorities in important leadership positions in organized sport is often based on racial myths and stereotypes. For example, many of you may remember the insensitive remarks made by Al Campanis in the late 1980s when he appeared on ABC TV's Nightline program hosted by Ted Koppel. Campanis was on the program to pay tribute to Jackie Robinson. He was asked to do so because he had been part of the Los Angeles Dodger baseball organization since the early 1940s and had helped develop the Dodgers' reputation for recruiting and playing minorities. However, Campanis sparked a national controversy when he explained that MLB did not have any (in 1987) African American general managers or managers because African Americans "may not have some of the necessities" for these occupations (Nixon & Frey, 1996, p. 240). Although Campanis apologized for his remarks the next day, calling the incident "the saddest of my career" (Associated Press cited in Nixon & Frey, p. 240), he was nevertheless forced to resign shortly thereafter. Although there has been some improvement in the wake of his remarks, in 1996, there were only two African Americans and two Hispanics who served as managers in Major League Baseball.

Stereotypes regarding racial minorities in sport are not confined to beliefs about leadership abilities. As Coakley (1986) points out, there is a popularly held belief that African American athletes owe their success to their natural abilities, suggesting that they have some genetic advantage over Whites when it comes to achievement in sports. In contrast, White athletes are said to achieve excellence in sport because of their discipline, intelligence, and hard work. Coakley insightfully argues that such beliefs are based on racist assumptions. Drawing a parallel with the dominance of Canadians in hockey, Coakley comments that: "No one claims that Canadians have naturally strong ankles, [or] an innate ability to withstand cold weather by storing body heat, . . . but when black athletes jump to the top in certain sports, . . . there is a widespread search for genetic explanations" (p. 154).

Racial minorities also are stereotyped in media coverage. In the 1994 study by the Amateur Athletic Foundation of Los Angeles, Duncan et al. found what they called a "hierarchy of naming" pattern, whereby those members of a less powerful group (i.e., minorities and women) were frequently referred to by their first name only, and those in more powerful groups (i.e., White men) were referred to either by their last name or their full name. In 90% of the cases where male athletes were referred to by first name only, the athlete was a person of color (Duncan et al., 1994). Some examples from professional sports will bring this point closer to home. All of us know who Michael, Magic, and Shaq are, but we do not think of Joe Montana and Cal Ripkin as Joe and Cal. Although certainly not intentional, this type of coverage can reflect and perpetuate a lack of respect toward minority athletes.

## Homophobia and Heterosexism in Sport

Sport sociologists are just beginning to address one of the more oppressive aspects of sport—homophobia and heterosexism. Homophobia and heterosexism exist in both women's and men's athletics. In terms of men's sports, Pronger (1990) has pointed out that being a male athlete and being gay is seen as a contradiction in terms. This is because traditional definitions of masculinity are synonymous with being a male athlete: Being physically tough and courageous are the cornerstones of being an athlete and being a man. At the same time, gay men are believed to be the antithesis of manliness in that homophobic assumptions stereotype them as soft, passive, and nonathletic.

Although homophobia is present in both women's and men's athletics, fears about homosexuals in sport have long been associated primarily with women's sports. Such concerns range from historical assertions that women's participation will harm their reproductive capacity (and thus make them unable to fulfill what are presumed to be appropriate heterosexual roles such as wife and mother), to modern claims that athletic involvement will turn females into males (Boutilier & SanGiovanni, 1983). One example of this latter concern is the commonly held assumption that female athletes, particularly those who engage in more masculine sports, are (or will become) lesbians.

Sport sociologists are becoming increasingly aware of the degree to which homophobic stereotypes prevent female athletes from gaining recognition, respect, and status. This is because to be pejoratively labeled a lesbian is to be stigmatized as abnormal or deviant and to be threatened with the loss of employment, career, and family (Cart, 1992; Griffin, 1993; Lenskyj, 1992). It is important to point out that this labeling process affects all female athletes, homosexual and heterosexual alike. Helen Lenskyj (1992) conducted one of the few studies that specifically addresses homophobia in women's sports. She found that sport and physical education climates were so hostile, not only to lesbians, but to women in general, that most lesbians, whether they were players, coaches, administrators, or faculty, remained invisible. Interviews with lesbian collegiate coaches and athletes also have revealed much prejudice and discrimination against lesbians (Krane, 1996).

An example of homophobia in women's athletics was the case of CBS Sports' golf analyst Ben Wright. Wright was quoted in May of 1995 as making derogatory remarks about the so-called negative influence of lesbians on the women's professional golf tour. Stating that "lesbians in the sport hurt women's golf" and that "when it [the presence of lesbians] gets to the corporate level, that's not going to fly," Wright also demeaned female athletes in general by suggesting that they are "handicapped by having boobs" that get in the way of their backswing (Gerdes, 1996, p. 1). Wright initially denied having made such remarks but was fired in January, 1996, after it was widely reported in the press that others had overheard him making such comments.

## Violence in Sport

Sport sociologists are just beginning to examine how violence is institutionalized in men's athletics (Crosset, Benedict, & McDonald, 1995). Messner and Sabo (1994) argue that in recent years, the image of the male athlete as hero has changed into one of an irresponsible, greedy individual who is often physically and sexually abusive toward

women. Examples of this latter image are rampant throughout sport. In 1996, O.J. Simpson was found not guilty of murdering Nicole Brown, his former wife. In 1988, however, he had pleaded no contest to a charge of spousal battery toward her (Nelson, 1994, p. 133). In a similar vein, professional golfer John Daly pleaded guilty to a misdemeanor harassment charge after he was arrested for "allegedly hurling his wife against a wall, pulling her hair and trashing the house" (Nelson, 1994, p. 133). We are also aware of the rape conviction of boxer Mike Tyson and the locker-room sexual assault of sport reporter Lisa Olson by several members of the New England Patriots. As Messner and Sabo (1994) point out, stories of sexual and physical abuse by male athletes appear to occur almost daily.

Why is this happening? A number of scholars suggest that for many males a central part of the sport experience is the glorification of violence—a glorification that encourages men to equate their physicality with behavior that demeans and sexualizes others (Curry, 1991; Kane & Disch, 1993; Melnick, 1992). Men's sports, particularly team

© Daily Illini

Some scholars propose the idea that an athlete's violence on the field, court, or rink could be an indicator, if not a cause, of violence in his life outside of sport.

sports that emphasize the physical domination and subjugation of others, have become a place where males learn far too often that violence is an acceptable way to relate to and control others, particularly when those others are women and homosexual men. As we begin to learn more about the athletic experience for males, it is important to ask ourselves whether the current model of men's athletics "reinforces and perpetuates social injustice and individual oppression" (Lopiano, 1994, p. 1).

## Learning Activity

Do you agree with sport sociologists that there is a strong connection between men's athletics and the glorification of violence? If yes, what specific strategies would you use as a sport manager (e.g., coach or athletics director) to stop such behavior? If no, how do you explain what appears to be an increase in the number of male athletes involved in such violence?

## Sport as a Vehicle for Social Transformation

Even though the four areas outlined previously represent the most problematic aspects of sport, sport can help us overcome prejudice and oppression. Created and reinforced with appropriate social values, the sport experience can instill in individuals a strong desire and commitment to make significant contributions to our society. McPherson et al. (1989) have argued that sport often has served as a catalyst for protest and social change. This in turn has created economic, political, and social transformations for society as a whole. The following example illustrates this point. In the early 1990s, Magic Johnson stunned not only the NBA but also all of America with the revelation of his HIV positive status. During that time, we were aware that thousands of people had died from AIDS and that millions more were infected with the deadly disease. We were even aware that such celebrities as Rock Hudson, Hollywood actor, and Freddy Mercury, lead singer for the rock band Queen, had died of complications due to AIDS. However, in the early 1990s, AIDS education, treatment, and research were not in the forefront of public consciousness. Magic Johnson's story demonstrates the power and widespread appeal of sport. In the wake of his press conference, the AIDS epidemic became *the* national story. Along with the well-publicized case of Ryan White, the story of Magic Johnson helped us move beyond the stereotypic and inaccurate perception that AIDS was confined to gay men. We learned to see AIDS as a tragedy that does not discriminate on the basis of sexual orientation.

Another example of sport as a vehicle for social change is women's involvement in sport. Before the early 1970s, many segments of society—including many sporting activities—were considered off-limits for most females. However, women and sympathetic men began to push for greater opportunities and a more level playing field for those females who wanted to participate. Such participation has made a difference in the lives of countless girls and women. Sport sociologist Mary Duquin (1989) has argued that sport can serve as an ideal setting for experiencing feelings of self-worth and empowerment. Through the physical, social, and intellectual challenges found in sport, women, like men, learn about their physical potentials; test their ambitions, goals, and dreams; and realize their ability to create their destiny, not only in sport, but also in society as a whole.

## Learning Activity

How can sport act as a vehicle for positive social change and transformation? As part of your answer, provide two examples that were not covered in this chapter.

## Implications for Sport Managers

Sport sociology has several implications for sport managers. We have discussed how individuals can gain feelings of self-worth, competence, and empowerment through the sport experience. We also have reported larger social phenomena, such as the economic impact of the sport and fitness industry. Finally, we have seen how organized sport can unify cities and nations and transcend bigotry and oppression. What all of these scenarios have in common is *people*. Knowing about people is critical to one's success as a sport manager because of the following:

Whether you are designing a fitness program, selling a program to the public, or hiring and supervising people to implement a program, you are first and foremost dealing with people. And dealing with people means learning how, when, where and why they do what they do. (Kane, 1990, p. 197)

In a similar fashion, Snyder (1990) points out that managing sport activities and facilities ultimately depends on people becoming involved in sport, whether as spectators or active participants. A sport manager's ability to get people involved in and stay committed to such activity requires understanding the social context of sport and the meaning attached to that context. A few specific examples relating to the positive and negative aspects of sport illustrate this point. In Minneapolis, Minnesota, sport managers were concerned with the lack of sport participation by adolescent African American females. They soon discovered that low participation rates were not due to a lack of interest but to barriers such as gender-role stereotyping and safety concerns that impacted girls more than boys (Steiner, 1991). For example, they discovered that adolescent girls (unlike their brothers) were expected to take care of younger siblings when the parent (usually a single mother) was at work. This barrier was removed by providing day care at the local parks and recreation facility. Another barrier was that girls often lacked transportation to and from the facility; this was particularly problematic for attendance at evening programs. This problem was solved when sport managers got volunteers to provide transportation. By developing a creative and aggressive outreach program, participation rates skyrocketed.

Another example of the direct connection between sport sociology and sport management relates to the notion of sport as a unifier. For example, since 1995 there has been a resurgence of interest in minor league baseball. We can link this resurgence to the larger social context and meaning of sport. The 1994 strike in Major League Baseball left many fans with a sense of disgust over what they saw as the greed, arrogance, and insensitivity of both players and owners. As a result, fans turned away in record numbers. In the vacuum created by the fans' exodus, many minor league and semiprofessional teams united cities around the country by attracting fans eager to return to a time when sport was played for the love of the game.

## Summary

Sport management embraces the concepts of sport and exercise psychology and sport sociology. The

## Learning Activity

Winning has become enormously important to most sport participants and spectators, from youth sport to the pros. What implications does this emphasis on winning have for sport managers? How can sport psychologists and sport sociologists address this concern?

individual aspects of sport and exercise participation are the foci of sport and exercise psychology, whereas sport sociology includes the cultural and societal aspects of sport and exercise participation. These two domains are intricately interwoven; the individual in sport and exercise is affected by the social and cultural environment, and vice versa. Sport and exercise psychology includes both research and applied components. Research sport and exercise psychology addresses issues of theory development, testing, and refinement, whereas applied sport and exercise psychology focuses on practically employing conceptual knowledge. These two spheres of sport and exercise overlay many perspectives. The perspectives within sport and exercise psychology include cognitive, developmental, health, performance enhancement, psychophysiology, and social.

Sport sociology involves the scientific study of the social context of sport. Sport sociologists are most concerned with describing the social dynamics of sport and exercise participation and social concerns in sport and exercise. Sport is an influential aspect of our society, shaping and perpetuating many social values. Positive social benefits of sport include teaching children valued social roles and unifying diverse people as they back a particular team. Sport also may contribute to disruptive social concerns such as sexism, racism, homophobia and heterosexism, and violence (both in and out of sport settings). Finally, sport may serve as a vehicle for social transformation. Sport figures may enhance awareness of social problems such as AIDS. Sport also can engender feelings of self-worth and a sense of empowerment.

Understanding and appreciating sport and exercise psychology and sport sociology will provide an important foundation for understanding sport management. To fully understand sport as a whole, as well as managing sport, it is necessary to be aware of its psychological and social aspects. Considering that sport managers work with individuals in social settings, it is imperative that they understand both the individual and the social environment. As we have indicated throughout this chapter, the individual and the environment are continuously interacting and affecting each other. The sport manager will have a strong impact on individuals in sport and exercise and will play an integral role in developing positive sport and exercise environments. The more positive the environment the manager creates, the more likely individuals will desire to participate in that environment either as athletes, exercisers, fans, clients, or consumers.

# For More Information

The following sources will provide you with more resources on the psychosocial aspects of sport.

## Web Sites

- http://yoda.ucc.uconn.edu/users/ yiannakisa/newslet2.htm
- http://www.hmse.memphis.edu/nasss/ nasshome.htm

## Professional Organizations

- American Sociological Association
- American Alliance for Health, Physical Education, Recreation and Dance (Sociology of Sport Academy)
- North American Society for the Sociology of Sport
- North American Society for Sport History

## Scholarly Journals

- *International Review for the Sociology of Sport*
- *International Review of Sport Sociology*
- *Journal of Sport and Social Issues*
- *Sociology of Sport Journal*

# Chapter 4

# Philosophical Foundations of Sport

**Joy T. DeSensi**
University of Tennessee-Knoxville

---

## Learning Objectives

After studying this chapter, you will be able to

1. identify the relevance, value, and use of philosophy and the philosophic process as related to sport, ethics, and social responsibility;

2. explain the concept of social and moral responsibility in relation to sport management; and

3. provide examples of the nature of personal and professional ethics in relation to managing sport.

---

Our values, beliefs, and actions are inextricably tied to how we regard life, ourselves, and others. Understanding what we know and believe and standing by beliefs in our actions is critically important. Learning to formulate critical questions and solve ethical dilemmas is what the study of philosophy is about. It is precisely this study that leads you to become a true professional.

The following scenario poses critical issues and philosophical questions similar to those all sport managers must confront. As you read this scenario, think about how understanding philosophy and critical thinking could help you make prin-

cipled decisions and act ethically. By the time you learn the concepts presented in this chapter, you should have some suggestions about how to resolve the situation.

In this chapter we will introduce you to the relevance, value, and use of the **philosophic process** as it relates to sport management. In addition to learning about philosophy, you will learn about ethics and moral and social responsibility, concepts that are perceived in a variety of ways (see figure 4.1). Perhaps this knowledge will lead you to possible solutions for the following dilemma, "Crisis in the Athletic Training Room."

## Crisis in the Athletic Training Room

You have just accepted an athletic training position at the college level, which enables you to work with one of the profession's noted senior members. Having been well trained, you learned that you should administer treatment to all athletes fairly and equally. The head athletic trainer, Jack Moran, has been at this institution since well before Title IX. After accepting this position, you find out that the coaches and athletes are not pleased with the treatment female athletes are receiving. In all instances, the women's sports are treated as though they were secondary to the men's sports. In addition, there is no athletic trainer assigned directly to women's sports. Mr. Moran has expressed openly that women are a nuisance, should not be involved in athletics, and should not take up time and space in the training room.

Jack Moran has worked at this college for many years and has his own standards established for the care of athletes. The coaches he works with have decided that fighting him does not work.

After completing your first month in this position, the following occurs: A female athlete is brought to the training room with a quadriceps contusion. You, as the assistant athletic trainer, make the immediate evaluation and decide on a treatment that requires the athlete to remain in the facility. When Mr. Moran arrives, he questions you about the athlete's presence and requests that you move her out before the guys start coming in from practice. Moving her is not of great consequence, but Mr. Moran's attitude in this situation is of obvious concern to you (adapted from Mangus & Ingersoll, 1990). Describe how you would handle this situation.

**Figure 4.1** There are better and worse ways to evaluate ethical behavior and social responsibility. Justice cannot be left to the spin of a wheel.
Reprinted from Wade Austin 1995.

# Philosophy and the Study of Sport Management

Many definitions of philosophy have been offered. Such definitions may include that philosophy is (a) a process of thought; (b) a product of logical discourse; (c) the love of wisdom; (d) a human endeavor that leads us to truth, meaning, freedom, justice, virtue, humanness, and choices; and (e) a way of life. Philosophy plays an extremely important role in developing the personal beliefs, values, and actions of all people. Philosophy is not reserved for those who are considered the elite or intellectual in our society, but for each individual. Because philosophy deals with the questions of everyday life and each of us engages in everyday life, the study of philosophy is for everyone and certainly for those with sport management responsibilities.

One purpose of philosophy is to assist individuals in evaluating their beliefs so the actions that follow are logical and consistent. Philosophy is a process that leads us to that understanding. Katen (1973) notes that a balance should occur in one's philosophical thinking and philosophical existence. "Thinking and experiencing should blend into a continuum and provide a richly unified existence" (Katen, 1973, p. 346). For example, after we establish our beliefs, they should parallel the choices we make and be consistent with how we experience people and things. In other words, a more unified existence is the result of consistency in thought and action or behavior. Although we may believe that philosophy is profound thinking, it is actually profound living. Our lives should be unified by a combination of philosophical thought and philosophical behavior.

Philosophy allows us to examine questions within the areas of metaphysics (the nature of things), epistemology (the nature of knowledge), and axiology (the value of things). It is the reflective, analytical, and speculative features of the philosophic process that offer individuals mechanisms for contemplation and problem solving. According to Kretchmar (1994),

> The philosophic process is the art and science of wondering about reality, posing questions related to that wonder, and pursuing answers to those questions reflectively. It is an art and a science because the philosophic skills of wondering, posing questions, and searching for answers are grounded partly on repeatable methods that can be objectified and explained (science) and partly on intuitions, tendencies, and flashes of insight that can neither be fully predicted nor accounted for (art). (pp. 4-5)

To better understand the concepts inherent in the philosophic process, we must understand the terms metaphysics, epistemology, and axiology. Metaphysics is a descriptive analysis of the nature of things. Questions in the area of metaphysics are concerned with describing the similarities and differences of physical and nonphysical things. This analysis in philosophy deals with inquiry regarding the kinds of things there are and their modes of being. Metaphysical questions or examination might include the nature of sport and how sport and dance are similar to or different from each other. In addition, the concept of believing and the characteristics associated with inanimate objects, such as a baseball bat or tennis racquet, might also be included within metaphysical analysis (Kretchmar, 1994).

**Learning Activity**

Discuss with a friend your questions regarding metaphysics. For example, discuss the similarities and differences among physical objects such as a tennis racquet, basketball, or hockey stick compared with nonphysical entities such as ideas, hopes, and dreams.

Epistemology deals with the concept of knowledge. What we know and how we know it are explored within epistemology. A question that arises in this area is the following: If we have not performed sport skills or had experience with dance or fitness activities, does that mean that we cannot teach, coach, or know what the experience is like?

**Learning Activity**

Discuss with a friend your questions regarding epistemology. For example, how do we come to know and understand through our participation in a sport?

The area of axiology is concerned with the value of things. Truth, excellence, quality, and how individuals should act and what should be is the focus within axiology. As a part of axiology, ethics allows us to explore our behavior and how we should treat each other. How our actions affect others is of great concern within ethics. Questions regarding what is honest and fair are ethical concerns.

**Learning Activity**

Discuss with a friend your questions regarding axiology. For example, what is the value of high school or college athletics in educational institutions? Are team sports at these levels of competition too violent?

In marketing sport programs, for example, is it honest to say that certain services will be provided, when in fact they are not? Is implementation of legislation such as Title IX ethical when it results in denying males or females access to athletic programs? For example, some schools have eliminated teams for males to finance teams for females. What are the ethical implications of these actions? Why do the athletics administrators at these schools believe they have to drop the teams for males? How might this situation have been avoided? Most organizations, such as the National Athletic Trainers Association, have codes of ethics designed to guide their professional

**Learning Activity**

Evaluate the strengths and weaknesses of the NATA Code of Professional Practice Ethical Principles found in figure 4.2. Using the information from this chapter, (a) explain each element and indicate how abiding by them would affect a person's behavior, (b) identify what has been omitted from the code, and (c) indicate any changes in the code you would recommend.

**NATA code of professional practice**

Ethical principles

1. Athletic trainers should neither practice nor condone discrimination on the basis of race, color, sex, age, religion, or national origin.
2. Athletic trainers should not condone, engage in, or defend unsporting conduct or practices.
3. Athletic trainers should provide care based on the needs of the individual athlete. They should not discriminate based on athletic ability.
4. Athletic trainers should strive to achieve the highest level of competence. They should use only those techniques and preparations that they are qualified and authorized to administer.
5. Athletic trainers should recognize the need for continuing education to remain proficient in their practice. They should be willing to consider new procedures within guidelines that assure safety.
6. Athletic trainers should recognize that personal problems may occur, which may interfere with professional effectiveness. Accordingly, they should refrain from undertaking any activity in which their personal problems are likely to lead to inadequate performance or harm to an athlete or colleague.
7. Athletic trainers should be truthful and not misleading when stating their education, training, and experience.

**Figure 4.2** NATA code of professional practices.
Reprinted, with permission, from *NATA Code of Professional Practice*, Winter 1990, as published in *Athletic Training, Journal of the National Athletic Trainers' Association*, **25**(4): 341.

behavior (see figure 4.2). Examining such codes of ethics helps prospective sport managers learn about professional expectations regarding ethical behavior.

Aesthetics is also a part of axiology, focusing on artistic quality. Questions such as what is beautiful, what is pleasing, and what is good from an artistic standpoint are examined. The judging of gymnastics, diving, ice skating, and dance falls into this category. When judging one of these activities, how do we determine the artistic quality of the performance, then transfer that judgment to a numerical evaluation? Establishing criteria that translate into a quality of the performance is not an easy task, and our definitions of what is good performance must be established through aesthetic examination.

Philosophic examination and reflection offers us many ways of thinking about issues and behavior. It is the most general form of human understanding and offers an inclusive perspective of

**Learning Activity**

Discuss with a friend your questions regarding aesthetics. For example, compare contests that measure beauty, grace, and style, in addition to athletic ability (e.g., figure skating and gymnastics) with contests that use scoring goals or points as the objective (e.g., volleyball, basketball, and hockey).

humankind. Philosophy is a process as well as a product. In posing our questions, philosophy assists us with understanding how we and others think, believe, understand, and subsequently act. By understanding the beliefs associated with metaphysics, epistemology, and axiology we gain knowledge that we can ultimately transform into action and insight into what others believe and value. Bressan and Pieter (1985) state that the process of philosophy is the "effort to transform the obscure, the ambiguous and the indeterminate into the evident, the explicit and the understandable" (p. 1).

Because this chapter will not cover everything there is to know about sport philosophy, it is important to further prepare and empower yourselves by taking additional courses in sport philosophy, social theory, critical thinking, ethics in sport management, sport sociology, and sport psychology to better grasp the implications that these areas have for sport management. Managerial responsibilities will test your decision-making abilities. Sound analytical and critical philosophical questioning applied to the management setting will assist you in making the best decisions.

Sport and sport management have a great need for social awareness and responsibility in the midst of theories, techniques, styles, and models of management. As a sport manager, you will be in a position to effect change. Understanding sport and management from a philosophical and social perspective will assist you in developing sound beliefs, a sense of social responsibility, and actions based on reason.

## Value of Philosophy in Sport Management

There is significant value placed on studying philosophy in relation to sport management. As a continuously evolving process, which ultimately leads to knowledge and understanding, philosophy offers us a tool to better explore our thoughts and actions related to sport in our society and the roles of the sport manager.

Through intellectual argument we generate new theories and ultimately initiate change. Philosophical examination may give rise to questions regarding the worth of sport programs, the concept of profit maximization, the responsibilities of a sport franchise to a community, the rights of spectators and athletes, moral and political actions in sport, and ethics and managerial behavior.

As we engage in sport, either as a participant or spectator, rarely do we examine the meaning of these activities and their relevance to our everyday lives. We gain understanding from different perspectives (e.g., player, spectator, manager, owner, referee) as we engage in reflective thinking and philosophic analysis. Meanings are revealed as we explore the nature of play, games, sport, dance, and fitness activities. Issues such as the body as subject (expressing through movement) or object (training the body as a machine) are viable philosophical questions. We may consider such questions as we envision the total body moving in expressive harmony compared with the concepts of training or using performance-enhancing drugs.

The art of movement and its various qualities spark much philosophical debate when individuals

© Daily Illini

Why do we view the grace and agility involved in athletics different from how we view grace and agility involved in dance?

define what is aesthetically pleasing to them as a participant or spectator. The question of how grace and other artistic qualities blend with more powerful athletic movement is an important concept to explore, particularly if the sport manager is dealing with marketing and promoting a specific event. How are these two areas reconciled, captured, and presented? We often do not equate the abilities of the dancer and athlete as similar, although both use grace, power, speed, endurance, flexibility, agility, and coordination to perform their skills. Why shouldn't we? Dance and athletic performance have been referred to as artistic expression, even though they occur in different settings. We might ask ourselves if we would consider advertising a dance presentation using phrases such as the "athletic ability of the dancer is equal to the grace of the football player" or the "grace of the rower is similar to the strength exhibited by the dancer." Philosophical exploration of the differences and similarities between sport and dance as artistic expressions is warranted.

Ethics, a subcategory of axiology in philosophy, has gained much attention lately, particularly regarding the athlete as hero or heroine, fair play and good behavior in sport (i.e., sporting behavior), and truth in advertising. How individuals *should* act is often set aside, using the more negative behavior (e.g., violence or the illusion of violence) as the marketing ploy to gain attendance at a sporting event. This strategy is particularly evident in sports such as boxing (both men and women), auto racing, ice hockey, women's and men's professional wrestling, and football.

Although philosophers have offered us many explanations regarding the concepts of truth, God, freedom, beauty, good, evil, existence, reality, and being, such questions can create unsettling feelings; this is the case with these issues as they apply to sport. How do we reconcile our religious beliefs when faced with obtaining a representative of the various religious denominations to offer the prayer at our high school or intercollegiate football games? Do we represent only one religion in this prayer or do we acknowledge the diversity of religious views in our society? Are all religious perspectives respected in how a prayer is worded? What about respect as well for agnostics and atheists? Additional questions arise when we consider offering prayer in a public institution. How do we evaluate the issue of the separation of church and state when we use prayer in a public institution? Debates regarding spirituality and

religion can invoke emotional arguments among individuals. For example, prayer in conjunction with an athletic or sporting contest has raised much controversy, especially within public arenas and educational institutions.

Certainly, none of the questions are dealt with easily, but they are more accessible through open deliberation and reference to rational, cognitive, or conceptual activities. It is these activities that characterize the process and product of philosophy. The spectator, participant, and sport manager all have the potential to pose questions dealing with meaning, definition, and justification. The philosophic process is vital to discourse regarding life and sport so we are not doomed to rely on the unsteady grounds of mere opinion or our narrow, personal experiences.

## Philosophical Questioning and Critical Thinking

Philosophical questioning and critical thinking go hand in hand. As we search for meaning, value, knowledge, and direction, we constantly encounter philosophical questions. These are easily recognizable if, as Kretchmar (1994) notes, we as individuals are conscious or awake and capable of dealing with ideas. Some individuals are more interested than others in addressing the philosophical questions associated with managing sport. However, no one who takes on such responsibilities can afford to set aside the issues that arise. If these issues are ignored, sport managers and the beneficiaries of their efforts are seriously disadvantaged. Included here are questions such as the following: What is the value of activities such as play and sport? Should individuals whose physical abilities differ from others have access to sport competition? What constitutes grace, beauty, and strength in sport performance? Is physical fitness spiritual in nature?

Critical thinking is directly associated with the area of epistemology or how we know what we know. It involves making sense of our world by carefully examining the thinking process to clarify and improve our understanding (Chaffee, 1991). Critical thinking involves thinking actively and for ourselves, carefully exploring situations with insightful questions, attempting to view situations from different perspectives, and discussing ideas in an organized way. This also involves being open to ideas and experiences other than our own, something that is easier said than done.

Philosophy is vital to the study of sport and sport management; it is an evolving process that leads to knowledge and understanding. As we engage in the philosophic process incorporating a critical thinking perspective, we will gain insight into the dilemmas within sport. For example, elite sport has set the pace for the increase in participation in all sport and physical activity. Consequently, the services provided to individuals through public and private sport facilities; recreational sport programs; professional sport; and school, college, and university programs have increased.

The increase in participation for many has been due to identification with the elite programs. Our increased exposure to sport through print and broadcast media constantly places the elite collegiate and professional performers before us. Unfortunately, elite programs are available to only the elite performers, and most of us are not elite athletes. Many of us participate vicariously in elite sport as spectators, yet some groups in our society are excluded from sport altogether due to gender; age; sexual orientation; skill level; and physical, emotional, or mental disabilities. Programs such as the Special Olympics, the Senior Games, the Gay Games, and the various state Sportsfests provide opportunities for individuals, but are still limiting because they occur only occasionally, rather than regularly. Even with Title IX legislation, sporting opportunities for some girls and women are still minimal. Many activities and programs for youth are directed toward those who are highly skilled, thus excluding those with the desire but not the abilities.

Each of these problems is directly associated with human issues. By incorporating critical thinking and the philosophic process, we hope to address and resolve inequities such as those we have noted. As previously indicated, philosophy offers us a way to examine basic problems of individuals and society. Sport managers can be practical philosophers in their work as they deal with critical issues for the sport participant and spectator. As a sport manager, you must be able to ask pertinent questions regarding life, reality, values and beliefs, and our moral actions. All of us who live and interact with others should question and explore such issues. The process of philosophy can help us integrate ideas and seek answers to such issues as value judgments, administrative decision making, and problems plaguing the sport world. Asking philosophical questions of yourself and of participants or spectators makes this area of inquiry a part of the life process.

## Learning Activity

In a meeting with several peers, plan how you will uphold the ideal of sport for all. This means providing sport opportunities to individuals of different age groups, ethnic groups, genders, abilities, and sexual orientations.

# Moral Dilemmas Within Sport Settings

The moral dilemmas of sport could easily fill volumes. It is not the intent of this chapter to cite every moral or ethical dilemma related to sport and the sport manager, but rather to alert you to the potential for moral problems and violations of ethics in certain settings.

The following are examples of moral dilemmas:

- As Director of Club Sports at a university, you are made aware of instances of improper behavior by players toward each other as well as toward the officials. What organizational reforms would you institute to eliminate such behaviors? Why would you institute such reforms?

- An Australian softball player was recruited by an NCAA Division I university. The team had already played 20 games in a 56-game regular season, but this athlete moved directly into a primary role as pitcher and led the school to a national championship. Several days after the final game, she dropped out of school and returned to Australia with no college credits because she received incompletes in the three classes in which she was enrolled. Ironically, the player was considered eligible by NCAA rules (Montville, 1995). What are the moral dilemmas of this scenario? What steps would you take to address each dilemma?

- People with differing physical and mental abilities have been denied the opportunities to pursue physical activity. The Americans with Disabilities Act (1990) requires that all individuals who are physically challenged be provided with access and opportunities to publicly funded and supported programs. What rationale could you use to demonstrate that this legislation is ethical?

- As a manufacturer of baseball bats, you are made aware that inferior materials are being used to produce this sporting equipment. Because your company is in a financial crisis, it is necessary for you to cut back on production expenses. What is your responsibility to the consumer?

© Daily Illini

Great athletes demand more of themselves than superior physical performance—teamwork and cooperation enhance moral excellence in the sport arena.

Individuals have given many reasons for not following high ethical or moral standards. Among them are the ideas that because everyone is doing the same thing, it can not be wrong, or if you are not caught, nothing wrong really happened. In addition, individuals have indicated that they have not been able to distinguish between what is part of a game and what is not. They believe that if the behavior is not specifically cited in a rule book, then it must be legal and, by extension, ethical. Lastly, it is difficult to discern legal strategy from win-at-all-costs manipulation. Whether or not these reasons are used for following unsound ethical standards, they ring familiar and have been incorporated into our reasoning regarding sport settings. Have you used such reasons to respond to these dilemmas?

## Ethical and Moral Development and Responsibility

Kretchmar (1994) points out that the terms ethics and morality are concerned with human responsi-

bility. Everyone has values and bases their judgments on those values. Not everyone, however, has high standards of morality or ethics. Because ethics and morality are directly associated with decision making, it is the sport manager's responsibility to be aware of what is worthwhile or valuable and to distribute that good fairly (p. 237). In other words, identifying and being sensitive to the moral issues in certain situations, attempting to have all parties involved share in the goods, or achieving a win-win solution are ways for meeting the objectives of ethics. For example, when mission statements for athletics departments, fitness clubs, and other sport settings incorporate ethical expectations, both the organization and the consumers of these programs reap the benefits. A mission statement that acknowledges the importance of ethical behavior is presented in figure 4.3.

When addressing the concept of moral development, we must remember that morality is learned from our experiences. We begin learning at an early age what is right and wrong, but where do we learn such lessons? Although parents and the

---

**Strategic planning model**

Indiana University Athletic Department

Focus—Academic support programs

*Indiana University, Bloomington mission statement*

The fundamental missions of Indiana University, Bloomington have remained unchanged for more than a century. The campus provides instruction, research, and professional service in a range of subject areas that are constantly changing but are delineated by custom, by tradition, and by regulation. As a public institution, Indiana University must pursue its missions for the greater benefit of those who support it. Pursuit of university missions will require not only responsiveness to the current needs of those state and national agencies, but also intelligent anticipation of changing needs within society. Thus, the Bloomington campus' goal in educating its students is not solely to certify them for professional employment, but also to help them develop ethical and social vision, a love of learning, and a complex and flexible intellect.

*Department of Intercollegiate Athletics mission statement*

The mission of the Department of Intercollegiate Athletics is to provide an athletics program committed to integrity, fairness, and competitiveness that is consistent with and in support of the mission of Indiana University.

*Department of Intercollegiate Athletics fundamental goals*

1. To have all student-athletes progress each year toward graduation, culminating in an Indiana University degree.
2. To be competitive in all sports.
3. To maintain an equitable, balanced, and well-rounded program for all participants.
4. To facilitate the integration of the athletics department and the student-athletes into the university community.
5. To comply fully with the rules of the National Collegiate Athletics Association (NCAA), the Big Ten Conference, and Indiana University.

---

**Figure 4.3** An intercollegiate athletics department mission statement.
Reprinted, with permission, from Indiana University Athletic Department.

home are the people and places from which we learn moral lessons, other settings and individuals impact us as well. Teachers, day care personnel, relatives, coaches, peers, television, and religious educators impress upon us certain behaviors. We are exposed to the teachings of morality at an early age, but it is much later before we acquire the capacity to think critically about such issues and to ask the ultimate question—why?

## Social Responsibility and the Social Contract

Within the concept of social responsibility, the relationships between society, sport, and the formal organizations of sport are raised. Social responsibility involves moral and legal accountability by individuals for the self and others. It is directly related to the social contract that exists between the business (e.g., sport) and the setting or society in which it functions (DeSensi & Rosenberg, 1996).

The social contract is composed of the duties, obligations, and relationships between organizations and the people, which relates to the corporate impact on the welfare of society. The social

responsibility of sport, as with any other business, is a significant part of the social contract (Steiner, 1972). The question does arise, however, as to whether social involvement and profit maximization are compatible concepts. They do not necessarily have to be mutually exclusive terms. It is possible that, with sound ethical judgment and moral planning, an organization could carefully formulate a mission statement including the intentions of the sport setting, and both goals could coexist. Although businesses give much attention to consumer satisfaction, community improvement, employee welfare, support for minorities, and environmental protection, these issues frequently are not written into the mission statements and are often ignored.

Robbins (1976) noted that, within management planning, the objectives selected by the organization may, in some cases, relate to social awareness or to being socially responsible and responsive. Nonprofit organizations are based on an awareness of real societal needs, such as providing food and clothing for the homeless or offering sport programs for those who do not have access to them. This is not the case, however, with profit-oriented organizations, such as professional sport and, in some cases, intercollegiate athletics. Frequently, the missions, purposes, and objectives of for-profit organizations do not reflect the concepts of social awareness and social responsibility.

## Social Responsibility and Intercollegiate Athletics

Professional sports teams have set the pace for college and university athletics departments. The effects of this influence have been both positive and negative. Many colleges and universities have lost their credibility with the critics as they stand closely in the shadows of professional structures. We even hear overtones of the professional ranks when directors of college and university athletics programs talk about the similar power structures and the labor force. We have been hesitant to acknowledge the businesslike structures of our athletics departments. Such organizations have had to hide behind a facade and purport a philosophy that in many cases has opposed the business model. For example, the NCAA as well as some athletics departments have purported concerns for athletes and schools when, in fact, revenue generation was the primary concern.

Intercollegiate athletics departments should not put forth one philosophy of operation (e.g., having great concern for the athletes' education or the educational model) and actually work under another (e.g., the business model of working to increase revenues). Athletics in many educational settings is a business, and the bottom line becomes more critical than the athletes' welfare. As soon as the organizations responsible for sport in the athletic setting acknowledge the similarities and differences (i.e., the production status, the emphasis on the win/loss record, and the need to increase revenues), they can establish sound foundational ethical standards.

One focus of social responsibility within the athletic setting has to do with ensuring that every athlete receives an education. In the current structure, athletics departments are caught in a paradox. The department attempts to please several conflicting social groups (i.e., players, alumni, administrators, and the NCAA), and the attempt to balance an educational model of athletics with that of a business model becomes unfeasible in certain cases. Perhaps the models should not be restricted to an either-or case. The business and educational models of athletics programs may possess separate aims and objectives; however, they may not necessarily be mutually exclusive.

An attempt to balance this thinking is a check on the ethical standards of the athletics organization.

This means making an honest effort at putting the *athlete* at the center of the intercollegiate program. Consider true concern and human regard for the individual athlete, her or his educational goals, the athletics program, those involved with these programs, and the community of spectators within the balance of the business and educational models.

## Social Responsibility and NCAA Certification

The recently established **certification** program of the NCAA addresses the concept of social responsibility. As a major part of the NCAA's reform agenda, athletic certification was approved for Division I institutions during the 1993 NCAA convention. The NCAA Presidents Commission, the NCAA Council, and the Knight Foundation Commission on Intercollegiate Athletics supported the certification program. This program requires NCAA Division I institutions to be accountable for their current practices regarding academic integrity, financial integrity, governance and commitment to rules compliance, and commitment to equity. In this case equity refers to gender; race; ethnicity; and equity along a number of lines regarding athletes, athletic staff, coaches, assistant coaches, graduate assistants, and nonathletes. The purpose of the certification program is to ensure the NCAA's commitment to integrity in intercollegiate athletics. Each institution is requested by the NCAA to engage in a self-study to examine the status of the four areas noted previously. The process of the self-study is to include participation by campus faculty, administrators, athletics personnel, athletes, and graduate and undergraduate students. After completing the self-study, a written document is submitted to the NCAA Review Team. An external Peer Review Team, composed of three to five members who are experienced educational and athletics personnel, then visits the campus to verify and evaluate the self-study. After a time, the institution is informed of its certification or areas that must be improved to achieve certification (NCAA Committee on Athletics Certification, 1993).

Benefits of the self-study for certification include (a) self-awareness, by opening the self-study to the public and educating the campus about the athletics program's goals, purposes, and how the program supports the institution's overall mission; (b) affirmation, by revealing parts of the athletics program worthy of praise; and (c) opportunities to improve, by revealing problems with the athletics program and identifying suggestions for improvement (NCAA Committee on Athletics Certification, 1993).

## Social Responsibility and Professional Sport

The responsibility of a professional sport franchise to a city or community is an issue within social responsibility. The team owners, individual professional players, sport managers, and administrators associated with such teams all have social responsibilities. The pursuit of profit maximization, according to Hemphill (1983), has taken first place at the professional level where sport management and labor have forsaken the public interest in favor of monetary self-interest. Issues such as the revenue generation potential of the sport franchise, the public interest in sport, and the social responsibility of the franchise owner to the community are called into question. These issues were particularly relevant to the moves of the Houston Oilers to Nashville, Tennessee, and the Cleveland Browns to Baltimore, Maryland.

Some sport franchise owners are aware of the social implications and meanings their franchise holds for a community. On one hand, fans become emotionally attached to and strongly identify with the home team, but in addition, the city depends on the revenue generated by a sport franchise. The sport team owner has three indirect obligations to the community: franchise location stability, the quality of team performance, and unpredictability of performance outcome. The owner's recognition of these points and action toward such ends ensures that the needs of the public are considered and that the franchise can be profitable.

Some professional team owners regard their teams as objects or toys to play with and manipulate (Flint & Eitzen, 1987). Some of these individuals know nothing about sport or its management and are more involved in the cartel-like power structures of business manipulation than in serving the community with socially responsible actions. Flint and Eitzen further substantiate this point:

> Because sport is still categorized as simple play, the power of wealthy capitalist owners can be overlooked as simple aberration or eccentric pastime. Although the meritocratic recruitment arguments are held high by the owners as well as the participants (players or consumers), little attention is given to the contradictory fact that owning a team is not based on merit but on enormous wealth. (p. 25)

Flint and Eitzen (1987) also note that the concept of ownership "defines a full range of economic relations, from entrepreneurial freedom of operation to the refined security of monopoly capitalism; from the independent pursuit of self-interest to the control of market exigencies by an interlocking corporate directorate" (p. 18). Individuals can achieve a socially responsible sport operation if they make changes that enhance the long-term operation of the professional sport franchise rather than sacrifice public interests for monetary interests.

### Learning Activity

Observe a professional team sport competition, considering the effort the sport managers (coaches, owners, marketing and promotions personnel, media personnel, business personnel, etc.) must put forth to have the event take place. Reflect on the social responsibility of each of those involved, including the players, the spectators, and others. What are the responsibilities of the players, owners, coaches, and spectators to each other? What does the professional sport team franchise owe to the community in which it plays?

## Social Responsibility in Sport and Fitness Clubs

Sport and fitness clubs are increasing in number to meet the exercise and fitness demands of society. Such clubs are not exempt from the concept of social responsibility. As with the intercollegiate and professional sport settings, certain legal and professional standards help keep this area in check. Social responsibility is the obligation that the owners and managers of the clubs have to their public or clientele. Such responsibilities might include a clean and safe environment; qualified and, in some cases, certified personnel to ensure safe practices in exercise prescription and adherence; good equipment in respect to functional assessment, safe and honest evaluation of performance, and stress tolerance; flexible hours of availability; appropriate facilities and equipment for both women and men; fair membership costs; information concerning the risks of activities; adaptability to the changes in society; programs and accessibility for all populations; and general care for the well-being of the clientele. While maintaining responsibility for these features of a health club, owners and managers can ensure an environment that is conducive for the programs it sponsors, the people it serves, and the overall sport management setting. Being socially responsible to the needs of the public goes hand in hand with survival in the business world.

Another area within the concept of social responsibility is interaction between individuals. Whether friendships grow out of social or business contexts, they involve definite responsibilities. Even the relationships that are developed solely for business reasons demand responsible attitudes. Business can not exist for long without mutual trust and goodwill among business associates.

## Learning Activity

Outline what you envision as your social responsibility in the sport management position you would like to hold. How will you ensure that you carry out this responsibility?

## Personal and Professional Ethical Responsibility

The mission and philosophy of a sport organization and those responsible for the leadership within these settings set the tone for the behavior followed in everyday operations. It is important that sport managers set forth clear ethical expectations and maintain an expectation of accountability (Branvold, 1991). The responsibility for ethical behavior is not limited to the leaders of sport organizations. It is the moral commitment of *all* the individuals in the organization. It requires personal moral and ethical development to produce responsible actions. No individual or specific office is exempt from the expectation of ethical behavior in sport settings. Ethical standards and behavior are not optional.

Because we all bring our own backgrounds and personal moral development to the professional setting, it is vital that sport managers engage in personal exploration and reflection from an ethical perspective to check their intentional personal and professional actions and behaviors. No mat-

ter the setting (e.g., a sport and fitness club, athletics, sport marketing, manufacturing of sporting goods, or intramurals), the ethical obligation on the part of the individuals within these settings is primary.

## Learning Activity

Write an autobiography about your participation in sport from as early as you can remember to the present. Indicate how you learned moral and ethical lessons. From whom and in what settings did you learn them?

## Ethical Decision Making

Decision making is part of a sport manager's role and responsibility. It is closely related to the managerial functions of planning, and it involves making choices or the best choice from the alternatives available. Once you identify and understand the goal you want to achieve, the decision-making process begins. Because decision making is rooted in philosophy, and specifically related to logic, reason, ethics, and moral judgment, the knowledge gained in this chapter should help you establish an ethical decision-making process.

Ethical judgments contain a moral component related to conduct or values, but these areas can differ. Many times the terms ethics and morality are used interchangeably, creating some confusion semantically. Ethics is considered on the level of theory or principles, whereas morals are observed on the level of practice (Billington, 1988). In ethics, one appeals to rules or maxims as a way to justify certain moral decisions, whether those decisions are right or wrong thus indicating good or bad ethics. Morals on the other hand usually describe a special set of values that frame the absolute limitations on behavior. "Do not steal," for example, would be a basic moral rule. The morals of sport managers would matter to their families and friends, which might differ from the ethical principles they apply in refraining from padding the budget (DeSensi & Rosenberg, 1996). In addition, Beauchamp (1991) describes morality as a "social institution with a code of learnable rules" (p. 6). The social nature of morality, its application of certain rules, and its expansive concerns separate it from ethics, which is embedded in theoretical concerns. Questions regarding how one should think and act arise in making

**Figure 4.4**   Are these the principles that you believe a good sport manager should live by? Keep reading.
Reprinted from Wade Austin 1995.

ethical decisions. A somewhat cynical view of ethical choices is shown in figure 4.4.

Laczniak and Murphy (1985) offer simple ethical maxims to guide behavior, including the following:

- *The Golden Rule:* Act in a way you would want others to act toward you.
- *The Utilitarian Principle:* Act in a way that results in the greatest good for the greatest number.
- *Kant's Categorical Imperative:* Act in such a way that the action taken under the circumstances could be a universal rule of behavior.

- *The Professional Ethic:* Take only actions that would be viewed as proper by an impartial panel of professional colleagues.
- *The TV Test:* Act in a manner that you would feel comfortable explaining to a national television audience.

Although these are simple and quick reference maxims, we should make ethical decisions with reference to a strong theoretical and philosophical base. We recommend an entire course in ethics related to sport management to develop this background. For now, the following summary of teleology and deontology theories will be helpful.

The term teleology is derived from the Greek meaning "end" and refers to evaluating the morality of actions or inaction on the basis of results or consequences. It is referred to as a results-oriented approach. For example, donating money for charity rather than spending it on a luxury may be based on the teleological premise of considering the consequences of such an act, seeking the greatest measure of this good, or weighing the benefits of an action. Utilitarianism, which follows the work of Jeremy Bentham (as cited in White, 1988 and John Stuart Mill, 1969), is a frequently used teleological theory. Within this approach, the good of the group is considered above the good of the individual; therefore, decisions are made by selecting the action or inaction that will produce the greatest social benefit. The results-oriented approach is best explained by White's (1988) "no harm, no foul" example: If slight contact occurs in a basketball game and there is little or no harm, the greatest good is achieved by allowing play to continue.

The term deontology is derived from the Greek for "duty." Kant's Categorical Imperative serves as a prime example here. It states that we should act in such a way that the action taken under the circumstances could be a universal law or rule of behavior. More specifically Kantian ethics indicates (a) that the moral action taken would make sense for everyone in a similar situation or be universalizable, (b) that it demonstrate respect for the individual and that others are not treated as means to an end, and (c) that it be acceptable to all rational beings (Branvold, 1991, p. 368).

Using part of Kant's theory, Ross (1930) developed another approach, which indicates that action is bound by duties such as fidelity, gratitude, beneficence, self-improvement, justice, and noninjury. These points are considered universal moral obligations, which supersede the law. Still another approach is the theory of justice postulated by John Rawls (1971). The theory of justice is based on the premise called the "veil of ignorance." That is, the rules and laws of society should be developed as if individuals did not know the roles they were going to play in the society. This in essence creates fairness and objectivity in our actions (Branvold, 1991, pp. 368-369).

Before analyzing our ethical decisions, the outline in figure 4.5 offers a view of selected ethical norms, which may assist you in understanding how to make ethical decisions. In this case, the ethical norms of utilitarianism, rights, and justice are presented. Utilitarian ethical norms support the organizational goals of satisfaction, minimizing external costs, and not jeopardizing organization goals with personal interests. The ethical norms of rights indicate that individuals have the rights of safety, truth, pri-

vacy, freedom of conscience, speech, and private property. Involved in the norms of justice are the areas of fair treatment of individuals, fair administration of rules, fair compensation, fair blame, and due process.

Figure 4.6 shows a process you could follow in making an ethical decision. The initial step is to obtain as much information as possible (gather the facts). Second, evaluate your action according to the three criteria of (a) utility—does the action optimize benefits? (b) rights—does the action respect the rights of those involved? and (c) justice—is the action fair? If the response is no to all the criteria, the action is unethical. If the response is yes to the criteria, the action is ethical. Also considered in this model are any overriding factors that may impact the decision. Overriding factors include the value or importance of one criterion over another, whether the action is freely

---

**Utilitarian**

1. *Organizational goals* should aim at maximizing the satisfactions of the organization's constituencies.
2. The members of an organization should attempt to attain its goals as *efficiently* as possible by consuming as few inputs as possible and by minimizing the external costs that organizational activities impose on others.
3. The employee should use every *effective* means to achieve the goals of the organization and should neither jeopardize those goals nor enter situations in which personal interests conflict significantly with the goals.

**Rights**

1. *Life and safety*   The individual has the right not to have her or his life or safety unknowingly and unnecessarily endangered.
2. *Truthfulness*   The individual has a right not to be intentionally deceived by another, especially on matters about which the individual has the right to know.
3. *Privacy*   The individual has the right to do whatever he or she chooses outside working hours and to control information about his or her private life.
4. *Freedom of conscience*   The individual has the right to refrain from carrying out any order that violates those commonly accepted moral or religious norms to which the person adheres.
5. *Free speech*   The individual has the right to criticize conscientiously and truthfully the ethics or legality of corporate actions so long as the criticism does not violate the rights of other individuals within the organization.
6. *Private property*   The individual has a right to hold private property, especially insofar as this right enables the individual and his or her family to be sheltered and to have the basic necessities of life.

**Justice**

1. *Fair treatment*   Persons who are similar to each other in the relevant respects should be treated similarly; persons who differ in some respect relevant to the job they perform should be treated differently in proportion to the difference between them.
2. *Fair administration of rules*   Rules should be administered consistently, fairly, and impartially.
3. *Fair compensation*   Individuals should be compensated for the cost of their injuries by the party who is responsible for those injuries.
4. *Fair blame*   Individuals should not be held responsible for matters over which they have no control.
5. *Due process*   The individual has a right to a fair and impartial hearing when he or she believes that personal rights are being violated.

---

**Figure 4.5**   Selected ethical norms.

Reprinted by permission of the publisher from "Organizational Dynamics," Autumn, 1983 © 1983. American Management Association, New York. All rights reserved.

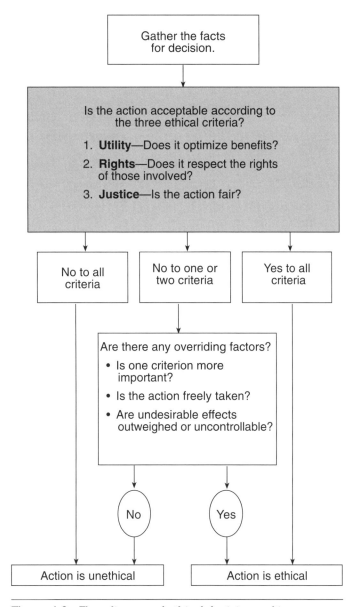

**Figure 4.6**   Flow diagram of ethical decision making.
Reprinted, by permission, from G.F. Cavanaugh, 1990, *American Business Values*, 3rd ed. (New York: American Management Assoc.), p. 195.

taken, and if the undesirable effects are outweighed or uncontrollable.

For example, if a baseball bat manufacturer decided to use inferior wood because the cost of materials was rising and the company was in financial jeopardy, this action must withstand critical evaluation. Facts that you must obtain include costs to the manufacturer and consumer, quality of the wood, the degree of financial difficulty being experienced by the company, and whether the product can be guaranteed. Analyze the acceptability of the decision in terms of its utility, its respect for the rights of the concerned parties, and its fairness. You must consider issues such as

what and whose benefits are optimized. Is the action justified by the manufacturer's benefit of selling an inferior product at a higher cost and ultimately making more money? Do both the manufacturer and consumer benefit from this action or is one or both disadvantaged and placed in jeopardy? Are the rights of those involved respected or is there a potential risk of injury to the consumer? Is it fair for the manufacturer to know the potential for injury exists yet do nothing about it? In this example, there are no overriding factors that would deem the decision ethical; therefore, because the answers to these questions are negative, the action would be unethical.

## Learning Activity

Write a paper explaining how personal moral and ethical responsibility could contribute to transforming sport.

## Summary

The content of this chapter can best be summarized by analyzing the athletic training scenario presented at the beginning of the chapter. First, we should consider several points: (a) the treatment of any athlete as a second-class citizen is disturbing and is in direct violation of the National Athletic Trainers Association Code of Professional Practice, which disallows discrimination; (b) Moran's tenure at this institution is a long one, and he will probably not change his way of thinking; (c) questioning Moran's actions might be viewed as insubordination, and your job could be in jeopardy; and (d) as the new junior member of this athletic training department, how do you follow the Code of Professional Practice regarding the equitable treatment of athletes and still remain respectful to the head athletic trainer? (Mangus & Ingersoll, 1990, p. 341).

As you consider the discussion in the chapter regarding social responsibility and ethical decision making, there are four courses of action you could implement in this scenario. It is important to remember, however, that you must consider how the results of each decision will impact you and others (Mangus & Ingersoll, 1990). The approaches to dealing with this dilemma and the possible consequences are the following:

1. Report Mr. Moran's unethical behavior to the National Athletic Trainers Association Board of Ethics or to administrators at the institution. Simultaneously, attempt to retain your position as assistant athletic trainer. As a consequence, Mr. Moran might resent your actions and make the work environment extremely difficult. He might even try to have you dismissed for insubordination.

   Alternatively you could attempt to resolve differences between Mr. Moran and yourself in a private discussion. This action might or might not change his thinking, but, on the other hand, he might permit you to practice athletic training as you see fit.

In either event, you must consider the amount of support you are receiving from your superiors. If the Athletics Director supports your reporting the behavior, retaliation from Mr. Moran may be reduced or eliminated. Your superiors might suggest that you pursue this complaint through institutional channels first, rather than taking it outside the college (Mangus & Ingersoll, 1990, p. 342).

2. Do not report the unethical behavior and remain secure in your position. This choice will be a way to avoid controversy and tolerate discrimination. You could possibly wait until Mr. Moran retires, then change the policy regarding women athletes. Tolerating unethical practice may make it appear that you condone the prejudicial treatment of some athletes. Providing care for women athletes in secret, which is also unethical, may result in your being discovered and charged with insubordination.

3. Report the unethical behavior and resign your position at the college. This action may result in a guilty charge for Mr. Moran, but does not insure that formal disciplinary action will be taken against him. There is no guarantee that he will lose his certification or receive any other punishment beyond a warning, and there is no assurance that the discrimination will stop. If you resign, you are no longer in a position to stand up for the rights of all athletes. On the other hand, perhaps a serious warning from the Board of Ethics will make Mr. Moran rethink his position.

4. Do not report the unethical behavior and resign your position. As in point 3, quitting your position at the college will probably have no impact on Mr. Moran's discriminatory practices. Is it not unethical for you to resign? Would you truly be acting in the best interest of the athletes? You have basically removed yourself from the problem, rather than acting in concert with the NATA Code of Professional Practice (Mangus & Ingersoll, 1990, p. 342).

From this scenario it is evident that sport managers need background in philosophical questioning regarding the issues of ontology, epistemology, and axiology to carry out daily responsibilities. The value and relevance of using philosophy in sport management is posed as a significant area of study, particularly as the sport manager deals with ethical and moral questions related to serving the public and working with employees in all types of settings. The need for developing logical reflective and critical thinking, social responsibility, personal and professional ethics is paramount for developing skills that will assist you in establishing a solid foundation from which you can assume the responsibilities of a sport manager.

## For More Information

Here are some more resources for you to take advantage of.

### Organizations

- NASPE Philosophy Academy
  American Alliance for Health, Physical Education, Recreation and Dance
  1900 Association Dr.
  Reston, VA 20191-1599

- The Philosophic Society for the Study of Sport
  HPER Department
  Kean College of New Jersey
  Morris Ave.
  Union, NJ 07083

- North American Society for Sport Management
  Ste. 344
  106 Main St.
  Houlton, ME 04730-9001

### Publications

- *Journal of the Philosophy of Sport*
- *Journal of Physical Education, Recreation and Dance*
- *Journal of Sport Management*
- *Quest*
- *Strategies*
- *Journal of Business Ethics*
- *Journal of Business Research*
- *Academy of Management Review*

# Section II

# Theoretical and Applied Foundations of Management and Organization

The following three chapters will enrich your understanding and appreciation of theoretical aspects of sport management. In chapter 5, you will learn about the evolution of contemporary approaches to management, how these approaches evolved, and why this knowledge is important for sport managers. In chapter 6, you will learn about organizational behavior theories and how they are used to analyze the structure and behavior of complex organizations. Finally, in chapter 7, you will learn how management and organizational theories are applied in the multifaceted business of sport.

When you enter the world of work, whether in a sport organization or another type of business enterprise, you will understand your environment better and be able to make more valuable contributions because you know the history of management thought and theories of organizational behavior. Your confidence and effectiveness as a manager will be enhanced by your ability to apply this information to managing sport enterprises.

# Chapter 5

# History of Management Thought

**Robert L. Minter**
Cleveland State University

---

## Learning Objectives

After studying this chapter, you will be able to

1. identify management style characteristics for each of the four schools of management thought;

2. identify major contributors and their contributions to management thought from the early 1900s to the present;

3. discuss the advantages and disadvantages of each school of management thought

regarding professional management opportunities and careers in sport management;

4. discuss the multidisciplinary bases for management theory development; and

5. discuss the characteristics of entrepreneurship as they apply to the sport management profession.

---

Before the turn of the century, a manager had little information to help in effectively operating a business. Because of the lack of literature during this period, managers had difficulty finding answers to critical issues regarding planning, organizing, and controlling the business operation; measuring work performance; delegating tasks; designing the organization and its work flow for maximum efficiency and overall effectiveness; motivating personnel; improving pro-

ductivity; determining an equitable wage and salary system; and setting prices for products or services.

Only since the beginning of the 20th century have major advancements in management thought and principles been developed, recorded, and published. This chapter will summarize management literature in units of information often referred to as **management movements or schools of thought**.

# Important Management Movements

The four movements we will discuss are often referred to as the administrative and scientific management movement, the behavioral management movement, the contemporary management movement, and the entrepreneurial movement. Table 5.1 highlights a sample of leading classic contributors and their major contributions to each movement.

Establishing specific dates as boundaries for each movement is somewhat arbitrary. For this chapter's purposes, the administrative and scientific management movement was dominant between 1850 and 1945, the behavioral movement was dominant between the 1930s and the mid-1970s, the contemporary movement began in the early 1970s and continues to the present, and the entrepreneurial movement has gained momentum within the past 15 years and will continue to be a popular school of thought well into the next millennium. The literature associated with these schools of thought reveals that the principles, theories, and concepts of management are derived from diverse fields or academic disciplines, as indicated in table 5.2. In the Learning Activities at the end of this chapter, you will have the opportunity to discuss various management practices in the context of sport-related businesses. Examples of direct application of these management concepts to sport management are provided in chapter 8.

# Administrative and Scientific Management Movement (1850-1945)

Administrative and scientific management concepts were usually not concerned with the welfare and working conditions of employees. The movement emphasized what management should do to maintain order, cut costs, and increase productivity through improved organization and management. It did not focus on improving employee working conditions. Unions emerged during this period, mainly because of negative working conditions and resulting employee dissatisfaction.

The contributions to management thought during this era were concerned primarily with

- increasing efficiency and effectiveness in the way work was designed and accomplished;

- giving management, rather than workers, control over planning and coordinating work;

- instituting pay structures and incentive systems;

- ensuring mandatory employee obedience and company loyalty (i.e., the interest of the employees or work groups should not supersede the organization's objectives);

- motivating employees primarily through monetary rewards; and

- creating division of work and job specialization (i.e., breaking jobs down to small units of work).

The major thrust of the management literature during this period was to develop a single set of universal management principles applicable to all situations.

# Behavioral Management Movement (1930s to mid-1970s)

Many disciplines contributed to developing this school of thought. Research in psychology, sociology, anthropology, and communication added to this knowledge base. The behavioral management movement focused on the employee as well as on management. Unlike the administrative and scientific management school, the behavioral movement was primarily concerned with the human aspect of managing the enterprise. This movement stressed the importance of human relations, employee attitudes and feelings, and the impact the informal organization can have on the day-to-day performance of employees.

Major contributions of the behavioral management school concentrated on improving the management of human resources in the areas of employee selection, employee counseling, employee compensation and incentives, work group behavior, organizational communication, human relations, employee job satisfaction and productivity, working conditions, employee morale, job enrichment, and managerial leadership. The behavioral management movement was the precursor of the field of human resource management. Human relations concepts emphasized company training programs, fringe benefit packages, social activities (e.g., picnics and employee interest clubs), and employee participation in management decisions.

A major problem emerging from this movement has been referred to as pseudo human relations. Managers practicing pseudo human relations

Table 5.1
## Leading Contributors to Management Thought

| Name | Major contribution |
|---|---|
| *Administrative and scientific management movement* | |
| Henrik Fayol (1841-1925) | Was one of the first to develop a theory of administration containing principles that could be taught to managers. |
| Fredrick W. Taylor (1856-1915) | Introduced time-study techniques to develop work standards. He is referred to as the father of scientific management. |
| Henry Gantt (1861-1919) | Developed a task-and-bonus system of wages, graphic charting techniques for charting productivity, and methods of production control. |
| Max Weber (1864-1920) | Was foremost contributor in developing a theory of bureaucracy and formal organization concepts. |
| Frank Gilbreth (1868-1924) | Developed the motion study techniques to improve on human efforts and physical efficiency in the workplace. |
| Mary Parker Follett (1868-1933) | Contributed to area of applying social sciences to industry. |
| Lillian Gilbreth (1878-1972) | Developed psychological principles to help management understand work behavior. |
| Chester I. Barnard (1886-1961) | Led in stressing the importance of understanding the informal organization, communication networks, role of authority, and decision-making processes. |
| James Oscar McKinsey (1889-1937) | Focused attention on the importance of budgeting as a major management tool. |
| *Behavioral management movement* | |
| Kurt Lewin (1890-1947) | Developed theories and conducted research on group dynamics and group participation. He is referred to as the father of group dynamics. |
| Fritz J. Roethlisberger (1898-1974) | Conducted pioneer research on human factors in management, later known as the Hawthorne experiments. Human relations principles emerged from this study. |
| Douglas McGregor (1906-1964) | Developed the Theory X-Theory Y managerial leadership model, which revolutionized the management/leadership concept. |
| Abraham Maslow (1908-1970) | Introduced a five-tier need hierarchy motivation model that pioneered the way for future motivation theories. |
| Fredrick Herzberg (b. 1932) | Developed a maintenance and motivation theory. He is often referred to as the father of job enrichment concepts. |
| Victor Vroom (b. 1932) | Developed an expectancy model of motivation, which provides a probability estimate that a given level of effort will result in a given outcome of performance. |
| David C. McClelland (b. 1917) | Introduced the achievement and motivation model, which specifically deals with high and low achievers in the work setting. |
| *Contemporary management movement* | |
| Ludwig von Bertalanffy (1901-1972) | Proposed a theory of general systems and subsystems that aided in explaining behavior in an organizational context. |
| Fred E. Fiedler (b. 1922) | Developed a contingency theory proposing that successful leadership depends on the match between the manager's leadership style and the demand of the situation. He introduced the notion that leadership is situational and that an effective leader in one setting may not be effective in another setting. |
| Victor Vroom (b. 1932) | Developed a contingency theory focusing on how a manager makes decisions. This theory assumes that the nature of problems vary and should be solved by different decision-making strategies. One decision-making strategy will not work in every situation. |
| Peter Drucker (b. 1909) | Developed the concept of management by objectives (MBO). |

*(continued)*

## Table 5.1 *(continued)*

| Name | Major contribution |
|---|---|
| W. Edward Deming (1900-1993) | Referred to as the father of total quality management. Developed Deming's 14 points for quality management. |
| J.M. Juran (b. 1904) | Known for his textbooks in quality management. Like Deming, he is considered as one of the pioneers in quality improvement. |
| Kaoru Ishikawa (b. 1915) | Developed the concept of *quality control circles*, which are small groups of employees who meet regularly to plan and implement changes to improve quality, productivity, and the work environment. |
| G. Taguchi (b. 1924) | Advocated that quality must be designed into the product; it cannot be inspected in later. He is well known for a number of Taguchi Methods to assist managers in their design of quality into the performance process. |
| T. Peters (b. 1942) | Provides direction for managers to cope with turbulent markets and economic climates in his books, *In Search of Excellence* and *Thriving on Chaos*. |
| J. Case (b. 1944) | Considered as a contemporary pioneer in writing about open-book management. |
| *Entrepreneurial management movement* | |
| P. Drucker (b. 1909) | Wrote the first book that considers entrepreneurship as a practice and a discipline in an entrepreneurial economy. |
| G. Pinchot (1865-1946) | Coined the term intrapreneurial to describe how corporate executives act very much like entrepreneurs in their own firms to make things happen within their organizations. |

## Table 5.2
## Disciplinary Bases for Management

| Discipline | Special emphasis |
|---|---|
| Industrial engineering | Measurement and analysis of physical factors to achieve work efficiency. |
| Economics | Allocation of scarce resources with orientation to the future. |
| Financial accounting | Recording, reporting, analyzing, and auditing past transactions. |
| Public administration | Forming a rational hierarchy for accomplishing activities. |
| Legal profession | Developing a consistent course of action based on precedents to achieve stability, order, and justice. |
| Statistical methods | Employing probability theory to infer facts from samples and to handle uncertainty. |
| Mathematics | Constructing models that explicitly state one's assumptions, objectives, and constraints. |
| Psychology | Scientific investigations concerning human needs, perceptions, and emotional factors. |
| Sociology | Study of interrelationships within and among work groups. |
| Anthropology | Cultural variations and discoverable patterns of behavior from history and environment. |
| Organizational communication | Study of formal and informal communication networks within organizational settings. |

Adapted, by permission, from Joseph L. Massie, 1987, *Essentials of Management*, 4th ed. (Prentice Hall, Inc., Upper Saddle River, New Jersey). 27.

attempt to make employees feel good about the company and the job even though they are not involved in making decisions that impact their jobs. A great deal of human relations hype during this period suggested that management should make employees feel important. The underlying theory that many managers accepted from the human relations movement in the 1940s, 1950s, and 1960s was the assumption that a strong positive correlation existed between employee morale and employee productivity. That is, as morale increases, so does productivity. This theory was debunked in the early 1970s. Current research indicates that, at best, the correlation is spurious.

The human relations fad seldom addressed the true nature of worker alienation, job dissatisfaction, job enrichment, and organizational health-related problems. Fortunately, other activities and theories emerged during the behavioral movement, such as human resource theory, contingency theory, and total quality management (TQM), that counteracted the human relations faddists, providing management with sound behavioral principles and techniques.

The impact of both the administrative and scientific and behavioral management movements has been enormous in terms of modern managerial thought.

## Learning Activity

Assume you have been hired as a consultant by a sport and leisure service business that specializes in vacation packages for adults within the age range of 25 to 55. The firm's name is SLS (Sport and Leisure Services). There are 100 employees distributed at three locations in the United States (California, Florida, Vermont). The firm's corporate headquarters is in California. Each facility has approximately 33 to 34 full-time employees. Of these employees, 15% are supervisors at each of the three locations.

Within the past 2 years SLS has experienced tremendous growth in sales at all three locations. However, the Florida operation is currently experiencing a 30% employee turnover rate among its nonsupervisory personnel. Assume you have been hired as a consultant to find out what is causing this high turnover at the Florida operation. Based on the content of this chapter, develop at least 10 questions that you would use when interviewing employees and supervisors at the Florida location. Once you develop the questions, write your rationale for asking each question. Be prepared to discuss your questions and rationale in class. The object of this exercise is to develop interview questions that will help identify management's philosophy at the Florida location only.

## Contemporary Management Movement (1970s-1990s)

We can trace development of contemporary management thought to both previous schools. The contemporary movement focuses on developing theories that shapers of the administrative and scientific and behavioral management movements either excluded, only lightly touched on, or were not aware of when developing their concepts.

Contributors to the contemporary school developed quantitative procedures to aid managers in making decisions under conditions of uncertainty relative to both short- and long-range planning. Although statistical procedures were applied to the area of quality control in the 1930s, computer and software developments within the past decade have made statistical concepts user-friendly for management decision making.

The contemporary management movement is based on contributions of systems theory, decision theory, human resource theory, contingency theory, total quality management (TQM), and open book management.

## Systems Theory

Systems theory views the organization as an open system. The theory assumes that (a) the organization is composed of interdependent subsystems and that a change in any subsystem (e.g., department, work unit, or work procedure) will have intended and unintended consequences for other subsystems within the organization; (b) the organization is dynamic and constantly undergoing change (both planned and unplanned); (c) the organization strives for homeostasis, or balance; (d) the total organization has multiple objectives that might conflict with one another; and (e) the organization is continually receiving inputs (e.g., money, people, raw materials, and ideas) that are transformed into new outputs, such as products, services, ideas, and other materials.

The manager must be able to manage the transformation processes that change the inputs to outputs. The effective manager must also learn to cope with many daily interactions relative to the tasks to be performed, the employees, the formal organization and its policies, and the informal culture of the organization.

## Decision Theory

Decision theory focuses on problem-solving and decision-making styles of managers. Although decision theory began in the 1950s, the concept gained momentum early in the contemporary management movement of the 1970s. Decision-making models provide rules (the ideal) for managers to follow in their problem-solving and decision-making activities. Decision theory has made contributions in such areas as identifying approaches to the problem-solving process; providing decision-making strategies for managers under conditions of certainty and uncertainty; providing a framework for identifying and using different problem-solving styles; using linear programming concepts to find the best solution to a problem; and developing decision matrices to determine various forms of payoffs for respective decisions.

Contemporary mathematical developments along with decision theory have created a new analytic specialty called *operations research management*, commonly referred to as OR. OR is a mathematical modeling approach using statistical and computer-based tools that permit the decision maker to manipulate several complex variables. You can apply linear programming, for example, to determine what combination of products, services, and raw materials are necessary to accomplish the objective. OR emphasizes using project teams composed of the organization's experts to solve complex problems. The National Aeronautics and Space Administration (NASA), for example, uses OR strategies to explore space. Spacecraft cannot be designed and launched without using complex mathematical calculations, computer-based decision models, and project teams consisting of many experts from diverse fields of specialization.

## Human Resource Management Theory

Human resource management theory (HRM) views the organization's human resources as assets or investments that can profit both the company and the employee if appropriately managed. The implementation of HRM philosophy establishes personal growth opportunities and planned career experiences for employees. These activities attempt to maximize employee personnel needs, potential for career enhancement, and overall organizational effectiveness.

The HRM approach contrasts greatly with the scientific management era, when managers viewed the employee mainly as a factor of production and designed work to be as simple and routine as possible to assume maximum output.

## Contingency Theory

Contingency theory considers the situation and environment in which the work is performed. Unlike the administrative and scientific management school, contingency management assumes that there is no one best way to manage or lead an enterprise. The contingency manager has no universal prescriptions, principles, or techniques that will work in every situation.

Contingency theory maintains that the organization's structure, processes, and situational characteristics work together. To understand this theory, you must view contingency variables as aspects of the situation that might influence the desired outcome. The manager must determine what factors to manipulate to bring about the desired change. Assume that the structure of a task can significantly influence the supervisor's behavior as well as employee job satisfaction. By changing the task structure, the manager may be able to improve his or her leadership style as well as employee job satisfaction. Each factor, task structure, and leadership style is contingent on the other.

## Total Quality Management

Total quality management (TQM) is a paradigm that was introduced in the United States by Edward Deming during the past 40 years. Deming, known as the father of total quality management concepts, was not taken seriously early in his career by many U.S. businesses. During the past two to three decades his ideas for improving quality and service in the workplace were considered by many American firms as too bizarre and expensive to implement.

Japanese managers, on the other hand, realized the merits of Deming's thinking and began implementing his TQM concepts shortly after World War II. For more than a decade, the Japanese have been an economic superpower, in part because of using total quality management concepts, and have created major competition for U.S. firms. These U.S. firms, both in manufacturing and service-related industries, have since realized that they must adopt TQM and employee practices to maintain their competitive edge in the international and domestic marketplace. The quality movement in the United States during the last 10 years has been rapidly gaining momentum.

TQM philosophy stresses that customer satisfaction is the responsibility of every member of the organization and can be accomplished only through a process of continually discovering ways to improve quality and service (see table 5.3).

The TQM model is eclectic in that it draws from the concepts associated with the four schools of management. TQM is a people-focused manage-

---

### Table 5.3
### Principles Underlying Quality Management

Customer-first orientation.

Top management leadership of the quality improvement process.

Focus on continuous improvement.

Respect for employees and their knowledge; employees are actively involved in the improvement process.

Reducing product and process variation to assure consistency.

Providing for ongoing education and training to employees.

Using statistical methods throughout the organization to measure quality.

Emphasizing prevention rather than detection of problems.

Viewing vendors as long-term partners.

Performance measures that are consistent with the goals of the organization.

Standardization for developing and adhering to the best known ways to perform a given task.

Product or service quality begins with its definition and design.

Cooperation and involvement of all functions within an organization.

Awareness of the needs of internal customers.

Involves substantial cultural change.

---

Adapted, by permission, from Ronald M. Fortuna, 1990, "The Quality Imperative," as it appears in *Total Quality: An Executive's Guide for the 1990s*, (Ernst & Young Improvement Consulting Group, Homewood, IL, Dow-Jones Irwin) 11-12.

ment system that stresses continual increase in internal and external customer satisfaction and continually lower costs. It works horizontally across functions and departments within the organization and involves employees at all levels.

## Open Book Management

Open book management (OBM) applies the ideas of the contemporary management school to three major elements:

- Employees learn to understand the organization's financial status and are trained to track the firm's performance. Employees are trained to determine if what they are doing is earning money for the organization.

- Employees learn that their job stability depends on moving the economic indicators of their job in the right direction. They are accountable to one another for their unit's outcomes.

- Employees are stakeholders in the organization's success and survival. OBM trains employees to think of themselves as businesspeople rather than as employees.

Open book management operates within an open system, sharing all financial data with employees so they can be well informed.

## Entrepreneurial Management Movement

The French economist J.B. Say coined the term entrepreneur approximately 200 years ago. Since then, there has been much controversy over the definitions of **entrepreneur** and entrepreneurship. For example, is an individual an entrepreneur who opens a retail sport equipment business? One predominant school of thought contends that this individual is not an entrepreneur if what he or she is doing is what has been done before by other sport equipment business owners. To be a true entrepreneur, the business has to be based on creating a new demand. For the venture to be considered entrepreneurial according to this definition, the business must take some existing service, product, or idea and add new dimensions to it to create new markets, opportunities, and customers. Entrepreneurship is a value-added concept.

Based on this contemporary view, entrepreneurs are in the minority among new business. Annually, more than 500,000 people start businesses in the United States, and within 12 months approximately 40% of the new start-ups will be out of business. Within 5 years of start-up, more than 80% or 400,000 will have failed. The majority of those that fail are businesses that attempt to replicate existing businesses and do not create new value for the customer. They are, by definition, not entrepreneurial.

Peter Drucker believes that the entrepreneurial movement in the United States is based on management, a new technology in our short history as a nation. He attributes the emergence of the entrepreneurial economy in our country to new applications of management principles. This evolution draws from the concepts of the four main schools of management thought discussed in this chapter. Drucker considers management to be the new technology that is making the American economy into an entrepreneurial society. The

## A Dream and a Nightmare

Let us assume that your dream career is to work in the front office of a professional baseball franchise, and upon graduation from college you are hired to work for one of the top three franchises in the North America. You are selected for this position because of your organizational skills, decision-making and problem-solving abilities, general sports knowledge, and budgeting and writing abilities. You have been assigned to the business office to work for Joe Romano, who never had the opportunity to go to college. He has been with the franchise operation for 15 years and has been a supervisor in the business office for 5 years. Early in his career he was a player in one of the minor leagues. However, as a player he suffered a knee injury that prevented him from playing in the major league.

Joe is in his 40s, does an excellent job as a supervisor, likes to work with minimal interruption, and until now did not have anyone to assist him. Joe has a high school education and deep down does not feel the job he's responsible for has room for both you and him. In fact, he is feeling threatened that top management has assigned you, with a college education and a major in sport management, as his assistant. You have also learned that Joe is a close relative of the franchise owner.

During the first month of the job, Joe has given you minimal training or instruction, asks you to report to him every 2 hours, and expects you to write all business reports for him. You discover, however, that Joe has little to do now that you've been hired and is critical of the work you show him for approval. He often has you redo work you thought was well done. He tells you only what you need to know to complete projects but nothing more. Obtaining information from him that will help you do your job is difficult. In fact, he does little things to make you feel incompetent. You have discussed your frustrations with Joe. He just listens and says, "Stick with it kid, things will get better," and walks away laughing. You are really frustrated at this point and feel you should discuss your problem with Joe's manager. However, you have heard that the manager is dating Joe's oldest daughter and that the manager and Joe are on pretty good terms.

Based on the content of this chapter, what school of management thought might describe the culture of this organization and Joe's behavior. You like your job, even though you don't like the way you are being treated. You have decided that you have no intention of leaving. If you stay long enough, you know there are excellent opportunities here. What do you plan to do in this situation? List the risk factors if you follow through on your plan.

challenge is for the entrepreneur to apply these management principles to new problems and new opportunities.

The life of an entrepreneur can be exciting and exhausting, in both personal and business relationships. Several studies have revealed that the following leadership characteristics of successful entrepreneurs are necessary for survival.

- Self-confidence
- Perseverance, determination
- Energy, diligence
- Resourcefulness
- Ability to take calculated risks
- Need to achieve
- Creativity
- Initiation
- Flexibility
- Positive response to challenge

## Summary

We should view the history of management schools of thought as continuous, evolutionary processes that are difficult to pigeonhole into discrete categories or units of time. You will find that management principles developed during one historical period are enhanced, value added, and even discredited during a succeeding phase. The concepts emerging from the four schools and their contributors within the past 200 years have provided a solid foundation of tested management principles for students entering the sport management professions.

Students interested in management careers within the sport industry need to be aware of the many management strategies in planning,

## Learning Activity

With this entrepreneurial readiness index, rate yourself using a 5-point scale on each of the following, as you perceive your readiness to become an entrepreneur in sport management (1 = None at this time, 2 = Some, 3 = Average, 4 = Quite a bit, 5 = A great deal).

1. What is your desire to start your own business within the next 10 years?
2. What confidence level do you have of your ability to start and manage a business?
3. What is your knowledge level about the type of business in which you would like to be successful?
4. What is your skill level to become a successful entrepreneur in the business venture you have in mind?
5. How much more do you think you need to learn to become a successful entrepreneur?
6. How good are you in handling stress?
7. To what degree are you willing to make sacrifices to become an entrepreneur?
8. How ready are you to experience failure in your first entrepreneurship venture?
9. To what degree are you willing to sacrifice your relationship with your immediate family for the good of the business?
10. What is the degree of risk you are willing to take as an entrepreneur with your personal finances?
11. How would you evaluate your level of creativity for a business venture?

Form discussion groups of three to five individuals to share your readiness for entrepreneurship profiles.

organizing, and controlling work performance and in human resource management. Many management concepts presented in this chapter are further discussed in chapter 6 as they relate to organizational behavior (e.g., Theory X and Theory Y perceptions of individual motivation and career development).

Becoming an effective manager in the sport management profession will depend on (a) the level of knowledge and understanding the manager has of the multidisciplinary approaches available when dealing with business and human resource issues, (b) the degree to which the manager can implement these skills, and (c) the manager's ability to exercise entrepreneurial strategies.

Sport-related enterprises that have survived the test of time generally reflect the characteristics of entrepreneurship mentioned in this chapter. They frequently exhibit a positive readiness profile relative to entrepreneurial leadership, and they continually provide value-added experiences and services for their customers. Sport management professionals are encouraged to experiment with the many management theories that have emerged from the four schools of thought. This experiential phase will no doubt spur the sport management profession to contribute new concepts to this growing body of literature.

# Learning Activity

Read each of the following managerial concepts, then determine which school of management thought is most closely associated with each concept by entering *A, B,* or *C* in the blank space to the left of the concept number:

  *A*—administrative and scientific management school
  *B*—behavioral management school
  *C*—contemporary management school.

Do this independently for all items in the exercise. Then, form small discussion groups to share your answers.

| Concept | Description |
| --- | --- |
| ____ 1. Theory Y | A fitness club manager assumes that employees are trustworthy, are not inherently lazy, and seek job challenges and self-actualization. |
| ____ 2. Theory X | An athletic director assumes that employees are generally lazy, require close supervision, cannot be trusted, will not assume responsibilities on their own initiatives, and are mainly motivated by money. |
| ____ 3. Time and motion study | A fitness director uses a stopwatch, film, videotape, or other observation methods to assess employee work efficiency. |
| ____ 4. Organization-sponsored clubs, events, and social activities | An organization emphasizes company-sponsored social activities to improve employee morale (e.g., bowling teams, ski clubs, camera clubs, investment clubs, and travel clubs). |
| ____ 5. Management by objectives (MBO) | A company uses a system whereby supervisors and their employees mutually establish performance goals with specific targets and deadlines. They usually do this at the end of each year. Employees are rewarded for results they achieve. |
| ____ 6. Human relations training | An organization emphasizes effective human relations between supervisors and their employees. Typical training subjects may be communication, employee morale, employee counseling. Although human relations training is emphasized, it does little to change the nature of employees' jobs. |
| ____ 7. Self-actualization | A club manager maximally uses human resource potential by providing employees opportunities to participate in planning and designing their jobs. |
| ____ 8. Human resource planning (HRP) | An organization has established a human resource planning system that provides employee career planning, identifies possible career tracks within the organization (i.e., related jobs that lead to career advancement), and identifies employee potential for advancement opportunities. |
| ____ 9. Job rotation | A club manager allows employees to rotate from one job to another. Each job is of equal complexity. Job rotation is practiced to alleviate boredom and to assure properly trained employees are available as backups for other jobs at similar pay levels. |
| ____ 10. Close monitoring of employee time | A company requires nonmanagerial employees to use a time clock to record when they arrive at work, take rest breaks, take lunch breaks, and leave at the end of the day. |
| ____ 11. Profit motive | An organization has an abundance of employee grievances relative to unsatisfactory working conditions. The organization has not made improvements in the work areas in years. Management believes that any profits should go back to the investors rather than use them to modernize equipment and workplaces. |

Form small discussion groups of not more than five individuals; then identify actual situations in sport and fitness that demonstrate the descriptions in this exercise.

Answers to exercise (1) B, (2) B, (3) A, (4) B, (5) C, (6) B, (7) B, (8) C, (9) B, (10) A, (11) A

# Chapter 6 Organizational Behavior

**Mary Kennedy Minter**
Management Consultant, Cleveland, OH

## Learning Objectives

After studying this chapter, you will be able to

1. demonstrate an understanding of organizational behavior from both macro- and microdimensions;

2. analyze and assess a sport management case study using the basic terminology of organizational behavior (OB), including management theories and the applied contingency approach (situational management); and

3. explain how subsystems and interrelationships of the open systems model are exemplified within an organization's structure, process, and individual and group behavior.

We can characterize organizational behavior (OB) as an eclectic field of study. For example, OB is interdisciplinary, drawing on the same disciplines as management, especially psychology, sociology, anthropology, and organizational communication (Hunsacker & Cook, 1986).

In studying OB, it is helpful to view it from both macrodimensions and microdimensions. For example, macrodimensions are the "big picture" of an organization, such as its structure, production/service subsystems, external environment factors, mission, culture, and climate. Microdimensions are emerging behaviors of individuals and groups within an organization and how those behaviors affect an organization's process, structure, and its management. The rationale for studying different perspectives is that understanding the macroview of an organization gives a better focus on the microview of individual and group behaviors. You can more easily see how both dimensions interrelate in producing a dynamic, ever-changing group.

Consider this brief example of a well-known sport organization as a corporate enterprise.

Visualize the environment surrounding a college football game. It is a sunny, crisp Saturday afternoon in the fall; you have finally found a place to park (for $10) and have walked a mile to the stadium. You give your ticket to the gatekeeper and pass by the souvenir stands, where you can't resist buying a logo cap for your home team; then you buy a program from one of the many passing vendors. In front of the stadium entrance is the long row of food concession stands (you, of course, stock up with your favorite drink and snacks). Once inside, the aura of the crowd engulfs you, yet you can observe many parts of the football organization operating (in addition to those you've just passed through). The band is organizing on the sidelines for the pregame show; the security officers patrol the field. You can also see groundskeepers attending to their duties and the sport medical and emergency teams standing ready. The cheerleaders, mascots, and student section leaders are all in action revving up the crowd for the big game. The referees are ready at center field. Last, but not least, both football teams are warming up with their coaches close at hand.

Now, we can consider this panoramic picture a macroview of what is going on and what has gone into preparing for this moment. When the game begins, what macro- and microperspectives will you use as a spectator? Will you pay close attention to the offensive team and analyze the coaching strategies that the players execute as they protect the quarterback on the third down? Will you criticize the coach of the defensive team for not having a better front line? Will you just concentrate on the cheerleaders? What would be different if you were working within the football organization? Keep this example in mind as you read through this chapter. Perhaps you will want to use the college football organization as a case study for practicing your OB analysis skills.

# Approaches to Organizational Behavior

Following are definitions of three approaches important to the topic of OB: management, organizational behavior, and the contingency approach.

## Management Approach

A commonly accepted definition of management is "working with and through individuals and groups to accomplish organizational goals" (Hersey & Blanchard, 1982, p. 3). This definition includes both the macro- and microperspectives of OB.

## Organizational Behavior (OB) Approach

Generally defined, OB represents the synthesis approach to management in that it recognizes the macrodimensions of the organization as well as the microimpacts of individuals and groups. As an interdisciplinary field of study, OB specialists analyze organizations using theories, concepts, and research models from all three management schools of thought (i.e., administrative and scientific, behavioral, and contemporary, see chapter 5). You can view OB as an applied approach to working with the behavioral and structural complexities of an organization to improve its effectiveness (Hunsacker & Cook, 1986).

## Contingency Management Approach

The contingency approach, which is especially helpful to OB practitioners, is the contemporary management orientation to analyzing management functions and organizational behavior. Contingency approach refers to a pragmatic view of organizations and management (i.e., a practical versus idealistic view). This view acknowledges that many interdependencies are inherent in the organization and will require *situational management*, which means that one management style will not be effective in all situations or with diverse human behavior.

# Macro- and Microdimensions of Organizational Behavior

The contingency and OB approaches are ways of thinking, analyzing, and managing organizational functions and resources. These concepts provide a framework for the macro- and microdimensions.

An analogy that may help you visualize the interrelationship of the macro- and microdimensions is that of an iceberg (see figure 6.1). Scientists estimate that the tip of an iceberg is usually only one third of the larger mass, with two thirds of the iceberg lying beneath the water's surface. From an OB perspective, the tip of the iceberg represents the formal organization, the prescribed processes and procedures (i.e., structure, subsystems, environment, development, and management) by which the organization should function. This formal organization is that part you

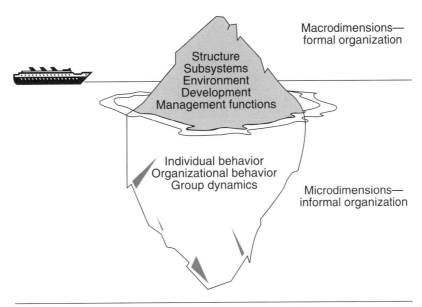

Macrodimensions—
formal organization

Structure
Subsystems
Environment
Development
Management functions

Individual behavior
Organizational behavior
Group dynamics

Microdimensions—
informal organization

**Figure 6.1**   An iceberg view of OB macro- and microdimensions.

can see documented in the organization charts and procedural manuals.

The formal organization (macrodimension) has been defined as an open system model. This concept of organization emerged in the 1960s to describe the structure and process of organizations. It was primarily based on Ludwig von Bertalanffy's (1968) general system theory, which originated from his holistic approach to biological science. His system model views organizations as composed of internal subsystems and external environment linkages that are interrelated. This view of an organization illustrates the permeable boundaries concept, that is, a structure and process in which subsystems intermingle and affect each other.

As figure 6.2 indicates, from a macro viewpoint the open system model is characterized by inputs transformed by processes into various outputs within the environment of the organizational structure. At any point, the open system may be affected by environments (internal or external); hence, the concept of permeable boundaries. We can analyze the outputs and feedback process from the levels of the organization, groups, or individuals. For example, the well-known situation of the 1994 national baseball players' strike clearly illustrates the open system's concept of permeable boundaries. As a brief scenario, the players and managers were in conflict with the team owners, which represented the internal environment of inputs being processed into a conflict output. However, a definite influence on the baseball organizations was eventually manifested by

their customers, representing the external environment. Based on the long-term strike, the return of the spectators to loyal customers was in doubt, and in fact, was slow to occur after the baseball strike ended. The boundary and decisions between the players and owners was definitely permeated (affected) by the actions of a key external environment—the spectators.

The microdimensions of the informal organization are illustrated (see figure 6.1) as the large mass under the water (two thirds of the iceberg), which represents the cultural forces of the organization that keep the macrostructure floating. This hidden mass of energy includes individual and organization behaviors (group dynamics).

In an open system (see figure 6.2), the microdimensions are represented by the transformation process, involving the contingency concepts related to task and person characteristics and to formal and informal social relationships. Leadership is an inherent function in the transformation process where people and tasks merge to produce organizational outputs. Fiedler and Chemers (1984) developed a contingency model of leadership based on their studies that distinguished between task-motivated and relationship-motivated leaders. Fiedler and Chemers found that situational leadership was a viable approach for describing how successful leadership depends on the match between the leader's style and the demands of the situation (Tannenbaum & Schmidt, 1958; Likert, 1961). In addition, a contingency approach incorporates the concept that conflict is healthy and that change (disequilibrium) is inherent in the

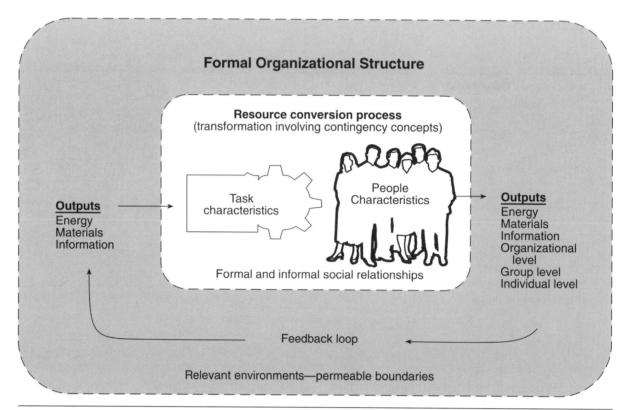

**Figure 6.2**   The open system model.

organizational process of growth and survival (Vroom & Yetton, 1973).

In summary, Katz and Kahn (1978) emphasized the phenomena of the microdimensions of emerging behavior of individuals within organizations, how these behaviors affect an organization, and how behaviors interrelate with the macrosystem elements: "Open system theory permits the use of both levels, the conceptual level for macro or system variables and the phenomenon levels [micro] for the actual facts to be gathered" (p.13).

# Understanding Organizational Behavior

We present the following case study* to give you a situation with which you can practice relating the OB dimensions as you continue this chapter.

## The Windansea Case

I came out to California years ago after getting my BS degree in mechanical engineering from the

University of Illinois. I accepted a job at a major aerospace corporation. But it wasn't long before I became more interested in surfing than in my job. First, I was into body surfing, then I learned how to use a surfboard and, for practice, a skateboard.

For the first year or so, I confined my surfing to weekends and after work. In those days we usually used much larger boards than today and we constantly discussed and experimented with various models. My engineering interest and competence led me to ponder endless variations in design. Finally, I decided to do something.

I rented a garage a block from the beach, purchased some fiberglass, some tools, and other equipment. I made a few boards and tried them out. A number of times people offered to buy some of them. I sold some and more and more people began asking me to custom-make boards to their specifications or to make one of my own models. At the end of about thirteen months of this, I found myself with more orders than I could fill.

Finally, I made the big decision to quit my job and go into business for myself. I formed Windansea Surfboards, Inc., and operated it alone for 6 months.

*Reprinted, by permission, from *Contemporary Management* (2nd Ed.) (pp. 112-113; 131) by D.R. Hampton, 1981, New York: McGraw-Hill. Copyright 1981 by McGraw-Hill. Reprinted by permission.

Business was even better than I expected and I found it necessary to hire first one, then another employee. After 2 years, I had seventeen employees and had installed our operations in part of a rented industrial building.

The way we had things set up was pretty informal. We were still making custom boards for individuals or small batches of our models. We rented a small store at the beach and displayed several models there. The company continued in this way until, after nine more years, it had over seventy employees, most of whom performed several operations in making a complete surfboard.

While sales continued to rise, earnings were rising at a lesser rate. It began to dawn on me that something might have to be done to control costs and streamline operations. It seemed like a particularly good time to face our problems because it appeared that surfing was about to become substantially more popular, and we wanted to be in a good position to take advantage of the potential. As president, I retained a management and industrial engineering consulting firm and told them I wanted them to study our business from stem to stern and make whatever recommendations they felt appropriate for our manufacturing processes, financial planning, marketing, and management.

They made a comprehensive study of our market and our operations. They agreed that we were on the brink of a major increase in volume. They made a number of recommendations in finance and marketing. They also recommended a transformation of our manufacturing system so that instead of its being a shop where each worker made a complete board, it was to become more like a mass production factory where boards flowed from one end to the other in an integrated sequential process. We would make large batches of one model, then another in this way. Most manufacturing employees would perform only a few repetitive operations.

They also proposed to rearrange and formalize the management of operations. For example, we had been operating without any particular person being responsible for either the planning of production or the inspection and quality control functions. Each employee was, for the most part, his or her own planner and inspector. The consultants, however, proposed to create a supervisor in charge of each of these functions. The supervisor of production planning would work out plans with the supervisor in charge of manufacturing operations. The supervisor of quality control would establish quality standards and use inspectors to check that they were being satisfied.

In short, it seemed that what they were proposing was, as I said, a mass- or large-batch production technology to replace our more self-paced system. To go along with this engineered system, they were proposing a more specialized and formal management system which would introduce new specialties and interpose a level of management between me and the workers.

I expressed some concern that even though I had a constantly changing workforce, the jobs would become so much simpler that the few long-term employees I had might be extremely disappointed. The consultants seemed to have anticipated this because they proposed to promote four of my most senior and valuable employees to the new management jobs. They said that I was correct and might disappoint some others, but that as we grew we might create more supervisory jobs. They also pointed out that it would cost less and take less time to train new employees for the simpler jobs.

I accepted their recommendations whole hog, but not without tossing and turning a few nights over the worry that there might be some problems we hadn't foreseen.

Anyway, within a year we had implemented virtually every one of the recommendations.

## What Happened in the Windansea Case?

For the most part, the changes worked out pretty well. Our volume of business did increase, and our "mass-production" setup with production planning, and our quality control with its standards and inspection, helped us produce the greater quantities we needed without any substantial loss of quality. We began to realize economies of scale from mass production better than we had been under our former system, and our earnings gain began to keep up with our sales gains.

One thing I regret, though, is that we never again did seem to have the pleasant atmosphere we had in the days when everybody was making complete boards. Things just became more factory-like. While we still have fairly good employee relations, the fact remains that more individuals and groups gripe about various problems with their equipment, with inspections, with production quotas, and so on than before. Even though most of our present employees weren't here before the changes, I think the changes make it more difficult to have good employee relations. Most of the old-time employees have been promoted, so they don't seem to have been hurt.

Frankly, the new organization worked so well that its success was a big factor in my agreeing to my husband's request that I take time off occasionally to have a baby. We now have two children, and the Windansea continues to prosper.

## Learning Activity

Several questions from the OB perspective arise from this case study. Before reading further about OB concepts, write down a few questions that come to mind about this organizational situation. It will be interesting to compare your questions from the case study with others listed at the end of the chapter.

# Macrodimensions of Organizational Behavior

Using the Windansea case study as a situational example, you can outline the macrodimensions of an OB approach as follows.

## Organizational Structure

The organizational structure of the Windansea company was small in size and informal in its production system. The tasks involved in producing a surfboard were completed basically by one individual, so that the work was autonomous, and each worker was essentially her or his own quality control inspector. The new structure significantly changed the design of the organization to a multiple-level one, with levels of management between the owner (president) and surfboard makers, each of whom completed only part of the total surfboard product.

## Learning Activity

Outline an organizational chart for both the original Windansea structure and the new multiple-level one. What do the different organizational charts indicate about potential problems in both kinds of organization? Remember that before the change in formal organization design and structure, about 70 employees worked for one manager, the president.

## Organizational Subsystems

A common definition of *system* related to organizations is an integrated network of tasks and processes (Hunsacker & Cook, 1986). Organizational systems are composed of *subsystems*, which are defined as smaller units within the total organization. As discussed previously, an organization's subsystems (networks) are often defined as an *open system,* which means they interact with each other (internal organizational environment) and with the external environments. You will concentrate on the internal organizational subsystems, but will also be aware of external forces. For example, in the Windansea case, the decision to reorganize the formal production system was influenced by the external factor that surfing was becoming more popular and the market for surfboards would increase.

Each subsystem has its distinct network of tasks and processes and usually has its own management. In analyzing the behavior of the organization, you would observe and study the five common subsystems.

1. *Informational subsystem*—the way necessary information flows through the organization to accomplish its tasks and functions

2. *Materials subsystem*—the way materials flow through the organization to be transformed into products or services (e.g., an assembly-line operation)

3. *Technological subsystem*—the way nonhuman and nonmaterial processes provide support to other subsystems (e.g., computers and equipment)

## Learning Activity

Look at your organizational charts for the original Windansea company. What subsystem factors contributed to the desire for a change in the organizational structure? What formal subsystems exist in the new organizational structure?

Summarize the effects of the subsystems on the human resources (employees) within the new Windansea organization. If you were the external consultant to this newly organized company, what recommendations would you make to the president to minimize employee dissatisfaction within the new production system?

4. *Economic subsystem*—the way funds flow through the organization (and to external environments)

5. *Social (human) subsystem*—the way human resources interact through the network of subsystems and contribute to organizational goals (Hunsacker & Cook, 1986, pp. 42-43)

In an organizational behavior approach to management, the human (social) subsystem is emphasized when completing an organizational analysis to aid in improving human interactions with the other subsystems. For the purpose of this chapter, the social (human) subsystem needs special attention.

# External and Internal Organizational Environments

Many concepts and variables exist within this macrodimension of OB, only a few of which are outlined in this overview chapter. Contemporary behavioral psychologists have concentrated on the following organizational and environmental concepts: external and internal factors, quality of work life (QWL), job design, organizational culture, organizational climate, organizational development, and management functions.

## External Environmental Factors

The organization is affected externally by markets (general), customers (specific), suppliers, regulators (governmental and others), and societal behaviors and norms. For example, you probably mentioned in your analysis of the Windansea case that the market demand for surfboards increased the orders and affected the company's production volume, which in turn indicated a change in production process.

## Internal Environmental Factors

The organization is affected internally by organizational variables (e.g., tasks, goals, structure, policies, and managerial practices); technological variables (e.g., complexity, standardization, and variability); and work climate (affected by organizational and technological variables and individuals such as needs, motives, values, personal goals, and education or training). In the Windansea case, the increased orders for surfboards was first solved by hiring more employees and continuing the one-person production process. However, this production process was complicated when the number of employees increased to about 70 and were all reporting to one person, the president. The span of management was not an efficient or effective one.

## Quality of Work Life

Another behavioral concept is quality of work life (QWL), which is contingent on the environmental variables outlined previously. The variable of work climate will impact the quality of work life and affect the worker's job performance and job satisfaction. For example, in the Windansea case the work climate was changed by reorganizing the process of producing surfboards, and different employees were hired who represented different individual variables, such as needs, motives, values, personal goals, and education and training levels.

## Job Design

An internal organizational variable that is a key factor in quality of work life is how the job is designed. For example, in the Windansea case the original structure was based on an individual, autonomous job (task) design in which each employee completed a surfboard. In contrast, the new structure functioned as a mass-production job design in which each employee only completed part of a surfboard, and the final quality check was made by a separate management person, not by the one-person artist of one surfboard.

## Organizational Culture and Climate

Organizational culture is a term related to the organizational environment dimensions and is often used synonymously with organizational climate; however, there is a difference. Generally defined, the cultural aspect of an organization refers to a culmination of all the variables mentioned thus far. Organizational culture encompasses the work group values, norms, and behaviors that emerge because of external and internal organizational variables and those, in turn, produce patterns of behavior unique to an organization. More specifically, culture is represented by characteristics identified as "deeply embedded and enduring" shared values and assumptions about an organization that develop over a long time (e.g., myths, rituals, and symbols) (Peterson, 1986, p. 82). In contrast, organizational climate refers to employees' "perceptions of their shared views and attitudes about current organizational patterns and outcomes" (Peterson, 1986, p. 82).

For example, there may be a culture of rituals within an organization (e.g., company picnics, workplace humor) that are perceived in different ways by various subgroups of employees (e.g., long-term versus newly hired employees). The culture of the organization has developed over a long time; the climate (or atmosphere) exemplified by the current employees may change daily, just like the weather, depending on internal and external environmental factors.

## Learning Activity

How do you think the organizational culture and climate in the Windansea case changed when the organization shifted from its original structure to the new production system? What effects did the change have on the quality of work life?

### Organizational Development

Organizational development (OD) is an approach to change that uses applied or action research to identify points in which behavioral science and management techniques might aid in organizational improvement. The OD research approach (that encompasses the dimensions of organizational behavior), originated in the contributions of Kurt Lewin (1951) and his field theory research method in group dynamics.

In the Windansea case, the president of the company asked an outside consulting firm to analyze the organization and recommend changes. That action is an example of an OD approach. However, the case study does not provide the details of how the OD consultants researched the situation or how they managed the intervention. This kind of information is significant and we would need it to analyze the effectiveness of the OD approach in this case.

### Organizational Management Functions

The last macrodimension interrelates with all others previously discussed. The standard management functions are commonly referred to as planning, organizing, motivating (communication and leadership), and controlling. We can consider these functions macrodimensions of an organization because they are broad conceptual factors that interact with the other macrofactors: structure, subsystems, environment, and development. However, management functions are unique in

that they represent a bridge between the substance and the heart of the organization—the human resources. This idea of management coordinating people to accomplish organizational tasks and objectives leads us into the concept of microdimensions of organizational behavior—the actions of people as individuals and within groups.

## Microdimensions of Organizational Behavior

Using the Windansea case study again as a situational example, you can outline the microdimensions of an organizational behavior by using theories about individual and group behavior and how they interrelate with and affect the organizations. Interrelationships and interdependencies of the concepts and processes occur within the contexts of individual behavior, individual and organizational behavior processes, and group dynamics. These concepts are emphasized because they represent the dynamic life of an organization.

### Individual Behavior

The workers in an organization bring to that group their individual personalities and motivations. A common contemporary management question illustrates the importance of individual behaviors to the organization: Is there a fit between the formal organization (i.e., the way the organization was designed to function) and the informal organization (i.e., what employees actually do)? In other words, is there compatibility between what the organization needs or wants and the employees' values, motivations, and job talents? This question implies another significant view of individuals within an organization. If an individual wants or needs to work in a particular organization but that organization's formal structure and culture do not fit the individual, then both parties will need to compromise to some degree or the employee will have to leave. For example, in the Windansea case, the president decided to significantly change the organizational structure to increase profits. The change resulted in a much different organizational culture and climate in which the employees would work. You could predict that those employees who could adapt to the new climate or structure did so; others who preferred the autonomous, individualized production system would probably elect not to accept the new structure. The point is that management of an organization has the right to structure the firm in ways that best suit the business needs, and the employees have the right to select organizations that best fit their personal needs and values. However, if employment options for individuals are limited, then they (and the organization) will need to develop coping strategies to produce an effective, mutually acceptable organizational climate.

## Self-Esteem and Attribution

Basic psychological concepts can help an individual understand and cope with the dynamic process of collaboration within an organization. For example, self-esteem refers to our personal, psychological judgments about ourselves regarding how worthy we feel about our general life experiences. Self-esteem has been defined as "the integrated summation of self-confidence and self-respect. It is the conviction that one is competent to live and worthy of living" (Branden, 1971, p. 110).

A more general personal concept encompasses the self-images we develop through our self-esteem perceptions and our social interactions. We can perceive the consequences of our personal and environmental (social) interactions in many ways (e.g., as threats or opportunities). We can cope with and reshape these personal and environmental relationships to maintain effective levels of self-esteem and self-image in our relationships with others. This process of perceiving ourselves and our environments and trying to cope with (manage) both is referred to as attribution. A key to the attribution concept is a phenomenon called locus of control. For example, persons who perceive themselves as in control of their destinies are attributing their life outcomes to their internal strengths (e.g., self-esteem or image) and to their

### Learning Activity

How can you use the concepts of self-esteem and attribution to analyze what changes in human behavior may occur with new Windansea organizational changes? How may management and employees in the new Windansea organization need to cope to produce an effective work climate?

The beneficial influence of positive group dynamics on self-esteem is evident in sport at all levels.

abilities to manage their lives. The individual is the locus of control. In the opposite attribution pattern, people may perceive external factors as attributing most often to their successes or failures. The predominant attribution pattern individuals develop is observable in the way they perceive themselves and their behavior with others.

## Individual and Organizational Behaviors

The personality factors of self-esteem and attribution are inherent elements in our self-motivation behaviors. However, when the individual operates within an organization, the motivation for work performance becomes a more complex phenomenon. This complexity of an individual's motivation within an organizational context has been the basis for many approaches to management and the OB field of study (e.g., Maslow's need hierarchy, McGregor's Theory X-Theory Y model, Herzberg's maintenance and motivation theory, and Vroom's expectancy model of motivation) (Maslow, 1962; McGregor, 1960; Herzberg, 1966; Vroom & Yetton, 1973; see also chapter 5).

OB practitioners focus on a microview of motivation within the context of different organizational processes. Within these processes, the following variables interact on an individual, group, and organizational basis: job performance (i.e., objectives, appraisal, and rewards), interpersonal relations and communication, leadership, power and influence, problem solving, decision making, and career development.

Analyzing interpersonal relationships and communication patterns helps improve overall effectiveness. For example, you can study communication within an organization as a series of networks (e.g., task related, informational, technical, or social) or as a vehicle for leadership, influence, or power.

Another process within organizational behavior is the problem-solving and decision-making activity, which is in turn interrelated to the key processes and variables of job performance, interpersonal relations and communication, leadership, and power and influence.

For example, in the Windansea case you have been asked to explain aspects of the communication networks that involve tasks, information, technical, and social factors that affected performance, communication, leadership, influence, or power. You may want to review your analysis. Are there other factors that you can identify related to individual and organizational behaviors?

## Career Development

This item is included in the list of key processes because it represents a contemporary microview of the individual within an organization. In this age of diversity among individuals and organizations, the concept of a career is, itself, a dynamic phenomenon. For example, a definite trend exists toward career clustering, whereby individuals can move among several organizations, depending on their transferable skills. In an OB approach, career development is usually viewed as a process in which the individual and the organization are responsible for input if both parties are to be effective. For example, in the Windansea case some experienced employees elected to stay with the company and advance their careers by becoming supervisors within the new production structure. Other employees elected to pursue their careers elsewhere after the reorganization of the Windansea company.

## Group Dynamics

OB practitioners also focus on the group dynamics within an organization. An OB approach would be to identify the formal group subsystems within an organization (e.g., departments and task-related groups in a mass-production, assembly-line operation), then to identify what informal groups have evolved that facilitate or hinder the production flow and total effectiveness of the formal systems. We can analyze the structure of these formal and informal groups by identifying communication networks within them to determine how the groups function internally. Then we can analyze the relationship between department or work groups (intergroup) in a similar manner to identify the dynamics (flow and movement) of the situation.

The microdimensions of organizational behavior can contribute to a better understanding of what is happening on the macrolevel in the dimensions of management functions (e.g., planning, organizing, and controlling), organizational structure, subsystems, environment, and development. For example, in the Windansea case a logical followup to the newly organized production approach would have been for the consultants to return to the company after a few months to interview employees (those who remained, the newly hired employees, and those who left the company). The consultants could have compiled information on how the group dynamics of the new organization may be affecting the new structure, subsystems, environment, and development of the company and its employees.

## Learning Activity

What were your first reactions to the conclusion of the Windansea case study? For example, had you made some assumptions that proved not to be true? What were those assumptions? What do such assumptions indicate about potential problems in organizational behavior? For example, what biases or stereotypes do individuals harbor that may affect their objectivity?

## Summary

Organizations need to be viewed as open systems both from the broad macrodimensions and from the specific microdimensions. These different perceptions help focus the study of variables operating within organizational behaviors. Organizational behavior (OB) involves individual and group actions and represents an interdisciplinary field of study that incorporates concepts from several academic disciplines, such as psychology, sociology, and anthropology. OB is considered an applied field of study because it helps managers analyze individual and group dynamics within the ever-changing environments of modern organizations.

This chapter has discussed basic concepts in an operational sense, that is, how you can use the conceptual definitions and apply them to real situations involving sport management. Because of the fluid nature of OB, a contingency approach is appropriate, directing you to analyze the situation and determine how best to manage the human resources and tasks involved. Awareness of the macro organizational subsystems and their interrelationships aids in discerning how to analyze and manage an organization's structure, process, and individual and group behaviors.

OB provides a framework for analyzing individual behavior that, in turn, helps determine how best to fit into an organization. The perceptions individuals have of their self-esteem and how they attribute who is in control of situational factors will determine how they cope with and manage their organizational behavior. Work motivation will be influenced by these personal perceptions and by attitudes toward priority needs, management styles, and what individuals expect from their work environment. Finally, an awareness of the multifaceted OB concepts can help analyze career development needs and how individuals relate within the group dynamics of an organization.

## Learning Activity

What may be some problems that the company president is not aware of within the macro- and microdimensions of the newly organized Windansea company? What are potential microdimension factors that may arise for the Windansea company and its employees?

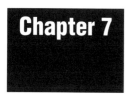

# Chapter 7 The Business of Sport

**Beverly R.K. Zanger and David L. Groves**
Bowling Green State University

---

## Learning Objectives

After studying this chapter, you will be able to

1. explain the three classifications of sport businesses;

2. discuss the economic impact of sport businesses;

3. explain the use of venture capital for sponsorship;

4. identify permeable boundaries in a sport-related business; and

5. explain the contingency theory as it would relate to inclement weather for a sporting event.

---

In an effort to examine how businesses function within the sport industry, this chapter applies some theories described in the preceding two chapters on management thought and organizational behavior. Specifically, we'll look at

- how to classify sport businesses by the way they generate revenue,

- the open system model as it applies to sport businesses,

- the management environment of sport businesses, and

- the permeable boundaries concept as it relates to the sport business.

## The Sport Industry

The growth of businesses within the sport industry results directly from the popularity of many sports. As the major sports in North America boom financially, the businesses directly or indirectly affiliated with them boom as well. Consider these figures: Clothing items with team logos account for 60% of the licensed pro sports merchandise sales—45% of Americans own at least one item. In 1995, sales of licensed merchandise were $3.15 billion for NFL (National Football League) products, $2.65 billion for NBA (National Basketball Association) products, $1.90 billion for MLB (Major League Baseball) products, and $1 billion for NHL (National Hockey League) products (Hall & Merrill, 1996). The numbers are high, but even more remarkable is how quickly they developed. If we could make a comparison with the auto industry, the sport industry exploded into prominence in a fraction of the time it took for the Model-T to reach maturity.

Sport has evolved worldwide into a major component of the economic marketplace, both on its own (as a percentage of the market) and as it relates to businesses within other industries. A sport business can be completely independent within the industry, as Major League Baseball is. It might be an organization like the Atlanta Olympic Committee, which solicited sponsorship dollars for the 1996 Summer Olympics from the Kodak Corporation. Or, it might be completely dependent on companies outside the industry, such as the Champion Apparel Company, which is owned by the Sara Lee Corporation. Sport businesses range from the smallest fitness club to companies such as Nike or Starter. Employment within the industry runs the gamut from volunteers at the concession stand to owners of professional sports teams. Like all other industries, the sport industry has had its ups and downs, from hugely successful events such as the Super Bowl, Wimbledon, and the Kentucky Derby, to failures such as the layoffs of apparel company employees, player strikes, and lockouts (Zanger & Groves, 1994b).

For the past 30 years, the sport industry has grown exponentially. Among many others, sport-related businesses include apparel companies, equipment manufacturers, media networks, arenas and stadiums, merchandise companies, players, sports teams, and professional leagues. We can see businesses outside the sport industry involved with sport businesses in corporate sponsorship of events, luxury boxes held by companies, endorsements of popular players, sales of sport-related products such as player cards, and exclusive television contracts for sporting events. Furthermore, corporate sponsorship of sporting events has become *big* business, and advertising during sporting events is one of the more successful methods of promoting products. The sport industry has certainly become lucrative, but how do particular sport businesses operate within this large and complex industry? We can best analyze this by looking at how sport businesses generate revenue.

# Classifying Sport Businesses

The most common way to classify sport businesses is by how the business generates income (or revenue). The three main classifications are

1. direct revenue,
2. supportive revenue, and
3. indirect revenue.

## Direct Revenue

Some organizations generate income through *direct revenue,* which is the income derived directly from a sporting event. Direct revenues include such income as gate receipts, revenue received from selling broadcast rights, and money earned through sponsorship. Direct revenue organizations include associations such as the National Football League, Major League Baseball, the National Hockey League, the National Basketball Association, and the National Collegiate Athletic Association, as well as each team and conference within these huge organizations. The criteria are that the team sells tickets, has sponsors, or sells broadcast rights; some small colleges are not direct revenue organizations because they do not meet any of these criteria. Some conferences (e.g., the Big 10) and prestigious universities (e.g., Notre Dame) that have traditionally obtained direct revenue from ticket sales and sponsorships are now considering selling or already have sold (in the case of Notre Dame) exclusive rights to broadcast some of their major athletic events, such as football games. As athletic associations receive more pressure to increase income, the big revenue generated by exclusive broadcast sales will likely become increasingly attractive—despite the position of some that this revenue undermines the integrity of the collegiate institution.

## Supportive Revenue

Some sport businesses, such as concession and souvenir stands, parking garages, and security companies, generate income through supporting a sporting event or activity. This income is called *supportive revenue.* The well-being of a typical support business is tied closely to the attendance at the sporting event, so the success of the direct revenue business heavily influences the revenue of the affiliated support business. The degree of success and the number of affiliated support businesses will depend on how well the direct revenue business is doing. Hugely successful franchises that get consistently large turnouts for their events—the Dallas Cowboys, Los Angeles Dodgers, and Chicago Bulls, among others—can support the revenue of thousands of smaller businesses related to the sporting event, but less successful teams or expansion teams cannot support nearly as many. Likewise, stadium and franchise owners may themselves operate the support businesses, thus bringing them under the control of those businesses that earn direct revenue.

## Indirect Revenue

The third way for a sport business to generate income is through *indirect revenue*. All companies that do not fit into the direct revenue or supportive revenue categories fall under this classification. These businesses do not depend directly on sporting events but on the popularity of particular sports and sports teams. Such businesses include those selling sports apparel and sporting equipment and those that generate revenue by sponsoring sporting events. For these businesses, attendance is not as important as it is for support revenue businesses; rather, the *popularity* of the affiliated sport or team is more significant. Thus, teams like the Charlotte Hornets of the NBA and the San Jose Sharks of the NHL, though only marginally successful on the basketball court and on the ice, can generate big profits for indirect revenue businesses because of their large national appeal.

Until the last 20 years, few sport businesses were generating much income through indirect revenue, but these businesses have now become major players in the sport industry. Through its endorsements of Michael Jordan, Sheryl Swoopes, Tiger Woods, and other sport superstars, Nike has been phenomenally successful in the sport apparel industry. Such stars are expensive, but Nike has found these endorsements extremely worthwhile. Similarly, Coca-Cola spent many millions on TV advertising during the 1996 Summer Olympics, but the increase in their worldwide sales showed that the money was wisely spent, at least from a financial perspective.

# Open System Model and Sport Businesses

The open system model was defined in chapter 6 as a view of modern organizations based on Ludwig von Bertalanffy's (1968) general system theory. It describes organizations as being composed of internal subsystems and interrelated external environmental linkages. The model consists of inputs (e.g., money or products) from external sources that are transformed into outputs by the company's internal element (e.g., management, employees, machinery). This provides financial returns via revenue generated outside the company (e.g., purchased apparel or exclusive television rights) that are used to purchase more input materials for the sport business. For a full review of how the open system model operates, see chapter 6. In a nutshell, the system works this way: **E** (an external source, such as spectators at a Major League baseball game) gives or sells **I** (input, such as the money paid by the spectators who attend the ball game) to **C** (the company or association who produces or presents the product, such as a baseball game). **C** then uses **I** to produce or present **O** (output, such as more expensive players or a new stadium). **O** provides **C** with **R** (revenue generated outside **C**, for example, the income a TV station pays **C** to broadcast its games because **C** acquired players that the spectators [the external source] want to see on TV). **C** uses this **R** to acquire more **I** from **E**, which starts the cycle over again. This is indeed a complex system. The main thing to grasp, though, is that the system could not work without **E**, the external source that provides the input.

At this point we'll present an overview of a sport business, the Nike corporation, in which the open system model is at work. The passage that follows is adapted from a study by the authors of this chapter (Groves & Zanger, 1994a), who completed a profile of Nike in 1993. After reading the passage, you'll have the opportunity to explain how the open system model applies to the way Nike does business.

Nike, whose primary marketing focus is doing business related to sport, provides financial support and apparel to many professional teams and universities. Nike generates substantial indirect revenue through sales of team-specific or athlete-specific apparel and gear, such as the Michael Jordan "Come Back in 95" T-shirt. They also own and run retail and outlet stores, provide sponsorship money for many sporting events, and advertise extensively to support their products.

Nike has become an icon within the sport industry, marketing its products worldwide and endorsing world-famous athletes like Michael Jordan, Michael Johnson, and Tiger Woods. As you would expect, Nike never sits still; it is an aggressive company that is constantly seeking new markets and developing new ideas to maintain its market share and competitive edge. For instance, to extend its visibility, Nike is currently reaching out to develop relations with universities.

Nike has developed its strong niche in the worldwide sport market by creating a product that is flourishing financially while competing internationally. The ongoing success the corporation enjoys is the driving force that motivates, structures, and propels the company to continually raise its achievement standards. Once a business has established itself as a leader in the industry, it must maintain an aggressive approach if it is to stay on top. The Chicago Bulls won five NBA championships in 7 years. Because of their great success, every team that the Bulls play during the regular season and the playoffs is gunning for them with an aggressive tenacity that isn't present when the Bulls' opponents play other teams. It works the same in business as it does in sport. Nike's competitors are always trying to gain on them and overtake them. Like the Bulls, Nike must keep changing their recipe for success. As other teams try new offenses and defenses, attempting to knock the leader off, the leader in the industry must adjust to keep the lead it has established. Usually, the "new" strategies employed by leaders and competitors are simply offshoots of tried-and-true business methods. The key factors that Nike and all other businesses must recognize and then manipulate according to circumstances have existed for centuries. What are these factors?

■ *Quality of the commodity.* Obviously, commodity quality is a key factor that Nike must always consider. If the product is not good, it's difficult to pretend it is (though some companies continue to try!). As you'd expect, product research is a constant process at Nike. The corporation is always looking for ways to (a) improve their product line (e.g., create new shoe designs), and (b) ensure that the current product line is being produced consistently well. The former concern rests with corporation researchers and engineers; the latter concern rests with the corporation's internal function (i.e., the production phase in the open system model). How highly skilled its labor force is, what technology they use, and the quality of the supervision during production are important factors in creating the product. If there's a slip in any of these quarters, the quality of the commodity will be significantly influenced.

■ *Communication.* As in all business environments, aggressive communication or promotion—including marketing and advertising—in the sports

industry is probably as vital to a company's success as the quality of their commodity. In fact, some cynics argue that success is more determined by promotion (the sizzle) than by the quality of the product (the steak). Here we won't enter the sizzle-steak debate—unquestionably both play huge roles in a business's degree of success. However, those who argue that aggressively communicating product information to the consumer and other interested parties is at least as important as product quality have a strong position. After all, what good does it do to have a wonderful product if no one knows about it? The Nike corporation, although faithful to its pledge of producing quality commodities, understands how crucial it is to communicate information about its products. Their extensive marketing and advertising staff is among the most creative in or out of the sport industry.

■ *Understanding the cultural climate.* Culture is likewise an influencing factor within the communication process. When comunicators attempt to deliver a message, it is imperative that they recognize the sociocultural position of the audience receiving the message. The Nike corporation is successful in communicating sport as a medium, relating product to culture, and interpreting its clients effectively. For example, Nike has taken full advantage of the fitness craze of the 1980s and 1990s. It is a climate in which people who *aren't* exercising feel guilty and even inferior because of their inactive lifestyle. Nike saturates the culture with their "Just do it" commercials, which encourage people to quit procrastinating and become active.

In summary, the factors that contribute to successful business practices are complex and varied. Not only do sport companies do business with companies inside and outside the sport industry, they must also effectively market their product to consumers (and in so doing deal with cultural and social issues), make sure that their product is of high quality, and above all maintain the competitive edge and forethought to stay one step ahead of competitors.

# Contingencies in the Sport Business

As you've learned from earlier chapters, success in sport management depends on applying principles that have evolved from sociology, psychology, philosophy, and other disciplines. Using the principles appropriately helps increase profits and ensure success, especially during economic stress. There is much more to developing a new business operation (or changing an ineffective one) than just managing the business to show a profit. How well or poorly a business will function depends on knowing which principles to apply under various circumstances. The idea that different circumstances require changing the application of principles is called the contingency theory of management (see chapter 6). To ignore this theory as you break into the sport industry is like ignoring the instructions to your parachute.

The contingency theory of management applies to the sport industry at least as much as it applies to other industries. However, as businesses try to force principles where they don't apply, the theory is often neglected. Many beginning sport businesses employ a trial-and-error method to solve the problems of their ailing sport enterprise. The result is often failure. Sometimes those who have been successful in an industry outside of sport will invest heavily in a sport enterprise and apply the same principles to the new business that made the other business a success. Again, the result is often failure. The denominator common to these two scenarios is a lack of understanding of the theories that apply to sport industries and an inability to apply principles appropriately (Zanger & Groves, 1994b).

Sport enterprises do not respond well either to traditional business theories such as supply and demand or to the traditional sport concept of winning and losing. Sport businesses benefit from a thorough understanding of general sport content and specific individual sports. For example, running an arena business for hockey is far different from running the same business for tennis. Hockey audiences are traditionally rougher and accustomed to more aggressive crowd participation, whereas traditional tennis audiences appreciate the game's civility, tradition, and ritual. Newcomers to the sport industry must gain quick sensitivity to the needs and expectations of different audiences or risk alienating the group they want most to embrace.

To stay creative and continue capitalizing on opportunities for success, sport business owners need to understand sport within a cultural context. Some university event directors, for example, manage football games assuming that all spectators are football enthusiasts. Other directors emphasize the pregame tailgate party and other so-

They look happy now, but as experienced people in the industry know, this group can be a fickle bunch. To succeed, newcomers to sport management must be sensitive to the needs and expectations of their audience.

cial aspects of the event, thus targeting a greater percentage of their audience. You don't have to be a football fan to enjoy attending a football game. A sport manager who doesn't know this will not appeal to all potential ticket buyers and, consequently, events will likely suffer poor attendance.

## Sport Culture

As discussed in chapters 5 and 6, the primary approaches for studying sport management are business or behavior oriented. A different method that has been successful is to take a cultural approach (Brunt, 1992; Fiske, 1992; Randall, 1994). In this approach the primary focus is not management or organizational behavior but how sport influences the culture and how culture influences sport. The information generated through this approach provides an environmental perspective to the sport enterprises.

In North America, the influence of sport on culture is pervasive (Dickerson, 1991). One obvious manifestation of *how* pervasive sport is in our culture is the association of individuals with a particular team or sport and how much money they spend to establish or prove this association. As we mentioned at the beginning of the chapter, the sport apparel business has exploded on our culture; we spend several billion dollars annually on clothing and other sport paraphernalia (such as squirt bottles, banners, and can "huggies") to

connect ourselves with our favorite teams or sports. There has been, and will continue to be, a tremendous market for autographs, baseballs, bats, jerseys, helmets, and other items associated with sport. Another interesting indicator of sport influence on the North American culture is the nostalgia associated with sports memorabilia, such as trading cards and programs. The same cards one generation typically tossed into the wastebasket have spurred a multimillion dollar business for the next generation. Another reflection of the impact of sport on culture is the hero syndrome (Levine, 1985; Meier, 1989; Wann & Branscombe, 1993). The more successful ad marketing campaigns have some association with a sport hero or a sport, which has increased the sales of many products. These are only a few manifestations of the North American culture's love affair with sport (Garfield, 1993; Levin, 1993).

The cultural climate in which sport operates provides the basis for understanding the environment in which the manager must work. Following is an abstract of a study analyzing the importance of environment (culture) on management styles in sport businesses. In 1995 Groves and Zanger studied the emotional elements that influenced the management style of the Detroit Tigers' baseball organization during the Tom Monaghan era (former owner of the Tigers) and the subsequent Mike Ilitch ownership. The study addressed management concerns through three primary actors: owner and management, players, and fans.

## Owner and Management

Detroit culture has been characterized as a management-labor, ethnic, automobile city with a simplistic approach to relationships and traditions. The culture reflects fierce loyalty and staunch independence. Change needs to be initiated from within; when imposed by an outside authority or power it usually meets resistance. This being the case, the Monaghan management style was less compatible with the culture than was the Ilitch management style. Tiger fans of the city of Detroit have wanted some control over the destiny of their club. Relationships have been equated with management-labor relations because this was the fans' perspective. Large companies and unions have been an important part of the Detroit culture, and these relationships transferred to the sports community. Monaghan's autocratic management

style was not compatible with the Detroit culture. The Ilitch management style was more conciliatory and, as a result, has been more successful. The breakdown of relationships with the Monaghan regime allowed a new ownership with an aspect of compromise to be an almost immediate success.

## Players

During the Monaghan era, the primary focus was to change the organization from one of ballplayers with a work ethic to a ball club of stars. The mediating force within this organization was Sparky Anderson, the manager, who was able to keep a balanced perspective during the Monaghan management period. Anderson used a combination of work ethic and star players that was compatible with management as well as the larger community of Detroit. When Bo Schembechler was employed, the autocratic management style was doubled. Sparky Anderson could no longer maintain homeostasis. In the Ilitch era, the ballplayers have been blue collar. We can characterize a blue-collar player as one with a good work ethic and a loyalty to the team. Such players have usually paid their dues, primarily through the farm system, and have come up through the rank and file. Because Detroit is primarily a union town that understands the work ethic, there has been a congruence between the blue-collar ballplayers and Detroit fans. The greatest influence on the players has been morale. Morale created an environment for players to reach maximum potential, achieve greater job satisfaction, and work together to achieve a goal.

## Fans

The fans in Detroit have vicariously lived their lives through the success or failure of the team, indicating both positive and negative motivation. To obtain this feeling, the fans of Detroit have spent their disposable income and more to attend a baseball game. If the team wins, the city takes on a feeling of success and a new atmosphere for development and pride. If the team loses, the fan support sags. Detroit fans seek success from their ball team using a style of play that suits their culture. During the later phase of the Monaghan era, fans were angry, both with the type of team that was being fielded and the lack of winning; there was a general feeling of defeatism. When Ilitch took over as owner and brought in players that suited Detroit's culture and won games, a new sense of pride ensued throughout the Detroit community.

It is the interactions of the owner and management, players, and fans that ultimately have developed the role of baseball within the Detroit culture. For ownership, the primary element in Detroit was control, for the players it was morale, and for the fans it was popularity and success. When the fans and the ownership moved in opposite directions, the impact was frustration and disappointment. When the goals of the ownership and management, players, and fans were congruent, a positive impact on the community was fostered. Sport has brought a community together to overcome differences. Owners and players had a profound influence on the motivation of fans, culture, and the community.

Tiger Stadium in Detroit, 1996.

© Robert Skeoch

# Permeable Boundaries

Sport enterprises must operate in an external environment in the world of business. Sponsorship is one example of how sport enterprises interact with the business world to the financial benefit of both. Sponsorship involves the return of dollars or benefits from an organization's investment in a game or event. Popularity of a sport increases the effectiveness of the outcomes for the sponsors. Based on the open system model, we could view sponsorship as a subsystem that penetrates the permeable boundary and interrelates within the company and the external environment (see chapter 6, figure 6.2 on page 82). For example, a corporation invests speculative dollars, referred to as venture capital (output) into sponsoring an event or league. The revenue from increased sales of the company's products as a result of this sponsorship goes back into the company as capital return or profit (input).

## Venture Capital

Venture capital consists of financial assets used for speculative purposes in the hopes of greater financial returns. Investment of venture capital is by its very nature risky; extensive planning and forethought is therefore necessary before venture capital is allocated. Sponsorship of sporting events has more and more become a lucrative market for those willing to provide venture capital.

Along with financial profits, companies providing venture capital as sponsorship dollars are hoping to increase (a) the visibility of the company and its product(s); (b) increased sales of its product(s); and ultimately (c) *name recognition* that increases inputs and outputs and therefore fosters future growth and profits (see figure 7.1). Just like the individual who puts money on a race horse—closely studying the racing reports (speculating)—measuring the odds for a financial return, corporations like Pepsi Cola closely study the market when providing millions of dollars to Dallas Cowboys owner Jerry Jones to be the exclusive soft drink provider for Texas Stadium. Yet unlike the bettor at the racetrack, Pepsi Cola's main goal is to create greater name recognition for their product, thus increasing sales well into the future. Thus, businesses within the sport industry must be ever watchful of the complex short- and long-term effects of their decisions.

For smaller companies, acquiring venture capital may be a stumbling block to providing sponsorship dollars. A company without adequate resources has several options to consider, including these:

- Exchange personal and professional expertise for investment dollars.
- Find new financing sources, either public or private, through creative ideas.
- Form a corporation and sell stock to the public.
- Take over a facility needing management expertise and put it on a sound financial basis for a percentage of the profits.

It is important to explore many investment avenues and understand various investment structures. An individual who does not have a large capital investment or expertise can enter into a smaller part of an operation. This usually occurs in auxiliary services involving independent operation and minimal investment, but can reap maximum profits and rewards (Groves, 1990).

## Financial Planning— A Critical Element for Venture Capital

Understanding business principles for providing quality products or services and applying those principles to the marketing function is how to create new demand. Consumer satisfaction determines the success of an operation and brings consistent growth. Sport managers must be able to deliver quality products and services to achieve high customer satisfaction and retention. Word-of-mouth advertising from satisfied customers is the least expensive and most effective form of promotion.

New business people frequently overlook the fact that only a specific population will support a particular sport enterprise and that a minimum number of people must demand a product or service to ensure success. An idea will not sell just because of its natural potential or attention. Experienced business owners know that demand may occur as a natural outgrowth of an activity itself, but more often it is the direct result of a conscious effort to create demand.

Understanding cost control within an operation is critical. In many facility-oriented parts of the sport industry, such as fitness clubs, the danger of excessive expenditures is inherent. Many sport facilities have failed because the owners did not know how to control costs. The key to cost reduction is efficient operation, and higher costs are not necessarily associated with higher quality services. Business owners, however, do not always

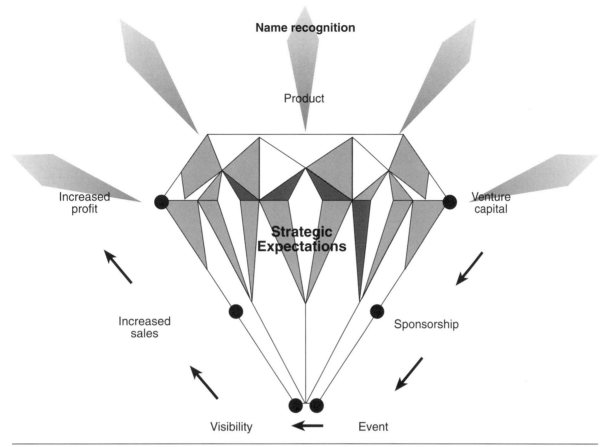

**Figure 7.1** Investing venture capital is a risk most major corporations take in hope of yielding the valuable "diamond" of name recognition.

understand this concept; the relationship between efficient operation and maximum profit is critical. Revenue centers must be well understood and diversified so that if one part of an operation fails, another will be able to pick up the balance. Examples of revenue centers are gate receipts and auxiliary services such as concessions, sponsorships, merchandising, and licensing. A financial plan must be developed to maximize the revenue centers; it must be detailed and directly tied to the initial planning stages of the business.

Crucial to a financial plan is developing a process for extracting dollars from consumers. Sport can be an intangible service, and money must be elicited from the patron effectively and efficiently to create satisfaction. Low gate fees are essential for maximum demand. Some events are natural attractions, and a capacity crowd is the result of the event itself. However, if demand does not exist, a high entrance fee will deter attendance.

Understanding motivation behind participation or attendance is important. The event itself is usually seen as the primary reason that people participate or attend, but often an event repre-

sents something else to the individual. Marketers must understand this concept to know how to promote an event. For the participant or spectator, sport is often not an end in itself but a means to something else (Groves, 1990).

## Sponsorship— A Vehicle for Venture Capital

Companies providing sponsorship dollars have realized the positive association with sport and use sport to popularize their products. When it pays off, sponsorship can therefore be a win-win situation for all involved: for the event (it helps defray the cost), for the corporation (it receives the coveted name recognition), and for the community (it receives a better quality event, and can get some name recognition for itself). There are some in sponsorship who see this endeavor as a social investment, but most of those providing the sponsorship money view it merely in terms of financial gains on both a short- and long-term basis. This does not suggest that they don't have some interest in the community or at least in presenting the image of being community conscious. Many corporations are realizing that sponsorship is a good way of getting additional image development while building brand loyalty, because many of those directly associated with a sport appreciate the sponsor and choose to support the sponsor by buying and promoting its products.

Corporate philanthropists are investing in the many benefits of corporate sponsorship, including a cost-effective exposure for a product, associating the company's product name with a specific event, and providing companies with high-visibility activities featuring athletic superstars (Mescon & Tilson, 1987). Sara Lee Corporation exemplifies the meaning of sponsorship for sport businesses with its Olympic Games involvement, as explained in their annual report: " 'Let the Games Begin.' When a global audience in the billions watches the 1996 Summer Olympic Games, one exceptional performer will climb to the medalist platform every time the American flag is raised. This versatile competitor, by any definition, is a true champion—*Champion* products that is" (Sara Lee Corporate Annual Report, 1995, p. 20).

As part of Sara Lee, both Champion and Hanes brands were sponsors for the 1996 Centennial Olympic Games in Atlanta. Champion provided the official U.S. Team opening and closing ceremony and medal presentation outfits, as well as the uniforms for the U.S. men's and women's basketball and volleyball teams. Hanes outfitted more than 7,000 staff and volunteers. Within the first months, the 500-day promotion (before igniting the Olympic flame in July 1996) raised $300,000 for the Children's Olympic Ticket Fund and the 1996 U.S. Olympic Team. A special limited edition of the Hanes Centennial Olympic Games T-shirt was auctioned every day in Atlanta or at a major event in the United States (Sara Lee Annual Report, 1995).

Sponsorship is a way of increasing visibility to a target audience that can develop an effective message. When individuals are watching or participating in their favorite sporting event or activity they are in a different frame of mind, and it is an appropriate time to reach these individuals with that message. A relationship is being built between the consumer and the sponsor. This two-way communication promotes interactions that allow both actors to obtain benefits now and in the future. Sponsorship is generally seen as a positive investment because it can develop community goodwill, provide a positive image and visibility, generate media exposure, allow the company to gain a competitive edge, and help develop the company's credibility. Sport is an especially good sponsorship investment because it develops company image, brand loyalty, and association with a positive experience in the consumers' lives.

## Visibility, Sales, and Profit— Components of Venture Capital

There is an adage that says you have to spend money to make money. We can apply this to the use of venture capital that finances a sport or event. The visibility the company gets from this sponsorship saturates the buyers market with its name or product. An increase in sales and subsequent profit for the company is the desired result. Brand loyalty is also a long-range expectation, involving customers buying only one kind of soft drink, wearing one kind of athletic shoe, or playing with a specific kind of golf club.

# Looking to the Future

With sport industry in its infancy, there is an opportunity to benefit from the mistakes of other industries. As Kofman and Senge wrote in 1993,

> In the United States, we tend to see competition among individuals as the ultimate mechanism for change and improvement in human affairs. We continually think in terms of war and sports analogies when we interpret management challenges. We need to "beat the competition," "overcome resistance to our new program," "squeeze concessions from the labor union," or "take over the market." We have a metaphorical tunnel vision. We rarely think about how the process of developing leaders may be more like parenting than competing, or how developing a new culture may be more like gardening than a military campaign. (Kofman & Senge, 1993)

Echoing the sentiment of Kofman and Senge, within our culture, our organizations, and our management of industries, it is time that we look to leaders who believe in cooperation and social responsibility as much as they believe in the bottom line. As we have seen, the business of sport is complex. Sport managers will need to keep abreast of the many faces of sport: sport culture, the vast growth and development of sport and the amount of money being invested in it, the future changes that are sure to come. It will most certainly take tenacious individuals to balance these needs with the profit margin.

# Segments of the Sport Industry

**A**s you have learned in the first seven chapters, the sport industry offers a variety of opportunities to aspiring sport managers. Each opportunity requires an understanding of management skills; therefore, chapter 8, the first chapter of this section, focuses on applying traditional management skills to sport organizations. The information in chapter 8 provides a framework for understanding the information in the following 11 chapters, which address intercollegiate athletics, campus recreation, sport communication, sport marketing, sport event and facility management, sports medicine, health promotion, sport tourism, professional sport, sport management and marketing companies, and international sport.

Understanding and appreciating the amazing diversity of opportunities in the sport industry will enable you plan your professional life more realistically. To fully understand the scope of sport management, we hope you will study the material in *each* chapter and reflect on the possibilities each area might hold for you, rather than concentrating only on the ones in which you are currently interested. Who knows? You might develop new interests and revise your career goals!

# Chapter 8

# Managing Sport Organizations

**Jerome Quarterman**
Bowling Green State University
**Ming Li**
Georgia Southern University

---

## Learning Objectives

After studying this chapter, you will be able to

1. discuss two reasons a course about management practice as a process for sport organizations is valuable to you;

2. compare and contrast the two major groups of workers in the sport industry;

3. list by title and briefly identify 10 technical specialists and 10 managers of various segments of the sport industry;

4. discuss the classifications of managers in the sport industry;

5. discuss the levels of managers in sport organizations;

6. define the underlying processes of management;

7. identify the roles and skills used by managers of sport organizations, and

8. discuss three challenges facing sport managers.

---

Students who aspire to management positions in the sport industry typically understand why they must take course work about the management process. However, other students enrolled in undergraduate sport management courses occasionally raise the question: Why do I need to learn about management as a process of sport organizations? This question is usually asked by students who are studying to become athletic trainers, personal trainers, exercise physiologists, sports writers, sporting goods sales representatives, fitness instructors, sport marketing representatives, and so on. The question is valid because many such individuals do not envision themselves as future **managers**.

Good reasons exist for studying management, whether you plan to work in professional sport, in the fitness industry, or in sport merchandising. First, it is obvious that prospective managers must understand the management process to qualify for responsible positions. Second, prospective technical specialists must understand management to develop insight into the link between management and staff. Such insight will make them better employees. Moreover, many individuals who start their careers with no desire to become managers frequently end up in management positions. This possibility exists because sport organizations are becoming larger and more complex, and they need well-prepared managers. Even though management isn't in your current plans, someday you might have the opportunity to become a manager. As mortgages, car payments, and family responsibilities loom larger in your life, the higher salaries paid to managers might make management more appealing to you. If so, you will need to know about management processes to qualify to take advantage of any opportunities that come your way.

The purpose of this chapter, therefore, is to provide basic information about applying traditional management principles to managing sport organizations. First, we will examine the two types of workers and managers in sport organizations.

Second, we will discuss the management process and practices. Third, we will outline the competencies required of sport managers. We will then address the managerial roles played by sport managers. The final part of this chapter will analyze challenges confronting sport managers in the future. We hope the information in the chapter will help you appreciate how understanding the management process is essential to your development as a competent professional, regardless of the specific position you seek immediately after graduation.

# Types of Workers in Sport Organizations

As in other businesses, there are two primary groups of workers in sport organizations: technical specialists (also known as operatives and support staff) and managers (also known as administrators) (Robbins, 1988). Both types of workers are needed and are important to the success of sport organizations. In figure 8.1, the lower rectan-

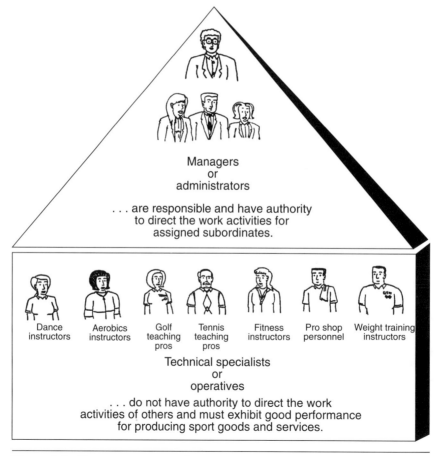

Managers
or
administrators

. . . are responsible and have authority
to direct the work activities for
assigned subordinates.

| Dance instructors | Aerobics instructors | Golf teaching pros | Tennis teaching pros | Fitness instructors | Pro shop personnel | Weight training instructors |

Technical specialists
or
operatives

. . . do not have authority to direct the work
activities of others and must exhibit good performance
for producing sport goods and services.

**Figure 8.1**   Two major groups of workers in the sport industry.

gular section represents the technical specialists and the triangular section represents the managers.

Technical specialists are workers who use specialized technical skills, knowledge, and abilities to produce the goods and services that sport organizations have been established to produce. They make up most of the workforce, and they have no responsibility for directing the work of other employees (Robbins, 1988). Although they are not officially designated as managers, these specialists do use management skills to accomplish their daily tasks (e.g., recording attendance in aerobics class, supervising student workers in intercollegiate athletics departments, inventorying golf equipment, ordering supplies). In fact, it is difficult to think of any jobs that don't use managerial skills to some extent. Some examples of technical specialists in sport organizations are

- wellness instructor,
- game official (referee),
- dance instructor,
- assistant athletic trainer,
- aerobics (fitness) instructor,
- sport promoter,
- personal trainer,
- business manager,
- tennis or golf teaching professional,
- sports journalist,
- pro shop attendant,
- sport nutritionist,
- sporting goods sales representative,
- sport statistician, and
- sport account executive.

The second group of workers are the managers. Although managers may use specialized skills, knowledge, and abilities, they also have formal authority for designing and directing the work activities of others (Robbins, 1988). Some examples of titles for managers in sport organizations include

- chief executive officer (CEO),
- assistant or associate athletics director,
- executive officer,
- head of the division or unit,
- president,
- unit supervisor,
- general manager,
- manager,
- assistant or associate manager,
- supervisor,
- head athletic trainer, and
- athletics director.

Both technical specialists and managers are responsible for getting the work done in sport organizations, but there is an important distinction between the two groups of workers. Managers are formally placed in their positions by appointment or by owning the organization; thus, they have the authority to direct the work activities of their assigned subordinates, who may be managers or nonmanagers. Technical specialists are not formally appointed to a position of authority to direct work behaviors of subordinates; therefore, they are responsible as specialized technicians for getting the work done under the supervision of managers.

## Learning Activity

Review the classified advertisement sections of a daily newspaper. Find an example of a job advertisement for a technical specialist in the sport industry.

All managers have formal authority for directing the work activities of others, but there are differences in the degrees of authority possessed by different managers. In the **hierarchy** of an organization, managers are usually classified as (a) top managers, (b) middle managers, or (c) supervisory managers (Glueck, 1980). In figure 8.2, the top-level managers are at the top of the pyramid.

## Top-Level Managers

This is the smallest group of managers. They are also known as executive or senior level managers, and they have the most power and authority. They are usually responsible for the total organization or a major part of it.

## Middle-Level Managers

These managers (also known as administrative level managers) are usually selected by top-level managers. Therefore, they are responsible to top-level managers and responsible for supervisory managers and sometimes for the technical

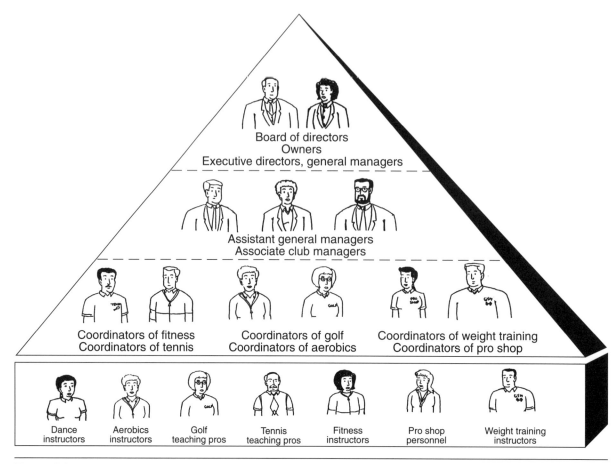

**Figure 8.2** An example of a private investor-owned health and racquet club.

specialists. In figure 8.2, the assistant general managers and associate club managers are the interface between lower management and upper management. They may often be confronted with contradictory demands from the two extremes of the organizational hierarchy.

To their subordinates, the middle managers are the source of information and solution of problems, because they know the technical side of the product and services. Consequently, a middle manager is often considered half generalist and half specialist (1975). The managers at the middle level are, in general, responsible for (a) managing a department or unit that performs an organizational function (1975), and (b) ensuring the assigned tasks are done efficiently. Middle managers are unique because they must be both leaders and followers. They are connected to superiors and to subordinates, both of whom are also managers.

## Supervisory-Level Managers

Theoretically, supervisory-level managers (also known as first-line managers or supervisors) re-

port to middle-level managers and are responsible for nonmanagerial employees. In figure 8.2, the coordinators of fitness, golf, weight training, tennis, aerobics, and the pro shop are examples of supervisory managers. Although such coordinators make up the largest number of managers, they have the least amount of authority. They are primarily responsible for a single area in a work unit, division, or department in the sport organization. In addition to the title coordinator, supervisory managers may have such titles as

- supervisor,
- department supervisor,
- department head,
- assistant director,
- chair,
- assistant manager, and
- unit supervisor.

Regardless of the title used for supervisory managers, they are primarily responsible for supervising nonmanagerial employees. It is their job to communicate with, inspire, and influence the non-managerial workers to get the job done in the most effective and efficient way. This makes their positions unique because they are the main source of contact between the nonmanagerial technical specialists and management. Examples of the titles of managers at different levels in three selected sport organizations are shown in table 8.1.

## Learning Activity

Review an issue of *Athletic Business*, *Fitness Management*, or the *NCAA News*. Find an example of a job listing for each of the following: (a) a first-line supervisory manager, (b) a middle-level manager, and (c) a top executive in a setting associated with sport organization management.

# Management as a Process in Sport Organizations

Over the years, in management textbooks, management journals, and speeches, management scholars have addressed the practice of manage-

ment as a process. The *process approach* implies that as managers practice their work in the sport industry they are using a set of ongoing interactive activities, commonly known as the underlying processes of management, for accomplishing the goals and objectives of their respective organizations, departments, or work units. Such processes were first introduced more than 6 decades ago as POSDCORB (Gulick & Urwick, 1937). POSDCORB is the acronym that describes the underlying elements of Planning, Organizing, Staffing, Directing, COordinating, Reporting, and Budgeting.

Contemporary sport management literature shows that the process approach is currently used to describe management for sport organizations (Chelladurai, 1986; Leith, 1983; Mullin, 1980). Although the models vary slightly from one scholar to another, there is general agreement about the nature of the management process: (a) typically, the process starts with planning and ends with controlling or evaluating; (b) there is no logical order in which practicing managers use the activities; and (c) managers may engage in several activities simultaneously as they carry out the responsibilities of their jobs. The model we use in this chapter to illustrate management as a process for sport organizations is shown in figure 8.3. This

## Table 8.1
## Titles for Managers at Different Levels in Three Typical Sport Organizations

| Levels of Management | Professional baseball organization | Investor-owned health and fitness club | NCAA Division I-A intercollegiate athletics program |
|---|---|---|---|
| Top-level managers | President<br>Chief executive officer<br>Vice presidents<br>• Business operations<br>• Baseball operations | Owner(s)<br>General managers<br>Regional directors<br>• Corporate wellness<br>• Health promotion | Board of trustees<br>University president<br>Athletics director<br>Head football coach<br>Senor associate AD |
| Middle-level managers | Director of public relations<br>Director of corporate sales<br>Director of marketing operations<br>Team manager<br>Director of scouting | Site managers<br>• Corporate wellness<br>• Health promotion | Head coaches—major sports<br>Associate ADs<br>• Director of fund-raising<br>• Director of development |
| Supervisory managers | Director of stadium operations<br>Director of broadcasting<br>Director of community relations<br>Director of baseball administration | Coordinators (supervisors)<br>• Aerobics<br>• Fitness<br>• Golf<br>• Pro shop<br>• Weight training | Assistant athletics director<br>Sports information director<br>Coordinators athletic training<br>Marketing director<br>Academic coordinator |

## The Sport Management Process

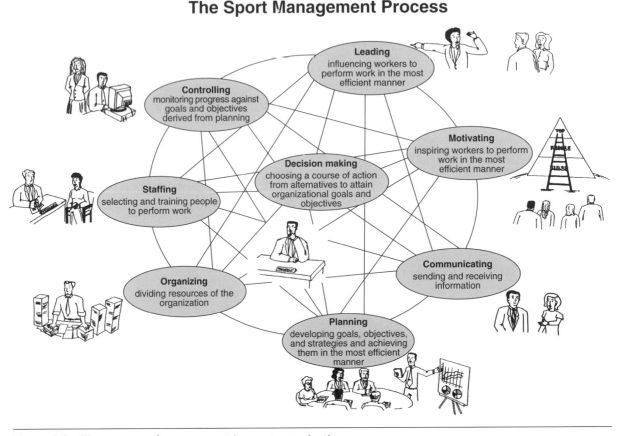

**Figure 8.3** The process of management in sport organizations.

model illustrates how decision making is inherent in each underlying process of planning, organizing, staffing, controlling, leading, motivating, and communicating. The model is further explained in table 8.2, in which we list each underlying process, followed by a simple definition and examples of how a general manager might practice the processes as he or she attains the goals of a private sport club.

## Time and Effort Spent in the Management Processes

All management positions are not the same, and managers spend varying amounts of time and effort using the underlying processes. The amount of time and effort that managers use in each process will depend on their level in the organizational hierarchy (Mahoney, Jerdee, & Carroll, 1965).

As figure 8.4 shows, supervisory managers, such as coordinators of recreation programs and coordinators of aerobic dance, spend the most time and effort in directing (e.g., communicating, leading, and motivating the technical specialists in performing their job assignments). In contrast, executive level managers, such as professional

team sport commissioners, intercollegiate athletics directors and commissioners, and general managers, are more likely to be planning long-range goals, organizing the overall formal structure, and controlling by monitoring the total organization's performance. These managers frequently engage in fund-raising, particularly when there is a need for venture capital (see chapter 7).

## Competencies Managers Need

Managers of sport organizations use several managerial skills and assume a variety of managerial roles. Management research has provided ways to identify and describe the skills that managers use and the roles they assume as they carry out the processes of management. This research has drawn on empirical studies of managerial skills (Katz, 1974) and managerial roles (Mintzberg, 1973, 1990).

### Managerial Skills

The term skill reflects the idea that one's ability to perform managerial tasks is not innate. It can be learned and developed through experience and formal training. Katz (1974) identified skills needed

## Table 8.2
## The Management Process of a General Manager in a Private Sport Club

| Underlying process | Definition | Example |
|---|---|---|
| Planning | Identifying the organizational goals to achieve, and developing and implementing strategies to achieve them | The general manager of a private sports club predicts the increase in enrollment at the start of the new year and arranges for the facility to be open 18 hours per day instead of 15 hours. |
| Organizing | Dividing the organization into work units and subunits so their efforts will mesh and fulfill the overall objectives | After conducting an assessment, the general manager establishes a work unit for teaching golf at the club. A full time coordinator is appointed who will coordinate three teaching pros and a new golf course with an adequate budget. |
| Staffing | Recruiting, selecting, hiring, orienting, training, developing, compensating, evaluating, and maintaining highly qualified human resources for achieving the organizational goals (selecting the right person to do the job) | The general manager advertises the positions: three teaching pros, one maintenance person, and one secretary. The general manager then holds interviews, checks references, makes job offers, and selects the staff needed for the golf program. |
| Leading | Influencing an individual employee or group of employees to better perform their jobs in attaining the goals and objectives of the organization | The general manager encourages the golf teaching pro to prepare weekend course packages for local executives who have expressed an interest in learning golf skills. |
| Motivating | Igniting the internal forces (inner drives and needs) and external forces that affect an individual or a group to produce goods and services in the most effective manner | The general manager announces the new system of rewards to the support staff (e.g., merit pay, profit sharing, stock ownership, flexible benefits). |
| Communicating | Sending and receiving information via a variety of channels to fulfill organizational objectives | The general manager holds individual conferences with the coordinator of golf and tennis each Friday to determine the activities for the next week. |
| Controlling | Monitoring progress against goals and objectives derived from planning; evaluating performance to determine if the goals were met as planned. | After 3 months, the general manager monitors the progress of the new golf program with the coordinator and discusses possible ways to make the program more attractive to lure new memberships. |
| Decision making | Choosing a course of action from alternatives to attain goals and objectives in the most effective manner | The general manager initiates a brainstorming session with the staff to develop alternatives in promoting another new sport program. |

by managers of all types of organizations as conceptual, interpersonal (human), and technical.

*Conceptual* skills are required for managers to see the sport organization as a whole and the relationships among the parts that make up the whole organization. For example, the commissioner of the National Basketball Association (NBA) uses conceptual skills to compare and contrast the total market share of goods and services produced by the NBA with the market share produced by each individual professional team that makes up the NBA.

Managers use *interpersonal* skills to interact with others and to coordinate individual and group efforts in achieving an organization's goals. Specifically, this implies that the manager must be able to work with both **internal constituents** and **external constituents**. For example, if you were the director of campus recreation at a university and you were confronted by minority students who were dissatisfied about how the facility was governed, your ability to use interpersonal skills would be important for dealing with such criticism constructively.

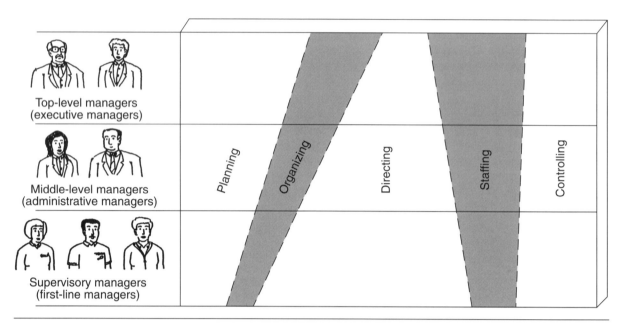

**Figure 8.4**   Relative proportion of time spent in the underlying processes of management.
Adapted, by permission, from Mahoney, T.A., Jerdee, T.H., & Carroll, S.J., 1965. "The job(s) of management." *Industrial Relations*, **4**(2): 97-110.

*Technical* skills include the specialized knowledge, tools, techniques, and resources used in achieving an organization's goals. It is important that managers are able to perform certain technical skills as well as being able to show their subordinates how to perform the skills. For example, if you were the marketing director for a national athletics footwear firm, it would be important for you to be efficient in preparing the annual report or annual budget for the marketing division of the firm. It would also be important for you to be able to teach others who work in your division how to prepare such reports.

All managers use conceptual, interpersonal, and technical skills, but they use them in varying degrees. For example, top managers often devote a major portion of time to long-range planning; therefore, they will typically spend more time using conceptual skills than will middle and supervisory managers. Paul Tagliabue, commissioner of the NFL, is a good example of a top-level manager who is recognized as using conceptual skills. "I don't want to be involved in things that are repetitive and things that are day-to-day," Tagliabue says. "If it involves a new concept, then I want to know the concept is being implemented the way I conceived it, not the way someone else dreamed of it. I don't want to micromanage" (Weisman, 1993, p. 2c). On the other hand, supervisory sport managers spend most of their time directing (motivating, leading, and communicating) non-

managerial staff; therefore, these supervisors use more technical skills than top-level or middle-level managers. Human relations skills are important to managers at *all* levels of sport organizations, because it is the responsibility of the managers to design ways for others to do the work; that is, they work through others to attain the goals of the organization.

An example of how different levels of management use different skills is shown in figure 8.5. In this sport club, supervisory (first-level) managers are called on to use more technical skills in sport activity performance and in producing the services of the club (e.g., showing the workers new teaching techniques, setting up equipment). However, the owners (executive directors or general managers) will use fewer technical skills and will spend more time using conceptual skills (e.g., developing and implementing long-range goals and monitoring the resources used by the club).

Program directors (middle managers) spend time using both technical and human relations skills. Note that human relation skills are used equally by all three managerial levels. Figure 8.5 also shows that technical specialists must be well trained in technical and interpersonal skills to perform their jobs and produce the services offered by the sport club. This does not mean, however, that technical specialists can't or shouldn't use conceptual skills; in fact, the best ones will!

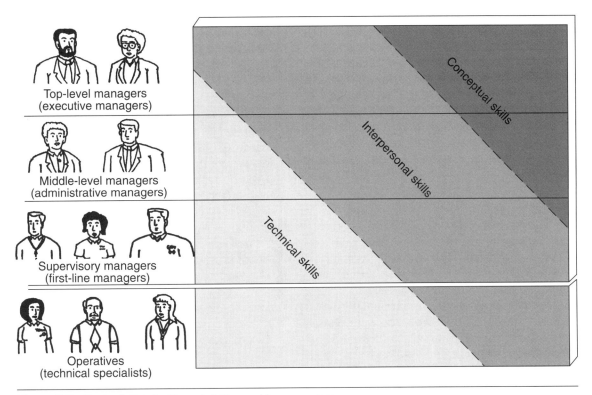

**Figure 8.5**   Typical distribution of skills used by managers.
Data from Katz, R.L. (1983). Skills of an effective administrator. *Harvard Business Review*, **52**(5), 90-101.

## Managerial Roles

In addition to using a range of skills, managers must assume a variety of roles as they carry out the traditional processes of management (Mintzberg, 1973, 1990). Mintzberg defined a *role* as a set of expected behaviors associated with a managerial position. Based on Mintzberg's theory, the typical manager portrays 10 roles, which are classified into three categories: interpersonal, informational, and decisional.

### Interpersonal Roles

Mintzberg (1990) identified three specific interpersonal roles: figurehead, leader, and liaison. When managers engage in these roles, they are primarily involved in interpersonal relationships with others. As figureheads, managers perform a variety of symbolic and ceremonial duties. Examples of the figurehead role are showing up at a subordinate's wedding, welcoming visitors to an organization, representing the organization at a public function, and cutting the ribbon for a new facility. One illustration of a top executive acting as a figurehead is a government official throwing out the first ball to open the professional baseball season.

The leader role relates to managers' relationships with their subordinates. As leaders, managers

© Anthony Neste

Paul Tagliabue talks to reporters in 1989 after being elected NFL commissioner: "I don't want to micromanage."

## Learning How to Be an Effective Manager

Several years ago, two students graduating from the sport management program at American Sport Marketing Institute were hired by Marketing International, a sport marketing firm, as project assistants. Two years later they were both promoted to project managers. As opposed to being paid for performing their specialty in designing promotional materials, they were now being paid for being managers supervising two different projects. At the end of the first 6 months, one of them, Antonio Demopolis, was experiencing considerable success and enjoying his new managerial job. Dolores Hayashi, the other manager, was not so successful. She was experiencing problems in meeting schedules and deadlines. There was unrest among several project representatives under her. She was also becoming discouraged and frustrated. Her immediate superior was concerned about her situation.

Antonio had adapted well to his new role. He realized that, in a way, he was embarking on a new and different career within the firm and had adjusted accordingly. More specifically, whether it was because of his personal insight or because he received help from his superior, he perceived his role and function to be different from what it used to be. Among the many things he did after being appointed manager was to delineate what objectives needed to be accomplished; the availability of the people in his unit to work toward those objectives; and the skills, strengths, and weaknesses of those individuals. He reviewed the work flow in his unit and formulated priorities and schedules. Through various meetings, he attempted to communicate these priorities and schedules to his subordinates, and he instilled his personal philosophy, which valued teamwork highly. He shared and discussed problems with his project assistants frequently. In addition, he was actively involved with helping individuals in his unit to set proper goals and realistically evaluate their performance.

In contrast, Dolores became overwhelmed by her new role. When she realized that she was no longer expected to complete the actual work for the project as she was used to, she became confused. She believed that to get each project done, she as a manager needed to make sure every aspect of the project was completed properly. As a result, she checked every assignment completed by her subordinates. When she found an error, she made the correction herself. She became convinced that checking was needed and was the only way to ensure no mistakes were committed. Dolores' obsession with detail led her to spending more time to make sure things were done right. Because she became so involved in checking, she neglected her other responsibilities. She did not file workload recording reports and employee evaluations on time. In addition, her staff assumed less responsibility for their work. They became passive, and two thirds of her staff changed jobs and left the firm within a year.

1. What processes of management did Antonio demonstrate?
2. What management skills did Dolores lack? What were her strengths?
3. If you were the top manager, how would you help Dolores improve her performance? How could you capitalize on her ability to check details?

recruit, select, properly train, motivate, evaluate, and direct the subordinates' energies and efforts toward accomplishing the organization's goals. Leaders are also responsible for coordinating the work of the subordinates. Examples of the leader role are conducting a workshop on computer programming for the support staff and rewarding staff for outstanding job performance. The director of ticket sales exhibits the role of leader when she or he provides flexible working hours for the telemarketing staff.

The liaison role refers to a manager's ability to develop and cultivate relationships with individuals and groups outside his or her work unit or organization. For instance, coordinators of concessions usually maintain contact with vendors to determine when there will be special sales on certain supplies. Directors of campus recreation often meet with peer directors to discern how they will vote on an important issue before the official voting sessions. These managers are acting in the liaison role.

### Informational Roles

When managers exchange and process information, they engage in the informational role. The role behaviors include monitor, disseminator, and spokesperson. As monitors, managers scan the environment for information that can affect the organization. They collect information from a variety of sources, including subordinates, peers, superiors, contacts, news media, electronic mail, the Internet, gossip, and hearsay. A supervisor who has a coffee lounge conversation with other supervisors about the organization's plans to downsize the support staff is engaging in the monitor role.

As managers collect information, they become the nerve centers of their work areas. When they transmit the information to others, they are disseminators and spokespersons. As disseminators, managers selectively pass on information to others in the organization or work unit. A supervisor who attends an athletics conference meeting then informs the subordinates of the rule changes that have been enacted is engaging in the role of disseminator.

As spokespersons, managers transmit information to persons or groups outside their respective organizations or work units. For example, a supervisor from the Blue Chip Athletics Corporation who speaks at the local Rotary Club luncheon might tell the members about a new style of athletic footwear the company has developed. In such a situation, the supervisor would be acting as a spokesperson.

## Decisional Roles

Decisional roles may be exhibited in four specific categories: entrepreneur, disturbance handler, resource allocator, and negotiator. As entrepreneurs, managers search for ways to effect change to improve an organization. A manager who provides the latest computer technology for the ticket office is acting in an entrepreneur role. Another example of the entrepreneur role is when the director of operations of a professional football team provides Internet access to each staff member to improve their capacity to find and use information worldwide.

As disturbance handlers, managers respond to unexpected situations that might disrupt the organization's normal operation. Usually managers must react to such disruptions immediately. For example, if all the support staff of a sport marketing agency became ill with influenza and could not report to work during the week of a major tennis tournament sponsored by that agency, the normal operation of the tournament would be affected. The event manager at the agency would need to

hire temporary help and recruit volunteers to effectively handle the disturbance.

As resource allocators, managers determine how to best allocate resources, such as people, money, equipment, supplies, time, and information, to each employee, group of employees, work unit, or the entire organization. For example, the coordinator of marketing and promotions of a state sport festival must provide the support staff and assistants with adequate office supplies to develop literature for informing the public about upcoming events.

As negotiators, managers confer with persons inside or outside the work unit or organization to obtain concessions or to agree on pivotal issues. Bargaining and reaching an agreement with the subordinates, a regulatory agency, an interest group, or a vendor are examples of the negotiating roles. A purchasing manager for the American Basketball League who negotiates with a vendor for lower prices and faster delivery times on equipment and supplies illustrates the negotiator role.

All managers, from top executives to first-line supervisors, perform these roles. However, the degree to which managers perform each role will vary according to the managerial level. For example, Pavett and Lau (1983) found that the disseminator, figurehead, negotiator, and spokesperson roles have been closely associated with top-level managers. On the other hand, the leadership, resource allocator, and disturbance handler roles more closely associate with first-line supervisory managers (Kerr, Hill, & Broedling, 1986). Table 8.3 illustrates the role delineation revealed in a study of athletics conference commissioners (Quarterman, 1994).

### Learning Activity

Review the article entitled "Managerial Role Profiles of Intercollegiate Athletic Conference Commissioners," (Quarterman, 1994). Compare and contrast the findings of that study with those of Pavett and Lau (1983) and Kerr, Hill, and Broedling (1986).

## Challenges Confronting Managers in the Sport Industry

In addition to becoming competent in a variety of managerial skills and roles, all workers in the sport industry, both technical specialists and managers,

Table 8.3

## Adaptation of Mintzberg's Managerial Roles for Intercollegiate Athletic Conference Commissioners

| Role | Description of Role | Examples |
|---|---|---|
| Interpersonal figurehead | Performing ceremonial duties on behalf of the conference | Welcoming dignitaries, greeting visitors, participating in groundbreaking ceremonies |
| Leader | Influencing subordinates to get the work done at the conference office | Conducting performance evaluations, acting as a role model in the workplace, praising an employee for doing a good job |
| Liaison | Maintaining a network of outside contacts to gather information for the conference | Attending meetings with peers, listening to the "grapevine," participating in conference-wide meetings |
| Informational monitor | Perpetually scanning the environment for information that may prove useful to the conference | Lobbying for information at an NCAA meeting, staying in contact with other commissioners by telephone, reviewing the athletic literature |
| Disseminator | Transmitting information received to individuals and/or groups within the conference | Sending information to the coaches and athletic directors, having a review session on NCAA rules with the athletic directors |
| Spokesperson | Transmitting information to individuals and/or groups outside the conference | Speaking at community and professional meetings, briefing the state legislature about athletics |
| Decisional entrepreneur | Searching for new ideas and implementing changes for the betterment of the conference | Initiating a new marketing concept for increasing revenue, bringing new technology to the conference |
| Disturbance handler | Making decisions to deal with unexpected changes that may affect the conference | Resolving a conflict among member institutions, dealing with changes in game schedules |
| Resource allocator | Making decisions concerning resource use—people, time, money, space, or the conference | Making a decision about a tournament site, adding or deleting a sports program |
| Negotiator | Bargaining with individuals, groups, or organizations on behalf of the conference | Negotiating a television contract, negotiating with vendors |

Reprinted, by permission, from H. Mintzberg, 1990. "The Manager's Job: Folklore and fact." *Harvard Business Review*, March-April. Copyright © 1990 by the President and Fellows of Harvard College; all rights reserved.

must be prepared to deal with challenges that confront sport organizations. Hendricks (1990) provided a list of management challenges that confront all private and public businesses in general, including "workforce diversity, workforce competition, technology, internationalism, financial accountability, and continuing education" (p. 17). In the following section, we address several areas that will influence sport managers' decisions.

## Workforce Diversity

The term workforce diversity has been used in management literature since the late 1980s (Johnson & Packer, 1987). DeSensi (1994) defined diversity as "differences of individuals within the workplace that are associated with any character-

istics that may set them apart as dissimilar" (p. 64). Carrell, Jennings, and Heavrin (1997) identified five groups of individuals whose entry into the workforce in large numbers has rendered it more diverse: (a) different racial and ethnic groups, (b) women, (c) older workers, (d) individuals with disabilities, and (e) people with various sexual or affectional orientations. It is estimated that the civilian labor force in the United States will increase from 127 million in 1992 to 151 million by the year 2005 (U.S. Bureau of Labor Statistics, 1994-1995). Although non-Hispanics have, until now, been the largest component of the workforce, they will be a smaller percentage by the year 2005. African Americans will be the second largest component, and Hispanics will increase by greater proportions than African Americans. African Americans, Hispanic Americans, and Asian Americans will account for roughly 35% of the labor force by the year 2005 (p. 11).

It is clear that, in the future, members of racial minorities and members of other diverse groups will hold greater numbers of sport management positions. The challenge is for managers of sport organizations to acknowledge and celebrate this diversity and to effectively use the energy and talent of these individuals in achieving organizational goals. Successful sport managers will be sensitive to social change, will anticipate the needs of society, and will embrace the opportunities that come with change (Clement, 1990).

## Workforce Competition and Equity

People want to be treated fairly. They frequently evaluate fairness by comparing their time, efforts, and rewards with those of others in similar work situations (Ivancevich & Matteson, 1990). Workforce equity in the sport industry usually is focused on salaries, frequently involves gender or race or both, and has been defined legally by federal law. "The Equal Pay Act of 1963 'requires that all employees, regardless of gender, receive equal pay for work that requires equal skill, effort and responsibility . . . performed under similar work conditions' " (Wong & Barr, 1993, p. 13).

Many of the workforce equity issues that have emerged in the sport industry have been in intercollegiate and professional athletics and have involved state or federal laws. For example, the equal pay issue has been hotly contested in intercollegiate basketball, where there are often significant discrepancies in salary between the women and men coaches. One of the first disputes arose in 1980 between the women's basketball coach and the College of William and Mary. Eloise Jacobs, the women's coach, "alleged that William and Mary violated the Equal Pay Act, because she was not given equal pay for equal work, compared to the men's basketball coach" (Wong & Barr, 1994, p. 12). In 1991, Sanya Tyler, an associate athletics director and women's basketball coach at Howard University sued the institution "claiming pay and Title IX discrimination" because she received a lower salary than did the men's basketball coach (Herwig, 1994, p. 8C). Tyler contended that she performed under similar work conditions as the male coach and had a better win-loss record. In this example, the female coaches compared their time, efforts, and rewards with their male counterparts and concluded that they were not being treated fairly.

Professional athletes and coaches evaluate pay equity by comparing their performances with other athletes and coaches in the league. Consider the examples of NBA stars Michael Jordan and Dennis Rodman and Coach Phil Jackson—all of the Chicago Bulls. Rodman's 1995-1996 salary was $2.5 million. After leading the NBA in rebounds and the Bulls to the 1995-1996 NBA Championship, he sought a 2-year deal of $8 million per year. Jordan's 1995-1996 salary was $4 million. After an amazing career

## Down the Road

Workforce diversity will bring with it questions about how businesspeople should conduct themselves. Baldrige (1993) captured the essence of the new demands created by the changing workplace when she stated the following:

> There is a new informality at work in how we meet and greet, entertain, dress, and socialize with one another, and yet a new formality as we deal with a diversity of people from and in other countries, where we increasingly do business.

> The needs of families, of women and men who are parents as well as respected workers, are increasingly sensitive issues in the workplace. The relations of men and women working together not only as equals, but also as new configurations of peer and superior in terms of gender and age, changes a lot of preconceived behavior codes. Also transforming life at work are the new concerns for the rights of the disabled, for more attention to ethnic equality, diversity and pluralism. (p. xxix-xxx)

Reprinted with the permission of Rawson Associates/ Scribner, a Division of Simon & Schuster from LETITIA BALDRIGE'S NEW COMPLETE GUIDE TO EXECUTIVE MANNERS by Letitia Baldrige. Copyright © 1985, 1993 Letitia Baldrige.

The Equal Pay Act of 1963 calls for equal wages for equal work.

in which he led the Bulls to four NBA championships (including the 1995-1996 crown) he sought a $20- to 25-million annual salary. Coach Jackson's 1995-1996 salary was $850,000. He had also garnered four NBA titles and was named NBA Coach of the Year while leading the Bulls to the 1995-1996 NBA championship. Jackson then sought $2.5 to $3 million annually (Dupree, 1996). In these examples, the players and the coach compared their accomplishments with other players and coaches in the NBA and sought additional compensation for exceptional performances that resulted in recognition for the Chicago Bulls.

## Technology

Computer technology has made extremely rapid advances in capability and sophistication and has changed the world of sport forever. For example, in a health fitness club, you can find audiovisual computerized aerobic training stations, body composition analyzers, digital electronic scales, computerized aerobic cycles and climbers, and computer software for in-house receivables and for managing the club facility. Computer systems have also been developed for many of the front desk functions, such as "lead tracking, hardware integrations, photo imaging, on-screen photos of members, member check-in, point-of-sale servicing, membership databasing, scheduling, accounts receivable tracking, electronic funds transfer, and multiple facility support" (Visani, 1995, pp. 68-69). Further examples include identity verification devices, such as card scanners, hand scanning devices, digital image scanners, keypads, and ticketing devices. These examples provide evidence that understanding computer technology is essential for managers in all segments of the sport industry.

A technological revolution occurred in the sport industry during the 1990s. Technological advances will continue to influence how sport managers use the processes of management as they attain the goals of sport organizations. Both specialists and managers must be familiar with and comfortable with technology, staying abreast of technological advances.

## Globalization of Sport

Throughout the 1990s, the U.S. economy will become increasingly integrated with the international economy (Cetron, 1994). As a result, international cooperation among sport organizations and businesses will increase considerably and will be necessary for competition and survival in the global business environment. In recent years, observable international efforts made by U.S. sport organizations include the NFL's development of an international football league and the NBA's addition of two Canadian franchises, the Toronto Raptors and the Vancouver Grizzlies.

To be prepared for the 21st century, sport management students should take advantage of course work in international business, specifically as it relates to sport, and international sport marketing. Future sport managers must be sensitive to diverse cultures and values and understand basic practices of conducting international business (see chapters 19 and 21).

## Financial Accountability

Many sport organizations report that they are experiencing financial difficulty. For example, most intercollegiate athletics programs operate in the red due to many factors, including inflation and high coaches' salaries in some sports. Some professional sport teams indicate they are in financial trouble, but the extent and cause of the problems is unclear (see chapter 17). One solution is for sport managers to make more financially accountable decisions. Financially accountable management means the sport manager needs to engage in good business practices and use cost effective and containment approaches to reduce unnecessary spending.

## Learning Activity

Find an article that addresses one of the following challenges in the sport industry: (a) internationalism (globalization), (b) cost containment, or (c) continuing education. For each challenge you select list the reference, state the main theme of the article, and explain the content of the article.

## Summary

The two groups of workers in sport organizations are technical specialists (nonmanagers) and managers (administrators). Technical specialists are responsible for producing the work of the organization or unit, and managers are responsible for designing and directing the work of the specialists. Understanding management processes is important for students planning to be either type of worker. It helps technical specialists understand the link between managers and nonmanagers; moreover, it helps them prepare for the day they might wish to become managers. An understanding of management processes will help prospective managers make better decisions.

Managers can be classified as top (executive), middle (administrative), or first-line (supervisory). All levels of management are responsible for carrying out the management processes of planning, organizing, staffing, controlling, leading, motivatng, and communicating to attain the goals of the organization or work unit. Managers use conceptual, interpersonal, and technical skills. They assume three roles: interpersonal (figureheads, leaders, liaisons), informational (monitors, disseminators, spokespersons), and decisional (entrepreneurs, disturbance handlers, resource allocators, negotiators). All workers must deal with challenges presented by workforce diversity, workforce competition, advances in technology, globalization, financial accountability, and continuing education.

## Learning Activity

It has been nearly 5 years since you graduated from college with a degree in sport management. During this time you have been employed as a sales representative for the Nike Corporation in Chicago. You have worked diligently and have earned a reputation as one of the better sales reps in the division of athletics footwear. Of 10 sales representatives, you are the senior person because you have the most clients and have been in this position longer than all your peers. You are happy with your work and schedule that you developed over the years. You and your spouse take the opportunity to attend various cultural, social, and sport events in Chicago. However, a week ago your supervisor called you in for a brief conference and informed you that she had been promoted to district vice president for the corporation and she was recommending you as the next supervisor of the footwear division. The supervisor thought the position would be perfect for you because you have been committed as a good sales representative.

You are wondering what you should do. You are familiar with the other salespeople in the division. Over the years, all of you had become good friends and occasionally met together for lunch as the schedule allowed. The position is being offered to you at a good time because the corporation has been selling a high volume of athletics footwear during the last year. Presently, 100% of your time and effort is assigned as a sales representative; however, for the new position as supervisor, your assignment will be 75% administrative and 25% sales. This means that 30 or 40 of your current clients would be assigned to the other sales representatives, and you would continue to serve no more than 10 clients.

You are knowledgeable about the footwear division; however, you do have some concerns about what managing the division will require of you. You are not certain that you will be happy with the new role as a supervisor. Some questions you have raised with yourself include the following: Could you get out to watch the Chicago Bulls, Cubs, or White Sox professional teams as you did before? Will you have the time to go fishing in your cabin cruiser? Will you still have the opportunity to go to lunch with your former sales representative peers? It was your observation that the former supervisor was usually busy and never had much time to really enjoy life.

1. If you decide to accept the position as supervisor, how will your work change?
2. List two advantages and two disadvantages in accepting the position as the next supervisor.
3. Because you were an excellent sales representative, will this provide you the advantage to become an excellent supervisor? Explain the reason for your answer.

# Chapter 9 Intercollegiate Athletics

**Robertha Abney**
Slippery Rock University
**Janet B. Parks**
Bowling Green State University

---

## Learning Objectives

After studying this chapter, you will be able to

1. define intercollegiate athletics;

2. demonstrate an understanding of the events surrounding the development of intercollegiate athletics;

3. describe the purpose of organizations governing intercollegiate athletics;

4. identify key athletics administrative personnel within intercollegiate athletics departments;

5. identify the duties of the various administrators who manage an intercollegiate athletics department;

6. discuss several current challenges within intercollegiate athletics; and

7. identify key associations, organizations, and publications related to intercollegiate athletics.

---

For fans of college sport, the excitement, hoopla, and anticipation of March Madness is an annual ritual. Basketball, basketball, basketball—it's on television and radio, in newspapers and magazines, on the Internet, on talk shows, and on millions of people's minds. The players and coaches are in the spotlight for weeks. It is *the* story, and wouldn't it be fun to be part of the action?

As you might suspect, being part of the action involves more than being among the fortunate fans to get tickets to the Final Four. Intercollegiate athletics in the United States is a huge, complicated, demanding, and controversial enterprise. Many people have a limited understanding of how intercollegiate sports started and what goes on behind the scenes. The purpose of this chapter, therefore, is to provide an overview of several aspects of contemporary intercollegiate athletics—a snapshot of what occurs away from the exciting and widely publicized action.

# Governance of Intercollegiate Athletics

Most secondary and postsecondary educational institutions in North America provide varsity athletics programs for their students. In secondary schools, these programs are called *interscholastic* athletics. Programs offered by 4-year colleges, universities, and junior and community colleges are known as *intercollegiate* athletics. Initially, intercollegiate athletics were student controlled. They began with class games that eventually became intercollegiate contests. In fact, they were so low-key that when the owner of a railroad proposed the idea of a regatta between the Yale and Harvard boat clubs in 1852, "The crew members thought of it as a 'jolly lark' which provided them with an eight-day, all-expense paid vacation on Lake Winnipesaukee" (Lucas & Smith, 1978, p. 197). As noted in chapter 2, this unpretentious event marked the beginning of intercollegiate athletics in the United States.

The nature of intercollegiate athletics quickly changed from social interactions to highly competitive events. By 1905, football competition had become so intense that some individuals urged that the sport be reformed or abolished. One way of implementing reform was to establish associations to govern intercollegiate athletics.

## National Collegiate Athletic Association

The Intercollegiate Athletic Association of the United States (IAAUS) was officially constituted on March 31, 1906, and took its present name, National Collegiate Athletic Association (NCAA), in 1910. The NCAA is currently located in Overland Park, Kansas, and will move to Indianapolis in 2000. The NCAA is an organization of more than 1,150 colleges, universities, and conferences that govern both men's and women's intercollegiate sports programs at its member institutions. Each NCAA member institution is classified within either Division I, II, or III (see figure 9.1). Division classification is based on several criteria, including, but not limited to, the size of the financial base, the number and types of sports offered, the focus of the program, and the existence of athletic grants-in-aid. Examples of Division II and III athletics department organizational charts are shown in figures 9.2 and 9.3, respectively.

Athletics programs at Division I institutions are major financial enterprises that generate significant revenue. These institutions have teams in football and men's basketball, offer full grants-in-aid based on athletic ability, are highly competitive, and consider many athletic contests to be entertainment for spectators. Depending on their resources, some of which far exceed others, Division I programs might be financed through student fees, gate receipts, television revenues, **licensing** revenues, and private donations. Division I institutions are further divided into Divisions I-A, I-AA, and I-AAA, each of which has specific classification criteria.

Division II institutions offer grants-in-aid based on athletic ability, but not to the extent offered by Division I schools. The major difference between Division I and Division II schools is that D-I schools strive for regional and national prominence, and D-II schools strive for regional recognition. In Division III, the largest division, with 401 members, the focus is on participation rather than competition or entertainment. In Division III schools, student athletes do not receive grants based on athletic ability, and they are treated the same as other students at the institution with respect to admission policies, academic advisement, and scholarship opportunities (Lessig & Alsop, 1990).

## Other National Governing Bodies

The National Junior College Athletic Association (NJCAA) was conceived in 1937 at Fresno, CA, and became a functioning organization in 1938. The goal of the NJCAA is to promote and supervise a national program of junior college sports and activities consistent with the educational objectives of junior colleges. The NJCAA membership is approximately 550 institutions. It is organized into 24 geographic regions and headquartered in Colorado Springs, Colorado (Karlin, 1995).

The National Association for Intercollegiate Athletics (NAIA), located in Tulsa, Oklahoma, was established in 1940 and has approximately 400 member institutions (Karlin, 1995). Membership is open to 4-year and upper-level 2-year colleges and universities in the United States and Canada. The philosophies and programs of NAIA member institutions are similar to those found in NCAA Division II (Lessig & Alsop, 1990). The organizational chart for the NAIA is depicted in figure 9.4.

The National Small College Athletic Association (NSCAA) was formed in 1966. Emanating from a group of 10 charter members, the association has grown large enough to sponsor national competition for eight sports. The primary function of the NSCAA is to provide opportunities for smaller

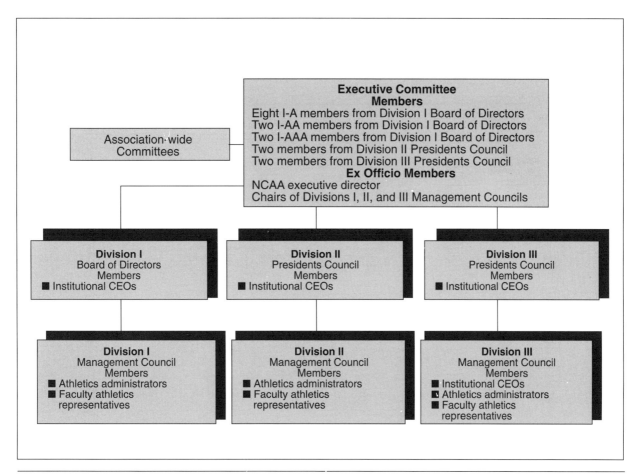

**Figure 9.1**   NCAA organizational chart/governance structure.
Data from NCAA News, August 4, 1997, 34(29).

colleges (fewer than 1,000 students) throughout the United States to compete with institutions of similar size (Franks, 1995-1996). The NSCAA is headquartered in Franklin, New Hampshire, and has 64 member institutions.

Another organization governing intercollegiate athletics is the National Christian College Athletic Association (NCCAA). Incorporated in 1968 and located in Marion, Indiana, the NCCAA focuses on "the promotion and enhancement of intercollegiate athletic competition with a Christian perspective" (Moss, 1995, p. 25). The NCCAA has 94 member institutions in two Divisions. Division I consists of 42 Christian schools and Division II consists of 52 Bible colleges.

A national governing body exclusively for women's intercollegiate sport emerged in 1971 when the Association for Intercollegiate Athletics for Women (AIAW) was established by women physical educators from colleges and universities across the country (Morrison, 1993). During its 10-year existence, the AIAW provided many opportunities for women athletes, coaches, and admin-

istrators. The organization also offered several national championships, many of which received television coverage. Eventually, however, the NCAA and the NAIA expanded their structures to include women's athletics, and in 1982, the AIAW was dismantled. Currently, both men's and women's intercollegiate athletics programs exist under the auspices of the same governing bodies.

## Conferences

A conference is a group of colleges or universities that govern the conduct of its member institutions' athletics programs. In addition to establishing rules of competition and conducting conference championships, conferences have functions related to (a) communication within and beyond the membership, (b) scheduling, (c) officiating, (d) crowd control and contest management, (e) compliance and enforcement (rules and regulations), (f) eligibility of student-athletes, (g) television contracts, (h) informational services, (i) merchandising (e.g., procuring commercial

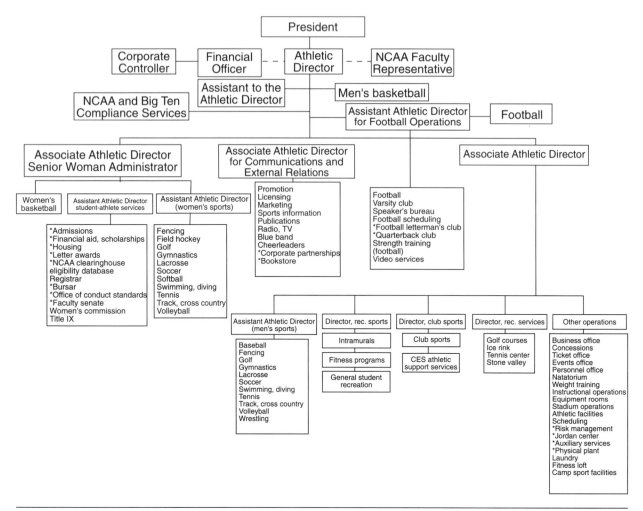

**Figure. 9.2** Organizational chart for an NCAA Division I athletics department.
Reprinted, by permission, from Penn State University.

sponsorship of conference championships or endorsement of an exclusive line of clothing or equipment), (j) conducting surveys of its members, (k) fostering collegiality among member institutions, and (l) record keeping (Kinder, 1993).

Examples of conferences are the Mid-America Intercollegiate Athletic Conference (MIAA), the Ivy League, the Atlantic Coast Conference (ACC), the Mid-Eastern Athletic Conference (MEAC), the Pennsylvania State Athletic Conference (PSAC), the Mid-American Conference (MAC), the Southeastern Conference (SEC), the Southwestern Athletic Conference (SWAC), and the Big Ten Conference. A typical conference organizational chart is presented in figure 9.5.

## Institutional Governance

Although national organizations and conferences exist to oversee and coordinate intercollegiate

athletics programs, the institution itself should be the first line of control. Institutional control, however, has been an elusive goal, particularly in so-called big-time athletics programs. In 1989, the Knight Foundation formed a Commission on Intercollegiate Athletics to study athletics in NCAA member institutions (Knight Foundation, 1991). After studying intercollegiate athletics for more than a year, the Commission published a report titled *Keeping Faith With the Student-Athlete: A New Model for Intercollegiate Athletics*. This report recommended four reforms designed to bring athletics back into line with traditional values and principles of higher education: presidential control, academic and financial integrity, and independent certification. The commission called this structure "the 'one-plus-three' model . . . in which the 'one'— presidential control—is directed toward the 'three'—academic integrity, financial integrity, and independent certification" (p. vii). Some major

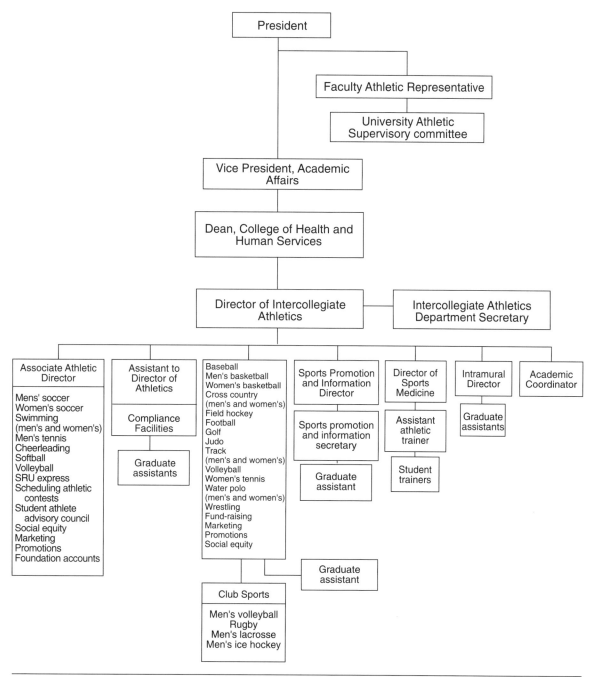

**Figure 9.3** Organizational chart for an NCAA Division II athletics department.
Reprinted, by permission, from Slippery Rock University.

provisions of these recommendations are discussed briefly here.

### Presidential Control

The presidents of the institutions will exercise the same control over athletics as they do over the rest of the university. The board of trustees, the athletics directors, the alumni, the boosters, and everyone else associated with the athletics program in any way must defer to the president in such matters.

### Academic Integrity

Student-athletes will not be admitted to the university unless they can be expected to graduate. Furthermore, every student-athlete's eligibility will be reevaluated each term and will be based on her or his continuous progress toward graduation.

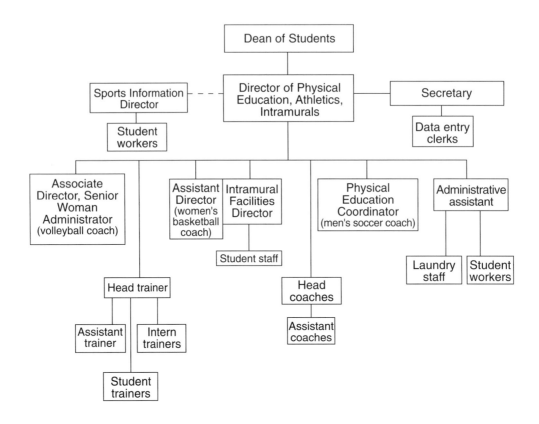

**Varsity programs (21)**

|  | Men (11) | Women (10) |
|---|---|---|
| Fall (7) | Cross country<br>Football<br>Soccer | Cross country<br>Field hockey<br>Soccer<br>Volleyball |
| Winter (6) | Basketball<br>Swimming, diving<br>Indoor track | Basketball<br>Swimming, diving<br>Indoor track |
| Spring (8) | Lacrosse<br>Tennis<br>Outdoor track<br>Baseball<br>Golf | Lacrosse<br>Tennis<br>Outdoor track |

**Figure 9.4**    Organizational chart for an NCAA Division III athletics department.
Reprinted, by permission, from Kenyon College.

The graduation rate of student-athletes should be comparable to the graduation rates of other students.

## Financial Integrity

All financial transactions, including those entered into by athletics foundations, booster clubs, and shoe and equipment contracts, will be under the direct control of the university. Athletics depart-

ments *will* be permitted to use institutional funds, thus affirming the "legitimate role of athletics on campus" (p. viii).

## Certification

Every year in the NCAA athletics departments that give financial aid based on athletic ability, an audit will be conducted on academic and financial matters. An outside agency will conduct a periodic

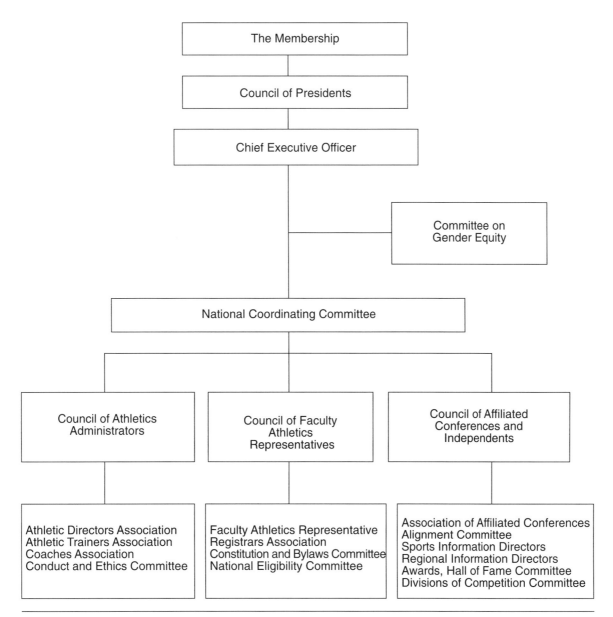

**Figure 9.5**   NAIA organizational chart.
Reprinted, by permission, from NAIA.

independent assessment of each athletics program to affirm academic and fiscal integrity. See chapter 4 for an in-depth discussion of the ethical implications of the NCAA certification policy.

The Knight Commission further stated that the dignity of the student-athlete should be maintained; that the health, welfare, and safety of student-athletes should be the primary concern of the administrators; and that all student-athletes, regardless of race, gender, or sport, should be treated fairly and should reap the educational benefits of the institution. This principle is a departure from the highly publicized emphases on revenue generation and win-loss records, particu-

larly in big-time programs. Clearly, the commission considered the *student-athlete* to be at the center of the program and expected institutional leaders to ensure that this philosophy was implemented.

## Learning Activity

Read an article about cost containment, corporate sponsorship, academic expectations, or financial compensation for athletes and make a report to the class.

© Daily Illini

The graduation rate of student-athletes compares very favorably to the graduation rates of other students.

## Intercollegiate Athletics Administrators

Administrative positions associated with intercollegiate athletics are found in junior and community colleges, 4-year universities and colleges, conference offices, and national governing bodies. The titles, nature, and scope of these positions vary widely. You should never assume that two individuals with the same title at separate institutions or governing bodies are responsible for the same duties. Each organization is structured differently, organizes their departments uniquely, and assigns responsibilities according to their human and financial resources. When looking for a position in intercollegiate athletics, study each job description carefully to determine if the responsibilities of a position are within your area of expertise.

Most of what we know about intercollegiate athletics administration today pertains to traditionally White institutions. The information revealed about those institutions, however, can not be generalized to historically Black colleges and universities (HBCUs), such as Tennessee State, Howard University, South Carolina State, Florida A & M, Tuskeegee University, and Grambling University. In many respects, HBCUs are similar to NCAA Divisions II and III and NAIA universities (see figure 9.6). In this chapter, we will discuss unique characteristics of HBCUs where appropriate.

In chapter 8, you learned about top, middle, and first-line managers. As figures 9.2, 9.3, 9.6, and 9.7 show, you can find all three types of managers in most intercollegiate athletics departments. An important point for you to remember is that many administrators will have assistants, the position in which novice athletics administrators usually begin their careers.

All athletics administrators must be able to fulfill the typical managerial functions of planning, organizing, staffing, directing, coordinating, reporting, and budgeting. Many positions with narrowly defined responsibilities will exist at most Division I-A colleges and universities, where staff members usually devote their entire workday to athletics. On the other hand, at smaller, less competitive institutions, you may not find as many positions. Athletics department personnel at smaller institutions might also have other duties, such as teaching part time in a sport-related academic area (Lessig & Alsop, 1990).

## Athletics Director (AD)

As the top manager, the AD oversees all department activities and must understand and approve the activities of each unit. Although middle and first-line administrators are in charge of their specific areas of the program, they must report to the AD. In most Division I universities, the AD reports to the university president or to the president through a vice president (Lessig & Alsop, 1990). In Division II and III institutions, the AD might report to administrators such as the Vice President of Student Affairs, the Dean of the College of Health and Human Services, or the Chair of the Department of Physical Education.

Among the AD's specific responsibilities are budget and finance, facilities, risk management,

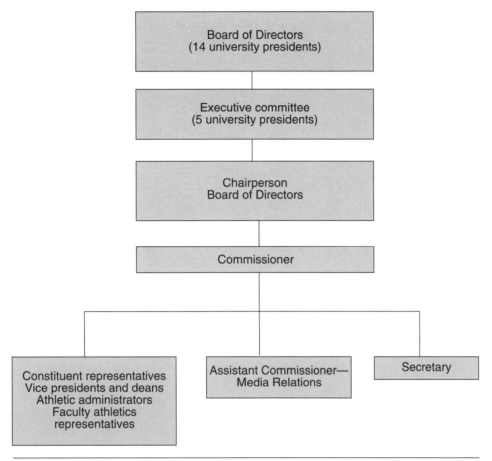

**Figure 9.6**  Organizational chart for the Pennsylvania State Athletic Conference.
Reprinted, by permission, from the Pennsylvania State Athletic Conference.

television contracts, compliance with laws and the regulations of national and conference governing bodies, academic progress of student-athletes, communication with the media, scheduling, marketing games and other events, corporate sponsorships, ticket sales, community relations, alumni relations, campus relations, fund-raising, and personnel management, including employment and termination of coaches (Karlin, 1995). Recently, the ability of an AD to raise funds for the athletics program has become a major prerequisite for employment (Lessig & Alsop, 1990).

## Associate or Assistant AD

Large athletics programs typically have at least one and perhaps two or three associate and assistant ADs (middle managers). In addition to working closely with the AD, associate and assistant ADs are in charge of specific work units, such as marketing, fund-raising, event management, facilities management, or sports information. Senior associate ADs are second in command and, among other duties, are usually responsible for operating the athletics department when the AD is out of the office. The titles associate and assistant AD do not reveal much about what the people in those positions do on a daily basis. You would definitely need to see a job description if you wanted to know the responsibilities of an associate or assistant AD at a specific institution.

## First-Line Managers

The first-line managers are responsible for specific work groups in the athletics department. These managers typically report to an associate or assistant AD.

### Academic Coordinator

This position is found in most NCAA Division I institutions and in some Division II schools. It might not exist in Division III schools, NAIA universities, or HBCUs because in most of those institutions, athletes and their nonathlete counterparts use the advising services of the university.

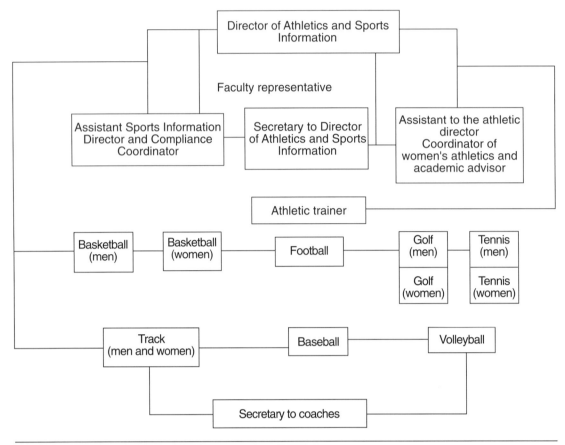

**Figure 9.7** Mississippi Valley State University Athletic Department organizational chart.
Reprinted, by permission, from Mississippi Valley State University.

Academic advising services are designed to enhance student-athletes' potential for academic success and graduation. The responsibilities of this office will vary according to the institution's admissions policies and level of competition. In general, athletic academic offices provide assistance to student-athletes in the areas of admissions, academic orientation, academic standards, registration, financial aid, student life (e.g., education about drug abuse, sexually transmitted diseases, domestic violence), and housing. The academic coordinator monitors the academic activities of all student-athletes and maintains records on their academic progress. Academic coordinators also work closely with coaches, faculty, the compliance officer, and other administrators to make certain the athletes are making progress toward graduation. Occasionally, the academic coordinator helps resolve problems related to athletes' academic performance.

Athletic academic advisors should have excellent interpersonal communication skills, be familiar with academic and career guidance techniques, and understand the processes of social adapta-

tion and human development. They should also possess evaluation, leadership, and instructional skills as well as knowledge of legal responsibilities and governing body compliance regulations (Gordon, 1992). Academic coordinators in large athletics programs might be in charge of several academic counselors, mentors, and tutors, some of whom will be undergraduate and graduate students. In this case, the coordinator should also possess excellent management skills.

## Business and Finance Manager

The business and finance manager assists with preparing, administering, and monitoring the athletic budget, which serves as a financial guide in determining the expenditures of each area of operation. Business managers process all reimbursements and payments and prepare monthly financial statements for coaches and staff members. They ensure that all expenditures are in accordance with policies and procedures that ensure strict compliance with sound business practices and the rules and regulations of the institution, the conference, and the national governing body.

## Compliance Officer

This is a new position in college athletics, spawned by the reform movement initiated by the Knight Commission. The role of compliance coordinators is to develop an educational process whereby everyone directly or indirectly involved with the athletics program understands and complies with the rules of the institution, the national governing body, and the conference. Compliance coordinators must know all the rules and conduct an investigation if they suspect any rules have been broken. They also submit reports to the NCAA and conduct training sessions for student-athletes, coaches, and other individuals at the institution (Karlin, 1995, p. 136).

## Development and Public Relations Director

This individual is responsible for raising funds to support the sports program; creating, developing, and implementing fund-raising programs; and cultivating potential donors. Development and public relations directors are responsible for coordinating, controlling, and monitoring the activities of booster or fan clubs. They must control the finances of these clubs and ensure that a booster club will serve, not damage, an athletics program.

Development and public relations directors must educate the boosters about the rules and regulations of the department, university, conference, and national governing body. They must maintain a positive relationship between the intercollegiate athletics department and the community, keeping the boosters involved and feeling valuable. It is imperative that development and public relations directors have a good rapport with the various publics (e.g., the media, community officials, and fans).

## Event and Facility Manager

Facility scheduling, maintenance, improvements, and contest management are the major duties of the facility and event manager. Facility and event managers make sure the athletic facilities are available, accessible, and risk free. They coordinate all aspects of game management for home athletic contests. This usually consists of such things as "security at games; hiring, training, and supervision of ushers; marking and lining of fields and courts; arrangements for ticket sellers and ticket takers; management of the time schedule of the game, including such things as the National Anthem, bands, and half-time shows, and attendance to the needs of game officials" (Lessig &

Alsop, 1990, p. 27). A more detailed description of event and facility management is presented in chapter 13.

## Marketing and Promotions Director

The marketing and promotions director strives to enhance the visibility of the athletics programs, increase attendance, provide a public service, and generate additional income for the athletics program (see chapter 12). The responsibilities of this position include providing **giveaways** and entertainment; promoting ticket sales for individual games, nonrevenue sports, season packages, and championship events; and promoting a complete line of apparel, fan support merchandise, and miscellanies for retail sale by direct mail, at the university's pro shop, and at concessions during sporting events; and developing corporate sponsorship packages. The marketing and promotions director monitors the use of the school's trademarked logo and licensing agreements, ensuring legitimate use of the logo and making certain that quality merchandise is being sold in the name of the university's athletics program. Marketing and promotions directors must fully understand trademark licensing and be familiar with trademark principles, terms, and definitions used in trademark law (Pitts & Stotlar, 1996).

## Sports Information Director (SID)

The sports information office is at the center of the action in intercollegiate athletics administration. Sports information directors prepare and disseminate information relevant to all intercollegiate teams and programs. They are responsible for publishing media guides; press releases; recruiting brochures; features on athletes for their hometown newspapers; announcements of schedules; and all other appropriate information pertaining to student-athletes, coaches, and administrative staff. The SID also assists the statistical staff for the various sporting events (Chamberlin, 1990).

The sports information department usually works closely with the news service and publications office of the institution. For example, announcements of appointments and resignations of high-ranking administrators and coaches might be coordinated by the news service. Signing of prospective student-athletes and announcements about less prominent administrators and coaches might be disseminated by the sports information office. The same rule holds true for press conferences and interviews with players, coaches, administrative staff, and others who are associated with the athletics program. The manner in which these communications occur will vary from institution to institution.

The SID communicates with both internal and external publics. Internally, the SID works with coaches, the AD, interns, graduate assistants, athletes, the development director, the marketing director, the university photographer, the recruiting coordinator, and the university public affairs director (McCleneghan, 1995). Externally, the SID works with radio play-by-play personnel, TV reporters, newspaper reporters, sports columnists, live TV game producers and directors, TV sports directors, newspaper sports editors, other schools' SIDs, local printers, and booster club officials (McCleneghan, 1995). Clearly, the SID is a busy person who must have excellent skills, not only in writing, computer use, and information organization, but also in getting along with people who are frequently working under a great deal of pressure (Chamberlin, 1990). The responsibilities of sports information directors are discussed further in chapter 11.

## Learning Activity

Obtain press guides, brochures, and so on prepared by the sports information office at your university and share them with the class.

### Ticket Manager

The primary responsibility of the ticket manager is coordinating all ticket operations. This person accounts for all money expended and received for tickets. A major resource for the ticket manager is Box Office Management International (BOMI), "a not-for-profit association dedicated to the improvement of ticketing operations worldwide" (Moss, 1995, p. 11). BOMI serves as a resource for ticket managers by sponsoring educational seminars through which they can learn about technological advances, such as computerized ticketing systems (e.g., Select Ticketing and TicketMaster) and new techniques related to the ticketing business. These seminars help the ticket manager to be efficient in coordinating and implementing all ticket sales, including season ticket orders, individual game tickets, and postseason competition ticket sales (Moss, 1995).

### Senior Woman Administrator (SWA)

The term Senior Woman Administrator is not a position title. It is an NCAA designation that goes to "the highest ranking *female* administrator involved with the conduct of a member institution's intercollegiate athletics program. She should be a full time institutional employee who has demonstrated an interest in athletics" (NCAA Education Services, 1996). The SWA might be an associate or assistant AD, the marketing director, or another female administrator, either in the athletics department or in the university. Typically, the SWA is *not* a coach, a faculty member, the AD, or the faculty representative to the NCAA.

The SWA usually participates in department, campus, conference, and national meetings, particularly those that address gender equity. Depending on the needs of the institution, other involvement of the SWA could include serving as spokesperson for the needs and interests of women in intercollegiate athletics, participating in decisions regarding budgeting and other issues affecting student-athlete welfare, being a role model for student-athletes, and educating them on issues that affect intercollegiate athletics (NCAA Education Services, 1996). It is important to note that SWA does not mean Senior Women's Administrator, a title that implies oversight of women's teams. The duties of the SWA are not necessarily associated with administering the women's sports program. Moreover, given that the designation SWA is restricted to females, the term should not be included in position descriptions for job listings. See figure 9.8 for more information.

## Learning Activity

Why is an SWA needed in intercollegiate athletics departments? Why shouldn't the designation SWA be included in any intercollegiate athletics position description?

## Additional Personnel

Two other positions in intercollegiate athletics that might interest you are equipment manager and athletic trainer.

### Equipment Manager

Equipment managers order, receive, and maintain inventory. They periodically replace equipment and supplies, including expendable items such as sports bras, athletic supporters, T-shirts, and socks that must be restocked frequently. The equipment manager is also responsible for storage, maintenance, security, and inventory of athletic equip-

**Who is a Senior Woman Administrator?**

The highest ranking female administrator involved with conducting a member institution's intercollegiate athletics program. She should be a full-time institutional employee who has demonstrated an interest in athletics.

**What is the purpose of appointing a Senior Woman Administrator?**

To involve female administrators in a meaningful way in the decision-making process in intercollegiate athletics. The position is intended to ensure representation of women's interests at the campus, conference, and national levels.

**Who appoints the Senior Woman Administrator and to whom does she report?**

Generally, the athletics director or the university president appoints the SWA, and the SWA usually reports to the athletics director.

**Figure 9.8** NCAA Senior Woman Administrator.
Reprinted, by permission, from NCAA brochure *Senior Woman Administrator.*

ment. All athletic equipment and supply requests go through the equipment manager, who is responsible for ascertaining whether such requested materials are necessary, based on current inventory and use. An annual inventory of all equipment is prepared at the end of each fiscal year. The inventory lists the items, quantity, quality, date of purchase, cost, vendor, service record, and other pertinent information. In addition to the managerial duties, this individual should know how to repair most pieces of equipment. Because the equipment manager deals with vendors who are eager to make a sale, they occasionally encounter challenging ethical situations regarding "freebies" or special gifts designed to entice them to purchase particular products. Each university will have a policy regarding these gifts (Kinder, 1993).

## Athletic Training Staff

In most athletics programs, you will find a head athletic trainer and any number of assistant athletic trainers, depending on the size of the institution. Frequently, graduate and undergraduate athletic training students work in the athletic training program as part of the National Athletic Trainers Association (NATA) certification process. Most full-time athletic trainers are certified by the NATA. Athletic trainers assume five roles in discharging their duties: prevention of injuries; recognition,

evaluation, and immediate care of injuries; rehabilitation and reconditioning of injuries; health care administration; and professional development and responsibility (NATA, 1995).

The health care administration role requires extensive managerial expertise. The NATA (1995) mandated that athletic trainers must be able to perform the following managerial functions:

- Use information systems to maintain records.
- Implement institutional, state, and federal standards to ensure a safe and sanitary environment.
- Write job descriptions, establish protocols, plan staff workloads, conduct performance appraisals, and supervise all personnel (including student athletic trainers) in daily operations.
- Standardize operating procedures by formulating policies and procedures.
- Use sound financial principles in ordering equipment and supplies.
- Communicate effectively with other health care professionals.
- Establish a sound risk-management plan relative to infectious diseases.

It is important for prospective athletic trainers to take course work in business and management so they can acquire the skills necessary to function effectively in these roles. It would also be a good idea for them to take a teaching methods course because they might have the opportunity to teach athletic training courses in an academic unit such as sport management or physical education.

Athletic trainers are responsible for ensuring the proper care, treatment, and prevention of injuries for all student-athletes at home and away athletic contests. It is the responsibility of the athletic training staff to assign personnel to all home and away events for which an athletic trainer is appropriate and to provide the necessary staff for all championship events. Decisions related to practice, competition, treatment, therapy, and rehabilitation are usually coordinated with the full participation of the student-athlete, the head coach, the athletic training staff, and other appropriate medical personnel.

## Administrators in Governing Bodies

Administrative positions in conferences and national governing bodies parallel many in colleges and universities. The major difference between them is that administrators in conferences and governing bodies must consider the welfare of many institutions and the conference as a whole, rather than focusing on a single university. As explained in chapter 8, conference commissioners in all NCAA Divisions perform their duties within three major role classifications: interpersonal, informational, and decisional (Quarterman, 1994). Examples of these functions are shown in table 8.3. You will notice they are similar to the roles of an AD, except the AD is acting on behalf of the university and the commissioner is acting on behalf of the member institutions. The organizational charts in figures 9.1, 9.5, and 9.6 contain additional positions in the NCAA, the NAIA, and conference offices.

## Learning Activity

Interview an athletics administrator and a coach at your institution. Ask them to discuss the role of the institution's athletic conference.

# Careers in Intercollegiate Athletics Administration

For some people, money, praise, prestige, and short work weeks are motivational factors for pursuing a career in intercollegiate athletics. Actually, those are the least likely benefits for the vast majority. Intercollegiate athletics administrative positions do not typically pay high salaries, you have to contend with "Monday morning quarterbacks" who are always willing to tell you how you could improve your performance, the hours are long, and the work is challenging. Rewards of your efforts might occasionally include the excitement of watching your teams in conference, regional, or national championship tournaments. More frequently, however, athletics administrators feel sufficiently rewarded to know that they are doing something they enjoy and, at the same time, touching the lives of young men and women and making a difference.

Career paths in intercollegiate athletics vary widely. There are no established paths that you can set out on to end up where you thought you were going. The following discussion of career paths of ADs and first-line administrators is designed to help you gain insight into this competitive career field.

## Becoming an Athletics Director

The traditional path to the AD position has been from collegiate athlete to collegiate coach to AD. Currently, however, there are at least two alternatives to that path. In some cases, athletics departments are recruiting successful businesspeople to take the helms of their financially challenged athletics departments. In other situations, individuals who aspire to be ADs are gaining formal education through sport management programs (Berg, 1990).

Although there is no one best path to the AD position, the appropriateness of the athlete-to-coach-to-AD path has been challenged, particularly for NCAA Division I institutions. Reflecting widely held sentiments, Cuneen (1992) stated that "managerial expertise and business acumen have become such essential characteristics for directors of major collegiate athletic programs that the long-standing career path of player to coach to athletic director is no longer sufficient" (p. 16). She suggested that prospective ADs should pursue a doctoral curriculum to prepare them in job responsibilities such as business management, strategic planning, marketing, facility management, legal aspects of sport, finance, accounting, organizational theory, and personnel management.

Fitzgerald, Sagaria, and Nelson (1994) examined the career patterns of 200 athletics directors in NCAA Divisions I, II, and III. They found that most respondents had been either college athletes or college coaches. Consistent similarities ended with that observation, however, as career paths differed unpredictably within Divisions and between genders. In HBCUs, the ADs have followed a slightly different path (Quarterman, 1992). Like their counterparts in predominately White institutions, most administrators at HBCUs were intercollegiate players and coaches before becoming ADs. The difference is that most of them also have teaching experience and are faculty members or coaches while they are serving as ADs. According to Quarterman, the career experiences of ADs in HBCUs (athlete to coach or instructor to AD) are similar to those of ADs in NAIA and NCAA Division II and III institutions.

## First-Line Administrators

First-line administrators, such as marketing directors, academic coordinators, and sports information directors, spend their entire careers within a work unit focused on one aspect of the program. For these administrators, career advancements

Some rewards of a career in college athletics are external—such as a trip to the final four—but far more are internal, including the knowledge that you are teaching young people and helping them grow.

are typically in the form of a vertical move from assistant director of a work unit to director of that unit. Occasionally, first-line administrators will relocate to similar positions at other universities (i.e., a horizontal or lateral move) to advance their careers. Other first-line administrators, particularly in NCAA Division I programs, might move into associate or assistant AD positions (Fitzgerald et al., 1994; Quarterman, 1992). As these administrators move vertically, whether to director of the work unit or to associate or assistant AD, additional managerial and administrative functions will be expected.

## Job Satisfaction

Intercollegiate athletics administrators have reported a high degree of satisfaction with most aspects of their jobs (Parks, Russell, Wood, Roberton, & Shewokis, 1995). Middle and first-line administrators, however, tend not to be satisfied with their salaries and their promotion opportunities (Parks et al., 1995). Dissatisfaction with salaries is probably a reaction to salaries in intercollegiate athletics being lower than salaries for managerial positions in other industries. The appeal of sport is so strong, however, that many individuals are

## Changing Plans

Curtiss Wayne is a first-year undergraduate sport management major. He participates in the sport management student organization, is in the marching band, is a varsity baseball player, and so far has managed to maintain a solid A grade point average. After the baseball season, Curtiss realized he would not be able to attain his goal of becoming a professional baseball player. He then decided he would pursue a career as an administrator in a Division I intercollegiate athletics department. What steps should Curtiss take to increase the possibility of achieving this goal? Choose one position discussed in the chapter and write a career plan for Curtiss.

Only in rare instances does this path lead to the top position (i.e., AD). Consequently, it is possible that first-line administrators might not perceive many opportunities for promotion.

## Learning Activity

Write a job description for each position identified on *one* organizational chart in this chapter. If possible, obtain actual job descriptions from your athletics department and compare your descriptions with them.

# Academic Preparation for Athletics Administration

The typical AD has at least one degree beyond the baccalaureate. In 1994, 85% of the ADs in NCAA I, II, and III institutions held master's degrees, with 21.5% of them possessing doctorates (Fitzgerald et al., 1994). Quarterman (1992) found that more than 95% of the ADs in HBCUs held master's degrees, and 36% of them had doctorates. An advanced degree was also prevalent among NCAA Division I-A middle and first-line administrators. Parks et al. (1995) found that more than 60% of these administrators held either master's or doctoral degrees. It is clear that if you want to pursue a career in intercollegiate athletics, a master's degree will probably be necessary.

content to work long hours for low pay. Moreover, the benefits that come with university employment (e.g., vacation time, life and health insurance, travel opportunities, access to academic courses, retirement benefits, association with student-athletes) are excellent, frequently offsetting modest salaries (see table 9.1).

The dissatisfaction of athletics administrators with opportunities for promotion is probably a reflection of the career paths in intercollegiate athletics. In this field, you typically start out as an assistant to a first-line administrator (e.g., assistant director of marketing) and eventually work your way up to the director of marketing position.

Table 9.1

**Mean Salaries of 608 NCAA Division I-A Athletics Administrators Who Had Been in Their Present Positions for an Average of 7.7 Years**

| Position | Maximum | Mean | Minimum |
|---|---|---|---|
| AD | $105,000 | $88,214 | $35,000 |
| Assoc. or Asst. AD | $105,000 | $52,150 | $15,000 |
| Academic Affairs | $75,000 | $38,064 | $25,000 |
| Business Manager | $85,000 | $45,975 | $25,000 |
| Event Manager | $55,000 | $40,000 | $25,000 |
| Sports Info. Director (SID) | $55,000 | $37,345 | $25,000 |
| Asst. SID | $35,000 | $25,000 | $15,000 |
| Ticket Manager | $55,000 | $33,445 | $25,000 |
| Developmental Director | $65,000 | $45,000 | $25,000 |
| Promotions Director | $55,000 | $36,600 | $25,000 |
| Compliance Officer | $55,000 | $38,846 | $25,000 |

Data from Parks, J.B., Russell, R.L., Wood, P.H. (1991). [Demographic characteristics of 608 NCAA Division I-A athletics administrators who had been in their current positions for an average of 7.7 years.] Unpublished raw data.

You can begin your career path in athletics administration by studying sport management at the undergraduate level, engaging in field experiences in athletics administration, and volunteering with an athletics department or a conference office. Your program should provide you with knowledge about sport in society and the role of athletics in institutions of higher education as well as an understanding of the business and technical aspects of the field. If you aspire to a position in an HBCU or an NAIA, NCAA II or III institution, it would be a good idea to develop a field of academic or coaching expertise too, because you will probably be a professor or a coach as well as an administrator (Quarterman, 1992).

Next, you should select a graduate school that will complement the knowledge and experience you gained at the undergraduate level. For students with no experience in intercollegiate athletics, an important element of the master's degree might be field experience with the university athletics department or conference office. This experience will permit you to learn more about the day-to-day operations of athletics administration. If you perform well, you will also begin to develop a valuable network of professionals who can vouch for your ability when you are looking for a job. If you want to be an AD, particularly at a major institution, you should include doctoral study in your professional preparation plans.

# Current Challenges

Numerous challenges await the next generation of intercollegiate athletics administrators. Major concerns include diversity, gender equity, racial equity, ramifications of the socioeconomic status (SES) of student-athletes, athletics program cost containment, corporate sponsorship of intercollegiate athletics programs, institutional control of athletics, academic integrity, and financial compensation for athletes. This list is not exhaustive, nor does space allow us to present any of these challenges in its entire complexity. In fact, we will discuss only the first three here. If you are interested in exploring these concerns in more depth, a good place to begin would be chapter 3, Psychosocial Aspects of Sport.

## Diversity

Current discussions of affirmative action and equal opportunity might lead a person to believe that a gender and racial balance has been achieved in intercollegiate athletics administration, particularly at the middle and first-line positions. To the contrary, recent studies of NCAA member institutions have shown a marked *lack* of diversity in athletics administrative personnel. For example, 92% of the 200 ADs in Fitzgerald et al.'s (1994) study were White, and 71.5% of them were men. Parks, Russell, and Wood (1993) found a similar racial and gender imbalance among 402 NCAA Division I-A top, middle, and first-line administrators, where 92% of the respondents were White, and 83% were male. The gender and racial imbalance found in these two studies presents a major challenge to the next generation of sport managers, who will be responsible for equalizing opportunities in intercollegiate athletics administration. In the more enlightened age of the 21st century, intercollegiate athletics administration should reflect greater participation, not only by women and minorities but also by people with differing abilities, a population that is currently underrepresented in athletics administration (Abney & Richey, 1992).

## Gender Equity

Title IX of the Education Amendments Act of 1972 requires athletics administrators to ensure equity in scholarship support, number of women coaches, promotions of women's athletics, salaries, scheduling of women's games, inclusion of women administrators up to the highest levels, and budgets (Tillman, Voltmer, Esslinger, & McCue, 1996). The Equity in Athletics Disclosure Act of 1994, which went into effect in October 1996, requires institutions of higher education to make public all information *by gender* about participation rates of student-athletes and expenditures associated with coaching salaries, grants-in-aid, recruiting costs, and equipment (Equity, 1994). Although this legislation enhances efforts to enforce the provisions of Title IX, equity in athletics is as much a moral responsibility as it is a legal mandate. The next generation of athletics administrators will be challenged to expand opportunities for women while controlling the costs associated with providing a quality athletic experience (Howard & Crompton, 1995).

## Racial Equity

With the increase in participation rates, the implementation of affirmative action policies, the passage of Title IX, and the Civil Rights Restoration

Act of 1988, one would anticipate an increase in the opportunities for minorities in coaching and managerial positions in intercollegiate athletics. This is not the case. African American male and female coaches and administrators have not attained parity and remain underrepresented in college athletics (Brooks & Althouse, 1993).

Abney and Richey (1991) investigated barriers Black women administrators face in HBCUs and in traditionally White institutions. In both settings, the women reported "inadequate salary," "lack of support groups," and "being a woman" as obstacles to their career development. The women who worked in HBCUs identified the additional barriers of "sexism" and "low expectations by administrators." The women who worked in the White institutions reported that "being Black" was an additional obstacle to their development as was the "lack of cultural and social outlets in the community."

In the 21st century, athletics administrators will be increasingly sensitive to the effects of gender and race on an individual's career aspirations. Abney and Richey (1992) summed it up when they stated, "For minority women to enjoy the benefits of Title IX, there must be individuals in positions that are knowledgeable, committed, and sensitive to the differences and the hiring of minority women. Until this occurs, opportunities will remain limited" (p. 58).

## Summary

Intercollegiate athletics began in the 1850s as class games and evolved into highly competitive programs. These programs are regulated by national governing bodies and conferences. The first line of control, however, lies with the institution. The Knight Commission on Intercollegiate Athletics (1991) issued a report calling for presidential control, academic integrity, financial integrity, and certification. Athletics administrative positions include athletics director, associate and assistant athletics director, academic coordinator, business and finance manager, compliance officer, development and public relations director, event and facility manager, marketing and promotions director, sports information director, and ticket manager. Additional personnel include the equipment manager and the athletic training staff. The SWA (Senior Woman Administrator) is the NCAA designation given to the highest ranking female athletics administrator.

Career paths in intercollegiate athletics vary widely. Most administrators have at least one academic degree beyond the baccalaureate. Individuals who want to become ADs in major institutions should consider earning a doctorate. Challenges with which intercollegiate athletics administrators must deal include diversity, gender and racial equity, ramifications of differences in socioeconomic status (SES) of student-athletes, cost containment, corporate sponsorship, institutional control, academic integrity, and financial compensation for athletes.

## Learning Activity

Write a position paper describing what you believe to be the major challenges facing intercollegiate athletics. Investigate the race and gender composition of the athletics administrators at your institution. How many of them are women, minorities, persons with disabilities?

# For More Information

The following sources will provide you with more information on the issues discussed in this chapter.

## Organizations and Associations

- College Sports Information Directors of America (CoSIDA)
- International Association of Auditorium Managers (IAAM)
- National Association for Collegiate Directors of Athletics (NACDA)
- North American Society for Sport Management (NASSM)
- Public Relations Society of America (PRSA)

## Publications

- *Athletics Administration*
- *Athletic Business*
- *Athletic Journal*
- *Chronicle of Higher Education*
- *Collegiate Athletic Management*
- *CoSIDA Digest*
- *Journal of Sport and Social Issues*
- *NCAA News*
- *Public Relations Quarterly*
- *Scholastic Coach and Athletic Director*
- *Sociology of Sport Journal*
- *Sport Marketing Quarterly*

# Job Opportunities

## Assistant Director of Marketing

Responsibilities of this position are to develop marketing and promotional strategies for ticket sales and nonrevenue sports; implement marketing strategies for teams involved in conference and NCAA championships; design and coordinate half-time activities and game-day promotions; design media campaigns; solicit corporate sponsorship; supervise interns and assistants; and report to the director of marketing. Bachelor's degree and 1 year experience in marketing and promotions in intercollegiate athletics required. Master's degree and computer skills strongly preferred. Beginning salary $23,688.

## Sports Information Director

A Sports Information Director position is being created at Bilgewater University. Responsibilities include writing news releases; contacting publications and athletic associations; maintaining team statistics; and supervising all sports information staff, including graduate assistants. Bachelor's degree in journalism, English, or related area required; 2 to 5 years experience in sports reporting, news reporting, and editing required. Will report to Assistant Director of Public Relations and Marketing. Salary range will be $20,000 to $25,000, depending on applicant's qualifications.

## Senior Associate Athletic Director

The Smoky Mountain State University needs a Senior Associate Athletic Director. Responsibilities include participating in management decisions concerning 20 men's and women's NCAA Division II programs; directing and evaluating the head coaches; analyzing department's needs, budget, and expenditures; overseeing department's compliance with gender equity and with Top 10 Conference and NCAA regulations. A bachelor's degree is required and master's preferred; seven to ten years of intercollegiate athletic administrative experience; excellent leadership and interpersonal skills; successful experience with Title IX, gender equity, and NCAA compliance; and excellent written and verbal communication skills will be required. Salary range: $40,000 to $50,000, commensurate with experience and qualifications.

## Recruiting Coordinator

John Quincy University is seeking a full-time Recruiting Coordinator-Academic Support Assistant. Responsibilities include meeting with the Head Academic Coordinator, coaching staff, and financial aid representatives to track the recruiting process. This individual will oversee the study programs, study tables, and mentoring. Salary competitive, with benefits. A strong academic record and experience with student athletes in college athletics at Division I or II a plus.

## Athletics Facilities Manager

Great Lakes College seeks an Athletics Facilities Manager. Duties include facility preparation, maintenance, and developing and scheduling sporting facilities. The Athletics Facilities Manager reports to the Director of Athletics and works closely with the Associate AD for Intercollegiate Programs. Background requirements include a master's degree with 4 years of experience. Salary commensurate with experience.

## Associate Athletic Director for Fund-Raising

Teton State University is accepting nominations for the position of Associate Athletic Director for the Women's Athletic Department. The Teton St. Freeze compete in the NCAA Division III High Plains Athletic Conference. Duties include administering ongoing annual membership programs of the Freeze Foundation, special fund-raising, developing a long-range giving program, and all Freeze Foundation social functions. Qualifications include master's degree in sport administration, prior experience in fund-raising and athletic administration. $40,000+.

## Athletics Director

Paradise Valley Junior College is accepting applications for an Athletics Director position. Candidates are expected to have a master's degree and 3 years athletic administration experience. AD reports directly to the President of the University, is responsible for the college's 10 varsity sports, and spends time in athletic fund-raising on behalf of student-athletes and the university. Applicants' knowledge of NJCAA compliance with Title IX regulations and commitment to diversity and gender equity within the athletic department will be evaluated. Minorities and women are encouraged to apply. Salary $42,000+.

# Chapter 10

# Campus Recreation

**Susan C. Brown**
Western Carolina University

---

## Learning Objectives

After studying this chapter, you will be able to

1. explain how campus recreation has evolved into the comprehensive organizational structure that we find today;

2. describe the competencies necessary to gain entry to this career path and be a successful manager;

3. define basic terminology;

4. identify the professional organizations that offer additional educational programs and through which you can obtain certifications;

5. describe the salary movement during the past 5 years in this field; and

6. describe how health, political, and social trends will affect the future of campus recreation.

---

Recreation on college campuses today is diverse. Programming provides students, faculty, staff, and other recognized members of the campus community an array of leisure and fitness opportunities. These opportunities may include but not be limited to intramural leagues, sport clubs, outdoor recreation trips, wellness and fitness programs, and informal recreation. Thus, campus recreation provides another employment setting for sport managers. In addition to sport programming skills, prospective managers should be competent in marketing, public relations, facility management, fiscal management, personnel management, and legal issues. A strong background in the exercise sciences is also necessary for anyone who wishes to pursue fitness management.

The purpose of this chapter is to provide a brief history of this management field and introduce you to organizational structure, salary expectations, necessary competencies, professional organizations, terminology, and information about the future direction of recreation on college campuses.

You will learn that a variety of job opportunities exist in today's recreational sport management setting.

# Historical Perspectives of Campus Recreation

Campus recreation is more traditionally known as intramurals, which is derived from the Latin words for within (intra) and wall (murus). However, the historical representation that follows will show how it has become much more than programming for individuals within an institution and has gone beyond sport as the only emphasis.

We can trace the origin of campus recreation back to the popular English form of sport known as sport clubs. On college campuses, students organized the clubs, helped finance their development, and played the roles of both coach and participant (Mull, Bayless, & Ross, 1987). Class competition (e.g., freshmen versus juniors) was a successful method of getting students to participate and became a strong tradition at some Ivy League schools. Between 1875 and the early 1900s, competition was mostly interschool and run predominantly by students (Means, 1973). In 1904, Cornell University proposed a system that would allow students to specialize in certain sports, and coaches provided instruction for these students who were not participating in college athletics. This was the first department to emphasize intramurals and the forerunner of what is known today as instructional sport. Between 1904 and 1912, student-controlled activities increased at such a pace that institutions began to exert control in the form of centralized authority. In 1913, The Ohio State University and the University of Michigan each inaugurated a department of intramural athletics (Mueller & Reznik, 1979). Although a faculty member was often assigned to run the departments and exerted control over field and facility assignments, students still formed the backbone of these programs. Due to the enormous popularity of intramural programs, separate facilities from varsity athletics were needed and the first building devoted primarily to intramurals was built at the University of Michigan in 1928 (Mueller & Reznik, 1979).

As intramural programs evolved in the early 1920s, athletic conferences and physical education associations began to hold annual meetings (Mueller & Reznik, 1979). After World War II, recreational programs grew even more and, in 1950,

Dr. William N. Wasson founded the National Intramural Association (NIA) at Dillard University in New Orleans. Today, the NIA is known as the National Intramural-Recreational Sports Association (NIRSA).

Organizational structure in the early development of intramural programs often placed intramural sports in the same department with physical education. However, as was documented by Voltmer and Esslinger (1949), in some institutions athletic programs were forced on physical education departments, and leadership struggles ensued. With one department now responsible for both programs, philosophical disputes arose and priorities became confused. Should physical education receive the greater portion of the budget because it would reach the greater number of students, or were the few athletically inclined to be the beneficiaries of the budget dollar? What would be left over for the intramural programs?

Times have changed dramatically. As we will illustrate later in this chapter, campus recreation directors now often report to a student development office. This is due largely to the positive role campus recreation plays in recruiting and retaining students and in the quality of student life. The traditional intramural sport program on the college campuses of yesterday is only one segment of the total campus recreation environment today. However, one historical element has remained constant. Student involvement in operating these programs is paramount. Although full-time staff are employed to oversee most management and fiscal responsibilities, campus recreation programs could not operate without student assistance.

# Program Goals

The goals of campus recreation programs, also known as recreational sport programs, may vary, but the main purposes have a central theme. The purpose for their existence is to provide a variety of programs for students, faculty, and staff and to enhance the quality of campus community life. Alumni and family are often allowed to participate in programs and use facilities and, thus, are identified as important to the campus recreation mission. We will discuss the scope of these programs later in this chapter, illustrating that they must meet the needs of many constituents. The traditional intramural program with team sport leagues exists to meet the needs of many college-age students. However, the astute programmer must not overlook the fact that not all individuals like team sports. The participation interests of international and nontraditional students and individuals with physical challenges might be different. The programmer must incorporate activities that serve these populations and, thus, reflect the program goals.

Governance of some campus recreation departments incorporates advisory boards. It should be a goal to involve members of the population being served (e.g., student, faculty member, international student) on committees that impact the recreation program and facility. Many institutions have recreation advisory boards that meet with the professional staff. Another common place for student input is on intramural appeal boards, which make decisions on participant suspensions from sport leagues, perhaps due to unsporting conduct. Campus recreation exists to serve the needs of its clientele. All program goals should be written and incorporated with the user in mind. Thus, input from the various user groups is important.

## Program Scope*

Programs offered within campus recreation departments vary dramatically from institution to institution. The following sections present appropriate terminology and describe the programming area and possible scope of job responsibilities.

Recreational sport is programmed sport activity for the sake of participation and fun. It is a diverse area that incorporates four program divisions: extramural sport, informal sport, intramural sport, and sport clubs. Each division represents varying levels of ability and diverse interests in

cooperative and competitive activity in the game form. Aside from identifying the four divisions, recreational sport is an umbrella term used synonymously with campus recreation. It also encompasses other programming areas as defined here.

Extramural sport is structured participation between campus settings. An extension of the intramural sport program, this programming area is primarily designed to use intramural champions by sending a team to participate in a tournament outside the home institution. An example of this would be the National Invitational Flag Football Championships held annually in New Orleans. Institutions are invited to send one championship men's, women's, and co-rec intramural team from their campus to represent the institution. Extramural sport can also incorporate sport extravaganzas, play days or festivals that may involve participation of many representatives from different settings.

Informal sport involves the process of self-directed participation. An individualized approach to sport, this program area acknowledges the desire to participate in sport for fitness and fun, often with no predetermined goals except that of participation (e.g., pick-up basketball, free swimming time). Informal sport requires minimal administrative or programming attention other than making sports facilities available based on the individual's schedule, interests, and resources.

Intramural sport is structured contests, tournaments, leagues, or other events in which participation is limited to the setting where the recreational sport system is located. Only those individuals within the setting (school, business, community, or military base) may participate. The participants

---

*Some of the information in this section was adapted with permission from the *Recreational Sports: A Curriculum Guide*, (1992), Corvallis, OR: NIRSA, pp. 7-8.

---

## Down the Road

Political, social, and economic trends impact the college environment tremendously. Brown noted in 1990 that "this nation has a roller coaster economy which changes every four or eight years when a new United States president is elected" (p. 32). Every part of society is intertwined and colleges must not only study these trends but also be prepared to operate

under anticipated and unanticipated changes. Legal issues will continue to be a difficult challenge for campus recreation directors. Negligence and sexual harassment lawsuits frequent court agendas. Discrimination and gender equity issues demand constant attention, and violence does not escape every college campus.

© *Daily Illini*

Recreational sport is programmed sport activity for the sake of participation and fun.

themselves may mandate eligibility restrictions through boards, committees, or councils. Most activities are structured into programs for men, women, and mixed participants (often called co-rec or coed), sometimes with varying levels of ability taken into consideration.

Groups with a common interest in a sport organize sport clubs. Clubs vary in focus and programming because the membership manages the operation. Membership interest may focus on teaching, team sponsorship, socialization, competition, or a combination of the four. Kent State University in Kent, Ohio, divides sport clubs into four categories. These include recreation, fitness and martial arts, special events, and competitive (McGregor, 1994). These categories depict different intents of the individuals involved.

Aquatic programming incorporates other avenues (e.g., instructional, intramural sport, informal, fitness) within the aquatic setting. For example, aerobics, a form of fitness programming, is often used in the aquatic setting and titled aquatic aerobics or some variation thereof. Intramural programming is used through swim meets between

fraternities or residence halls, and informal programming is incorporated by allowing free swim time throughout the pool's operating schedule.

Instructional programming, sometimes called noncredit instruction, involves arranging the teaching of sport skills, strategies, appreciation, rules, and regulations to educate the participant and improve performance. Methods such as clinics, short courses, and lessons incorporate individual or group teaching. Usually there are three levels of instruction: beginner, intermediate, and advanced. This differs from educational sport, defined as courses in which individuals may enroll and receive a grade at the course's completion. These educational sport courses, more frequently titled physical education classes, are offered through the appropriate academic department at the university. Aerobics, racquetball, or tennis are other examples of activities that fall under the instructional programming format.

Outdoor programming is defined as arranged experiences that involve outdoor activities, using resources such as mountains, lakes, rivers, parks, and caves. This area may also include the use of indoor climbing walls or pools to instruct students before participating in the natural outdoor setting. Planning trips to incorporate outdoor activities is a popular programming avenue for this portion of campus recreation.

Special events are arranged activities that introduce new programs or expand existing ones within and beyond sports. Examples of special events can be a holiday basketball tournament, an annual new student orientation activity week, or a dive-in movie night held in the campus pool. The special event is further defined as an event that may happen one time or annually. It is an event that generally takes a great deal of planning time, often incorporating more than one programming area or institutional department. However, one common element defining a special event is that it is concluded over a short time, usually lasting no longer than a week.

Special population programming targets students other than the traditional 18- to 24-year-old, able-bodied student who lives on campus in structured housing. Special programs or facility usage times may be targeted to include but not be limited to families of approved users; graduate students; commuters; or students who are physically challenged, international, or nontraditional.

Wellness programming can be broad and may incorporate the seven dimensions of wellness (physical, **social**, **spiritual**, **emotional**, **intellectual**, **career**, and **environmental**) (Jones, 1994, p. 67). The physical concept is the most widely used in campus recreation and may include cardiovascular training; body fat composition, nutrition and flexibility assessment; aerobic and weight training classes; as well as access to fitness facilities for self-directed participation. The remaining six concepts can be programmed by providing seminars, martial arts instructional classes, and cultural events, or by incorporating other programming avenues. Other campus departments are often involved in the programming aspect. For example, promoting Wellness Week on a college campus may involve individuals from the offices

## Learning Activity

Interview a sport or fitness manager working in the campus recreation field. Inquire about how he or she got into the field, certifications, association memberships, and recommendations for new managers attempting to gain employment.

of student development and the health center, as well as the campus recreation office.

## Financial Operation

Managing many campus recreation departments is the same as managing a large business. The amount of autonomy and responsibility the director has depends largely on the organizational structure of the institution. In the institutional setting, large or small, where there is a multimillion dollar recreation center or a program with diversified offerings, many directors are required to be profit centered. In other words, the facility should be run and programs offered in such a manner that revenue is generated to help offset their cost. Often faculty and staff must pay membership fees to use the facilities, and students gain access by paying fees through their tuition. At East Carolina University, students began paying a recreation facility fee of $16 per year 6 years before the opening of their $18-million facility. Fees were increased several times and, upon the 1997 opening, students were paying $200 per year as part of their student fee assessment. The faculty and staff membership fee for facility usage was initiated at $20 per month (N. Mize, personal communication, February 10, 1997). This plan is one example of what is becoming a common method of financing the multimillion dollar recreation facilities being constructed on college campuses today.

However, generating revenue by charging for access to the recreation center is not the only avenue available. Pay for play is common, in which intramural teams pay a small entry fee to participate. Operating dollars can also be raised by charging participants for the instructional programs, offering a towel service, and charging a locker rental fee.

Finally, it is important to realize that revenue generation is not a goal of every campus recreation department. Many institutions still fully support the recreation programs and the facilities in which they are housed through student development funding or physical education and athletic budgets. In many cases, a small recreation fee is charged each student, but rarely does it offset the entire cost of the college recreation program.

## Organizational Structure

Students and their parents are cost conscious in today's society and want the best value for their high tuition dollar. With modern recreation facilities and diversified program offerings, campus recreation departments can assist in recruiting and retaining students and faculty. Thus, a service-oriented recreation organization run as a business venture is becoming more common. To generate money, operate a modern recreation center, and offer diverse programming with quality service, universities must hire qualified individuals. The modern campus recreation department can employ several full-time recreational sport and facility managers and hundreds of student employees to meet the paying customer's needs and desires. Figure 10.1 illustrates the diversity of staff positions in the Department of Recreational at The

Ohio State University. This organizational chart was incorporated in 1995 as the department began master planning for the 21st century (J.M. Dunn, personal communication, February 12, 1997). Many positions shown can be staffed by sport management practitioners whose academic preparation was not focused on this setting. Examples of such positions are facility operations, marketing, and athletic training. These three career employment opportunities are gaining in popularity and necessity in this environment. Individuals gaining experience in these specific areas generally do not turn to campus recreation for employment. Thus, their

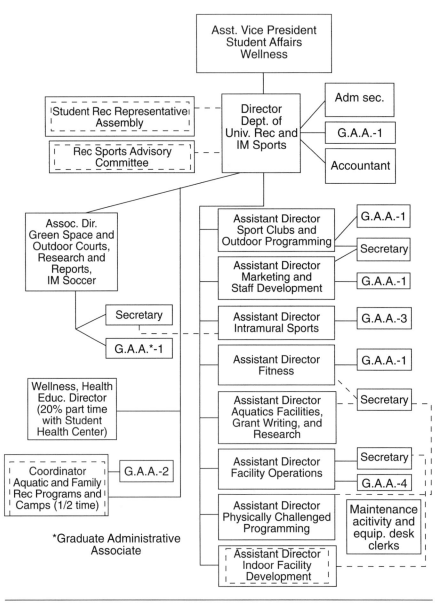

**Figure 10.1**  Ohio State University organizational chart for IM-Rec Sports.
Adapted, by permission, from Ohio State University.

uniqueness to this setting requires additional discussion.

## Learning Activity

Invite full-time employees of different university campus recreation departments to speak to your class about varying responsibilities. Ask them questions regarding organizational structure, future plans, services offered, and revenue sources to determine direction and emphasis for each institution.

### Facility Management

Employment in the facility management sector of campus recreation requires an individual who understands recreational sport programming formats and has a working knowledge of legal concepts, facility systems, terminology, and management concepts. Personnel management, particularly as it relates to students and motivational strategies, must be a strong asset for these individuals as they often hire all staff who clean, maintain, schedule, and supervise the facility. Management of the University of Georgia's Ramsey Center for Physical Activity, which opened in the fall of 1995, was assigned to campus recreation under the umbrella of student affairs. This facility, which houses recreation, physical education, and some athletic programs, encompasses 420,000 square feet and had a $40-million price tag, which included $3 million in moveable equipment (J. Russell, personal communication, February 10, 1997). Managing such a facility requires a great deal of expertise, and campus recreation managers must be prepared to accept these responsibilities. Discussions of various aspects of facility management are presented in chapters 9 and 13.

## Learning Activity

Visit institutions as a class project or during summer and spring breaks. Call in advance to schedule a tour of the recreation facility and offices. Prepare questions about programs offered, funding sources, program goals, facility management, and personnel development.

### Marketing and Promotions

These positions are important in the campus recreation setting, especially on campuses that must reach many students, particularly commuters. When a programmer initiates a new program, its success initially depends on how well the target market is understood and eventually on the promotional campaign used to attract participants. On a large campus, this can be a full- or part-time position or a requirement of each person's position. See chapters 9 and 12 for more information on marketing.

### Athletic Training

Athletic training is the newest employment position beginning to appear on campus recreation organizational charts. Although many universities use student trainers who need clinical hours for certification, some campus recreation departments are hiring NATA certified trainers to be available and supervise students in this area. The role of the athletic trainer in this setting is to handle emergencies when possible, but primarily to run a training room accessible to the campus recreation participant. Athletic training is discussed more fully in chapters 9 and 14.

## Careers in Campus Recreation

The recreational sport manager working in the college environment must have diversified skills and competencies. To be prepared for this field, an individual must gain a strong background in concept knowledge, develop a variety of competencies, and prepare for the future of this growing field. Later in this chapter, we discuss the political and social issues and trends within society that impact all higher education and, thus, are important to those studying for a career in campus recreation management. Understanding how society will impact this environment will help you become more adequately prepared for this employment path.

### Levels of Management

The NIRSA has identified three professional levels of employment. Level one is considered an entry-level leadership position. Examples of positions in this category may include programmer, program supervisor, activity instructor and specialist, or coordinator. NIRSA targets the undergraduate curriculum as the appropriate educational level at which the concept knowledge and competencies for level one positions should be gained.

Level two positions are considered middle management and could involve positions such as assistant director, coordinator, program supervisor, facility manager, and programmer. Competencies for these positions have been targeted as appropriate for the graduate-level curriculum. Level three includes the top management positions. Individuals who fall into this category have considerable experience and usually are in charge of the campus recreation program or a significant portion thereof. They may have several full-time employees under their supervision. Titles such as director, associate director, sports director, or recreational sport manager can fall into this category (National Intramural-Recreational Sports Association, 1992). Competencies at this level are usually gained exclusively through on-the-job training, advanced graduate-level study, or at specially designed institutes targeting the campus recreation or management setting. Please note, for all levels, job titles and responsibilities can differ among institutions and often relate to the size of the student body.

In general, an entry-level manager will start as a programmer with personnel management duties that involve supervising students and graduate assistants. As entry-level managers gain experience, they may move into middle management, where they take on more budgetary and strategic planning responsibilities. Personnel management may now involve supervising full-time employees. At the top level of management, the campus recreation director oversees the entire operation and becomes an advocate for the department. The director may serve on many university committees and be responsible for the overall fiscal operation. The director is often the facility manager thus she or he must be extremely knowledgeable regarding facility systems and maintenance. Reading and understanding architectural drawings and overseeing a facility construction project are not uncommon responsibilities for a top-level manager.

The competencies and concept knowledge necessary for individuals to gain entry into this career field vary greatly. Table 10.1 displays what NIRSA has identified as undergraduate- and graduate-level competencies necessary to compete for a position at one of the three management levels. Understandably, there is some overlap of information that you could learn either in an undergraduate or graduate curriculum as each institution will have different academic requirements. On-the-job training will be necessary to acquire some competencies. You can gain experience by working in your campus recreation program; student union programs; or any sport, recreation, or wellness facility within the community.

It is important for students to learn concept knowledge through appropriate college courses at both the undergraduate and graduate levels of study. It is not uncommon for an institution to require a minimum of a master's degree for entry-level positions. Additionally, many institutions are listing the Certified Recreational Sports Specialist (CRSS) certification as a required or recommended prerequisite for employment. Other certifications that are common prerequisites for employment may include the following, depending on the job description:

- First aid
- Cardiopulmonary resuscitation (CPR)
- Lifeguard certification
- Water safety instructor (WSI) or water safety instructor trainer (WSI-T)
- Certified pool operator (CPO)
- Varying levels of aerobic instructor, exercise leadership, or strength and conditioning certifications

## Salary Expectations

The NIRSA conducts an annual survey of its member institutions and universities that have at least one professional NIRSA member on staff. The 1995-1996 salary survey information was provided by 303 collegiate institutions for 14 professional categories typically found in the campus recreation setting. Table 10.2 illustrates the average salary provided by all institutions that responded and provides a comparison with results received from the 1991-1992 survey. According to the survey, the greatest salary gain in the past 5 years has been for individuals holding the title of assistant intramural director. The average salary reported was $28,900, which was a 23.5% increase over the 1991-1992 levels (National Intramural-Recreational Sports Association, 1996).

The average salary reported for a director of campus recreation in the survey was $45,400. Of course, the size of the institution plays a role in these numbers. You could reasonably expect a higher salary at a larger institution. As reported in the 1995-1996 survey, the average salary for a campus recreation director increased in 9 of the 11 enrollment categories as the size of the institutional enrollment rose. Salary ranges for this position, which were also listed in the survey, showed $20,000 to be the lowest individually reported salary, with the highest being $94,999. This highest

Table 10.1

## Competencies in Campus Recreation Management
## for Undergraduate and Graduate Study

| Knowledge area | Undergraduate level<br>Entry to middle management | Graduate level<br>Middle to top management |
|---|---|---|
| Foundations and philosophy | Knows basic recreational sport terms<br><br>Understands theories of competitive and cooperative play<br><br>Recognizes the philosophical values of recreational sports to the individual | Applies knowledge of the philosophical values of recreational sport to individuals<br><br>Understands the broad spectrum of recreational sport opportunities<br><br>Demonstrates a strong philosophical basis of recreational sport<br><br>Applies recreational sport terminology to all aspects of the program<br><br>Implements the theories of cooperative and competitive play<br><br>Differentiates among the philosophical purposes of recreational sports in relation to physical education and other departments and agencies administering recreational pursuits<br><br>Understands organizational and operational aspects of sport clubs or organizations |
| Management | Understands entry-level concepts in management<br><br>Understands the importance of effective communications with coworkers and other personnel<br><br>Understands leadership techniques and group dynamics<br><br>Understands principles of time management | Uses effective decision-making skills<br><br>Understands techniques in effective meeting management<br><br>Develops and maintains standards of quality for programs and services<br><br>Understands personnel selection, management, and evaluation<br><br>Develops and applies appropriate departmental policies and procedures<br><br>Demonstrates knowledge of organizational theory and behavior<br><br>Prepares and reviews committee, program, and informational reports<br><br>Evaluates and documents program development<br><br>Understands and implements strategic planning concepts<br><br>Demonstrates methods of securing participant involvement in leadership roles<br><br>Applies leadership techniques operational in recreational sport |
| Risk management and legal concepts | Recognizes factors that lead to accidents<br><br>Relates accident trends to eliminating hazards<br><br>Ensures safety through equipment maintenance | Comprehends legal implications in recreational sport<br><br>Processes contractual agreements for facility use and other recreational sport applications |

*(continued)*

### Table 10.1 *(continued)*

| Knowledge area | Undergraduate level<br>Entry to middle management | Graduate level<br>Middle to top management |
|---|---|---|
| Risk management and legal concepts *(continued)* | Familiar with effective decision-making techniques dealing with accidents<br><br>Understands specific risks inherent in managing sport<br><br>Understands the basics of tort law<br><br>Understands proper supervision and conduct of activities<br><br>Understands federal and state legislation that affects sport and the workplace | Applies appropriate federal and state legislation to programs and office environment<br><br>Develops and implements a risk-management plan<br><br>Understands aggression, its relationship to the sport participant and spectator, and possible criminal law implications<br><br>Understands collective bargaining<br><br>Understands and applies the legal aspects of product liability as a distributor |
| Facility management | Understands administration of a facility reservation system<br><br>Understands maintenance needs of facilities and equipment<br><br>Understands policy and procedure regarding inspections of facilities and equipment, inventory and storage of supplies, and user eligibility | Recognizes program needs in facility design<br><br>Comprehends design specifications of equipment and facilities<br><br>Develops and maintains planning schedules, both long and short range, for improvement, construction, and maintenance of facilities<br><br>Administers a facility scheduling and event management system<br><br>Organizes a reporting system of maintenance needs and routine investigations of facilities and equipment<br><br>Understands efficient use of facility systems |
| Governance | Identifies procedures to regulate the conduct of spectators and participants<br><br>Understands procedures for settling protests<br><br>Prepares written documentation of cases dealing with protests<br><br>Understands supervisory controls that prevent participant misuse of a facility<br><br>Understands participant development | Demonstrates ability to organize an advisory or appeals board<br><br>Develops and implements a code of conduct and appeals for participants |
| Public relations, marketing, and promotions | Maintains effective communications with the public<br><br>Identifies and encourages participants for programs<br><br>Understands basic practices for effective program promotion | Promotes effective communications with public and staff<br><br>Coordinates interagency cooperation<br><br>Prepares and delivers public presentations<br><br>Develops a system that identifies new initiatives for program and facility development<br><br>Develops publicity approaches for encouraging program participation<br><br>Understands marketing research and its application in campus recreation |
| Computer and technological applications | Understands basic computer terminology and commercial software applications | Identifies and selects appropriate computer hardware and software |

| Knowledge area | Undergraduate level<br>Entry to middle management | Graduate level<br>Middle to top management |
|---|---|---|
| Computer and techno-logical applications *(continued)* | Familiar with software available for recreational sport, fitness programming, and facility supervision<br>Knowledge of basic computer skills | Understands available technology for the purpose of improving employee productivity<br>Coordinates department's use of technological applications with other departments and agencies |

| Undergraduate level | Graduate level |
|---|---|
| **Programming techniques**<br>Understands organizational and operational aspects of recreational sport programming<br>Demonstrates ability to schedule tournaments, leagues, and meets<br>Develops and maintains procedures for postpone-ments, rescheduling, and forfeits<br>Observes and supervises recreational program participants<br>Knows and understands levels of competition in sport<br>Understands participant recognition and its importance<br><br>**Exercise science and fitness/wellness research**<br>Understands basic anatomy and physiology<br>Understands scientific applications to exercise and fitness<br>Understands the importance of exercise testing and prescription<br>Understands wellness concepts and their program-ming application<br><br>**Officiating**<br>Understands basic officiating skills and techniques, game rules, interpretation, and application<br>Handles player misconduct in the game environment<br>Understands effective organization, training, schedul-ing, and supervision of officials<br><br>**Certifications in specialized activity areas**<br>Understands components of the Certified Recreational Sports Specialist (CRSS) certification<br>Obtains necessary certifications in CPR and First Aid<br>Understands basic certifications available for aquat-ics, aerobics, fitness management, and martial arts<br><br>**Recreational sport skills acquisitions**<br>This section implies that an individual could acquire an entry-level position with instructional sport responsibilities. An individual may wish to become proficient in one or more sport skill areas (e.g., racquetball, tennis, aerobics). | **Psychology and sociology**<br>Knows levels of competition in sport<br>Recognizes aggression problems of participants<br>Understands socialization process evident in sport<br>Understands the effects of recreational sport on personality and attitude<br><br>**Research**<br>Applies statistical tools to program evaluation, financial analysis, and planning<br>Understands survey methods for program analysis<br>Understands the process of creative writing and publishing<br>Knows existing research in recreational sport<br>Collects and analyzes program participation statistics<br>Knows measuring instruments appropriate to statistical analysis<br>Constructs problems appropriate to recreational sport research<br>Understands outcomes assessment, its use, and importance particularly in the educational setting<br>Understands and applies the guidelines of human subject research<br><br>**Budget and finance**<br>Prepares and defends a budget proposal<br>Understands fiscal management including revenue control<br>Identifies sources of income for budget<br>Applies purchasing policies and procedures<br>Prepares financial reporting statements<br>Initiates effective office procedures for handling registrations, forfeits, and other program components involving monetary income<br>Develops, implements, and evaluates program fee structures |

Adapted, by permission, from *Recreational sports: A curriculum guide*, 1992. NIRSA, 8-12.

Table 10.2

**Five-Year Comparison of Salary Averages by Campus Recreation Employment Position**

| Position | 1991-92 avg. | 1995-96 avg. | 5-year comparison |
|----------|--------------|--------------|-------------------|
| Rec Spts. Director | $38,700 | $45,400 | +17.3% |
| Assoc. Director | $35,400 | $41,500 | +17.2% |
| Asst. Director | $28,500 | $31,900 | +11.9% |
| IM Spts. Director | $28,800 | $33,700 | +17.0% |
| Asst. IM Director | $23,400 | $28,900 | +23.5% |
| Sport Club Director | $30,600 | $33,400 | +9.15% |
| Informal Spt. Director | $27,300 | $32,500 | +19.0% |
| Facility Director | $31,500 | $33,100 | +5.08% |
| Instructional Prgm. Director | $30,600 | $33,100 | +8.17% |
| Outdoor Rec Director | $28,500 | $30,400 | +6.67% |
| Aquatics Director | $28,800 | $31,600 | +9.72% |
| Ice Arena Director | $32,700 | $34,600 | +5.81% |
| Fitness Director | $28,200 | $31,000 | +9.93% |
| Wellness Director | — | $31,300 | — |

Adapted, by permission, from *NIRSA Newsletter*, Spring, 1996, (Corvallis, OR: NIRSA) 8.

salary was reported by an institution that had an enrollment between 30,001 and 35,000 students (National Intramural-Recreational Sports Association, 1996).

# Challenges for Campus Recreation Managers

History has seen the campus recreation environment move from an alternative employment setting for physical educators and coaches toward a specialist's profession. As mentioned earlier, students and parents are becoming consumer oriented in their search for a postsecondary institution and demand the best in facilities, programs, and services. With tuition increasing every year, institutions will continue to compete for students. Colleges that recognize the value of campus recreation, hire professionally prepared managers, and insist on building quality and aesthetically pleasing facilities will be the winners in recruitment. Between 1994 and 2005, college enrollment is expected to increase by 1,188,000 students while high school graduates during this time are expected to increase by only 535,000 ("Fact File," 1995). This continues a long-term trend noticed during the first half of the 1980s. Forecasters predicted a college enrollment crash because the number of high school graduates was declining, but enrollment actually increased by 7% (O'Keefe, 1985).

What the forecasters did not consider was the nontraditional population enrolling in increasing numbers.

In the 21st century, we will see dramatic changes in postsecondary education. Technological changes will be the front runner. **Distance learning** has been around for a long time in the form of correspondence courses. However, with satellites, the Internet, fiber optic cables, virtual reality, and other technological advances, the way students learn 10 years into the 21st century may be quite different than our educational system today. Will students actually come to campus to obtain their degrees or will an entire college education be garnered over the computer screen? We hope not, as much can be said for human interaction in the learning and mentoring process.

If we apply technological advances to the physical fitness and recreation realm, campus recreation managers will certainly have to stay abreast of the changes. How will people exercise? We already see computers in exercise equipment. Will we obtain fitness with ease by enhanced technology that has not yet become part of our thinking?

Society's impact on the recreation field is ever changing. With more women working outside the home and more households having two incomes, some perceive the amount of leisure time available to be shrinking. Will this stay the same? Many individuals have observed the downfall of the family unit in society and consciously choose to

As time for leisure shrinks in our culture, we need to strive to make the most of the hours we do have.

4 years to complete college due to numerous part-time jobs and having to pay for their rising tuition costs. Campus recreation managers must understand these societal changes and plan their programs and facilities around the campus community. This will assist the university in attracting and retaining students, faculty, and staff because of the increased services offered.

Finally, what will campus recreation managers be programming? Many campuses have seen a decrease in participation in traditional intramural programs and have had difficulty attracting female participants. Perhaps some programmers are already behind the trends. In 1992, rugby was the fastest growing sport among women in the United Kingdom, and the United States had more than 162 women's rugby clubs; more than half the boxers at West Los Angeles's Bodies in Motion gym were women; and 10% of travel fell into the outdoor recreation category (Aburdene & Naisbitt, 1992). How many colleges have in-line hockey leagues? In the 21st century, campus recreation will have to compete for the student's leisure time, and activities will have to be entertaining. The programming agenda will increasingly include ideas that emphasize recreation as an alternative to drugs and alcohol and perhaps a safe haven away from the violence of the streets. The recreational agenda must change with society.

## Learning Activity

Apply for a part-time job or volunteer to work in your institution's campus recreation department, other departments offering recreation programming, or a sport and fitness facility. Learn about all facets of the organization.

stay at home with children, sacrificing a larger family income. As a result, job sharing is becoming more popular as are flexible work schedules.

To accommodate flexible work schedules, Brown (1990) predicted that by the year 2000, 24-hour campus recreation facilities may be common. Many campuses are using a 16- to 17-hour operating schedule with ice rinks pushing the open times into the early hours of the morning. Further proof of this shows high schools are seeing the value of holding classes in the afternoons and evenings to allow students to work and help support their families (Thurston, 1995). Increasingly, students are taking more than the traditional

## Summary

Campus recreation programs (also known as recreational sport programs) had their beginnings in sport clubs, an English tradition. Originally, these clubs were managed by students, but faculty eventually gained control. Today, campus recreation programs exist to provide a variety of programs for students, faculty, and staff and to enhance the quality of campus community life. Campus recreation programming varies widely from campus to campus. Examples of the types of programming that exist are recreational sport (extramurals, informal, intramurals, and sport clubs); aquatics, instructional, and outdoor programs; special events; programs for special populations; and wellness programs.

Campus recreation programs are financed in several ways. Some are funded by membership fees, whereas others charge fees to participating teams. Fewer and fewer are supported solely by the university. In all cases, however, the facility and the program must be managed professionally and usually must generate some revenue to defray costs.

Large campus recreation departments might employ several full-time sport and facility man-agers and hundreds of students. Employment op-portunities are particularly optimistic in facility management, marketing and promotions, and ath-letic training. The National Intramural-Recreational Sports Association has identified the competen-cies required for three levels of employment in campus recreation. Campus recreation profession-als must be aware of the influence their services have in recruiting students, conversant with mod-ern technology, informed about legal issues, and abreast of social change.

# For More Information

Please utilize the following resources to learn more about the campus recreation field.

## Governing Bodies

- National Intramural-Recreational Sports Association (NIRSA)
- Canadian Intramural-Recreation Associa-tion (CIRA)

## Professional Publications

- *NIRSA Journal*

- *Canadian Intramural-Recreation Association Journal*
- *Athletic Business*
- *Fitness Management*
- *Aquatics International*
- *Journal of Physical Education, Recreation and Dance*

# Job Opportunities

## Assistant Director of Recreational Sports

The University of Mont-Blanc invites applicants for the position of Assistant Director of Recreational Sports. Position involves full management of campus intramural sports program, management of informal recreation program, and development of special events for the department. Master's degree in a recreation- or sport-related field and minimum of 2 years practical experience in recreational sports program management required. Excellent written and oral communication, interpersonal, and organizational skills desired. Applicants with experience in computer operation, budgeting, fiscal and statistical management, program evaluation, and risk management preferred. NIRSA Recreational Sports Specialist certification appreciated. Flexible work schedule; salary commensurate with experience and qualifications.

## Coordinator of Outdoor Recreation Program

Mesa University is seeking an individual to manage the Outdoor Recreation Program. Responsibilities will involve management of outdoor equipment rental; equipment maintenance and inventory; documentation of financial records; fiscal and personnel management, including staff recruitment and training; and development and management of trips and clinics. Master's degree in a recreation, sport, or higher education administration area and 3 years experience in outdoor recreation management required. NIRSA Recreational Sports Specialist, first aid, and CPR certifications preferred. Salary is $28,000 to $30,000, plus full benefits depending on qualifications.  Full-time, 12-month appointment.

## Coordinator of Intramural Sports

South Baja College is seeking an individual to coordinate the Intramural and Special Events Program.  Responsibilities include  budgeting; program development; and staffing, supervising, and evaluating all full- and part-time employees (student-staff included). Master's degree in a sport- or recreation-related field and a minimum of 1 year intramural sports management experience required. Experience in staff supervision and proven good personal skills preferred. First aid and CPR certification desired. Full-time, 12-month position, with salary commensurate with education and experience.

## Campus Recreation-Intramural Director

Southern Vermont University is seeking a qualified individual to serve as Intramural Director. Job duties include managing rosters, scheduling contests, managing intramurals, and tracking and monitoring attendance. A bachelor's degree is needed and Certified Recreation Sport Specialist preferred. Also need experience and proficiency in intramurals. Salary is $22,500.

## Fitness Facility Director

The Mt. St. Margaret University invites applicants for Director of the Campus Five Fitness Centers. Administrative responsibilities include (a) training, scheduling, and supervising staff; (b) maintaining equipment and supplies; (c) establishing and enforcing program guidelines; and (d) budgeting for all resources. A bachelor's degree required; master's degree preferred. Three years experience in managing fitness facilities desired but not necessary. Position open until filled.

## Fitness Center Coordinator

The Fitness Center Coordinator at Aspen State University will be responsible for programs involving the campus fitness center. Responsible for programming wellness and special events, sport club advertisement and staffing, and part-time strength and conditioning of student athletes. A 12-month commitment is required. Master's degree preferred; however, those individuals with a bachelor's degree in the appropriate area of specialization and 3 years experience will be considered.  Must be committed to working with diverse populations.

## Director of Recreational Sports

Southport University is seeking qualified individuals to fill the position of Recreational Sports Director. Requirements include 5 years experience in collegiate physical education, recreation, or student affairs related programs. Educational requirements include a master's degree in physical education, sport management, or related field. Primary administrative duties include direction of personnel, programming, and financial resources of Recreational Sports. Responsible for the informal recreation, recreational sports, intramural and sport clubs, and outdoor recreation programs. Salary is commensurate with education and experience.

# Chapter 11

# Sport Communication

**Catherine A. Pratt**
Bowling Green State University

---

## Learning Objectives

After studying this chapter, you will be able to

1. explain the breadth of sport-related careers that depend for their success on solid communication skills;

2. understand the skill and knowledge base necessary to pursue a sport communication career;

3. discuss the journalistic process with examples of how the print and broadcast media function in covering sport;

4. identify ways that communication technology has affected sport communication;

5. recognize the power inherent in many sport communication careers; and

6. discuss ethical issues associated with careers in sport communication.

---

Most of us who fantasized about a career in sport realized early that professional participation as an athlete was beyond our talents. This reality, however, does not have to eliminate a career that involves a primary focus on sport. Many of you might find just such a career in the field of communication. Nearly every newspaper, magazine, broadcast station, and cable network has one or more sports journalists—those writers, photographers, and videographers who cover the sports beat. In addition, many athletic and fitness organizations employ individuals for **promotion** or publicity purposes under titles or designations that may include terms like sports information, public relations, or community relations.

In this chapter, you will learn about four primary aspects of sport communication. First, you will learn about the communication process— what it is, why an understanding of it is essential, and how you can improve your communication skills. Second, you will learn about communication career opportunities specifically related to sport. These opportunities are presented in two categories. The first type of communicators are the journalists—the individuals who work in the print or broadcast media to convey information to the public. The second category is the insider type of communicators—those individuals who work in specific organizations or agencies to convey information from the inside to the media and to the public. You will learn that if you prepare yourself appropriately and work hard, there could be opportunities for you in both categories.

The third topic addressed in this chapter is technology and its effect on the communication process. We give specific attention to the impact of technological advances in television and computers on sport communication. Fourth, we discuss the area of ethics. Understanding and appreciating socially responsible behavior is a bottom line requirement for a career in sport communication.

# Importance of Communication Skills

Regardless of the setting, all the occupational choices in this chapter share a common denominator: the ability to communicate well. Creating a message that accurately and effectively communicates your ideas to the audience you want to reach is the foundation for success in these fields. Failure to understand effective **communication** techniques is usually a prelude to unproductive or counterproductive efforts.

Every activity that involves more than one person includes some form of interpersonal, group, or **mass communication**. In fact, because everything we do has a communication component, you could argue that it is impossible to *not* communicate. However, not all communication is successful communication. Remember the popular game called gossip that involved whispering a sentence to the person in the next seat, who then whispered it to the next person, continuing until the message had been passed along by everyone playing the game? The outcome is a final message that differs radically from the original whispered communication. Although this may be an amusing game, the results are not funny when we fail to communicate our message in situations in which accurate communication is important. Imagine what would happen if coaches failed to communicate game strategy to

their players or if the brochure you received in the mail heralding the opening of the city's new recreation facility included an incorrect opening date. Imagine how frustrating it would be to read a story about yesterday's big sports contest, only to find out that the report was so jumbled and inaccurate, you could not figure out who won the game!

## Becoming a Good Communicator

In most communication situations, we want our audience to understand and, frequently, to act on our communication in a predictable or preferred manner. Although good communication is a necessary tool in nearly every human endeavor, sports information and sports journalism rely on communication as a primary function. Individuals in these occupations need a solid understanding of the communication process to do their jobs effectively.

So, how do you become a proficient communicator? There's the old cliche: "How do you get to Carnegie Hall? Practice, practice, practice!" Certainly practice (i.e., experience) is an important ingredient. Even individuals looking for a first job in most communications fields are expected to have picked up some experience, whether through education, internship, or volunteer activities. In addition to experience, understanding how we communicate and how we can help or hinder communication effectiveness enhances the learning potential of our communication practice. Reinventing the wheel is a waste of time! Individuals who study the established principles of effective communication can avoid mistakes and eliminate wasted effort.

## Model for Being a Good Communicator

Communication scholars have suggested that theoretical ideas are easier to understand if they can be presented as a diagram or model. Several communication models, from basic to sophisticated, have been developed to explain aspects of how we communicate, how we ought to communicate, obstacles to communication, and communication effects. The most well-known and useful models share an approach that treats communication as a process, with identifiable components arranged to explain the process. The most commonly accepted components are the source, the message, the channel through which the message is delivered, and the receiver. When combined with the concepts of **encoding**, **decoding**, feedback, and noise, these components offer a useful description of the communication process with a practical advantage: The better we understand the process the more likely we are to communicate well.

In the model we present in figure 11.1, the communication source could be a person speaking, a photograph in the newspaper, a sports reporter's story on the evening news, or a billboard announcing the opening of a new fitness facility. The channel through which the message is delivered could be face-to-face spoken words (and the accompanying voice, expression, and gesture cues), print media (e.g., newspapers, magazines), or broadcast or cable media (i.e., radio, television). The receiver of the communication could be one or several individuals involved in a conversation, the readers of a magazine, or the viewers of a prime-time sporting event on television.

The encoding and decoding components of the communication model refer to the inescapable fact that every sender and receiver of communication assigns meaning to the communicated message. This meaning may or may not be readily apparent. Think about the times you've heard or seen something that did not make sense to you. Think, too, about instances when you thought you knew the meaning of some communication, but later you discovered your interpretation was incorrect. Maybe this helps explain why seeing isn't always believing!

Feedback refers to communication that returns to the original sender through deliberate or inadvertent responses on the part of the receiver.

Feedback helps the communicator understand whether or not the correct message is being received. It provides information for future communication. The number of fans who respond to a game promotion or show up at team photo night, phone calls concerning a change in the services offered by a recreation facility, and a letter to the editor about one of your sports stories in the paper would be considered feedback.

Noise can be literal: Fans yelling at a sporting event may drown out the field announcer relaying an important message. It can also be figurative: A badly printed brochure with smeared type or colors out of register would hinder communication effectiveness and, thus, be a form of noise. The goal in communicating is to minimize or eliminate noise so there are as few impediments as possible in the communication process.

It is also important to remember that even the best-intentioned and best-fashioned communication may be ignored, misinterpreted, or forgotten. The terminology for these pitfalls are **selective attention**, **selective perception**, and **selective retention**. Selective attention refers to the tendency we all have to seek communication that relates to topics in which we already have an interest. Selective perception refers to interpreting information to reinforce what we already believe. Selective retention describes our inclination to remember those things we find comfortable and useful, forgetting the things we dislike or make us uncomfortable. Each concept feeds on the basic human need to avoid conflict or *cognitive*

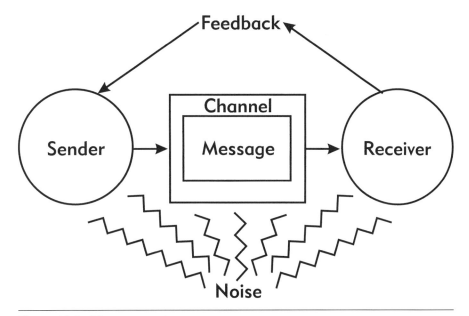

**Figure 11.1**   The communication process.

*dissonance*—the emotional or intellectual discomfort we feel when messages conflict with our strongly held beliefs. Effective communication requires an understanding of human nature and its need to protect itself through strategies like selective attention, perception, and retention.

Here is one additional concept that might make the communication process clearer. Schramm, a highly respected communication scholar, and Porter argued that for communication to exist, the sender and the receiver must share something: a common language, vocabulary, or interest in the subject. The more the sender and receiver share, the easier it is for them to communicate effectively. Schramm and Porter's point is a useful one to consider whenever you communicate. Ask yourself how much you and the receiver of the communication share. If you can increase the level of shared interest, you will increase the likelihood that your communication efforts will be successful.

Individuals with strong communication skills and an interest in sport can pursue a communication career that builds on that interest. Sport communication career opportunities include options such as a collegiate sports information director; promotion director for a community fitness and recreation facility; health promotions manager; public relations officer or marketing director for a professional sports team; and such diverse media communication careers as print or broadcast sports reporting, broadcast sports production, and creating fitness books, videos, or television infomercials on fitness products.

## Sports Journalist

Sports journalists might work as reporters, covering news and writing articles for a newspaper or magazine. They might work for a radio, television, or cable outlet, covering and packaging reports on sport-related topics. Sports journalists might be photographers for print publications or videographers and editors for television. Although the most prominent area of coverage has traditionally been competitive sport, individuals working for the media outlets in sports journalism cover a variety of topics, including nearly every recreational sport activity.

Success in sports journalism may lead to a similar position on a bigger publication or in a larger market, but it can also result in a position of greater authority at the same media outlet (e.g., an editor's job or a promotion into management).

Some sports journalists cross over from the journalistic side of covering athletics to promotion and public relations jobs with professional or collegiate athletics organizations. People working in the field range from your local newspaper's sports reporter to the person in charge of sports programming for a major network, plus everything in between. Because the field's most prominent jobs are those connected with network television and professional athletics, sports journalism has an aura of glamour. Many people head into the field without giving enough thought to the demands of a career in this area, and many people fail because they didn't obtain the proper academic and extracurricular preparation necessary to land and succeed in that critical first job.

It has been said that journalists write the first draft of history. Sports journalists are no different from other journalists in that respect. Some recent articles written about sports have included events more likely to be found on the front page of the news section than on the sports page. Drug abuse in professional and college athletics, the controversy over whether college athletes are getting a real education, and other negative stories may not be what sports fans want to read about, but these stories are news, and a journalist's job is to investigate the news and get the facts to the public.

These investigations, however, are not usually part of the daily routine of the sports journalist. A sports journalist working in a small city might be most interested in high school and amateur athletics, and a sports reporter in a city with one or more professional sport franchises might cover a professional team exclusively. Day-to-day work includes both news (e.g., game stories, unusual events from player trades, or a change in ownership) and feature stories (e.g., player profiles, background pieces on the competition, or a history of the team name or mascot). A sports reporter also frequently offers an analysis or commentary about the prospects of the team or the strengths and weaknesses of some aspect of the team or game. News reporters don't routinely write these stories because news commentary is usually reserved for the editorial page. Sports reporters, however, frequently include opinion, commentary, and more emotion-charged adjectives in their analysis than their news counterparts.

Of course, the most thorough coverage is always reserved for special events in sports: the Olympics, the World Series, the NCAA Men's and Women's Final Four, or the Super Bowl. During these major events—and in the weeks (sometimes months) preceding them—a plethora of stories appears from all levels of sports reporting. National publications cover the upcoming events in great detail, and local publications frequently send sports reporters to cover the event itself or pre-event activities. If the national event involves participation by a local athlete or team, even the small town sports reporter can become involved in the continuous coverage that includes preevent predictions, event coverage, and postevent analysis.

Whatever their specific jobs, sports journalists work in one of two categories: print journalism or broadcast journalism. Print journalism includes newspapers—from your local paper to the *New York Times*—and magazines such as *Newsweek* and *Esquire*, which may do occasional stories on athletics, or *Sports Illustrated* and *Sporting News*, publications that concentrate exclusively on covering athletics. Broadcast journalism includes local radio and television stations as well as networks like NBC, ESPN, and CNN. ESPN and CNN are cable networks, not traditional broadcast networks. Technologically, there are differences, but from the perspective of the sports journalist, the differences are negligible. Although print and broadcast journalists share many tasks, there are differences, both in the prerequisites for getting into the field and in the daily routine once there.

## Careers in Print Journalism for Sports Journalists

Sports journalists working for newspapers usually start as reporters and may eventually work into an editor's slot. Reporters are assigned a specific area of coverage or "beat." On a small newspaper this may mean all area high school sports. On a larger newspaper the total sports coverage is likely to be greater and the staff larger, so the beats may be more narrowly assigned. A reporter working in a market with one or more major college or professional teams may cover a single college or team during the season, writing game stories and news about the team as well as generating feature stories.

Reporters for small newspapers sometimes take photographs in addition to writing about sports, but most papers have full-time photographers. Magazines like *Sports Illustrated* have an entire staff of photographers. A photographer interested in sport is likely to start as a general assignment photographer and, with luck and talent, eventually work into full-time sports photography for a large paper or magazine.

Novice journalists generally have difficulty landing a full-time job on a magazine. Many magazines keep their full-time writing staffs small and rely on freelance writers. Editors at magazines are rarely entry-level personnel, and photographers usually have significant experience before joining the staff.

## The World of Print Journalism

Every day, 113 million adults read some part of a newspaper (*Standard Rate and Data Service (SRDS)*, 1996). The 1996 edition of *SRDS* lists more than 1,500 daily newspapers and nearly 7,500 weekly newspapers in the United States, and most of them cover sports to some extent. Although the number of staff members exclusively handling sports journalism assignments may be limited on small papers, a mid-1980s newspaper survey cited in *SRDS* found that, among the surveyed papers, an average of 19% of the reporters were assigned to sports, the largest percentage in any category—even general assignment! *SRDS* also noted that 90% of adults in the United States read one or more magazines regularly, and many of them select one or more of the 100 magazines devoted entirely to sports. Some of these magazines cover a variety of sports, like *Sports Illustrated*, which is the only sport publication among the top 20 nationally circulated magazines (*SRDS*, 1996). Other magazines find success with coverage of a single sport. *Golf Digest* and *Golf*, examples of single-sport publications, rank among the top 50 nationally circulated magazines (*SRDS*, 1996).

## Characteristics of Print Journalism

Working for a newspaper or magazine as a sports journalist requires a talent for writing with speed, clarity, and accuracy. On a daily newspaper, the deadlines come every 24 hours or more frequently. On a weekly newspaper the deadlines are less pressured, but they are not leisurely. Magazines have several deadlines, depending on the kind of material involved. For a journalist, deadlines are part of the career package. A person who cannot adhere to established deadlines should steer clear of a career in journalism.

The clarity and accuracy aspects of journalism are just as important for sports journalists as for journalists covering any other story. Journalists write in a style that may vary with the paper or magazine, but, in general, a career in journalism involves communicating in a clear, crisp style that is as objective as possible. Even beginners in the field are expected to have mastered the basics of journalistic writing, such as using the **inverted pyramid style**.

The field also requires a healthy curiosity. Being a reporter means spending time figuring out the right questions to ask and how to get the answers. There is a lot of homework involved in sports journalism, much background research you must do before the interview or story begins.

If you are interested in becoming a sports reporter or photographer for a newspaper or magazine, get as much experience as possible while still in college. The first step is usually to volunteer for your college paper. Sometimes that is not as easy as it sounds, because the sports section is usually a popular place for volunteers. You may have to be persistent and write a few stories on *spec*; that is, cover the event without a promise that the paper will use your story. Then submit it to the sports editor to demonstrate your writing skills. In addition to good writing skills, college newspapers also hold dependability in high regard. Because most staffers are not paid, editors know that the sports writer has some other reason for grinding out the copy. If you see your college paper as a stepping-stone in your career path and can convince your editor that you are willing to work hard and are dependable, you have a good shot at climbing the first step in the proverbial ladder of success.

A good second step is to approach the sports editor of your local newspaper with several of your best *clips*, stories with your by-line that have appeared in print. Some local newspapers will hire college students during the school year or in the summer either as interns or as *stringers*, part-time writers who get paid only when they are given a specific assignment or when the paper accepts something they write. Small newspapers with limited staff resources are especially interested in good stringers during high school tournament time, when the regular staff may be stretched in many directions.

The experience you gain while still in school should minimize the most frequent problem college graduates encounter when they look for their first job: no experience. Although your full-time experience will be limited, your job search should be easier because you will already have clips to show a prospective employer as proof that you can produce good copy. If the stories carry your name or by-line, all the better. You should neatly collect your clips, using the actual newspaper copies, not your original copy, in a portfolio and present it during your job interview or, in some cases, send it to the prospective employer before the interview. The portfolio can be as simple as several stories neatly placed in a manila folder or as formal as a collection presented in a three-ring binder. The important thing is to collect clips that best showcase your ability to cover a variety of assignments well. Your first full-time sports reporting job is likely to be with a small newspaper, but this should lead to a job at a larger paper and perhaps a position as sports editor.

## Learning Activity

Collect 1 week's worth of sports pages from your local newspaper, and analyze the stories included in the sports section. Try to determine which stories are hard news and which are feature stories.

Look at the stories that have by-lines and those that don't; notice which are written by local reporters and which are from the wire services. Compare several stories with stories from the front page of the paper. Do their styles differ? Does the sport story contain more reporter opinion? If you live in a community that does not have a professional or major college team, go to your library, find a copy of a daily newspaper from a large city like New York or Chicago, and compare the sports section of that paper with your local paper.

## Careers in Broadcast Journalism for Sports Journalists

Sports journalists who would like to work either in **broadcasting** or cable television reporting usually want to be on-air sports reporters. Major radio stations in large markets and television stations in smaller markets have at least one full-time sports reporter who also serves as the sports anchor on newscasts. These reporters frequently carry the title of sports director or sports editor. Many stations also have one or more assistants in the sports department who handle stories assigned by the sports director and perhaps handle on-air anchor assignments during weekends. At small stations these assistants may spend only part of their time covering sports and the rest as general assignment reporters. In a market that occasionally broadcasts the games of local sports teams, the local radio or television sports reporter may have the opportunity to do play-by-play or color commentary. If a specific station broadcasts all the team's games, a contractual agreement between the station and the team may determine who anchors the broadcast.

Radio sports reporters usually work alone, sometimes using a portable cassette recorder to get the voice of the person being interviewed for on-air use. Television sports reporters have to think of visuals for the story as well as the sound. At small stations, the reporter may have to handle a video camera and recorder, acting as reporter and videographer for routine assignments. In larger stations and at most stations with union labor contracts, the reporter is assigned a videographer who operates the camera while the reporter directs the story and conducts the interview. At most television stations, reporters edit or help edit their stories, using a variety of videotape and digital technologies.

Deadlines are as critical in broadcast journalism as in print journalism. A story finished at 6:30 P.M. cannot be used on the 6:00 P.M. news. Radio stories frequently require audio production time, and television stories usually include video that must be shot, selected, and edited with the journalist's voice over. These additional requirements mean that preparation time in broadcast sports journalism is sometimes tight.

Behind-the-camera jobs in sports broadcasting are not always technically considered journalism careers, but they are certainly related to the business of sports journalism. These jobs include the directors, producers, videographers, and other technical personnel necessary to air a sports event or a news program. Many broadcast journalists get valuable experience or make important industry contacts early in their careers by working as freelance production assistants on sports productions.

## Characteristics of Broadcast Journalism

All the concerns about writing well and quickly apply even more strongly to broadcast journalism, where deadlines may be hourly, not daily, and where stories usually have to be told in 30-second or 1-minute packages. Writing for the ear rather than the eye requires straightforward sentence structure and the ability to condense sometimes complicated ideas into a clear, concise style.

## The World of Broadcast Journalism

There is no shortage of radio and television stations in the United States and no shortage of audience willing to listen and watch. There are about 584 million radios in the United States, with about 373 million classified as home or personal radios and the remainder designated as out-of-home (mostly car) radios, according to the 1995 edition of *Broadcasting and Cable Yearbook (B and CY)*, a standard industry reference. *B and CY* also listed more than 1,500 television stations and nearly 12,000 radio stations (4,923 AM and 6,778 FM). Just over 98% of U.S. homes have at least one television set and almost two thirds of those homes tune in on an average night in prime time (8-11 P.M.) (*B and CY*, 1995). Schaaf (1995) reported a study revealing that Americans watched an average of 179 hours of sport programming annually.

Some television and radio stations are noncommercial or educational, but most are commercial stations. Television stations are either affiliated with a network (e.g., ABC, CBS, NBC, Fox) or operate as independent stations with limited or no network affiliation. Most network affiliates have local news and, thus, sport programming. Television networks have additional sport personnel to cover events on a regular or special basis, for example, NFL football or a championship tennis match. Obviously, ESPN and ESPN2 require a large number of sports reporters and anchors to handle their all-sport format. Some programs that air on ESPN, however, are sold to the network as a package, complete with announcers and commentators under contract to the company producing the program, not the network airing it. Radio stations are less likely to have full-time sports journalists on staff, but in big markets the top stations may have someone who handles sports reporting. Radio stations with all news or talk formats usually have a sport staff as well.

The healthy curiosity required of print journalists is just as important in broadcast journalism. However, in addition to researching the story and asking the right questions, broadcast journalists must also think about the audio and video aspects of media. Radio reporters, including sports reporters, always look for a good **actuality**, a quote from the news maker that is sandwiched into a news story to allow the listener to hear the words

## Hear, Hear!

Broadcast writing style differs from the style that print journalists use. Broadcasters use the present and present perfect tenses in their reports, whereas print journalists usually write in the past tense. Thus, a print journalist might write the following: "The coach *said* the team is ready for the playoff game" (past tense of *to say*). A broadcast journalist would phrase the copy one of these two ways: "The coach *says* the team is ready for the playoff game" (present tense of *to say*). "The coach *has said* the team is ready for the playoff game" (present perfect tense of *to say*). This differing style has developed, in part, because of the distinction traditionally cited between print and broadcast journalism: Print journalism provides a relatively permanent record of news events and offers the opportunity for in-depth analysis; broadcast offers more immediacy and brings us the latest-breaking news events but is frequently limited to the highlights of an individual story because of time constraints. Broadcast journalists also use more contractions and less formal construction than print journalists. The reason for this, of course, is that print journalists write to be read; broadcast journalists write to be heard.

## Learning Activity

Select a favorite sport or team and research the information necessary for a color commentary during the team's next competition. If you have access to a VCR and an audiotape recorder, tape both television and radio coverage of the same sporting event. Listen to the similarities and differences in how the announcers handle the play-by-play and the color commentary.

of the person being interviewed. Television reporters have to be aware of possible pictures to go along with their stories: the video that shows people working out in the community's new fitness facility or a feature on a local high school basketball player explaining in her own words—a sound bite—how she developed her unstoppable hook shot.

Broadcast journalism has some requirements that do not pertain to print journalism. These center on the performance aspect of broadcasting and include the reporter's voice and appearance. Although broadcast journalism is frequently criticized as a place where pretty people make happy talk, jobs in this field are not limited to attractive, deep-voiced males and pretty, perky women. However, the ability to speak well, think quickly, and maintain composure on the air is critical.

Both print and broadcast journalists need to understand the legal implications of covering events and publishing stories to a wide audience. Broadcast journalists, however, operate in a much more regulated environment than print journal-

ists and must know the rules and regulations of such governmental entities as the Federal Communications Commission (**FCC**).

The career path for a successful sports journalist in broadcasting would probably involve several moves from smaller to larger markets (i.e., bigger cities with larger news and sports operations) and might lead to a job with one of the networks—either with the sports division of a major network, like ABC Sports, or with an all-sports network like ESPN. If you are interested in a career in broadcasting as a sports journalist, you should look for experience while still in college. Many colleges have campus radio stations and some have campus television stations. If these stations broadcast news programs or cover sporting events, you have a great opportunity to establish yourself in the field while still a full-time student. Opportunities can include reporting on sports, play-by-play or color commentary, and hosting a sports talk show. At this level, your knowledge of sports and your dependability will be key assets. Once you get the opportunity to do on-air coverage, you will begin building the experience that will help open the doors to an internship or part-time work at a local radio or television station. Your initial experience could even include nonsport broadcast work, such as doing voice overs for your local television station's on-air promotion spots.

Some local stations have internship programs available for college students, but many more would probably be willing to set up some supervised work experience if you can convince the sports editor or director that you have something to offer: even if it's just your services as a gofer (go-fer-this, go-fer-that) during a live telecast of your university's basketball team. Getting your foot in the door and showing that you are able and willing to help is the first hurdle. Once you're there, you can work your way up to doing some reporting or writing—perhaps eventually getting on the air with your stories. This initiative will pay off when you look for your first full-time job.

## Learning Activity

Carefully watch and take notes during a televised sport event on network television. Pay attention to how much information the sportscasters relate to the audience during the game. Pay *particular* attention to events that have many pauses in the action (for example, between plays during a football telecast or between batters and innings of a baseball telecast).

In addition to these obvious places to hone your skills, you can find other places to start. Because voice considerations are important in broadcasting, your college debate club can provide you with excellent experience in public speaking and thinking on your feet. Theater productions are also a source of good experience. The performance nature of these activities can help reduce the initial nervousness that invariably results from knowing that an audience is listening to you. The best kind of broadcast voice is strong, confident, and free from pronounced regional accent.

Your career path in broadcast sports reporting is likely to be much less predefined than one in print journalism. The big names in broadcast sports journalism today have a great diversity in backgrounds and experiences. Many, like NBC's Ahmad Rashad, come from the ranks of professional players. Others have worked their way up from local radio and television stations to the network level. A few, like the late Howard Cosell, don't seem to follow any traditional career path, but instead have been in the right place at the right time for their talent to be noticed. Probably the best known—and by all accounts one of the most respected—of the new generation of broadcast sports reporters is Bob Costas, whose insightful commentary on the 1994 Major League Baseball strike was impressive and who has hosted a popular late night talk show for NBC.

## The Insider

Many men and women use their communication skills in the field of sports information and promotion by working for a specific enterprise or entity, such as a recreation facility, a college athletic program, an amateur sport governing body, a health agency, or a professional sports team. These positions exist under a variety of designations, such as sports information, community relations,

## Down the Road

In 1987, Gayle Sierens became the first female sports reporter to do professional football play-by-play commentary on network television. Since that time, the number and stature of women in print and broadcast journalism have increased. NBC Sports reporter Hanna Storm was part of the network team covering the 1995 World Series and the 1996 Olympic Games (Brady, 1996). She and other women sports journalists, like ESPN's Robin Roberts and Lesley Visser of CBS Sports, have worked hard to establish a high level of personal reporting credibility, as have their print counterparts, such as Christine Brennan of the *Washington Post*. Since Gayle Sierens shattered one of sport's "glass ceilings" in 1987, it has become less surprising to see women reporting the sports news.

Most sports journalists have been involved with organized sport, either as participants or as fans. It seems likely that the increase in the number of young women participating in sports will lead to a corresponding increase in the number of women who make the transition from player to commentator. Moreover, Koppett (1994) suggested that access to sports knowledge is now more available to women because of the extensive media coverage devoted to athletics. Koppett argued that this "electronic fan training course" is helping women to be more comfortable with and excited about sports. This extensive media exposure, coupled with an increase in sport participation by young women, is likely to generate greater numbers of women interested in and prepared for careers in sports journalism.

marketing, public relations, media relations, advertising, promotion, and publicity. Some organizations have staffs large enough to include separate information and promotion functions, but many organizations employ a single individual who handles information, promotion, media relations, customer or fan relations, and miscellaneous marketing and public relations duties. Success as an insider sports communicator requires a genuine interest in the field, strong interpersonal and written communication skills, and the perseverance to unearth and secure internship and entry-level job opportunities in a highly competitive field.

## What Insider Sports Communicators Do

Sport communication professionals who work for a team, facility, or organization are responsible for creating, coordinating, and organizing information about that entity and disseminating it to the public through the mass media (publicity or media relations), direct contact (promotional brochures, marketing, or community relations events), or paid advertising. For example, Chamberlin (1990, p. 66) indicated that if you were a sports information director with a college or university, your duties would include

- writing news releases;
- updating hometown newspapers;
- writing feature stories;
- filing game reports;
- writing, editing, and laying out brochures;
- preparing game programs;
- selling advertising space;
- overseeing promotional activities;
- compiling records and statistics;
- organizing a photo file system;
- planning and conducting press conferences;
- answering requests from publications and organizations;
- managing a press box staff and managing the press box on game day;
- organizing a radio or television network; and
- any other duties assigned by the athletics director or other supervisor.

Chapter 9 has more detailed information on the duties and career paths of collegiate sports information jobs. Communication managers in profes-

sional sports perform many of these functions, although for major league teams, staff responsibilities might be spread among more individuals. Sports communicators who work with sports recreation facilities also perform some of these functions, but the focus is on the community opportunities available at the facility and the events or activities scheduled.

### Learning Activity

Develop an information sheet that athletes at your college or university could use. The sheet should request biographical information as well as anything that might be used in promotional copy or news releases. Remember to ask for the athlete's home town and high school information because the local angle is usually a critical one!

## Insider Sports Communication Careers

There are thousands of colleges and universities; hundreds of major and minor league professional sports teams; and one or more sport, fitness, health, or recreation facilities in most cities in North America. Each enterprise needs to get information to the public, and many of them employ at least one professional communicator to handle the job. This means there are many opportunities to be employed as sports communicators. You must remember, though, that the field is so popular and so competitive, your career success depends on recognizing and sometimes *creating* opportunities to get your foot in the door. Prospective employers will be looking for a solid educational preparation that includes strong communication skills. Typical majors are sport management, journalism, public relations, and communications. Beyond your basic education, however, you should capitalize on your sport interests to discover or create volunteer or internship experiences so that when you graduate you will have more on your résumé than the name of your degree.

Your career in this field might begin with an internship or volunteer stint with your college's sports information office. Because most college sports information programs include a group of dedicated but overworked sports communicators, you can frequently find good quality internship opportunities, although you might have to help create the parameters of the internship yourself. Many beginning interns are assigned routine duties during the season, such as keeping team statistics. As they prove their reliability and skills, interns may eventually be assigned additional duties that provide valuable on-the-job experience.

A good internship can do more than simply give you experience; it can also give you a network of sports communicators to contact for job opportunities, not to mention essentials like letters of reference. There are some internship opportunities with professional teams, but because the competition to be involved in the "glamorous" world of professional sport is so intense, these internships are not as common. Your best bet would be to try minor league teams or teams in sports other than football, basketball, baseball, and hockey. Don't forget to look for internship opportunities with community recreational facilities such as the YM and YWCA and Jewish Community Centers. Tight budgets and limited staff resources can make these organizations appreciate dedicated volunteer and internship help.

Your first full-time job will probably be as an assistant to the sports information director or the promotions director at a college, a team, a governing body, or a facility. If you do your job well and keep your ear tuned for advancement opportunities, that assistant's job could lead to a sports information director's job or a job as promotions or public relations manager for an organization connected with sport or fitness. This first job should provide you with a broader network of contacts that will be valuable as you prepare yourself to move into positions with larger organizations or into a manager or director job.

The competitive nature of insider sports communication jobs can not be overstated. Although the number of available positions has increased as colleges, facilities, and teams acknowledge the connection between publicity and profit, the number of individuals competing for the jobs has also increased. Salaries are not always commensurate with similar communication positions in the corporate world because of the many people who seem willing to work in sport almost for free.

# Communication Technology and Its Impact on Sport

Media technology, particularly television, has had a tremendous impact on sport. Some people think our national sport shifted from baseball to football because the pace and segmented action in football made for better television. Certainly, televised Major League Baseball has had a negative impact on minor league attendance. The influx of television dollars into professional competitive sports and such amateur sport events as the Olympics, has affected everything from salaries to rules. Television was the impetus behind night baseball and obviously plays a central role in making the Super Bowl a super event! In fact, much technology now routinely used in television production (e.g., minicams, satellite relays, split screens, miniaturized computer graphics) was developed during the 1970s—primarily by the team under Roone Arledge at ABC Sports—and financed by a dramatic increase in the advertising dollars spent to sponsor professional and big event sport coverage.

The amount of money spent on media sport coverage is staggering (Robinowitz & Youman, 1990). In the early 1990s, Fox spent $395 million to out-bid CBS for National Football League broadcast rights, moving the NFL games that had been at home on CBS for 38 years to the young, aggressive,

## The Bottom Line

Perhaps the most dramatic example of just how big the price tag on sports coverage has grown is the Olympics. In 1960, the TV rights to the Winter Olympics cost a mere $50,000. The Summer Olympics that year were a bit more expensive—$394,000. Just 20 years later, the 1980 TV broadcast rights cost $15.5 million for the Winter Games and $87 million for the Summer Games. The TV rights for the 1984 Winter Games jumped to $91.5 million, and the Summer Games carried a $225-million price tag (Schaaf, 1995). According to NBC, the 2000 and 2002 Olympics will carry the peacock logo, because the network agreed to pay an incredible $555 million for the 2002 Salt Lake City Winter Games and a whopping $715 million for the Sydney Summer Games in 2000. Remember, this is just the cost of buying the rights to televise the Games. It does not include production costs!

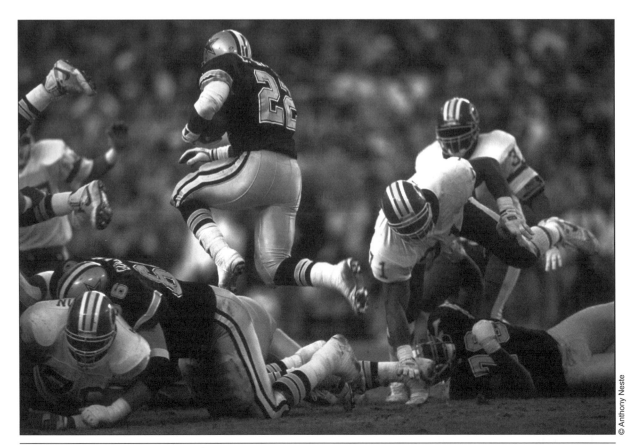

© Anthony Neste

In the early 90s Fox Network spent $395 million for the rights to broadcast Emmitt Smith of the Cowboys along with other NFL regular season games.

youth-oriented Fox Network. Television rights aren't the only expensive aspect of sport telecasts. A 30-second commercial aired during the 1995 Super Bowl telecast cost over a million dollars! (*Broadcasting & Cable Yearbook*, 1995).

## The Ever-Increasing Impact of Computer Technology

There is an old Chinese curse: "May you live in interesting times." The briefest look at the implications of computer-driven communication technology helps explain what the insightful author of that curse might have meant. Although we are living in an era of unparalleled available communication opportunities, our times are so interesting many individuals are confused and somewhat alarmed. We are well on our way to establishing an **information society**. The proliferation of technical information necessary to handle something as basic as ordering telephone service has left many of us concerned that we will end up as roadkill on the information superhighway.

From surfing the **Internet** to **virtual reality technology**, our interesting times have given us the capacity for instantaneous communication with individuals and access to a pool of information that perhaps should, more accurately, be renamed an ocean. With a basic computer, modem, and connection to an on-line service, we can get the day's sports scores without soiling our fingers with newsprint ink. We can engage in a spirited discussion about potential team trades with fans in other parts of the world without using our voices. Virtual reality technology will eventually allow us to attend a sporting event or even play as a member of the team without ever leaving our homes. Certainly, this technology creates the potential for both positive and negative sports communications implications. Instructional video can progress from a "watch me do this" to a "do it with me" level. Exercise equipment sales may go up and golf scores may go down with this individual instruction potential. Fans may be more likely to try a game or event previously unfamiliar to them if the extent of their commitment is hooking themselves into a virtual reality apparatus. They might even be inspired to attend future games. On the other hand, you might find that fan support diminishes when you can get all the excitement without the cost and hassle of being there, especially when you can enhance the contest or event by virtual reality participation. Most of us would rather be the quarterback than the fan—especially if we don't feel the pain from the tackles!

If you are interested in pursuing a career in sports information you need to become familiar with this technology. You're going to be left at the post if you don't know the difference between sneaker net (walking to the computer store to buy a program and walking back home to load it into your hard drive) and Internet (a network of computer networks that communicate through a common language and sublanguages or protocols such as World Wide Web and E-mail). Marshall McLuhan, whose 1966 *Understanding Media: The Extensions of Man* was embraced, ignored, and recently revived by communication scholars and media enthusiasts, said "the medium is the message." He was right. Technology isn't an option in sports communication; it is the absolute—or virtual—reality.

## Learning Activity

Investigate the computer technologies available at your school, in particular any instructional sessions available free to students on computer networks and technologies. Become familiar with some basic publications that deal with computers (there are dozens), and keep track of any innovations that receive publicity during this school term. Try to determine their implications for sport communication professionals.

## A Word About Ethics

No discussion of an activity as powerful as communication should end without some attention to relevant ethical issues. Sports reporters should remember that they are members of the journalism profession, not fans who just happen to be covering the game. Journalists are obligated to provide objective, fair coverage of events, not personal vendettas disguised as commentary. Good reporters, whether they are covering sports or any other beat, are interested in facts, not rumors. Good reporters investigate lots of leads that never become news stories. In addition,

journalists do not accept "freebies," because that compromises both the appearance of and the adherence to standards of objectivity, and most news organizations have developed specific rules about what can be accepted and what must be purchased. For example, seats in the press box and access to the athletes are usually considered part of the job, not a freebie, but many news organizations will not allow their reporters to travel with the team unless the news organization compensates the team for the cost of the travel.

Individuals in sports information promotion fields share some ethical concerns with sports journalists. Both careers include access to a great deal of information—much of it personal. If you are in an insider sports communication position, you need to be sensitive to this and carefully guard proprietary information concerning the organization and the privacy of the individuals involved. Sports journalists, although traditionally considered messengers, not repositories, must still be aware of the delicate balance between the public's interest in a person or issue and the privacy rights of the individuals involved. Today's ever-expanding—and intrusive—technology will only increase concerns in this area.

## Summary

A number of media and nonmedia sport-related jobs depend on excellent communication skills for success. A thorough understanding of the way we communicate can help you secure your first job in the field and launch your successful career.

Sports communication careers fall into two categories: media jobs and nonmedia or insider jobs. Media jobs include sports reporters and editors for newspapers and magazines as well as broadcast reporters and anchors who handle sports coverage for local radio and television stations or for one of the networks. Individuals in a nonmedia job might direct promotion activities for a fitness facility such as the YMCA or provide communications expertise publicizing the athletic program at a college.

Jobs in communications are varied and numerous, and the competition for them is usually high. The challenge is to get into the information loop so that you can find out about job opportunities. One way to do that is to get some good internship or volunteer experience while you are still in college. Everyone you meet while working in the field can become an important contact for future opportunities.

In addition to the rapidly changing technology of broadcasting, you must consider the impact of computer technology on sports coverage. Everything from the Internet to virtual reality technologies may alter the way we receive our sport information in the immediate future. It is critical to stay current with the rapidly changing world of communication technology!

## For More Information

Following are more sources for you to look at.

### Professional Organizations

- American Marketing Association
- Baseball Writers Association
- College Sports Information Directors of America (CoSIDA)
- Football Writers Association of America
- International Association of Business Communicators
- National College Baseball Writers Association
- National Recreation & Park Association
- North American Society for Sport Management
- Public Relations Society of America
- United States Basketball Writers Association

### Professional Publications

- *Athletics Administration*
- *Athletic Business*
- *Auditorium News*
- *Broadcasting*
- *CoSIDA Digest*
- *The Chronicle of Higher Education*
- *Journal of Sport Management*
- *NCAA News*
- *NCAA Public Relations and Promotion Manual*
- *Sporting News*
- *Sports Illustrated*
- *USA Today*
- *Parks & Recreation*
- *Public Relations Journal*
- *The Sport Marketing Institute Manual*
- *Sports Market Place*

# Job Opportunities

## Promotions Director

Health facility in urban area seeks a self-motivated individual with three to five years of experience working in promotion or public relations, with some experience in a sports- or fitness-related field. A bachelor's degree in journalism, communication, or sport management strongly preferred. Strong writing and speaking skills, good organization, and a high level of creativity and flexibility a must. Job responsibilities include special events planning, press relations, membership promotion, and marketing. The individual will work closely with the facility director and the facility's 20-member community board.

## Television Sports Reporter

A spot on an Emmy-winning television sports staff is available for an experienced, talented sports reporter. This station's top-rated sports team covers local, professional, collegiate, and community sports events as well as a number of national and international sports events. The station's expanded local coverage and frequent specials provide a great opportunity for both feature coverage and in-depth news analysis of sports-related issues. Applicants must have very strong writing and interviewing skills and solid video editing experience. The job may include some weekend anchor opportunities. All station reporters take an active role in community events and activities. Minimum five years experience in broadcast sports reporting required (at least three years in television sports reporting).

## Newspaper Sports Reporter

Entry-level reporting position available on small-city daily newspaper with 15,000 circ. Bachelor's degree required: journalism degree preferred, but evidence of solid news writing experience (part- or full-time) will be considered. Applicant must be comfortable covering wide range of elementary school, high school, and college sports as well as sports-related community events. Strong writing and interviewing skills are required.

## Assistant Sports Information Director

Mid-sized university with Division I athletic program for a wide variety of men's and women's sports is looking for an addition to its sports information team. The successful candidate will have a bachelor's or master's degree in journalism or a sports-related area and at least two years of sports information experience with a college, facility, or professional sports team. Superior oral and written communication skills a must! Primary responsibilities include writing and editing press guides and programs. The position requires extensive evening and weekend work. Salary is commensurate with experience.

## Radio Sports Reporter and Call-In Talk Show Host

WWOW-AM/FM radio in Baltimore, MD is seeking a dynamic, motivated personality to handle sports reporting duties and host one of the station's live call-in sports programs. If you're interested in joining a team that likes to "work hard and play ball" and you have the right blend of experience and enthusiasm, you might find yourself behind our microphone. Minimum three years full-time broadcast sports experience required; talk format experience preferred. Must be flexible in working hours and job assignments.

## Assistant to Public Relations Director, Sports League Office

Write press releases, prepare daily sports circulation report, and distribute internally to all executive offices; prepare statistics and other materials required to print media guide for special events (exhibition games, All-Star Game, League Championsip Series); assist with press conferences. Candidates must have expertise in writing press releases and in presenting sports statistics for publications. Must also have excellent computer, communication, and interpersonal skills.

# Chapter 12 Sport Marketing

**F. Wayne Blann**
Ithaca College

---

## Learning Objectives

After studying this chapter, you will be able to

1. recognize how a marketing plan is linked to an organization's mission statement and core values;

2. assess the future market climate for a sport or event by conducting a SWOT (strengths, weakness, opportunities, and threats) analysis;

3. analyze a sport product, such as the game itself (e.g., New York Yankees or Colorado Silver Bullets) or an event (e.g., Masters Golf Tournament or Dinah Shore Classic);

4. define product positioning and market niche;

5. give an example of a sport product that communicates a distinctive image;

6. recognize how you can communicate images and messages of a sport product in ethical and socially responsible ways;

7. define market segmentation and target audiences;

8. explain the four factors for developing a pricing strategy;

9. explain the five elements that comprise a promotion strategy;

10. discuss how sports are distributed to consumers;

11. define "place" of a sport product;

12. define packaging and selling a sport product;

13. explain what is meant by the "promise" of a marketing plan; and

14. identify two sport marketing needs in the 21st century.

---

Marketing is one of the most complex and important functions of sport organizations. Through their marketing efforts, sport companies must promote and sell products to prosper. You probably have heard the term sport marketing in many contexts, and you might be wondering exactly what it means.

That's a good question because sport marketing is composed of several elements and the term sport marketing frequently is used incorrectly. People tend to define marketing in terms of their experiences, instead of recognizing the role of marketing as carrying out the mission of an organization.

For example, some corporate executives might describe sport marketing as selling goods and services to generate a profit. Sport marketing is *more* than selling. People working in advertising and public relations might consider sport marketing as obtaining Super Bowl tickets for clients or entertaining a corporate sponsor at the U.S. Open Golf Tournament. Sport marketing is *more* than advertising and public relations. Individuals providing services for professional athletes might view sport marketing as arranging for athletes to attend the grand opening of a shopping mall or arranging to have corporate executives play tennis with Andre Agassi or Steffi Graf. Sport marketing is *more* than community relations.

Pitts and Stotlar (1996) define sport marketing as "the process of designing and implementing activities for the production, pricing, promotion and distribution of a sport product to satisfy the needs or desires of consumers and to achieve the company's objectives" (p. 80). Marketing is a complex function, and sport marketing is even more complex because sport has certain characteristics that make the sport product unique. A brief examination of some unique sport qualities proposed by Mullin, Hardy, and Sutton (1993) will show how sport as a product differs from other goods and services and must, therefore, be marketed uniquely.

First, sport is intangible and subjective because the impressions, experiences, and interpretations about a sporting event vary from person to person. If two individuals attend the same field hockey game, one person may view the game as low scoring and unexciting. Yet, the other person may appreciate the strategy involved in the game and consider it interesting. It is difficult for a sport marketer to predict what impressions, experiences, and interpretations consumers will have about sporting events.

Second, sports are inconsistent and unpredictable because of injuries to players, the emotional state of players, the momentum of teams, and the weather. These factors contribute to the uncertain outcome of sports. Sport marketers have little control over these factors, yet the unpredictability has great appeal to spectators.

Third, sport is perishable because the sport event as it is being played is what spectators want to see. Few people are interested in seeing yesterday's soccer match or field hockey game. Consequently, marketers must focus on advance ticket sales. If the team's performance is poor or not up to expectations, gate receipts will suffer.

Fourth, sport involves emotions. Some spectators become emotionally attached to their sports teams and are referred to as fanatics or fans. Other consumers might purchase licensed products with team logos and uniform replicas as a way of identifying with their sports teams.

Given these unique characteristics, what factors should we consider in making decisions about marketing, promoting, and selling sport products? What changes will be needed in marketing, promoting, and selling sport products in the future? In this chapter, you will learn about the marketing mix; how companies develop a socially responsible sport marketing plan; and how they position, promote, and sell sport products. In addition, you will learn to appreciate dilemmas faced by sport managers in implementing sport marketing plans. Finally, we will discuss future challenges and trends in sport marketing.

## Developing a Sport Marketing Plan

The four primary elements involved in marketing are called the marketing mix. The marketing mix consists of product, price, place, and promotion. These elements are well established in the marketing industry and are universally known as the four Ps. A *product* may be a tangible good (object), a service, or an intangible quality that satisfies consumers wants or needs. *Price* represents the value of the product and the costs the consumer must accept to obtain the product. Consumers determine the value of a product by balancing the expected benefits of buying the product against the expected costs of the product. When the benefits derived from a product exceed the costs attached to the product, then consumers believe the product has value. *Place* represents the distribution channels where consumers may obtain a product. *Promotion* involves using techniques to communicate images and messages about a product to motivate consumers to buy the product. This chapter examines the unique characteristics of the sport product and presents strategies for pricing, distributing, and promoting the sport product. When you study sport marketing in subsequent courses, you will learn about each of the four Ps in greater detail.

To maximize their success, marketers manipulate the four Ps in a variety of ways, depending on the missions of the organizations and the fluctuations of the market (Pitts & Stotlar, 1996). This manipulation is critical to carrying out a marketing plan successfully. In this chapter the process we use in developing a sport marketing plan is 10-step process expressed as the 10 Ps. This process, shown in figure 12.1, elaborates on the original four Ps, which remain central to the process and represent its core elements.

## Purpose of a Sport Marketing Plan

Step 1 involves clarifying the purpose of the sport marketing plan and linking the plan to the organization's mission and core values. Before marketing, promotions, and selling can occur, sport marketers must establish a context to provide an orientation and direction for why they will develop marketing, promotions, and sales programs and how they will implement them. Establishing a context requires sport managers to examine the organization's core values as described in its mission statement. If the organization does not have a mission statement, then a mission statement that identifies core values must be written. It is important that all individuals in the organization be involved in the process of writing a mission statement so everyone will be committed to carrying out the mission and acting in accordance with the core values. Covey (1989) says, "an organizational mission statement is important because it creates in people's hearts and minds a frame of reference, a set of criteria or guidelines by which they will govern themselves. . . . They have bought into the changeless core of what the organization is about" (p. 143).

A sport marketing plan derived from and consistent with the organization's mission statement and core values is necessary to ensure that

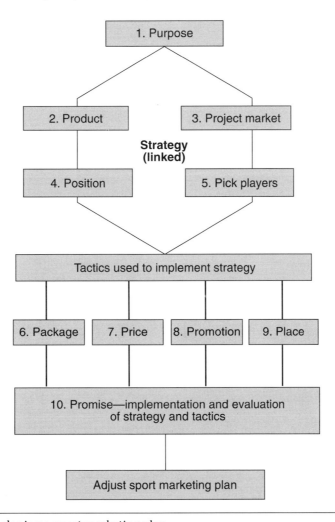

**Figure 12.1**  Steps in developing a sport marketing plan.

Adapted, by permission, from B.G. Pitts and D.K. Stotlar, 1996. *Fundamentals of sport marketing*. Morgantown, WV: Fitness Information Technology, Inc., 81.

**The NBA's mission is to be the most respected and successful sports league organization in the world.**

**We aim to achieve our mission, and thereby continue to enhance the economic value of our teams, by**

working to make basketball the most popular global sport and to maintain the NBA's position as the best in basketball; creating and maximizing business opportunities and relationships arising from basketball; and capitalizing on our key assets and strengths—our people, skills, experience, reputation, and innovative and entrepreneurial spirit—to expand beyond basketball into related activities worldwide.

**We have a commitment to excellence**

We do every task as well as it can be done, reflecting quality and attention to detail at every stage—from inception, to planning, to execution.

**We strive at all times to live by and act in accordance with the following core values:**

**Innovation**   We encourage entrepreneurship and innovative thinking. We create opportunities and do not merely react to those that come our way. We aim always to be on the cutting edge and ahead of all competition.

**Integrity**   We conduct ourselves in accordance with the highest standards of honesty, truthfulness, ethics, and fair dealing.

**Respect**   We value our individuality and diversity. We are civil and respectful to each other, to our fans, customers, and business associates. We take pride in our success, but we are not arrogant.

**Social responsibility**   We recognize and embrace our responsibility—as a corporate citizen in the world, in the United States, and in local communities to support causes that help people to achieve an improved quality of life.

**Teamwork**   We work hard together in a true cooperative spirit and without regard for departmental lines or individual goals. Our priority is always to provide the best possible service to all our constituencies.

**Workplace environment**   We believe in equal opportunity, the importance of job satisfaction, and that each employee has an important role in achieving our mission. We empower each employee to make job-related decisions commensurate with the employee's experience and level of responsibility. We promote and reward our employees solely on the basis of merit, and we evaluate not only achievement but also whether the employee's conduct reflects conformity with our mission and values.

**Figure 12.2**   Mission statement of the National Basketball Association.
Reprinted, by permission, from the National Basketball Association.

marketing, promoting, and selling will be conducted in socially responsible ways. The National Basketball Association's (NBA) mission, presented in figure 12.2, provides a good example of a mission statement with core values.

## Learning Activity

Using the NBA mission as a guide, write a mission statement and core values for a sport product of your choice.

## Analyzing the Sport Product

In step 2, the marketer analyzes the sport product and determines whether the product is a tangible good, a game or event, or a service. The sport product is three dimensional (Pitts, Fielding, & Miller, 1994). It is composed of tangible goods, support services, and the game or event itself.

Goods include tangible items such as clothing (e.g., shoes, aerobic apparel) and equipment (e.g., automobiles and car parts, tack used in horse racing, mountain bikes). Services include activities or programs that are ancillary to sport but necessary for its operation (e.g., game officials, athletic trainers, sport psychologists). The game or event itself is the core product of sport and is usually viewed as a form of entertainment (e.g., NY Knicks versus Chicago Bulls, U.S. Open, Super Bowl, World Series, NCAA Basketball Championships).

Brooks (1994) proposed the following four tangible elements in the core sports product:

- The type of sport—football, basketball, gymnastics
- The participants—athletes (beginner, elite, professional), coaches (volunteer, part-time salaried, full-time professionals), and environment (challenging golf courses, difficult mountains)

- The team—Notre Dame, Michigan, Dallas Cowboys
- The competition—local and regional, national championships, Super Bowl

In addition, Brooks (1994) pointed out that the sport product has an intangible dimension, which is internally generated and represented by the psychic side of sport—the participant's emotions and experiences. Examples include

- the high individuals experience when running their personal best time,
- the thrill individuals feel when winning a contest,
- the satisfaction individuals derive when overcoming challenges posed by competitors or the environment, and
- the pride individuals or teams feel when they compete to the best of their ability.

You must fully understand and appreciate these unique characteristics of the core product (i.e., the game or event itself) before you can develop an appropriate and effective marketing plan.

## Learning Activity

Using the four elements of a sport product as a guide, analyze a sport product of your choice.

## Projecting the Future Market Climate

Step 3 is analyzing, projecting, and forecasting the future market climate. Assessing the sport climate requires examining internal and external factors as they impact marketing efforts. For example, internal factors affecting the climate of Major League Baseball include players, owners, team management, and staff personnel. The media, corporate sponsors, advertisers, spectators, and federal government represent examples of external factors that affect the climate of Major League Baseball.

In 1994, Major League Baseball (MLB) was having one of its best years ever. Several players were striving to break long-standing records, and teams that had not contended for a league championship in many years were leading their leagues in the standings. Newly aligned divisions had created another tier of playoffs and wild card possibilities. This created great interest among spectators,

which resulted in increased attendance and heightened press coverage. The game was reinvigorated and seemed to be making strides to reclaim its place as America's national pastime. Then the dispute between players and owners regarding possible implementation of a salary cap resulted in the longest players' strike in the history of American professional sport.

The strike ended the 1994 season on August 11; there were no league championships or World Series. Even the beginning of the 1995 season was delayed because the dispute between players and owners remained unresolved. MLB withdrew its participation in the newly formed Baseball Network and, thus, limited its television market. Finally, the courts forced the league to begin operations in May, 1995, because the players and owners still had not settled their differences. In the fall of 1996, the owners and players' association signed a new collective bargaining agreement. Although the terms of the agreement might not resolve the problems faced by MLB, it will provide stability for the league through the year 2000.

From a marketing perspective, MLB was faced with a disaster following the 1994 players' strike. The spectators viewed the players and owners as selfish and greedy and believed they did not care about the fans or the game. The situation had serious negative financial consequences for everyone directly or indirectly involved with the industry. Team management and staff personnel; the media; corporate sponsors and advertisers; food, beverage, and lodging businesses; and other support services in the communities all lost in the process. MLB needed a new marketing strategy to promote and sell the game.

It is important to analyze the past market climate to project the future market climate. For example, what impact have the media had on

## Learning Activity

Suppose you were hired as the new director of marketing for MLB to recommend a marketing strategy for the 1995 season and the future. An analysis of the present market climate surrounding Major League Baseball in 1995 might have indicated that marketing efforts would be affected by spectators' negative views; strife between players and owners; negative attitudes of corporate sponsors, advertisers, and the media; and threats of intervention by the federal government. Where would you begin?

baseball in the past? What impact will the media have on baseball in the future? What actions have been taken by the federal government in the past regarding the baseball industry, and what actions might the federal government take in the future? What kind of relationships have advertisers and sponsors had with baseball owners in the past, and what benefits did each party derive? How might the relationships of advertisers and corporate sponsors with baseball owners change in the future?

Assessing the past market climate enables managers to identify factors associated with successful or failed marketing efforts. On the other hand, forecasting the future market climate requires re-examining the organization's mission. Assessing the strengths and weaknesses of an organization or event and the opportunities and threats faced by an organization or event is called a SWOT analysis (Rowe, Mason, & Dickel, 1986). A SWOT analysis usually results in developing a new mission statement, which, in turn, will affect the marketing plan.

For example, an assessment of the past market climate of MLB between 1990 and 1995 might reveal the following information: escalating player salaries, confrontations between players and owners, federal court actions to settle disputes between players and owners, declining TV viewership, declining ticket sales, and the public's growing disenchantment with the game. A SWOT analysis of the future market climate of MLB might forecast the following:

- Strengths—history, tradition (America's national pastime), established spectator markets
- Weaknesses—game too slow and too long, lack of TV viewership resulting in loss of advertisers and corporate sponsors
- Opportunities—improve marketing of star players, interleague competition to stimulate team rivalries and spectator interest, new stadiums
- Threats—popularity of professional basketball and football; lack of interest in baseball

© Anthony Neste

Opening day at Shea Stadium, home of the Mets. Under the media's influence, will the non-weekend day game become a thing of the past?

among youth, women, and minority ethnic groups; erosion or loss of antitrust exemption

Given this past, present, and future market analysis, MLB may need to reexamine its mission statement and core values and determine a new mission.

---

## Learning Activity

Using the SWOT analysis for MLB as a guide, conduct a SWOT analysis for a sport product of your choice.

---

## Positioning the Sport Product

Step 4 involves positioning the sport product. Positioning is what you do to influence the mind of the consumer. The objective of positioning is to differentiate the sport product from competing products by creating a distinctive image of the product. Images can be communicated through logos, symbols, and messages, such as TV and radio advertisements, public service announcements, jingles, press releases, news articles, and feature articles. For example, in 1995 Reebok developed a new TV advertisement about girls' participation in sport. This advertisement communicated a distinctive image to capture the attention of girls and women sport participants, spectators, and volunteers:

*Video:* Scenes from high school, many focusing on girls' sports: team practice, competition, traveling on the bus, hanging out at school, ultimately capturing moments of closeness between the players.

*Audio:* (girl) If you don't play . . . you can hang out . . . you can watch . . . you can brush your hair a lot . . . but you can never say, I was a player. And you can never say, I was on the team. And worst of all, you can never do all this incredible, exciting . . . hilarious stuff . . . with these girls who are like sisters. So all I'm trying to say is . . . my question is . . . wanna play?

*Video:* Just Another Chance to Play on Planet Reebok.*

A sport product perceived by consumers as being unique is well positioned to compete successfully in selected markets, provided the images are positive. For example, communicating the image of unity positioned the 1994 Gay Games for success with consumers in particular markets. The unique image also conveyed messages that were positive and socially responsible. Likewise, the Paralympics does an excellent job in communicating a positive image of elite world-class athletes who are physically challenged.

In their landmark work on public relations theory, Grunig and his colleagues (1992) suggested several elements of effective communication practices. Among these elements were the suggestions that we should (a) use open and honest communications with the public, (b) make sure the images and messages are socially responsible, (c) work cooperatively with the public and respond to their interests, and (d) establish good faith relationships with the public.

A story about the Washington Bullets demonstrates how Grunig and White's four steps might be applied. During the 1995-1996 season, Abe Pollin, owner of the Washington Bullets, decided the team nickname conveyed a negative image, because Bullets had nothing to do with basketball but everything to do with people being injured or killed by shooting incidents in Washington, DC and the surrounding communities. Pollin used open and honest communications with the public about the need to change the team's nickname (step 1). He involved the public in a promotional contest to determine a new team nickname, one that would convey a positive and socially responsible image of the team (step 2). The contest was an example of an organization working cooperatively with the public and responding to the public's interest (step 3). A corporate sponsor contributed prizes for some contestants, thus generating interest and publicity and establishing a good faith relationship with the public (step 4). Moreover, an antiviolence campaign was launched in conjunction with the team nickname contest. This campaign communicated the message that the Washington Bullets organization was a good corporate citizen wanting to help the community solve an important social problem. By the way, the promotional nickname contest resulted in the team being renamed the Washington Wizards.

Viewing marketing as a means of honest communication that creates a distinctive and socially responsible image of a sport product is the best way to position a sport product in the market. There are six distinct markets for sport: primary markets composed of participants, spectators, and volunteers and secondary markets composed

---

*Reprinted, by permission, from Reebok International Corporation.

of sponsors, advertisers, and athletes' endorsement of products and licensed products (Brooks, 1994). Examples of niches in primary markets include the following:

- Participants—athletes, coaches, and game officials
- Spectators—stadium attendees, television viewers, radio listeners, and newspaper or magazine readers
- Volunteers—social hosts at sports events, statisticians, team managers

Secondary markets could include the following:

- Advertisers—use sports to target and communicate their products to large groups of spectators (e.g., stadium banners and signs, TV and radio advertisements)
- Corporate sponsors—use sports to target and communicate positive and distinctive images about their products to large groups of spectators (e.g., Cadillac as sponsor of golf tournaments, Volvo as sponsor of tennis tournaments)
- Athletes' endorsement of products and licensed products—use sports personalities and celebrities or distinctive symbols, logos, or trademarks to have consumers perceive products as popular or prestigious

## Learning Activity

Describe how you might develop a distinct and socially responsible image for a sport product of your choice. Explain how you might position this product in a niche in the market.

## Picking the Players— Analyzing and Targeting Consumers

In step 5, the marketer analyzes the market and targets consumers, a process that we can envision as picking the players. This involves grouping consumers according to common characteristics. To sell sport products, marketers must have information about consumers. According to Crispell (1993), market research is conducted to obtain information about sport consumers in four areas: demographics, **psychographics, media preferences,** and **purchasing behavior** (see figure 12.3).

Information collected through market research enables marketers to segment consumers into clusters according to selected characteristics. This process is called **market segmentation** and identifying **target audiences**. A sports equipment manufacturer might identify the primary target audience as male, 12 to 16 years of age, interested in in-line skating, and watches MTV. Target marketing is zeroing in on specific consumers who are most likely to find your product appealing, rather than attempting to sell your product to all consumers. This is called picking the players.

Once target audiences are identified, a marketer can develop a strategy to reach them. A key to success is communicating an image for the product that will appeal to your target audience. For example, the 1994 Gay Games and Paralympics advertisements communicated honest and positive images that encouraged participants, spectators, and sponsors from specific target markets to get involved in these events.

## Learning Activity

Using the characteristics of target audiences as a guide, explain how you might segment the market and identify target audiences for a sport product of your choice.

## Packaging the Sport Product

Step 6 is packaging and selling the sport product. This process includes presenting the product in the best possible manner to encourage selected target audiences to purchase it. Because consumers differ, it is necessary to present the product in different ways. Packaging tangible or industrial sport products involves explaining the benefits of the products: strength and longevity of metal bats, comfort and safety of helmets, expanded sweet spot of oversize tennis rackets. However, packaging the core product of sport (game or event itself) involves communicating about the expectations of the product and providing information before the point of purchase. For example, sport marketers might package the game or event as family entertainment and offer family ticket plans. Or, marketers might package sport as a good place to make business contacts and offer corporate-business ticket plans. A sport organization might wish to be packaged as caring about the community and, thus, offer group discount ticket plans for social service and charitable organizations.

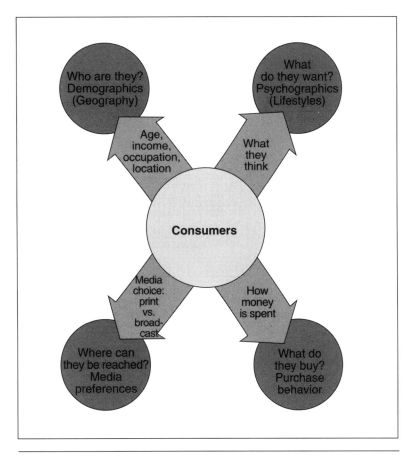

**Figure 12.3**  Types of information generated by consumers.
Reprinted, by permission, from P. Francese, 1990, *The insider's guide to demographic know-how*, (Ithica, NY: American Demographics), 11.

Packaging the sport product to secure financial support from corporations is an especially important aspect of the marketing plan. A sport marketer must conduct research to learn what benefits corporations are seeking through sponsorship. This information is necessary before beginning negotiations with corporate sponsors. In negotiations, you must be flexible so you can modify packages to meet the interests and needs of the corporate sponsor. However, flexibility does not mean that the sport product should be misrepresented or that claims of benefits be exaggerated. What is being exchanged between the sport product and corporate sponsors must be honest and fair so you can maintain and strengthen trusting relationships with corporate sponsors (McCarville & Copeland, 1994).

## Pricing the Sport Product

Step 7 is pricing the sport product—determining the value of the product by assigning it a price. Price is the element that is most visible and flexible because of discounts, rebates, and coupons. Developing a pricing strategy is important because it significantly impacts the success of the marketing plan. According to Pitts and Stotlar (1996), you should consider four factors in developing a pricing strategy:

- The consumer—analyze all aspects of the consumer, including demographics, psychographics, purchasing behaviors, and media preferences.

- The competitor—analyze the consumer's perception of the product value compared with all competing products and analyze the competitor's prices.

**Learning Activity**

Describe what packaging strategies you might use in selling a sport product of your choice.

- The company—analyze the costs involved in producing the product (materials, equipment, salaries, rent) and set a minimum price to cover the costs.

- The climate—analyze external factors, such as laws pertaining to pricing, government regulations, the economic situation, and the political situation.

Normally, money is exchanged for products. In sport marketing, trading is a common practice that does not involve money. According to Gray (1996), sport organizations or events frequently trade tickets, stadium signage, and scoreboard advertisement for goods and services. For example, marketers of a tennis tournament might make trades with corporate sponsors to include tickets for tennis balls, stadium signage for food and beverages for a hospitality tent, and scoreboard advertisement for the use of vehicles to transport players and officials.

The value of a product is determined by factors other than price. Each consumer holds attitudes, preferences, beliefs, and has available a certain amount of expendable money. Besides price, these factors influence how individuals determine the value of a product. Because the value of a product is unique to each consumer, it is important to develop a pricing strategy that will appeal to as many different consumers as possible. For example, sport franchises set different prices for corporate season-ticket holders, charitable organizations, group ticket purchasers, miniseason ticket purchasers, family ticket purchasers, and single ticket purchasers.

Consumers tend to equate price with value. Therefore, a new sports franchise would be better to price tickets comparable to competing products (other sporting events, movies, theater, other entertainment) rather than set a lower price. Consumers might equate a lower price with an inferior product.

Lead time is a concept that is important to sports pricing. There are more day-of-the-game or walk-up sales at a Major League Baseball game than for an NBA basketball game, because there are many more games and seats available at lower prices in baseball than in basketball (Mullin, Hardy, & Sutton, 1993).

Sports pricing is complex and critical to the success of the marketing plan. In the final analysis, sport marketers must determine how consumers perceive the value of the product compared with all other competing products and determine an appropriate price.

## Learning Activity

Using the four factors outlined previously as a guide, describe a pricing strategy you might develop for a sport product of your choice.

## Promoting the Sport Product

Step 8 is promoting the sport product—communicating the product's image to selected target audiences. Promoting sport products involves implementing a mix of activities that will best communicate your desired image of the product to selected target audiences. Elements that compose a promotion strategy include advertising, publicity, promotions, public relations (including community relations and media relations), and personal selling.

- Advertising—presenting a one-way paid message about the sport product (newspapers, magazines, TV, radio, direct mail, scoreboards, in-arena signage, pocket schedules, game programs, posters, outdoor advertising).

- Publicity—a nonpaid communication about a sport product in which the sponsor is usually not identified and the message reaches the public because it is newsworthy (news releases, TV and radio public service announcements).

- Promotions—inducements to encourage consumers to purchase the sport product (giveaways, coupons, free samples, cash refunds, contests, raffles).

- Public relations—a sport organization's overall plan for communicating a positive image about its product to the public, including implementing community and media relations activities and programs.

- Community relations—activities and programs arranged by a sport organization to meet the interests and needs of the public and, by so doing, establish good faith relationships with the public (youth sports clinics, athlete autograph signing opportunities, collecting food items at sports arenas to help people in the community).

- Media relations—maintaining networks and positive relations with individuals in the media to obtain positive media exposure for a sport product (schedule informal and formal information sessions with media representatives).

- Personal selling—direct interpersonal communication with individuals, groups, or organizations to persuade them to purchase the sport product.

The successful use of these promotional elements requires setting clear objectives, identifying appropriate elements of the promotional mix to use, and coordinating the promotional mix elements into a strategy that will achieve the objectives.

## Placing the Sport Product

Step 9 is analyzing the place of the sport product. Place refers to the location of the sport product (stadium, arena), the point of origin for distributing the product (ticket sales at the stadium, sales by a toll-free telephone number), and the geographic location of the target markets (global, national, regional, state, communities, cities). Fac-

## Learning Activity

Using the elements listed previously as a guide, describe some activities you might use to promote a sport product of your choice.

tors related to the location of the sport can impact the marketing plan either favorably or unfavorably. To ensure a favorable impact on the marketing plan, it is important that the sport facility be easily accessible (highway systems, parking, walkways, ramps); have an attractive physical appearance (well maintained and painted); have a pleasant, convenient, and functional environment (quick and easy access to concessions, clean bathrooms, smoke-free and odor-free environment); and have safe and pleasant surroundings (adequate public safety and security personnel, attractive neighborhood).

Sport is unique in the way it is distributed to consumers. The production and consumption of the product occur simultaneously at the same

© Robert Skeoch

For a favorable marketing impact it's important that the sport facility be easily accessible. Of course it also doesn't hurt for the facility to be magnificent to look at, like the Sky Dome in Toronto, home of the Blue Jays.

place for spectators attending sports events in stadiums or arenas. The sport product is also distributed through print media (newspapers, magazines). However, the sport product is most widely distributed to consumers, nationally and globally, through the electronic media (TV, radio, 1-900 sports telephone hot lines, World Wide Web, pay-per-view TV).

Ticket distribution is critical to marketing sport. The objective of a ticket distribution system is to make consumer purchases accessible, easy, quick, and convenient. Some approaches used by sport organizations include outside companies such as TicketMaster; ticket outlets at local banks, shopping malls, grocery stores; mobile van units that transport ticket personnel and operations to various locations throughout the community; on-site stadium and arena ticket sales with expanded hours of operation, toll-free telephone numbers, and will-call pick up arrangements.

---

## Learning Activity

Describe strategies you might use to distribute a sport product of your choice.

---

## Promise of the Sport Marketing Plan

Step 10 is evaluating the extent to which the marketing plan met its promise to help achieve the organization's mission. This evaluation requires obtaining feedback (from inside and outside the organization) about the marketing plan. The feedback must then be analyzed and evaluated. The evaluation should focus on determining the extent to which the plan helped the organization achieve its mission by acting in accordance with the core values of the organization. For example, Reebok might establish a mission "to diversify its products to appeal to girls and women" based on a core value of "establishing positive relationships with all segments of the community." Obtaining feedback from girls and women about the Reebok TV advertisement would allow an evaluation of this element of the marketing plan. The evaluation might conclude that the TV advertisement achieved the mission and did so in a manner that was consistent with the core values.

In some cases, a marketing plan might not have a clear purpose linked with the organization's mission and core values. In these cases, an evaluation of the marketing plan might show that it is not helping the organization achieve its mission and, even worse, that the manner in which the plan is being implemented reflects poorly on the organization. For example, the Washington Redskins might establish a mission to "be the most respected and successful football team in the NFL," based on a core value of "being civil and respectful to each other, to fans, and business associates." Obtaining feedback from fans, business associates, and others might indicate that the team nickname Redskins is offensive to some people. An evaluation of the team nickname, as an element of the marketing plan, might conclude that the nickname is not helping the organization achieve its mission, and even worse, is communicating a negative image of the organization. In this case, the management of the franchise might consider selecting a new team nickname that will communicate a positive image and be viewed as socially responsible. The mission and core values of the organization should be considered in selecting a new team nickname.

As these examples indicate, linking the purpose of the marketing plan to the organization's mission and core values helps ensure that the plan will be socially responsible. Sport marketers who develop marketing plans linked to the organization's mission and core values are being proactive. According to Covey (1989), "reactive people are driven by feelings, by circumstances, by conditions, and by their environment. Proactive people are driven by values—carefully thought about, selected, and internalized values" (p. 72). Sport marketers who are proactive will achieve the promise of the marketing plan because their actions will be socially responsible and will help fulfill the mission of the organization.

---

## Ethics and Social Responsibility

A sport marketing plan derived from and consistent with the mission statement and core values is necessary to ensure that marketing, promoting, and selling will be done in socially responsible ways. Viewing marketing as a means of honest communication that creates a distinctive and socially responsible image of a sport product is the best way to position a sport product in the market. Sport marketers who are proactive will achieve the promise of the marketing plan because their actions will be socially responsible and will help fulfill the mission of the organization.

## Learning Activity

Select a sport product and explain how you would determine the extent to which a marketing plan might fulfill its promise.

# Challenges and Directions in Sport Marketing

In many segments of the sport industry, pressure is placed on sport marketers to increase their product sales and generate revenues for their organizations. This pressure to increase sales of sport products poses a challenge for sport marketers. Because sport marketers are involved in persuading consumers to buy their products, they run the risk of exaggerating or misrepresenting their products in an effort to sell them. Today, and in the future, sport marketers should recognize this risk and monitor their marketing strategies to ensure that they communicate honest images and messages about their products that are consistent with the core values of their organizations.

Another challenge sport marketers face is the rapidly changing demographics in society, which are becoming more diverse. In addition, sports, like other businesses, are operating in a global market. This trend of diversity in the national and global market will pose a special challenge for sport managers in the 21st century (DeSensi, 1994).

Sport marketers will need to learn how to market their products to diverse consumer groups in socially responsible ways. This will require them to develop communication skills that enable appropriate and acceptable intercultural communication with diverse audiences. Sport marketers will need to adapt different ways of seeing the world to understand and be understood across cultural boundaries—within their own countries and in other countries.

# Summary

This chapter outlined a 10-step process that you can use in developing a sport marketing plan (see figure 12.1). The core of this process includes the primary elements in marketing, traditionally known as the four Ps and called the marketing mix (product, price, place, and promotion).

A sport marketing plan will most likely succeed when marketing is viewed as a means of communication. Marketing strategies should communicate a distinct, positive, and honest image of a product and should position the product in a particular niche in the market. Selling the product requires using effective pricing, promotions, and distribution strategies that will reach target audiences. Finally, a sport marketing plan will fulfill its promise when communications and sales of a sport product are conducted in honest and socially responsible ways that are linked to and consistent with the mission and core values of the organization.

# For More Information

Here are some more sources for you to consider.

**Governing Bodies and Professional Associations**

- American Marketing Association
- American Sports Data, Inc.
- The Academy of Marketing Sciences
- The Direct Marketing Association
- The Society of Consumer Affairs Professionals
- International Sports Marketing Association
- Licensing Industry Merchandisers Association (LIMA)

**Conferences and Special Events**

- National Association of Collegiate Marketing Administrators Conference
- National Girls and Women in Sports Day
- North American Society for Sport Management Conference
- Women's Sports Foundation Summit
- Women's Sports Marketing Conference

**Related Publications**

- *Advertising Age*
- *Journal of Marketing*
- *Marketing Communications*
- *Sport Marketing Quarterly*
- *Team Marketing Report*
- *The Women's Sports Experience*

# Job Opportunities

### Assistant Director, Special Events and Promotions

Responsible for writing press releases, developing mailing lists, making telephone calls, and assisting with implementation of special events promotions. Candidates must have strong writing, oral, and computer skills and knowledge of the sport industry.

### Assistant Sport Marketing Director

Assist Ticket Coordinator in all aspects of ticket sales and promotions; assist Event Director with planning and execution of on-site advertising and operations; assist Volunteer Coordinator in organization and administration of event volunteer workers. Candidates must have communication, organizational, and sales skills.

### Assistant Public Relations Director

A professional sports league office is seeking a self-motivated individual with at least three years experience working in a public relations office with a professional sports team. A bachelor's degree in communications or sport management/communications is required. The candidate must also demonstrate excellent writing and computer skills. Job responsibilities include writing press releases, preparing and distributing a daily sports circulation report, compiling, organizing, and printing statistics for media guide publications for special events such as the All-Star Game Series and League Championship Series and preparing written materials for press conferences.

### Coordinator of New Business Development

The Florida Fleet, a new professional women's ice hockey league is seeking an individual with at least five years management experience with a professional sports team or league office. A bachelor's degree in sport management, management, or marketing is required. Demonstrated skills in strategic management planning, marketing, and community relations is desirable. Job responsibilities include working with the Vice President of Marketing and Special Events in developing strategic plans for expanding markets and spectator audiences, strengthening and expanding community grassroots involvements in the sport, and attracting new corporate sponsors.

### Tournament Operations Manager

A sports management firm responsible for marketing a professional women's tennis tournament is seeking an individual with one to three years experience in professional sports tournament operations. A bachelor's degree in sport management is preferred. Job responsibilities include assisting the tournament director with food and beverage operations, facilities management, and coordinating and servicing on-site booth operations for corporate sponsors. Excellent planning, organizational, interpersonal, and communications skills are required.

### Director of Marketing

A major university is seeking an individual with three to five years experience in marketing or sports marketing. A bachelor's degree in marketing or sport management is preferred. Previous work experience in an NCAA Division I athletic department or with a professional sports team is desirable. Job responsibilities include ticket sales and promotions, promoting individual sports teams, securing corporate sponsorships, selling stadium advertising space and program advertisements, and developing and implementing other marketing and promotions strategies.

### Director of Community Relations

A new expansion team in a minor ice hockey league is seeking a creative and highly motivated individual to develop and implement a community relations program. A bachelor's degree in sport management is preferred. Job responsibilities include arranging speaking engagements for coaches and players, organizing youth ice hockey clinics, organizing appearances of coaches and players with charitable organizations, developing other strategies for involving coaches and players in community activities and events. The individual must have excellent planning and organizational skills with the ability to handle details.

### Director of Marketing and Promotions

The Santa Fe Bladerunners is looking for an individual to direct marketing and promotions. This position includes raising awareness and interest in a sport never played professionally in this area. Applicants must have at least five years of experience with sports promotion/marketing; preference will be for candidates with previous professional sports promotion/marketing experience. The marketing and promotions director will report directly to the team owner and work closely with the general manager and other team personnel.

# Chapter 13

# Sport Event and Facility Management

**Rob Ammon, Jr.**
Slippery Rock University

---

## Learning Objectives

After studying this chapter, you will be able to

1. identify steps in conducting an event or managing a facility;

2. explain the need for effective risk management of facilities;

3. identify differences between public assembly facilities and those managed by private companies;

4. discuss similarities and differences between event and facility management; and

5. demonstrate comprehension of current trends in sport and public assembly facilities.

---

Managing sport and entertainment productions and the facilities in which these activities occur requires many skills and competencies. Employment positions exist for individuals who can schedule events, work with facility operations, oversee facility finances, equip the facility with TV and video connections, provide maintenance and custodial services, conduct facility marketing and promotions, engage in event merchandising, and provide risk-management services. These are only a few of the diverse opportunities that exist for students who desire to become involved in facility

management. As a manager or director in one of these positions, you must know the responsibilities and skills for that specific area and understand facility management.

Obviously, individuals who administer events and facilities use many skills and competencies managers in other professions need. In what areas will they need training to address unique challenges and opportunities? This chapter divides the field of study into three components: (a) event management, (b) risk management, and (c) facility management. Each area is unique, but they are also interwoven to the point that it is sometimes difficult to identify which one is being performed at any time. In fact, most of the time, at least two and perhaps three of them are occurring simultaneously. Therefore some skills and competencies will be similar in each component.

# Event Management

An event could be a sporting contest, a circus, or artistic productions such as plays, symphonies, dances, and concerts. Each event has a demonstrable existence. Each event is a product, an outcome, and an occurrence. An event will occur in a specific year and month, on a specific date, at a specific place. All preparation must be completed before the event begins. The total effort is much like the prepared actor waiting in the wings for the cue to go on stage.

## Scenario 1: Troubled Tammy

Tammy Mondra worked for the athletic department at Regular University. She was managing a 5K fun run that would take place on the university campus. During the 2 weeks before the race, Tammy conducted preliminary planning meetings with other athletic department staff, campus police, and local volunteers. She was confident that most logistics were in place and that the road race would be successful.

On Friday, the day before the race, the graduate assistant responsible for laying out the race course discovered it to be 1/10th of a mile too short. After several discussions, the course was extended the additional distance onto a local grocery store parking lot. The owner of the parking lot, an RU alum, assured Tammy there would be no problem with extending the finish line from the edge of campus onto his store's lot.

Friday at 4:00 P.M., after solving the distance problem, the only remaining pre-race agenda item was the delivery of the race T-shirts. More than 500 contestants had prepaid the $12 entry fee, which included a multicolored, long-sleeved T-shirt to be received on completing the race. Tinker Wannabe, Tammy's assistant, convinced her to go home while he awaited the tardy shipment.

Around 5:30 P.M., after a relaxing dinner, Tammy received several disturbing phone calls. Chuck Bidnot, the vendor for the T-shirts, called to explain that the manufacturer had production problems and the race T-shirts would not be completed until Monday morning. He apologized profusely,

but said little could be done at this time. No sooner had Tammy hung up the phone than Stacy Counselor, the university lawyer called. She explained to Tammy that because the finish line had been extended 1/10th of a mile off campus property, a city permit was necessary before the race could begin. Unfortunately, the courthouse wouldn't open until 10:00 A.M. and the race was scheduled to begin at 8:00 A.M.

Tammy had not anticipated these problems, and she was stunned and confused. In addition to everything else, Tinker called again and said the city paper was attempting to contact her for a race update to be run in their morning edition. Tammy was paralyzed with indecision. What should she do?

Event management includes planning, coordinating, staging, and evaluating any event. Successful event management requires attention to each area listed here, several of which Tammy did not address completely.

- Recruitment and training of personnel
- Planning emergency medical services
- Risk management
- Facility rental
- Alcohol management and training
- Box office management and ticketing
- Food service management and catering
- Building maintenance
- Marketing, advertising, and public relations
- Securing proper permits and licenses
- Contract negotiations with promoters
- Merchandise and novelty sales
- Crowd management
- Parking and traffic control
- Evaluating the final result

Whether the event is a small 5K run or a Chicago Bulls basketball game, these components are crucial to the success of the production. How many of these responsibilities and to what extent and detail each is needed depends on the kind of event, the time, place, and clientele. For example, in Tammy's situation, there would be no box office or ticket management because there was no seated audience. On the other hand, a ticket to a Bulls game is a prized possession. Think of the preparation of the building maintenance crew for a Bulls game! Even Tammy had to deal with parking lot logistics for the 5K run. Marketing and merchandising are strategic assignments for Tammy and the Bulls personnel. Good recruitment policies for both volunteer and paid personnel are an important element in event management. Training these personnel could make or break the success of the event. A good training program will pay for itself many times by providing quality performance for a quality event.

# Event Personnel Assignments

The event coordinator has the most direct responsibility for managing the individual events. This staff member oversees the setup and takedown of the event, hires and trains the event staff—ushers, ticket takers, guest relations personnel, crowd management staff, and food service employees. This individual may be an employee of the event itself or, in many cases, of the facility where the event is taking place. All events—from Tammy's fun run to the Olympics—need an effective management plan. A management plan will include six basic steps: scheduling, negotiating, coordinating, staging, settling with the promoter, and evaluating.

## Scheduling the Event

Scheduling includes determining what the event will be, where in the facility it will occur, and when it will happen. The philosophy of a facility will dictate the types of events that are scheduled in it. For example, if a facility identifies profit as its primary purpose, events held in it would be sport, entertainment, or artistic productions that would generate sufficient revenues to maximize the return on the investments. Examples of these types of facilities are the Astrodome (Houston), the MCI Center (Washington, DC), Red Rocks Amphitheater (Morrison, Colorado), and Key Arena (Seattle). On the other hand, some facilities are more concerned with providing services for the community. These facilities would schedule nonprofit events, such as trade shows, garden shows, or intercollegiate athletics contests. Examples of nonprofit facilities are coliseums, fairgrounds, community centers, and high school gymnasiums.

Each event being considered must be investigated to discover if it would be a good fit with the facility's philosophy. Basic research about the event begins with a representative of the facility, usually the event coordinator, examining the reputation, qualities, and merits of an event and its **promoters**. A **cost analysis** will be conducted to determine if the event will be profitable (in the case of a for-profit facility) or will at least break even (in the case of a nonprofit facility).

There might be several activity spaces in a facility, making it possible to schedule more than one event in the same building at the same time. The person responsible for scheduling, therefore, must be detail oriented and must maintain accurate records, keeping in mind that the goal of all sport and event facilities is a full schedule of confirmed events that are compatible with the facility's philosophy.

## Negotiating the Event

Once an event is formally scheduled, it is considered booked. At that point, preliminary negotiations occur between the event coordinator and the promoter or representative of the event. These negotiations determine the terms of the contract regarding such items as the facility rental fee and ticket prices. In addition, any sources of revenue that may be shared or **split,** such as money generated from tickets, concessions, parking, and advertising, will also be negotiated. Financial negotiations are a critical factor in establishing the cost of an event, and if the dollar amount is too high, additional negotiations ensue to determine which costs to eliminate and which splits to modify.

## Coordinating the Event

Once the contracts have been signed, the event coordinator designs a plan or work order for all employees to follow. This instrument is the game plan for the event. It documents all the requirements discussed with the promoter or other company representative. An additional purpose of the work order is to define the time it will take to do each assigned task. As this plan develops, problem areas pertaining to the original contract may occur, and the contract is often revised. An example might include technical problems in staging, such as lighting or sound systems, size of stage, or placement of the mixer board. It might even be a contract rider concerning the specific kind of bottled water or snacks provided in the catering room.

In the first scenario, Tammy failed to plan properly. One secret to successful planning is the ability to plot the event's time restrictions. Start with the date of the event and calculate the time needed for each step, from last-minute tasks just before the event back to the initial meeting for the event. Allow additional emergency time within the work order. Examples of the application of this procedure are high school plays that can be factored on a 6-week chart from opening night back to casting the roles. Another example is preparing a multicourse meal, such as Thanksgiving dinner. The cooking time for the thawed turkey is determined and the potatoes are mashed 5 minutes before serving time. Everything has to come out of the oven and off the burners at their right times. All the food must be hot and on the table at the same time. Timing is a key ingredient. When the kitchen crew makes it happen, the result is a Happy Thanksgiving; when the event staff makes it happen, the result is a successfully managed event!

After the event management personnel have designed, evaluated, and refined the event coordinator's plan, orientation meetings are scheduled with the ticket takers, ushers, crowd management, concession, and parking staff to address specific concerns. The event coordinator presents the work order at this orientation meeting. Also at this time, all new volunteers and employees will be identified for specific training.

Various preliminary planning meetings should take place with all staff members and other people whose cooperation is critical to the success of the event. In Troubled Tammy's case, people such as personnel from the athletics department, campus police, and local volunteers, should be consulted, informed, and involved at each step along the way. During this process, any necessary permits should be obtained, a factor Troubled Tammy neglected to consider. Also, the organizers must continually anticipate potential problems, thus avoiding surprises like the ones Tammy had to face.

## Learning Activity

You are the event coordinator at a university sports arena. The Harlem Globe Trotters and the noted rock band, Mogen David and the Grapes of Wrath, have been scheduled for a special event. The Trotters will be flying into the nearest airport, whereas the Grapes have their own bus. Both groups will stay overnight and will leave the following morning. Make a list of the details you must handle.

### Staging the Event

After much planning and anticipating, the day of the event arrives. In small events, such as 5K races, the organizers make certain that items such as start and finish lines, award tables, and porta-

johns are properly located. For large events, such as concerts and ice shows, the truck(s) carrying the equipment for the event will arrive and an entire day is usually allowed for load-in and setup.

At the designated hour on the day of the event, the doors or gates are opened, the crowd flows inside, and the event begins. At this point, the event coordinator discovers if he or she was effective in planning and coordinating the following facets of staging the event: parking, seating, alcohol policies, and crowd control.

## Learning Activity

The Volvo International Tennis Championships are scheduled for your facility. Prepare an event-management plan. Begin by listing all the activities that need to take place before the event. Include such items as reserving the facility, advertising, hotel accommodations, ticket printing and sales, and personnel scheduling. Next, place all the activities in the sequence in which they must occur. Now, calculate the time needed to accomplish each task. Finally, place the items on a project calendar that shows each activity in sequence, the time required to complete it, and the overall chain of events.

**Parking.**   As with every plan, the various groups involved (campus, city, county, and state patrol) must be allowed to provide input to the work order, in this case regarding parking and traffic. Some parking spaces may be lost due to weather (mud or large puddles of water) or because of special promotions, such as fireworks, and traffic flow problems may exist due to limited access. Providing bus lanes and alternative methods of transportation will diminish the total number of vehicles parking at your event. The intersections that have higher than normal accident rates must be identified and extra officers should assist out-of-town fans through these problem areas. Posting adequate signs on major thoroughfares to direct arriving spectators also decreases potential problems. Altering the duration of signal lights during ingress and egress assists vehicular traffic through most congested areas. In addition, notifying local residents and businesses of event-day traffic plans helps community relations. Finally, by establishing emergency routes for police, fire, and medical personnel, dangerous situations may be quickly and safely overcome.

**Seating.**   Most events in the United States provide either general admission, reserved, or festival seating (a misnomer because no seats exist, just open floor space). With the use of trained ushers and an effective crowd-management plan, most events encounter minimal problems with reserve seating. Festival seating, however, which allows spectators to crush up against the stage in a general admission setting, has proven tragic in several instances. In 1979, 11 patrons were killed as a result of festival seating and the fact that facility doors were not opened on time before a Who concert at the Cincinnati Riverfront Coliseum. In 1991, three teenagers died in Salt Lake City as a result of a crowd surge at an AC/DC concert (Lewis, 1992). Festival seating was in effect at the concert in spite of legislation that prohibited its use. Later that year, 5,000 patrons tried to cram into a 2,700-seat facility on the campus of New York's Harlem City College, resulting in 9 deaths and 29 injuries (Newman & Dao, 1992). Festival seating allows promoters to sell more tickets than reserved or general admission seating and continues to be a controversial topic in event management.

**Alcohol Policies.**   For many individuals, sporting events are social outings, and sometimes the consumption of alcohol is involved. Although millions of sport fans drink alcohol responsibly, a minority are irresponsible, and their "good times" become a major headache for an event manager. Alcohol can be sold and managed effectively at sporting events, but managed improperly, alcohol sales may become an onerous liability. An effective alcohol policy will make the difference (Ammon, 1995).

Many individuals in the sport industry argue that revenue generated from beer sales at athletic contests is substantial and worth the risks entailed. In fact some programs, especially universities with small attendance figures, would find it difficult to generate a profit if it were not for home game beer sales. Other programs have determined that alcohol sales are not worth the liabilities associated with this increased revenue. A potential liability exists if alcohol is served; therefore, a comprehensive alcohol policy should be an integral part of any event-management plan. The written alcohol policy should be filed with proper authorities, and signs should be posted on the premises. If drinking alcohol is not permitted, signs should be posted in full view of the patrons stating: "Alcoholic beverages are prohibited." If alcohol consumption is permitted, event managers must be prepared for the problems that might occur. Intoxicated patrons create many safety concerns for themselves and others (Ammon, 1995).

> **Learning Activity**
>
> You are the facility director of a new multi-purpose facility. Present an argument against the sale of alcohol in your new building. What factors do you need to consider?

**Crowd Control.**   You need to formulate an effective crowd-management plan for every event. The components of these plans are similar, regardless of whether the event is a fun run or a major spectacle such as the Super Bowl. Miller (1993) listed seven criteria that juries have considered in determining whether or not crowd-control measures were adequate and appropriate: (a) type of event, (b) surrounding facilities and environment, (c) known rivalries among schools, (d) threats of violence, (e) existence and adequacy of emergency plan, (f) anticipation of crowd size and seating configuration, and (g) use of security personnel and ushers. If you have attended a high school championship athletic contest, you have seen each of these components in action.

A basic crowd-management policy should parallel your event philosophy of providing a safe, enjoyable, and secure environment for all who attend. This may be accomplished by following five basic steps. The first component of an effective crowd-control policy is providing adequate informational signage. These informational and directional signs build a support network between fans and your event-management staff. Spectators appreciate having direction and will normally abide by facility directives if previously informed.

Second, the crowd-management plan should delineate procedures to use in ejecting disruptive, unruly, or intoxicated patrons. As previously mentioned, the prime focus of an effective crowd-management plan should be to provide for the safety and security of the fans, which includes protection from violent third parties. Therefore, removing any disruptive or intoxicated fan will provide a safer environment for the remaining spectators and a measure of protection against **litigation**. As the event coordinator you must be prepared to document ejections with appropriate paperwork. This is a critical step in the ejection process, as it will be necessary in the event of a lawsuit.

© Daily Illini

Whether your event attracts thousands of spectators or dozens, your crowd-management policy should be to provide a safe, enjoyable, and secure environment for all who attend.

Third, you must employ a trained and competent staff to carry out the crowd-management policy. For example, if the event is extremely popular and has a limited seating capacity, your ticket takers and ushers might need to be prepared for counterfeit or duplicate ticket problems. Using trained personnel who have progressed through a licensing program provides you, as the event coordinator, with better qualified employees.

Fourth, you are obligated to provide fans with a safe and secure environment. For example, promotional giveaways (e.g., bats, helmets, balls) may attract customers, but they may also cause problems. These items pose safety concerns because they frequently become missiles that unruly fans launch at each other and at the players, officials, and coaches. Moreover, if the giveaways are the type that will need to be cleaned up after the event, they will increase the workload of the housekeeping and custodial departments.

In the past, it was assumed that all customers were ambulatory, had 20-20 vision, normal hearing, and were otherwise free of any physical or mental differences. In recent years, however, we have acknowledged the fact that variations exist in people's abilities, and we must make our facilities accessible and pleasant for everyone who wishes to enjoy them. To ensure accessibility for all citizens, Congress passed the **Americans With Disabilities Act (ADA)** in 1992. The ADA has had a major impact on sport, entertainment, and arts facility design. Among the mandates of the ADA is a requirement that physical barriers in existing public accommodations must be removed, if possible. If these architectural changes are financially or structurally impossible, alternative methods of providing services must be offered. New construction must also meet the requirements of the ADA. Sport and entertainment event managers must be familiar with other requirements of the ADA as they pertain to facility features such as signage, restrooms, telephones, parking, and shower stalls. The ADA is only one of many state, federal, and local laws to which event managers must adhere.

The fifth component of an effective crowd-management plan is an effective communication system. Multichanneled radios are an integral element in implementing such a communication system. Each group involved in the event (facility, medical, security, and law enforcement) must have the ability to discuss immediate problems quickly.

### Settling With the Promoter

If the event is for profit, the promoter and the event coordinator sit down together for the **settlement** while the event is in progress. This process involves reconciling the revenues versus the expenses and splitting any resulting profit between the promoter and the facility representative (Farmer, Mulrooney, & Ammon, 1996).

### Evaluating the Event

After the event is over and the crowd has filed out, the equipment used in the event is gathered up and put away or stored in trucks, and the cleanup of the facility commences. Usually another entire day is permitted for the load-out. Immediately following the event, the event coordinator meets with the management team to evaluate the entire process. **Documentation** of the entire process is critical, not only for protection against subsequent litigation but also for reference in planning future events. Now let's see how a prepared event manager would conduct a 5K race.

## Scenario 2: The Mondra Model or Terrific Tammy

Tammy Mondra worked for the athletic department at Regular University. She was managing a 5K fun run that would take place on the university campus. A year ago when the project had been assigned, Tammy had planned the event in detail, using a work order that included times, schedules, deadlines, and committees. The race course layout was approved by the track coach and appropriate authorities. The runners' shirts and awards were bid by contract with delivery guaranteed 2 weeks before the race day. The university legal counsel reviewed all facets of the project's risk-management plan. The marketing plan was successfully implemented (see chapter 12), and news releases and interviews were well received by both print and broadcast media (see chapter 11). All project personnel were well prepared and on task. Every committee coordinator performed well. After the 5K fun run, Tammy's team of volunteers and the athletics administrators evaluated the event. All comments, complaints, and suggestions for improvement were included in Tammy's event

folder for implementation next year. The 5K fun run was a success with a great student turnout and good weather! By the way, Tammy has been working on more than this event. The Alum Golf Outing is coming up and she is ahead of schedule with her event planning.

## Risk Management

Risk management is an integral element of any facility management operation, and we can not overstate the importance of a risk manager (Berlonghi, 1990; Cotten, 1993; Sharp, 1990; van der Smissen, 1990b). Risk management has been practiced for a long time in the business industry, yet has taken many years to become a concern to sport managers. Review of the sport-related literature before the late 1960s revealed limited information pertaining to risk management. Safety practices and legal liability were discussed, but little was mentioned about problems specific to the sport industry (e.g., trampolines, protective gear such as football helmets) (van der Smissen, 1990b).

Millions of individuals are injured each year while participating in or attending sporting events or recreational activities. Before the 1970s, most participants or spectators who were injured during an athletic event assumed the injury was a risk inherent to the activity and rarely considered litigation. During the 1970s, however, the theory that participants assumed their own risk was eroded by judicial interpretation, and legal action became a common recourse to resolve a loss. Because of increased litigation and high monetary awards by juries, the cost of insurance coverage escalated, and many sport and recreation programs were forced to limit their offerings.

A risk is the possibility of injury or damage occurring during an activity or event. Managing risk is a legal duty of administrators, educators, and managers to provide a safe and enjoyable environment to their spectators (Ammon, 1993). An individual employed to anticipate risk and reduce these problems is a risk manager. The United States is a litigious society; therefore, prospective event and facility managers must become aware of their legal **duty of care**, the responsibility for safety that facility managers owe to patrons and spectators.

Usually, an event or facility manager's duty of care is divided into three areas of responsibility: (a) to provide a safe environment from injurious or defective products, (b) to exercise care in maintaining the facility and its equipment, and (c) to protect patrons from injurious acts by third parties (Wong, 1988). In many facilities these functions are assigned to risk managers or are addressed by a safety committee. Without the assistance of a risk manager, a breach of any of these duties could occur, thus subjecting the facility director to a lawsuit for negligence. The following list identifies areas that risk managers at sport and public assembly facilities participate in daily:

- Conduct regular training programs.
- Originate simple but understandable signs that communicate facility policy to fans.
- Document everything to decrease potential liability.
- Eliminate activities with high risks and little rewards.
- Inspect all facilities and equipment.
- Make certain supervision is adequate and proper.
- Ensure that all employees are trained and competent.
- Schedule trained personnel for treating injuries at every event.
- Create emergency medical plans.
- Design and implement emergency evacuation plans.
- Produce incident reports for all injuries and ejections.

With today's astronomical negligence awards and the amount of publicity that surrounds sport controversies, a logical assumption would be that the cost of a risk manager would be outweighed by the gain of avoiding litigation. In addition, the negative publicity resulting from litigation could affect community support for your event. It would, therefore, be prudent for event and facility managers to employ a full-time risk manager. This is a new occupational classification in which interested sport management students with a knowledge of law and facilities could secure a position in the facility management field.

## Learning Activity

Think about why there are more lawsuits in sport and recreation today than 10 to 15 years ago. How could risk management help eliminate some litigation cases?

# Facility Management

Facility management is the process of planning, administering, coordinating, and evaluating the day-to-day operations of a facility. These duties encompass a wide array of responsibilities, including marketing the facility, promoting facility events, facility maintenance, and hiring and firing facility personnel.

## Facility Personnel

Most sport facilities are managed by a facility director. Directors are ultimately responsible for facility planning and administration. Often the director is appointed or hired by the city, so many of his or her duties will be political in nature. An additional duty will be negotiating major contracts pertaining to the facility, sometimes including events being scheduled in the facility.

The director of operations is the primary assistant to the facility director. This person is heavily involved in coordinating the day-to-day facility operations. His or her duties include making certain the facility is kept clean, proper signage is posted, minor repairs are completed, and supplies and equipment are delivered as ordered. The operations director also evaluates many facility employees, including maintenance workers, ticket takers, housekeepers, construction workers, and ushers. In addition, the operations director usually oversees many functions pertaining to the facility itself.

As previously mentioned, the event coordinator has the most direct responsibility for managing the individual events. Most facilities have their own event coordinator, and this individual will be the liaison between the event and the facility management. He or she manages the event for the facility; however, the director of operations is ultimately responsible. Additional information about managing sport facilities is presented in chapters 8, 9, and 10.

## Facility Ownership

An important concept in facility management is the understanding that how these processes will be accomplished depends on who owns the facility. Many facilities are privately owned by an individual or a corporation. Examples of privately owned facilities are Texas Stadium in Irving, Texas (Jerry Jones), Pro Players Stadium in Miami, Florida (Wayne Huizinga), and the Forum Arena in Los Angeles (Jerry Buss). Other facilities are publicly owned and are operated by local municipalities or government entities. Examples of public ownership are the Civic Arena (Pittsburgh), the Kingdome (King County, Washington), McNichols Arena (city and county of Denver), as well as **stadiums** and **arenas** on public university campuses.

The primary objective of a privately owned facility is to make a profit for the owners and stockholders. The manager focuses on maximum return on investment. If publicly owned, the facility will usually have a profit-oriented philosophy; however, in some cases the primary objective will be to provide a service to the community or campus. In these instances the facility needs to generate enough revenue to stay in business, but income beyond expenses goes back into operations. These different goals directly affect facility managers' decisions.

## Privatization

City governments are not in the business of managing facilities; therefore, operational efficiency and financial performance of these municipally managed facilities are often less than optimal. Consequently, many publicly owned and managed facilities across the United States operate at a deficit, a situation that has led to services and events being reduced or eliminated. As facility management has become more complex and demanding, many facilities have turned to private companies to handle management tasks. Privatization is the term used to describe this move from public to private management.

Do not confuse private management with the previously discussed issue of private ownership. The facilities are still owned by the municipalities. Each of these companies specializes in facility management and, therefore, are contracted to independently manage facilities (Stotlar, 1990). Private companies can negotiate contracts more effectively, be flexible in negotiating deals, and establish relationships with promoters to increase the number of events. In addition, their priority is to make a profit.

Currently, there are four major private facility management companies in the United States: Spectacor Management Group (SMG), Ogden Allied, Centre Management, and Leisure Management International (LMI). Although most privately managed facilities are in the United States, several of these companies have expanded internationally to Europe and the Far East. The first facility to be privately managed was the Louisiana Superdome in 1977. Some estimates have indicated that 20% of all stadiums, arenas, and convention centers in the United States are now managed by private companies (Sauer, 1993).

Many individuals feel that one possible solution for cities in financial woes will be to privatize in areas other than facility management. Municipalities may desire to contract with private management companies because these companies could provide efficient services to entities such as school districts, parks, sanitation services, and safety services. Some mention has even been made of privatizing the U.S. Postal System. The future of privatization contains many possibilities.

## Learning Activity

You are the facility manager of an 18,000-seat municipally owned arena in a midsized city in the central United States. The facility has not shown a profit in the past 3 years, and you have been requested to make a presentation to the city council describing the benefits and detriments of hiring a private company to manage the facility. At this meeting the council expects you to make a recommendation as to which option they should choose. What will you say?

## Types of Facilities

There are many types of sport facilities and ways to categorize them. In this chapter, we classify facilities according to the types of events and activities held in them. In some situations, the purpose is broad and incorporates many sports or activities. For example, a multipurpose high school gymnasium might be designed for interscholastic sports practices and competition, physical education classes, school plays, and graduation ceremonies. On the other hand, some facilities, such as a **natatorium**, are designed for a specific purpose. Softball complexes, golf courses, bowling alleys, motor sport tracks, and skating rinks are single-purpose facilities. Field houses, gymnasiums, and fitness centers usually provide space for a variety of sports and other activities. These facilities are designed primarily for activity; therefore, spectator seating usually is limited. A fitness center might provide activity spaces for gymnastics, swimming, tennis, racquetball, jogging, and a cardiovascular area that includes fitness machines and free weights.

Facilities such as field houses and fitness centers must also provide several ancillary areas, support areas used in the facility's functioning. Typical ancillary areas include locker, shower, and dressing rooms for men and for women; administrative and staff offices; lounge and reception areas; public restrooms; custodial closets; pro shops; equipment storage and issue areas; health and nutrition bars; kitchens; and mechanical and chemical filtration rooms.

Arenas and stadiums, on the other hand, provide space not only for activity but also for spectators. These facilities are known as spectator facilities. The Pyramid in Memphis, Tennessee, is an example of an arena. The $60-million structure has more than 450,000 square feet and is built in the shape of a pyramid (Cohen, 1993). As a major tourist attraction, this multipurpose facility sponsors a variety of events from basketball games to tractor pulls. Some facilities are single purpose in that they are designed for only one sport. Camden Yard (Baltimore Orioles) and Jacobs Field (Cleveland Indians) are examples of one-sport facilities.

Originally, stadiums were outdoor facilities; however, in recent years, many covered stadiums have been built. You might be familiar with some of these, such as the Superdome in New Orleans, the Skydome in Toronto, and the Alamodome in San Antonio. In addition to hosting professional and intercollegiate sport competitions, these large, covered spaces are used for events, such as concerts, truck pulls, motocross races, home and garden shows, and recreational vehicle shows. Most covered stadiums have large video screens and video monitors that provide close-ups, instant replays, and special features to entertain the crowd. Movable stands and convertible floors enable these massive stadiums to accommodate a variety of events, from small gatherings to large concerts, ice extravaganzas, conventions, athletic events, and festivals.

The purpose of stadiums and arenas is to provide entertainment; therefore, it is necessary for these structures to include specific amenities. Amenities are special features added for the convenience of the facility's users—the spectators, patrons, and players. Amenities include food, beverage, and merchandise services; restrooms; spectator seating; and parking lots. The number of amenities provided will depend on the size of the facility or event. For example, the Louisiana Superdome houses a gift shop, a Stadium Club, two restaurants, four large ballrooms, five cocktail lounges, and eight bars. On a smaller scale, Terrific Tammy probably provided amenities such as water

stations and several porta-johns for the contestants in her 5K run.

In addition to more elaborate spectator facilities, interest has grown in erecting nontraditional facilities. An ice arena is a specialized facility that can be used for figure skating competitions, ice hockey, **curling**, and instructional and recreational skating. Growing interest in adventure activities has produced indoor rock climbing centers. Amusement parks and water sport parks are becoming extremely popular. Even some shopping malls have gotten into the act by including various sport facilities in their structures. An ice skating rink, a miniature golf course, an underwater activity area for scuba diving, a gambling casino, and an amusement park are some of the features of the West Edmonton Mall in Alberta, Canada.

# Summary

Event management includes the planning, coordinating, staging, and evaluating of an event. For an event to be successful, the event coordinator needs to complete each of these important tasks. Scheduling and booking an event begins the overall process, and a cost analysis is a critical element in this initial operation. After the event coordinator has decided that the event will be held, the necessary contracts are signed, and a game plan or work order is created by the event manager and communicated to the others on the event-management team. This document provides the guidelines for the organizers to follow. Once the event is completed, the management team meets to evaluate and to ensure the proper documents are filled out. In addition, this meeting makes certain that a blueprint exists for similar events to be held in the future.

Risk management is an important component for all personnel working in sport facilities. The duties owed to spectators and fans create the need for an individual who can anticipate potential areas of loss and injury and can take action to decrease them. Employing an individual to reduce these risks is a less expensive alternative than the potential litigation that exists without such a person. Interested sport management students with a knowledge of law and facilities could obtain a position in the facility risk-management field.

Facility directors, operation managers, and event coordinators each have specific responsibilities for a facility. How these individuals manage the facility will depend on whether it is owned by private citizens or the taxpayers. Regardless of ownership, the management of sport facilities is increasingly falling to private management companies. Private management has been successful in some sport and public assembly facilities across the United States. For example, presently four companies manage more than 76 facilities on a national and international scale. Due to the increase in privatization, many job possibilities exist with these companies at the corporate level and at each facility location.

Fairs, festivals, water sport parks, and various events all have one common denominator: they take place in some type of facility and each facility needs individuals to manage them. For some facilities, the purpose will be singular, such as for entertainment events. For others, it will be athletic events. Some will have community events as their focal point, and for some multipurpose facilities, it may be a combination of all three.

---

# For More Information

Please take advantage of the following sources in order to obtain more information on event and facility management.

## Professional Associations

- AAHPERD Council on Facilities and Equipment
- Association of Higher Education Facilities Officers
- International Association for Sports and Leisure
- International Association of Auditorium Managers
- National Institute of Parks and Grounds Management
- National Spa and Pool Institute
- Resort and Commercial Recreation Association

## Related Publications

- *Aquatics International*

- *Athletic Business*
- *Collegiate Athletic Management*
- *IAAM Newsletter*
- *Journal of Sport Management*
- *Recreation Resources*

## Web Sites

- Sports Technology Hotlist: http://www-white.media.mit.edu/~intille/sports-technology.html
- World Wide Web of Sports: http://www.tns.lcs.mit.edu/cgi-bin/sport
- Sportsline-Sports in the Courts: http://www.sportsline.com/u/page/courts/index.html
- The Sports Network: http://www.sportsnetwork.com
- Online Sports Career Center: http://www.onlinesports.com/pages/CareerCenter.html

# Job Opportunities

## Food and Beverage Manager

Looking for a general manager to oversee all aspects of our small arena concession business. Major responsibilities include event-day operations, developing and implementing operation and inventory controls, training programs for concessions employees, and special projects. The candidate must have excellent organizational and interpersonal skills.

## Event Coordinator

Established Mid-Atlantic municipal arena seeking applications for hands-on event coordinator with additional responsibility of employee training. Include resume and salary history.

## Director of Arena Operations

Full-time position available for a director of operations responsible for day-to-day operation of the arena, including ticketing, guest relations, security, and first aid. Duties will also include assuring guest satisfaction through employee hiring and training, design of safety and risk-management programs, and the day-to-day supervision of six managers and staff.

## Promotion Manager

Stage Inc. is currently seeking an enthusiastic, creative, and results-oriented promotion manager who is eager to promote live sporting events. Will be responsible for researching assigned markets; ticket pricing and sales; setup; media planning, buying, and negotiating; local sponsorship sales; and event publicity planning and coordinating. Candidate must have a degree in marketing or sport management. Travel required. Excellent compensation and benefit package.

## Operations Manager of Aquamarine Water Park

This position reports to the corporate offices in New Mexico and is responsible for the day-to-day operations of the water park. Primary responsibilities include facility maintenance, aquatics, park services, guest services, and admissions. Secondary responsibilities require supervising group services and marketing.

## Sport Facility Manager

Professionally based sport and entertainment group seeking individual to manage its stadium and ancillary facility development process. The ideal candidate should possess experience in facility development and start-up, along with related aspects such as concession negotiations and supervision of facility architectural firms. Facility operations experience a plus

## Branch Managers and Guest Services Managers of A1 Event Management Company

Event staffing company is seeking dynamic individuals to fill immediate and future openings in major arenas and stadia. Proven management skills and hands-on experience in the crowd and facility management industry preferred. Financial management and budgetary planning experience a plus. Communication and leadership skills are necessary to excel in this rewarding environment.

## Public Facility Manager

Bernard Amphitheater is seeking a public facility professional to assume the position of facility manager. This position requires supervising marketing and box office personnel, negotiating with all outside promoters, and coordinating all self-promoted events. In addition, the facility manager will supervise and oversee all group sales and special events. Individuals should possess a background in facility management.

# Chapter 14

# Sports Medicine

**Lynn A. Darby**
Bowling Green State University
**Kathy D. Browder**
Georgia Southern University

---

## Learning Objectives

After studying this chapter, you will be able to

1. define sports medicine;

2. identify the disciplines that provide the knowledge base for professions in sports medicine;

3. specify careers in the fitness, exercise, and athletic training areas of sports medicine;

4. describe professional responsibilities and academic preparation necessary for each career;

5. compare and contrast criteria for programs and settings in which sports medicine information is disseminated and procedures implemented;

6. define the three classification levels (i.e., apparently healthy, at risk, or with disease) that determine the extent and type of exercise testing and prescription appropriate for an individual;

7. explain the need for classifying individuals before exercise tests, prescriptive exercise, or rehabilitative programs;

8. identify professional associations in sports medicine and explain the purpose and benefits of membership in them; and

9. discuss future challenges in sports medicine.

---

Most people know that exercise is necessary for overall health and rehabilitation. Many people, however, don't know how to exercise safely and effectively. For example, the six individuals we describe here need assistance, but they are unsure how to get it. As you read the chapter and learn more about specific career opportunities in exercise and athletic training, think about how the information relates to these individuals and their needs.

*Bobbie.* Bobbie has been *sedentary* for a long time. For her, exercise has always been difficult, something "to do tomorrow," and she doesn't want to exercise with a group of people. Bobbie finally decides to start an **exercise program** to *lose weight*, but is unsure whether to lift weights or jog.

*Jay.* Jay has always been *active and runs approximately 8 to 10 miles per week.* Recently, while running Jay turned his ankle and the *pain* was so severe that he could not complete the workout.

*Chip.* After 2 weeks in the hospital following a *heart attack*, Chip was eager to get home. All these hospital staff were poking, prodding, and coercing Chip to exercise. Now, to his consternation, he must attend *exercise programs* three times a week *at the hospital.* He has signed up for **cardiac rehabilitation**, but is unsure what this entails.

*Lucia.* Lucia, recently retired, *gets plenty of activity* working in the yard and bicycling. However, Lucia wants to sign up for the *senior* walking class at the *community recreation center* to meet other people, learn the guidelines for walking as exercise, and *have fun.*

*Rick.* Rick's parents work out regularly. Recently, the *health and sports club* at which they exercise advertised that personal trainers are available. Rick's parents want to enroll Rick because his physical skills have developed slowly. His parents are unsure about the *quality of instruction* Rick would receive.

*Katie.* Katie has been a *personal trainer* for some time. Many of her clients have commented that she is an excellent motivator and *exercise leader.* Her number of clients has increased dramatically lately. She is having a difficult time keeping all the client information, *fees, and so on organized.*

In this chapter you will learn about the knowledge, skills, and settings necessary for delivering and managing exercise programs. Then, at the end of the chapter, with an understanding of the field of sports medicine, you will match the client with the appropriately skilled sports medicine professional or experience.

# Nature and Scope of Sports Medicine

Sports medicine is a term that includes a broad range of clinical and scientific aspects of sport and exercise (Lamb, 1984). For example, exercise thera-pies, such as ultrasound or electrical stimulation, are considered forms of sports medicine. Exercise prescriptions, such as weight training, and endurance (aerobic) running, jogging, and walking are also forms of sports medicine. Likewise, the exercise sciences, athletic training, and nutrition are part of the larger concept known as sports medicine.

Sometimes people are confused about the meaning of sports medicine because terms associated with it are often used interchangeably. Therefore, in an effort to clarify sports medicine and its terminology, we present in figure 14.1 our version of the Sports Medicine Umbrella, a concept that was first suggested by Lamb (1984). Additionally, tables 14.1 and 14.2 provide a framework for organizing sports medicine information and should help you understand how the components of the umbrella interrelate.

The cover, or canopy, of the umbrella in figure 14.1 shows that disciplines such as physiology, biology, and kinesiology provide the overarching knowledge base for sports medicine. A strong disciplinary background is essential for prospective sports medicine professionals. These individuals must make knowledgeable decisions based on theory and scientific research that is a fundamental part of each discipline. They can not engage in trial and error practice on clients. Each client's situation is unique, and the competent sports medicine professional blends theory with application to help the client.

In the shaft of the umbrella, you see the exercise sciences (e.g., **biomechanics**, exercise physiology). Sometimes called **subdisciplines**, these fields of study use theories and knowledge from the disciplines as they specifically relate to sport and physical activity. These disciplines and subdisciplines provide the specialized scientific information that sports medicine professionals need to provide quality service to their clients.

Around the handle of the umbrella, several sports medicine professions are shown. These are examples of careers in which you could apply the knowledge you gain through studying the disciplines, subdisciplines, and exercise sciences of sports medicine. For example, the **athletic trainer** and the **strength coach** are practitioners who provide unique services in sport and activity settings. Athletic trainers frequently prescribe range of motion exercise in the whirlpool, and strength coaches will provide instruction on proper body positions for weight lifting. To be effective, the athletic trainer must understand the effect of heat

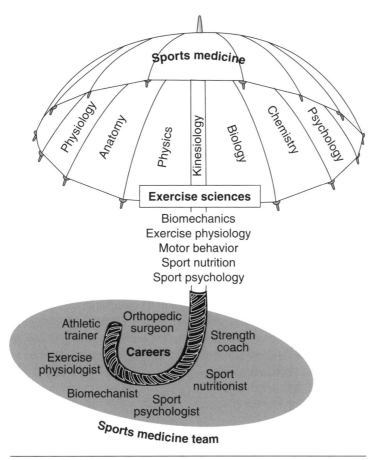

**Figure 14.1**   Sports medicine umbrella.

and movement during whirlpool therapy (exercise physiology), and the strength coach must understand the angle of pull and force generated by muscles during a lift (biomechanics). Therefore, both professionals rely on knowledge from the exercise sciences to perform their duties.

When several sports medicine professionals work together *and* a medical doctor (e.g., orthopedic surgeon or athletic team physician) is part of the group, the unit is known as a **sports medicine team** (note the shaded area under and encompassed by the sports medicine umbrella in figure 14.1). You are probably familiar with this concept as it is used in association with **sports medicine clinics**, a relatively new concept that has captured the imagination of health care professionals during the past decade. Sports medicine clinics may be associated with hospitals or be managed privately by a sports medicine team. These clinics have emerged because of the wants and needs of a diverse group of participants in sport and physical activity who seek the varied sports medicine information and services described throughout this chapter.

# History of Sports Medicine

As Ryan (1989) describes in detail, sports medicine can be traced to ancient civilizations (e.g., Greece, Rome, China). However, the first modern use of the term sports medicine was in 1928, during the Second Olympic Winter Games in Switzerland. The term was used to describe clinical practice and research focusing on the performances of Olympic athletes. During this time, the Association International Medico-Sportive was established to (a) promote scientific research in sciences related to sports, (b) promote the study of medical problems encountered in physical exercise in sports, and (c) organize international congresses on sports medicine (Ryan, 1989).

The Harvard Fatigue Laboratory (1927-1947) was established to conduct physiological research on industrial hazards (Powers & Howley, 1994). The research conducted under the auspices of the Harvard laboratory extended well beyond industry, however, as the scientists studied the effects of phenomena such as aging, altitude, and metabolism. This early research laid the foundation for

Table 14.1
## Criteria to Designate Type of Fitness and Exercise Programs and Settings

| Criteria | Recreational | Prescriptive | Rehabilitative |
|---|---|---|---|
| Objective | Fun! Enjoyment<br><br>Get some exercise<br><br>General health maintenance | Effect change (e.g., weight, cardiovascular, strength, muscle tone)<br><br>To enhance health and reduce risk factors | Remedial, therapeutic |
| Clientele | Apparently healthy—the normal person | May have high-risk factors<br><br>Generally wants to shape up | A disability, disease in which therapeutic exercise program is part of medical treatment plan<br><br>All ages, but tend to be adult |
| Leadership | Activity leader<br><br>Knowledge about conduct of activities being sponsored or offered; ability to observe, in general, the condition of individual<br><br>Improper leadership usually results in negligence action, in contrast to malpractice suit | Exercise specialist<br><br>Knowledge about physiology, kinesiology, and so on; the conduct of exercise related to intensity, which changes impact; and possesses level of expertise appropriate to health-disease status of clientele<br><br>*Beware* unauthorized practice of medicine; malpractice suits use physician standard of care!<br><br>Consulting physician mandatory | Physician directed and monitored<br><br>Exercise specialist one of health team<br><br>Improper performance, practice of medicine results in malpractice suit |
| Program or activity | Any organized competitive or other recreational activity; may have facility available for individual or group informal participation; may be special event or ongoing program | Generally aerobic or strength oriented. Although done individually or in groups, prescription is for individuals after testing or classifying in other manner<br><br>Physician-specified parameters (intensity, nature, type of movement, et al.) and exercise specialist selects and conducts the exercises within such parameters | Activity selected specifically for its therapeutic value to an individual (part of medical treatment) |
| Testing | Not usually part of program<br><br>Informal self-testing (e.g., weight, timed runs, pulse count) | Essential for determining exercise prescription<br><br>Exercise protocol recommended by ACSM, AHA, AMA, APTA<br><br>Must be done by trainer, preferably certified, exercise specialist<br><br>Direct physician monitoring, depends on clientele condition and nature of testing<br><br>Where prescription calls for exercise "on own" and self-monitoring (e.g., take pulse), client must be trained in technique and be capable of recognizing conditions of danger | Under physician monitoring and at physician's direction |

Table 14.2
**Agencies and Programs in Recreational, Prescriptive, and Rehabilitative Settings**

| Setting | Recreational | Prescriptive | Rehabilitative |
|---|---|---|---|
| Agencies | Recreation center (community or university) City park building YMCA or YWCA Senior citizen centers | Corporate fitness center Hotel or resort exercise facilities Training facilities for athletes Fitness or health club Senior citizen center | Sports medicine clinic Hospital Training room for athletes |
| **Programs** | **Fitness programs** | **Exercise programs** | **Therapeutic programs** |
| Examples | Community recreation program Senior exercise program Walking program | Strength training Aerobic training Sports conditioning | Cardiac rehabilitation Pulmonary rehabilitation |

*Note:* Some agencies are listed in more than one setting because program objectives are different, but program sites are the same.

many of our present exercise guidelines.

In 1954, the American College of Sports Medicine (ACSM) was established to bring together professionals interested in sharing and disseminating sports medicine information. Today, this organization provides services for many professionals associated with the sports medicine team.

Before the 1960s, departments of physiology at several universities conducted an impressive amount of **work physiology**. This type of work occurs today under the title exercise physiology. Interest in exercise physiology continues to flourish in contemporary industry and academia. Research projects studying human reactions to various environmental conditions (e.g., altitude, space flight, gravitational forces, heat, cold) and the effects of work-related situations (e.g., work stations for lifting, building, assembling) are found in universities and in private and governmental laboratories of **ergonomics** or bioengineering.

Following WW II, increases in health care costs, incidence of obesity, and heart disease prompted attention on exercise and health (Nieman, 1995). Then, in the 1950s, it was noted that American school children were not as physically fit as their European counterparts. Moreover, autopsies on 18- to 20-year-old soldiers from the Korean War revealed significantly advanced **coronary heart disease** (Powers & Howley, 1994). Advisory boards were established to investigate these findings. These boards evolved into our current President's Council on Physical Fitness and Sports (Powers & Howley, 1994).

During the 1950s and 1960s, exercise goals were revised as more medical research on the benefits of exercise was conducted. In the United States,

the primary message to the public was that the risk for coronary artery disease, a leading cause of death, could be reduced through participating in regular aerobic exercise. In the case of cardiac patients, this message was in contrast to the previously accepted thought that bed rest and no activity were the best treatments for cardiac patients (Wilson, 1988). Armchair exercise and walking programs for cardiac patients were introduced in 1952, and by the late 1960s and early 1970s several noted researchers were studying the benefits of exercise. In the mid-1970s and into the early 1980s more formalized programs for cardiac rehabilitation were established. In 1975 ACSM published its first edition of the *Guidelines for Exercise Testing and Prescription*. The American Heart Association, the American College of Cardiology, and the American Association of Cardiovascular and Pulmonary Rehabilitation have continued to develop guidelines, and cardiac rehabilitation is now accepted as a viable, clinical procedure (Wilson, 1988).

According to Nieman (1995), the late 1960s were times of heightened awareness of the benefits of exercise. Kenneth Cooper published *Aerobics* and *The New Aerobics*, and many Americans began to participate in regular exercise. Through the 1970s and 1980s several forms of aerobic exercise, such as jogging, walking, cycling, swimming, and aerobic dance, became habitual activities for many individuals. To meet the needs of these exercisers, health clubs proliferated in the 1970s and 1980s (Nieman, 1995). This proliferation of exercisers and health clubs led to an increase in the need for all types of sports medicine professionals. Although many people believe the fitness

© Mary Langenfeld

Studies from the 1950s through the 1990s have shown that children in the United States are not as physically fit as children in Europe.

boom has plateaued somewhat in the 1990s, the incidence of coronary heart disease, obesity, and health care costs have not been reduced (Nieman, 1995); therefore, there is much work yet to be completed by sports medicine professionals. Millions of current and potential exercisers continue to seek sports medicine professionals and the information and services they offer. Where should these individuals seek information? In the next section, we will describe settings in which sports medicine professionals complete this important work.

## Choosing a Sports Medicine Program, Agency, and Setting

The individuals described at the beginning of the chapter need to make informed choices about which **program** is best for their needs. Confusion exists with the public and even with many sports medicine professionals because there are varied programs that different **agencies** offer. Many partnerships and affiliations are possible between and among agencies. For example, the number of

hospitals with **satellite facilities** is increasing, and more private health clubs are aligning in some way with sports medicine clinics. As Moss and Parks (1991) have noted, it appears that the concept of large wellness centers will be expanded in the future. For example, large facilities under one roof will have cardiac rehabilitation at one end of the building, family workout areas at the other end, and health education classes in another part of the building. This type of agency may also offer other sports medicine services. A model for grouping agencies was presented by van der Smissen (1990b). As shown in table 14.1, agencies can offer fitness and exercise programs in three settings: (a) recreational, (b) prescriptive, and (c) rehabilitative.

## Criteria That Differentiate Programs, Agencies, and Settings

van der Smissen's model was originally intended to group only programs offering fitness and exercise; however, we are suggesting that these criteria may also serve as a beginning framework differentiating where other therapies, programs, or services offered in sports medicine agencies could be found. In this chapter we define the word settings as the three categories in which we can group sports medicine agencies and programs according to criteria proposed by van der Smissen. The five criteria that are important for our clients to consider in selecting the appropriate program and setting are (a) clientele, (b) objective, (c) type of program or activity offered, (d) testing, and (e) leadership.

In table 14.1, specific characteristics of the participants who should be participating in programs at agencies in each setting are found under the heading Clientele. The clientele who can safely exercise in each setting are determined from examining their **risk factors for coronary heart disease** and functional status. ACSM suggests three classifications for clientele: (a) apparently healthy, (b) at risk, and (c) with disease. The apparently healthy individual has no symptoms of coronary heart disease and has no more than one of the seven risk factors for coronary heart disease. The at-risk client is a person with signs or symptoms suggestive of possible cardiopulmonary or metabolic disease, or two or more of the risk factors. A client with disease has been diagnosed as having cardiac, pulmonary, or metabolic diseases (American College of Sports Medicine, 1995). Qualified sports medicine professionals should classify clients before they participate in any exercise testing or prescription.

Objective refers to the goal or purpose of the program (e.g., to improve fitness or to rehabilitate after an injury). Type of program is defined as the content of the program (e.g., activities or movements intended to improve health or exercises intended to effect change). Testing refers to the variety of physiological tests that are available for the qualified professional to administer to assess the client's abilities and progress after or during training and rehabilitation. Leadership includes the knowledge, qualifications, and competencies of the professionals administering the programs.

## Agencies and Programs in the Three Settings

Examples of agencies and programs in the three settings are shown in table 14.2. These settings may be recreational, prescriptive, or rehabilitative.

### Recreational Setting

Examples of agencies in a recreational setting include community and park recreation centers,

hotel or resort fitness centers, and retirement centers. Clientele should be apparently healthy participants. In this setting, fitness programs would be offered. The term fitness implies activity for improving overall health. These fitness programs have the objective of getting the participants moving with the goal of enjoyment for the client; therefore, no testing is usually involved. It is important that program names accurately denote the objective of the program. The title Water Fun for Seniors would be appropriate for a water fitness program in a recreational setting.

### Prescriptive Setting

Agencies such as sports medicine clinics, corporate fitness centers, and private fitness and health clubs are found in the prescriptive setting. Participants may be classified as apparently healthy or at-risk clients. If the clients are at risk, then qualified professionals may be needed to supervise their activities. Exercise programs in which the objective is much more specific (i.e., to effect change) than in fitness programs are typically offered in agencies in the prescriptive setting. The term exercise implies that a specific physical characteristic will be improved. These programs may be aerobic or strength-training programs with guidelines (e.g., intensity, frequency, duration, sets, repetitions) designated by knowledgeable professionals. Agencies in the prescriptive setting could conduct testing to determine muscular strength, percentage body fat, and cardiorespiratory fitness level. An appropriate title for a water exercise program in a prescriptive setting would be Water Workouts.

### Rehabilitative Setting

Sports medicine clinics, hospital physical therapy departments, cardiac rehabilitation clinics, or school athletic training facilities are examples of agencies in the rehabilitative setting. These agencies offer **rehabilitative programs** with the objective of restoring the injured or limited client to some normal level of function. Hence, the clients are in the category "with disease." Testing often involves sophisticated technology and may be an **invasive** or **noninvasive procedure**. Some examples of procedures that would have to be completed in a rehabilitative setting because of the necessity of physician supervision or specialized equipment would be graded exercise testing, isokinetic muscular strength evaluation, muscle needle biopsies, surgeries, CT scans, and other imaging techniques. Therapeutic programs are often prescribed by a physician. Exercise programs for clients with special needs may include therapeutic programs for cardiac, pulmonary, cancer, diabetic, or obese patients. An appropriate title for a therapeutic water program in a rehabilitative setting would be Aquatic Therapy.

Understanding titles and types of programs, objectives, and classification of clients is important for *all* fitness managers. Of course, the manager must be mindful of the welfare of the clients. The manager must also be aware of legal liability concerns for themselves and their organizations. van der Smissen (1990b) noted that "There are differences in the standard of care required for each of these programs, according to the nature of the program" (p. 144). If correct exercise prescriptions or therapies that fit the client's needs are not offered, sports medicine professionals may be liable, negligent, or both if they have not provided a **reasonable standard of care** that is commonly agreed upon by the profession.

The six individuals introduced at the beginning of the chapter now have an idea of *where* they might find a program appropriate for them. What additional information do they need to make an informed decision about *who* will provide the program? Which sports medicine professionals work in these agencies with apparently healthy, at-risk, or with disease clients?

# Career Opportunities in Sports Medicine

Objectives of the program, clientele, and type of program or activity determine who will be qualified to provide leadership in the various settings (see Leadership, table 14.1). It is critical that program leaders do not attempt tasks beyond the scope of their academic preparation, abilities, or objectives of the setting. It is also important that the site manager communicate this requirement to the leaders and guarantee that the scope of the program is not exceeded.

In a recreational setting, the leader should be qualified to lead exercise and other types of recreational activities. The objective is to have fun, so extensive programming should not be attempted. In the prescriptive setting, however, exercise leaders and exercise specialists should have more advanced levels of expertise to lead the activities and manage the site. In a rehabilitative setting, consistent with the objective of being remedial or therapeutic, an **exercise specialist** (cardiac rehabilitation), an athletic trainer, or other allied health

professional (physical therapist, occupational therapist) would carry out the therapeutic exercise programming. Other sports medicine professionals (e.g., physicians, physical therapists, occupational therapists, nurses) are not discussed in this chapter because their academic preparation is completed in professional schools (e.g., medical school) specific to their professions.

The American College of Sports Medicine (ACSM) lists 46 occupational codes or professions in its membership directory (American College of Sports Medicine, 1994). Ryan (1989) has identified sports medicine practitioners as "physicians, coaches, athletic trainers, exercise physiologists, psychologists, sociologists, physical educators, and others whose special interests are less well-defined" (p. 13). Because all these professionals are drawing from the same disciplinary base, overlap among duties and responsibilities may occur on the job. Due to budgetary constraints, it may be necessary to have a less than optimally trained professional fill a void at an agency. However, based on the history and development of each profession, we can identify certain characteristics unique to each of them. Broad descriptions of five sports medicine professions are provided in table 14.3. Actual job descriptions, with some names changed, that have been published in career bulletins from various professional organizations are shown on page 214.

Table 14.3 also presents information on the academic preparation, employment settings, and certifications for some sports medicine career fields. The academic preparation of professionals will vary depending on the college or university at which the student earns a degree. Although some overlap may be present among degrees with titles such as exercise science, exercise specialist, kinesiology, and health promotion, each degree program should have a particular focus. For example, academic preparation for an exercise specialist would focus on exercise testing, prescription, and management. On the other hand, health promotion students would focus on disseminating health information (e.g., fitness, smoking cessation) and educating the client (see chapter 15). Students should try to match their career goals with the knowledge and skills specific to an area of study.

## Disciplines in Sports Medicine

There are many disciplines, or bodies of knowledge, within sports medicine that offer career opportunities. Following is a list of some major disciplines:

Table 14.3
## Professions in Sports Medicine

| Profession | Athletic trainer | Exercise leader | Exercise specialist | Exercise physiologist | Strength coach |
|---|---|---|---|---|---|
| Academic preparation | Bachelor's or master's | Bachelor's | Bachelor's or master's | Master's or doctorate | Bachelor's or master's |
| Job responsibilities | Specialized in the care and prevention of illness and injury in sport and in maximizing performance of the athlete. Tasks include preventing injury, evaluating injury, first aid, rehabilitation, organization and administration counseling and guidance, education. | Leads safe, effective, and enjoyable exercise programs for apparently healthy individuals. Responsibilities include floor supervision, exercise prescription, spotting, exercise record keeping. | Conducts graded exercise testing, exercise prescription, and exercise leadership in preventive and rehabilitative exercise programs for individuals with cardiovascular, pulmonary, and metabolic disease. Exercise specialist cardiac rehabilitation—same as exercise specialist but works in a cardiac rehabilitation program. | Studies the muscular activity and functional responses and adaptations during exercise. | Knowledge of all types of strength training programs desired, especially free weights and Nautilus; administer and supervise strength and conditioning programs for athletic teams. |
| Agencies for employment | Athletics, professional sports, sports medicine clinics. | Fitness and health clubs, corporate fitness center, hotel or resort. | Fitness and health clubs, corporate fitness center, hotel or resort, cardiac rehabilitation, retirement communities. | University settings, federal agencies or grants, cardiac rehabilitation. | Athletics, professional sports, private clubs. |
| Certifications | NATA certified athletic trainers | ACSM exercise leader, ACE personal trainer, IDEA personal trainer, NSCA certified strength and conditioning specialist (C.S.C.S.) | ACSM preventive levels: health and fitness director, health and fitness instructor | ACSM rehabilitation levels: program director, exercise specialist, exercise test technologist | NSCA certified strength and conditioning specialist (C.S.C.S.), YMCA certifications |

Professional organizations: ACE—American Council on Exercise; ACSM—American College of Sports Medicine; IDEA—International Association of Fitness Professionals; NATA—National Athletic Trainers Association; NSCA—National Strength and Conditioning Association

Adapted, by permission, from B. van der Smissen, 1990, *Legal liability and risk management for public and private entities*, (Cincinnati, OH; Anderson Publishing Co.), 145-147.

■ Anatomy—the study of the structure of the body. Application—by understanding where muscles are located and attached to bones, we can identify muscle groups to improve with strength training.

## Learning Activity

Contact a professional in your desired field of study. Spend a day observing and shadowing this professional on the job.

■ Biology—science of life (*Webster's Dictionary*, 1987). Application—by understanding tissue and cell processes, an athletic trainer has the information to decide what may be the better therapy for treating an injury (e.g., ultrasound or electrical stimulation).

■ Chemistry—the study of matter; the science of the properties of substances, combination of substances, and chemical reactions. Application—cellular imbalances of ions may cause muscle cramps. Knowledge about these substances may help prevent or treat cramps.

■ Physics—the discipline that deals with matter, energy, motion, and force (*Random House*, 1993). Application—in the branch of physics called mechanics, forces, torques, acceleration, friction, and so on are studied. To improve any motor skill (e.g., pole vaulting), understanding the forces involved could help the coach, teacher, or athlete identify and correct problems in the technique or execution of the skill.

■ Physiology—the study of the function of the body. Application—knowledge of how the body regulates its temperature (e.g., sweating) is necessary for making decisions regarding fluid replacement during exposure to heat (e.g., water or Gatorade).

■ Psychology—study of the mind and mental processes and how these affect behavior. Application—by understanding what motivates individuals, we can design programs to help individuals adhere to a prescribed regimen (e.g., taking a medication, completing an exercise program, modifying diet).

■ Kinesiology—the study of movement, or more generally the study of physical activity (Newell, 1990). Application—when movement or exercise is added to a disciplinary fact, we must consider a new set of factors. Interdisciplinary questions emerge such as the following: What are the determinants of the energy cost of activities in children? Scientists could study and answer this question through collaboration. The scientists who look for the answers to these questions may come from exercise physiology, biomechanics, and motor development.

## Subdisciplines and Exercise Sciences in Sports Medicine

Along with the major disciplines found within sports medicine, there are several subdisciplines and exercise sciences focusing on particular aspects of sports medicine. Here are some subdisciplines and exercise sciences:

■ Exercise sciences—a subset of kinesiology; the description and explanation of natural phenomena associated with physical activity and sport; includes specialty sciences of exercise physiology, motor control and motor learning, biomechanics of exercise and sport, sport psychology, and sociology (Lamb, 1984). Application—we can not answer many modern sports medicine questions by work from a single discipline. Scientists might complete collaborative research to determine factors that could be altered to permit optimal performance in athletes (e.g., physiological, biomechanical, psychological).

■ Biomechanics—the application of mechanical principles to biological systems. Application—understanding the forces that act on the knee joint during normal walking is necessary for rehabilitating the injured person to recover to a normal gait pattern.

■ Exercise biochemistry—study of the chemistry of biological substances and processes during exercise (ACSM, 1994). Application—lactic acid, a chemical compound, is produced during exercise. By monitoring its increases in the blood during exercise, scientists can determine how intense the activity is for the exerciser.

■ Exercise physiology—the study of how the body functionally responds and adjusts to exercise, both acute and chronic. Application—analysis of expired air during exercise allows us to determine the caloric cost of activities. We can use this information to instruct individuals how to lose or gain weight.

■ Motor behavior—the study of the movement process; study of how movement is acquired and developed. Application—we can evaluate movement by qualitative observations and descriptions. Although a child and an older adult may both complete a walking gait using the same scientific principles, the manner in which each accomplishes this may be qualitatively different (e.g., posture, arm movement, carriage of the body, center of gravity, stride length, cadence).

■ Motor control and learning—the sciences that describe and explain the neural bases of planning, executing, controlling, patterning, and learning movements (Lamb, 1984). Application—

researchers in this area study how individuals obtain, retain, and use information for executing a motor skill (e.g., swinging a golf club).

■ Sports nutrition—the study of nutrient intake and use during exercise and sport activities, the optimal provision of nutrients for sport, and the prescription of altered patterns of caloric intake and expenditure to achieve optimal body weight and body composition (Lamb, 1984). Application—by understanding how the muscle stores energy, scientists can determine if eating greater than normal amounts of carbohydrate will increase performance.

■ Sport psychology—the study of mental activity in sport and exercise situations associated with sport and exercise (Lamb, 1984). Application—using mental imaging or practice may improve sport performance. For example, an athlete may imagine or visualize a high-pressure, competitive game situation. By visualizing this situation, and mentally planning and practicing his or her response, when the real life situation occurs, the athlete may perform better.

## Graduate Study in Sports Medicine

Many sports medicine job descriptions in the job Bulletin Board on page 214 require graduate study or other professional experience. Masters and doctoral programs are designed to enhance students' disciplinary knowledge base, provide opportunities for them to learn research skills, and help them gain practical experience under the tutelage of researchers and scholars. Advanced degrees are often required before staff are placed in leadership, management, or supervisory positions. In some situations, certifications, **licensure**, or other professional preparation external to the academic setting may be required (see table 14.3 and the job Bulletin Board).

### Learning Activity

Visit a university and investigate major curricula related to sports medicine. Also, join and become actively involved in the student club associated with your academic major (e.g., kinesiology club, sport management club).

## Management and Administration

Regardless of the setting, most sports medicine professionals work in agencies that have to be managed to carry out the mission of the organization. As you can see in figure 14.2, either medical, academic, community, or private businesses may manage the agencies, programs, or services that sports medicine agencies deliver. Within every agency, the amount of administrative or management experience necessary for each profession will vary. Some professions have more administrative responsibilities than others. Many professions that use management skills typically require on-the-job experience or a graduate degree(s) (i.e., master's or doctorate).

Individuals who are competent in organizing, planning, budgeting, designing facilities, maintaining equipment, record keeping, and scheduling activities may opt for professions in management (see chapter 8). Individuals who desire to work directly with the clients and observe and measure changes brought about through exercise may opt for the professions in programming. All professions associated with sports medicine include some management or programming responsibilities. These responsibilities are delineated at each job site and are specified in job descriptions. Many times, increased management and administrative responsibilities will result in an increase in salary.

### Learning Activity

Investigate salaries of sports medicine professionals in your geographic area. In public agencies, find out where you can obtain salary information. In private organizations, investigate whether this information is published in the yearly report.

## Professional Development in Sports Medicine

Sports medicine is rapidly changing as advances are made in technology, procedures, drug therapies, equipment, and modalities. Professionals should stay current in their field, and they can do this in several ways.

### Professional Organizations

One way is to join professional organizations composed of other professional colleagues with simi-

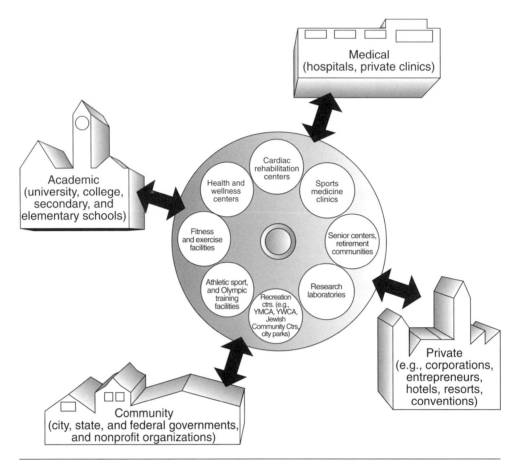

**Figure 14.2**   Types of organizations that administer sports medicine programs and agencies.

lar interests. These associations sponsor national, regional, and state conferences for their members. Professionals might want to earn continuing education credits by attending professional meetings or workshops and learning about new techniques and approaches. Several sports medicine professional associations are shown in the For More Information section of this chapter. Many organizations have regional as well as state chapters that are excellent for beginning involvement by students. This section includes only selected professional organizations related to sports medicine, and there are numerous resource (special interest) groups.

## Journals in Sports Medicine

Sports medicine professionals can also participate in regular developmental activities, such as reading current journals and other publications to stay up-to-date on sports medicine research and information. Many professional associations publish the most recent research in their scholarly journals. As specified in For More Information on page 209, these journals contain research and other

### Learning Activity

Contact one professional organization and ask for membership information to be sent to you. Many professional organizations offer reduced membership fees to students.

factual information, and the intent is to inform the professional. On the other hand, the magazines listed are designed to entertain a readership and might or might not contain accurate and current technical information from sports medicine research findings. Active involvement with professional associations and reading current journals and magazines helps sports medicine professionals continue learning and stay current in their field of study after they have earned academic degrees.

## Certifications

In many sports medicine professions, certifications are part of the job requirements and may be required by law (see table 14.3). These certifications signify to a potential employer that candidates for positions not only have the requisite academic background but also have competencies that are comparable to other certified professionals in their occupational field.

The National Athletic Trainers Association (NATA) is the certifying agency for athletic trainers. The most prominent certifications for exercise leadership are those offered by the National Strength and Conditioning Association (NSCA), American Council on Exercise (ACE), and American College of Sports Medicine (ACSM) (see table 14.3). In addition, the ACSM offers more advanced certifications for professionals working with at-risk and with disease clientele. Before investing your time, energy, and money in a certification, you should ask university faculty or practitioners for advice.

## Choosing a Career Within Sports Medicine

Now, using the information you have learned in this chapter, consider the advice you would give to Bobbie, Jay, Chip, Lucia, Rick, and Katie. For example, which setting is appropriate for each of them? What types of activities or programs should they seek? How would you describe the clientele group to which each individual belongs? With what sports medicine professionals or experiences should they become involved?

## Learning Activity

Currently, prospective certified athletic trainers complete a baccalaureate degree from an accredited university. In addition, you must be certified in first aid and basic cardiopulmonary resuscitation, accumulate directly supervised clinical hours, and verify that 25% of the athletic training experience hours were attained in actual (on location) practice or game coverage with specific sports. A NATA Certified Athletic Trainer must endorse the application for certification, and you must pass the certification examination (Arnheim & Prentice, 1997, p. 24). Contact five universities and inquire about their athletic training curricula. Compare and contrast the information you receive.

Contact an organization that certifies fitness and exercise professionals. Ask the following questions to gain information about the certification: (a) Is it a well established professional organization? (b) If a fee is included, what does it cover? (c) Is the certification recommended, recognized, or required for typical positions in any sports medicine profession? and (d) Are there preexamination requirements that you must meet (e.g., baccalaureate degree, first aid or cardiopulmonary resuscitation (CPR) certifications) before taking the certification written or practical exam?

## For More Information

The following professional associations will help you to learn more about sport medicine.

### Recreational and Prescriptive

- Aerobics and Fitness Association of America (AFAA)
- American Council on Exercise (ACE)
- American Alliance for Health, Physical Education, Recreation and Dance (AAHPERD)
- Association for Worksite Health Promotion
- International Association of Fitness Professionals (IDEA)
- International Health, Racquet, and Sportsclub Association (IHRSA)

### Prescriptive and Rehabilitative

- American Association of Cardiovascular and Pulmonary Rehabilitation (AACVPR)
- American College of Sports Medicine (ACSM)
- American Physical Therapy Association (APTA)
- American Society of Biomechanics (ASB)
- International Society of Biomechanics and Sport (ISBS)
- Kinesiotherapy
- National Athletic Trainers Association (NATA)
- National Strength and Conditioning Association (NSCA)

Here's a hint: The criteria you should consider for your decision are italicized in the descriptions at the beginning of the chapter.

*Bobbie.* Bobbie called the local fitness club. Her club offers a class collaboratively with the local hospital. The class is under the supervision of a dietitian and an exercise specialist or a certified strength and conditioning specialist. Bobbie's exercise needs to be specific to achieve her goal of losing weight. Bobbie is classified as at risk so she will need an individualized exercise prescription. Bobbie should seek help in this prescriptive exercise setting. Perhaps a weight-loss class is what she needs.

*Jay.* Jay went to the local sports medicine clinic that was affiliated with the hospital. The physician evaluated him and referred him for treatment to the athletic trainer. After the initial treatment in this rehabilitative setting for this injury, he will complete a short rehabilitation period with the athletic trainer.

*Chip.* Because Chip is a cardiac patient, he is classified as with disease. Chip will need to exercise in a supervised cardiac rehabilitation program (i.e., rehabilitative setting). In his Phase II cardiac rehabilitation program (i.e., outpatient exercise three times per week, weekly health education sessions), Chip will complete a variety of exercises under the supervision of the cardiac nurse and exercise specialist. The goal is to restore his physiological and psychological health and to change his poor health habits.

*Lucia.* Lucia wants to have fun and doesn't want to be regimented in her exercise program. Therefore, participation in a recreational fitness program led by an exercise leader would help her meet her goals. She is apparently healthy, although her age will make it necessary for her to have her physician give medical clearance for participation in the program.

*Rick.* Rick's parents, just as if they were selecting a personal trainer for themselves, found a qualified instructor. There was a personal trainer who had a degree in exercise science and a minor in child development. In addition, he had taken special workshops to learn how to lead children in exercise.

*Katie.* Katie needs to interact professionally with other personal trainers or exercise specialists. Workshops on budgeting, managing clients, and entrepreneurship are offered at national or regional meetings of many professional organizations (e.g., ACE, IDEA, NSCA).

# Challenges for the Future

The sports medicine of the future will be characterized by rapidly advancing technology, a more diverse clientele, and a heightened emphasis on preventive medicine. Sports medicine professionals will need to engage in lifelong learning that will enable them to successfully meet the challenges these developments will present.

## Technology

Nuclear magnetic resonance imaging; isokinetic muscular strength testing; drug testing; injury statistics; Holter monitoring; computer databases for membership accounting, fitness programming, and logging—these are a few examples of changes in technology that have affected sports medicine. With new technologies comes the need for professionals with the expertise to use the technology. This need should create more jobs, and perhaps specialized jobs, in sports medicine. Well-prepared, experienced sports medicine professionals who possess critical thinking skills, decision-making abilities, sound ethics, and problem-solving expertise are essential for the emerging technology to be used safely and effectively.

Although it is difficult to speculate how technological advances will affect the next generation of sports medicine professionals, one thing is certain: No technology can replace the empathetic, caring human interaction that must occur between the sports medicine professional and the client.

## Diverse Clientele

As clients from more diverse populations seek sports medicine information, professionals will need to change to meet their needs. Women, older adults, children, and clients with unique needs will want specialized sports medicine information. The number of women participating in all types of sports will continue to increase as more opportunities are available. The older population will have greater disposable incomes to spend on exercise, fitness, and information. The number of children exercising and seeking sports medicine information outside the school system will continue to increase. All types of clients with special needs (e.g., people with diabetes, cardiac problems) will be more educated about the benefits of exercise and will participate in organized programs. Sports medicine professionals must be able to under-

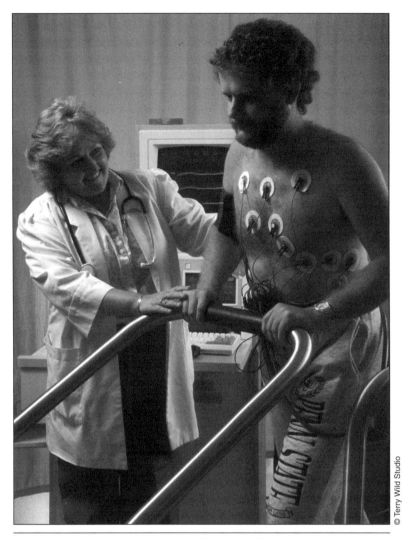

As newer technology is developed, there will be a need for sports medicine professionals who know how to use the specialized equipment—this need might create more professions in the field.

stand diverse needs and direct clients to the most appropriate settings and activities.

## Preventive Medicine

Some efforts have already been made to reduce health care costs through preventive medicine. For example, some insurance companies offer special rates to nonsmokers. Other insurance policyholders who may reap benefits from healthy behaviors are those who engage in regular exercise programs, enroll in smoking cessation courses, or get annual mammograms. Sports medicine professionals can contribute to the benefits of preventive medicine by developing programs that encourage people to adopt healthy lifestyles. Exercise leaders can motivate individuals to exercise to decrease the risk of heart disease, minimize absenteeism, and reduce hospital stays.

Although interest in home-based exercise programs and equipment has risen, a report by the International Health, Racquet & Sportsclub Association (IHRSA, 1995) indicated that people will continue to exercise at clubs because of the socialization and instruction they can obtain there. There will be an increasing demand for professionals to develop, design, evaluate, market, and sell exercise equipment and other equipment for all areas of sports medicine.

Industrial agencies are just beginning to design workstations and use ergonomics to prevent injury. Work hardening programs to rehabilitate workers after occupation-related injuries are a growing part of outpatient sports medicine clinics. We will continue to need biomechanists, exercise physiologists, athletic trainers, and other sports medicine personnel in these specialty areas to carry out therapies, conduct research to establish new therapies, and gain new knowledge through research. Collaboration and cooperative operating agreements among agencies (e.g., sports medicine clinics, corporate fitness programs, training facilities), the organizations that administer these agencies (i.e., academic, community, medical, and private), and the sports medicine professionals whom these agencies employ should continue into the next century (see figure 14.2).

## Lifelong Learning

Step aerobics, in-line skating, bench aerobics, cryotherapy, electrical stimulation, new therapies and drugs—it is essential that sports medicine professionals stay up-to-date with new procedures by earning academic degrees beyond the baccalaureate, attending workshops and professional meetings, reading professional journals, and engaging in other lifelong professional learning. As mentioned previously, technology will change quickly and so will the wants and needs of clients. For example, computer feedback from exercise devices will need to be explained to exercisers. Competent professionals will need to understand how to determine exercise workloads for each individual, how to derive caloric costs of exercise, and how to individualize exercise prescriptions for each client. Exercise testing is popular to monitor a client's progress in an exercise program. The sports medicine professional must determine what test is appropriate for each client and must carefully interpret and explain test results. Video technology is often used to motivate clients to exercise. For each client, the sports medicine professional will need to decide how and when to use video data and when to give personal attention.

## Summary

Sports medicine is a broad term that encompasses several professions that provide information and therapies for a variety of clients. Their knowledge is drawn from disciplines, subdisciplines, and the exercise sciences, as well as practical experiences. A variety of professions exist under the umbrella of sports medicine, and professionals in each area have specific duties that are characteristic of the setting in which they work. Sports medicine programs and settings differ by criteria such as objective, type of program, and clientele. Clientele should be classified as apparently healthy, at risk, or with disease before exercise testing, prescription, or treatment. To stay current in their fields, sports medicine professionals should obtain certifications and belong to professional organizations, such as the American College of Sports Medicine, the National Strength and Conditioning Association, and the National Athletic Trainers Association. As technology changes, the clientele become more diverse, and preventive medicine is emphasized, sports medicine professionals will need to engage in lifelong learning. The human interaction that occurs between client and professional can not be replaced by technology when rehabilitating an athlete back to participation, prescribing exercise, and observing improvements in each client's abilities.

# For More Information

There are many Web sites and list servers for sports medicine and all subdisciplines. To find information, search the Internet using any related word in the glossary. Here are a few examples of Web sites in sports medicine or related topics:

## Web Sites

- http://www.humankinetics.com/Infokinetics —information on associations, classified ads and jobs, conferences and events, journals, careers, and links (to physical activity on the web) all specific to physical activity.
- http://www.exer-phys.club.com.
- http://www.nata.org/.

## Conferences

Regional and national meetings are held for all professional associations. For a list of conferences contact the professional associations or http://www.humankinetics.com/Infokinetics.

## Publications in Sports Medicine

- *Journal of Cardiopulmonary Rehabilitation*
- *Research Quarterly for Exercise and Sport*
- *Medicine and Science in Sports and Exercise*
- *Journal of Applied Physiology*
- *Journal of Clinical Biomechanics*
- *Club Business International (CBI)*
- *Journal of Applied Biomechanics*
- *Athletic Training*
- *Journal of Strength and Conditioning Research*
- *Strength and Conditioning*
- *The Physician and Sportsmedicine*
- *European Journal of Applied Work Physiology*
- *Fitness Management*
- *Journal of Orthopedic and Sports Physical Therapy*
- *Journal of Physical Activity and Aging*
- *Journal of Sports Medicine and Physical Fitness*
- *Pediatric Exercise Science*
- *Physical Fitness and Sports Medicine*
- *Sports Medicine*
- *The American Journal of Sports Medicine*
- *American Health*
- *Fitness*
- *Health*
- *Living Fit: Fitness for Women at Any Age*
- *Men's Fitness*
- *Muscle and Fitness*
- *Self*
- *Shape*
- *Women's Sport and Fitness*
- *Walking*

# Job Opportunities

## Personal Trainer and Fitness Staff

West Cleveland health and recreation club seeks service-oriented exercise instructors for our state-of-the-art fitness department. Personal trainer positions are available for those with degrees in a health-related field.

## Exercise Physiologist

Certified professional needed at sports training center to develop training programs of elite cyclists. Must test athletes with available state-of-the-art equipment for determining performance limits. Knowledge of factors limiting performance and training on isokinetic muscle strength testing equipment desirable.

## Health and Fitness Director

State fire organization seeks qualified individual to develop, validate, and implement occupational-related tests to include physical fitness and agility testing and coordination. Must develop occupational standards for fire employees. Must develop and implement health management program for the agency. Masters degree in exercise physiology preferred. This person will also provide consultation, design individual exercise prescriptions, and analyze and validate all data for occupational standards. A strong research and computer background and administrative and management experience required. Must pass background investigation. Salary range $28,500 to $44, 550.

## Athletic Trainer

University of Portage seeks NATA certified athletic trainer with PdD or EdD in science-related area (e.g. exercise physiology, biomechanics) to teach undergraduate courses and conduct research. Expertise in obtaining extramural funding desirable. Salary commensurate with experience.

## Fitness Director

Administrator wanted for health and racquet club in the Midwest. Position requires ACSM certification and one year experience in a health club atmosphere. Duties include overseeing all fitness center, aerobic, and event programs and establishing a personal training client base. Salary commensurate with experience.

## Clinical Coordinator

Individual sought to oversee and direct the cardiac and pulmonary rehabilitation service, including Phases I-V and lifestyle modification training, and patient education services. Master's or doctorate in health-related field with 3 to 5 years of direct cardiac rehabilitation experience preferred.

## Athletic Trainer

Private sports medicine clinic seeks NATA certified athletic trainer to work mornings in the hospital located clinic and afternoons supervising high school athletics. Clinical experience working with age group athletes desired. Master degree in exercise-related area preferred, but not required. Salary commensurate with other allied professionals under subcontracted sports medicine clinic contract.

## College Professor

Cambridge College invites application fo a full-time tenure track exercise physiologist position as an assistant professor specializing in exercise biochemistry. Doctorate in biochemistry, pharmacology, or related field required. Responsiblities include teaching undergraduate and graduate exercise physiology courses, directing the exercise physiology laboratory, and other departmental and curricular service activities.

## Health Fitness Instructor

Individuals qualified to instruct group exercise, exercise prescriptions, and supervise healthy and diseased clients. One to two years of college in a related field or one to two years experience in a health and fitness environment and certification by a nationally recognized accrediting body (ACSM, NSCA, ACE). Also required are CPR and first aid certifications; demonstrable knowledge of health appraisal techniques and risk factor identification; and the ability to recommend safe, effective exercise programs. You'll enjoy a competitive salary and excellent benefits as part of our team.

# Chapter 15 Health Promotion

**Stephen M. Horowitz**
Bowling Green State University

---

## Learning Objectives

After studying this chapter, you will be able to

1. define health promotion, optimal health, epidemiology, lifestyle, risk factors, and heredity;

2. identify programs that address the five dimensions of optimal health: physical, emotional, social, spiritual, and intellectual;

3. list the academic areas that contribute to the field of health promotion;

4. describe the job titles, responsibilities, and educational and experiential requirements for at least four careers in health promotion;

5. identify a minimum of 10 settings in which health promoters work;

6. list at least three national health promotion associations or organizations; and

7. identify at least three health promotion scholarly journals and three professional publications.

---

Health promotion is a new field of study that primary care and sports medicine physicians, nurses, athletic trainers, and health educators are looking at with increasing interest. Its primary value may come from its efforts to promote good health and athletic performance, reduce risk of disease and injury, and facilitate recovery when disease or injury do occur.

Health promotion is a comprehensive field that addresses many aspects of a person's health. It helps individuals achieve balance in their emotional, physical, social, intellectual, and spiritual needs, which results in enhanced well-being and athletic and job performance. For example, the physically well-trained athlete can further improve his or her performance with the knowledge and skills that promote proper nutrition, weight control, and stress management.

Health promotion is such a broad discipline that students wishing to pursue a career in this field must obtain a wide spectrum of knowledge and skills to be successful. There are many job settings that health promoters may work in, as well as diverse careers that they may pursue based on their personal interests and goals. In this chapter, you will learn about future trends in health promotion, possible career opportunities, a suggested academic curriculum, professional associations that students can contact for more information, and publications to which you may wish to subscribe. Additionally, you will learn about some challenges facing many health promoters and have an opportunity to complete learning activities that will familiarize you with some job responsibilities a worksite health promotion professional handles.

## What Is Health Promotion?

Health promotion is the science and art of helping people change their lifestyles to move toward a state of optimal health (O'Donnell & Harris, 1994). People can achieve optimal health, or wellness, when there is a balance between the physical, emotional, social, spiritual, and intellectual dimensions in their lives (see figure 15.1). An additional occupational or vocational dimension has recently been proposed, but many health promoters often include this dimension within the realm of the other five. In addition to focusing on individual health habits, health promotion also addresses the social, political, economic, and environmental factors that positively and negatively influence a person's health. We will discuss these areas later in this chapter.

Many people believe that health promotion is synonymous with physical fitness. Physical fitness is just one component within the physical dimension of optimal health. Physical health dimension refers to the physiological condition of your body (O'Donnell & Harris, 1994). The effects on health from smoking, physical activity, alcohol, and nutrition have been clearly demonstrated in the scientific literature. Most health promotion programs typically address the physical dimension of optimal health, and it is most often the area that overlaps with other areas, such as exercise physiology and kinesiology, sport management, fitness and conditioning programs, and recreation and leisure. Although health promotion may address components within each previously mentioned field, it usually encompasses a more comprehensive approach to well-being (Chenoweth, 1987; Everly & Feldman, 1985; Parkinson & Associates, 1982; Patton, Corry, Gettman, & Graf, 1986; Rainey & Lindsay, 1994).

The emotional health dimension refers to your mental state. It addresses such issues as self-esteem, leisure pursuits, and reactions to and coping with life's stressors. Health promotion programs designed to address these issues would be

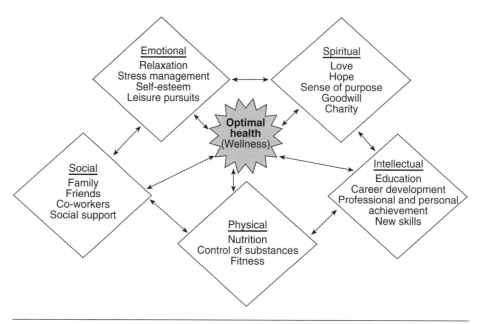

**Figure 15.1**   The five dimensions of optimal health.

stress management, employee assistance programs, and recreation and leisure activities.

The social health dimension deals with your relationships with others, including family, friends, coworkers, and neighbors. Research has clearly demonstrated the beneficial effects of social support on individual health, and on lowering mortality and disease rates. Examples of social health programs are group recreation and workplace sport teams, positive parenting groups, communication skills programs, assertiveness training, and behavior support groups for smoking cessation and weight management.

Spiritual health refers to the condition of your spirit, having a sense of purpose in life, being able to give and receive love, and feeling goodwill toward others. Health promotion activities contribute to spiritual health in the form of life-planning workshops, and charity or volunteer work with nonprofit agencies.

The final dimension, intellectual health, relates to health that results from educational, vocational, and cultural pursuits. Health promotion programs might address activities such as learning needlepoint, calligraphy, or flower arranging and group trips to the theater or historical sites. It might also include learning new skills, such as first aid and cardiopulmonary resuscitation (CPR), or attaining professional certifications as a personal fitness trainer or American Red Cross HIV and AIDS instructor.

The key to health promotion is establishing a balance among all the dimensions, because overemphasizing one area usually results in sacrificing well-being in other areas. An example might be people who work in a demanding, but fulfilling, career and spend 60 or more hours each week dedicated to their profession. They take no time to exercise, eat most meals at fast food restaurants, and are rarely home. As a result, they might be physically unfit, overweight, have high cholesterol and blood pressure, and have poor relationships with their families and friends (Boyer & Vaccaro, 1990).

Health promotion is usually facilitated through a combination of efforts to enhance awareness,

Health promotion has been defined as the science and art of helping people change their lifestyles to move toward a state of optimal health.

## Learning Activity

For each dimension of optimal health, describe at least one example of a healthy lifestyle habit and an unhealthy lifestyle habit that you practice regularly.

change unhealthy behaviors, and create environments that are conducive to good health practices (Dishman, 1986; Gerson, 1987; Steinhardt & Carrier, 1989; White, 1993). Health promotion efforts focus both on a person's unhealthy lifestyle habits (microenvironment) and on the social and political environments (macroenvironment) that have detrimental effects on health. The macroenvironment includes such things as organizational policies and procedures, government legislation, and social norms, as well as the physical world around us. For example, health promoters may help design a smoke-free workplace policy or develop programs that reduce the harmful effects of organizational stressors (Bellingham & Cohen, 1987).

## Learning Activity

Find five different advertisements, greeting cards, and cartoons that relate to health. What is the general point they are making? Who is the audience the message is targeting? In your opinion, is the health message positive or negative? Why?

## Value of Health Promotion

In 1979 the U.S. Surgeon General's report brought to national attention the significant contributions that lifestyle and the environment play as risk factors for death from the major diseases of the time. This report highlighted the fact that, during the 20th century, the leading causes of death changed from infectious diseases, such as tuberculosis, pneumonia, and influenza, to chronic diseases, such as coronary heart disease, cancer, and stroke (U.S. Department of Health, Education and Welfare, 1979). Health promotion targets these lifestyle-related diseases to decrease the rate of premature death and disability. The incidence, prevalence, and patterns of these diseases have been identified through the science of **epidemiology**.

Epidemiological studies have also found a relationship between many causes of death and the quality of medical care, the environment, lifestyle, and heredity (Anspaugh, Hamrick, & Rosato, 1994). For example, poor quality of medical care can result in adverse reactions to prescribed medications and surgical complications, and can, therefore, impact your risk of dying prematurely. The environment includes the air you breathe; the water you drink; the food you eat; and your physical surroundings at work, home, school, and play. Second-hand tobacco smoke, air pollution, waterborne contaminants, and extreme climatic conditions are environmental factors that can contribute to mortality.

Lifestyle is defined as the type of health habits you practice regularly. The things we do regularly can positively or negatively influence how and when we die. For example, lack of exercise, cigarette smoking, high blood pressure, and high cholesterol are primary risk factors for heart disease. Exercising regularly improves heart and lung function, reduces the negative effects of stress, and increases longevity, whereas smoking cigarettes is associated with developing lung cancer, heart disease, and emphysema.

Heredity refers to those biological predispositions to health that we inherit from our families. Many diseases and conditions, such as hypertension, cancer, and heart disease, are influenced by our genetic background. Your heredity can

## The Bottom Line

Health-screening services for detecting health-risk factors are becoming a mainstay for early detection. Due to the increase in health insurance costs and physical examinations, most companies will be turning more to screenings for assessing employee health. Health-risk appraisal (HRA) instruments are frequently used due to their cost-effectiveness in raising health awareness. Health promoters will need to focus more on linking a person's HRA results to individual counseling and behavior change efforts, rather than arbitrarily selecting behaviors to modify.

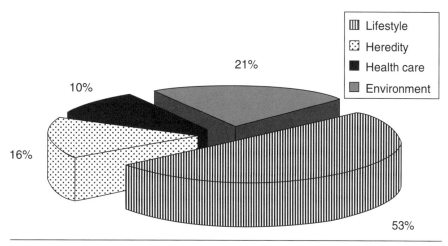

**Figure 15.2**   Factors that influence mortality.

work either for you or against you. For example, if your father has high blood pressure, or your mother has breast cancer, you have a higher risk of developing those diseases than someone whose parents did not have these health problems. On the other hand, having hardy parents and grandparents who live long, healthy lives can make you more resistant to the effects of an unhealthy lifestyle. Although heredity can buffer the effects of unhealthy habits, an individual's lifestyle is still the major influence on premature death and quality of life. Figure 15.2 illustrates this relationship.

Health habits are usually modifiable and are often within the individual's personal control. In the past decade, emphasis has been more on preventing disease than on the traditional medical approach of treating disease after it is in progress. The impetus for this change originated in business. Each year companies were spending more of their profits on health care costs. Because it generally costs less to prevent disease than to treat it, investing in programs that could accomplish this

made good business sense. Health promotion, which plays a significant role in disease prevention and health maintenance, became a popular alternative to the high cost of treating illness (Harris, 1994b). Today, private industry, the health insurance industry, and primary care physicians are increasingly looking toward health promotion to reduce the frequency and severity of health-related problems (Eddy, Gold, & Zimmerli, 1989; Kernaghan & Giloth, 1988; Opatz, 1987). You will be a sport manager who understands the importance of such programs, and you might even initiate one at your worksite.

## Levels and Components of Health Promotion Programs

In general, workplace health promotion programs have three levels of effect (O'Donnell, 1992). They can increase awareness and knowledge, help employees make appropriate lifestyle changes, and help create environments that support healthy

## The Bottom Line

Based on health-screening results, incentive-based (i.e., risk-rated) insurance plans are being implemented. These programs reduce costs for companies as well as for individuals by using the health of an individual as the basis to determine annual and monthly health care fees or premiums. For example, an employee who has high cholesterol or is hypertensive might have to pay a higher monthly premium than another employee who has

normal blood pressure or cholesterol levels. These programs are controversial in that insurance ratings are based on group, rather than individual, statistics. In other words, an employee with high blood pressure may not require increased use of medical care, whereas another employee with normal health values might generate health care costs two or three times higher than we would expect based on group statistics.

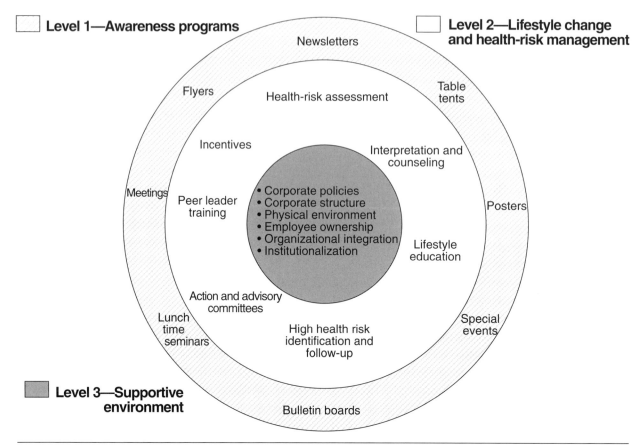

**Figure 15.3**   Levels and components of health promotion programs.

lifestyles (see figure 15.3). The impact of each level on health behavior change and maintenance increases as you move toward the center of the concentric circles. Health promoters who create supportive environments (e.g., develop health-related policies and physical structures such as an on-site fitness facility), have the greatest chance of success in helping employees develop and maintain long-term healthy lifestyle practices (O'Donnell & Harris, 1994).

## Functional Areas Contributing to the Field of Health Promotion

As you can see from the following list, a variety of areas of study directly or indirectly contribute to the field of health promotion. Having basic knowledge or experience in these disciplines can help you be a more effective health promoter.

- Athletic training
- Behavioral medicine
- Biomechanics
- Computer technology

- Economics
- Epidemiology
- Ergonomics
- Exercise physiology
- Health care administration
- Health education
- Management
- Marketing
- Nursing
- Nutrition and dietetics
- Organizational behavior
- Physical education
- Physical therapy
- Psychology
- Recreation
- Recreation therapy
- Research and development
- Safety

Furthermore, the following list illustrates the diverse settings in which you will find health promoters employed. Depending on its organizational structure, profit-making status, and clientele, each type of location may require different qualifications, skills, and knowledge.

- American Red Cross
- American Cancer Society
- American Heart Association
- Commercial fitness clubs
- Community recreation
- Consulting companies
- Continuing and adult education
- Corporations and industry
- Exercise equipment companies
- Government agencies
- Health education materials companies
- Health maintenance organizations (HMOs)
- Health promotion software companies
- Hospitals and health care institutions
- Independent consultant
- Insurance companies
- Jewish Community Centers
- Luxury cruise lines
- Military services
- Older adult and retirement communities
- Preferred provider organizations (PPOs)
- Private spas
- Schools and academia
- YMCA and YWCA

# Job Roles, Opportunities, and Responsibilities in Health Promotion

In 1993, the Association for Worksite Health Promotion (AWHP) conducted a national survey of worksite health professionals. The report includes an excellent cross section of the fitness, wellness, and health promotion industries. It was found that within the fitness and wellness industries, there is a variety of titles and required education and experience criteria for similar positions. This is due, in part, to how young the health promotion field is, as well as to its rapid growth.

According to the AWHP survey, jobs in the health and fitness field can be classified into four categories: technician (prescriptive exercise and health promotion), coordinator (prescriptive exercise and health promotion), management (health promotion manager and director and fitness director), and sales and marketing (representative and manager).

## Technician

Jobs in the prescriptive exercise category typically involve competency in electrocardiographic (ECG) interpretation, flexibility and muscular strength and endurance testing, body composition assessment, blood pressure monitoring, administering graded exercise tests, developing exercise recommendations, and motivating individuals to comply with the recommendations. (Refer to chapter 14 for additional information regarding careers associated with exercise science.) Individuals interested in these types of positions tend to have a greater academic preparation in kinesiology, exercise physiology, and related fitness concentrations than the traditional health promotion curriculum. Examples of prescriptive exercise position titles are exercise specialist, exercise instructor, fitness instructor, fitness consultant, exercise physiologist, and exercise technician.

Health promotion technicians may be involved in performing blood pressure and cholesterol screenings, lifestyle counseling, and leading health education seminars and training workshops. As teachers, health promoters provide basic health education knowledge and skills that address disease prevention, health maintenance, or rehabilitation from an illness or injury. Workshop trainers focus more on developing specific lifestyle behavior skills (e.g., learning how to read food labels or do progressive muscle relaxation) in small groups, usually within a workshop format where individualized instruction often occurs.

Health counseling is an integral component of a health promoter's responsibilities. The counselor's purpose is to help people learn how to achieve personal growth, improve interpersonal relationships, resolve problems, make decisions, and change unhealthy lifestyle behaviors.

## Coordinator

Responsibilities can vary considerably but typically include coordinating, scheduling, evaluating, and presenting fitness and health promotion programs. Prescriptive exercise coordinators focus on fitness-related activities and programs, such as fitness testing, aerobics classes, and use of resistance and cardiovascular training equipment. Titles for this position might include fitness center coordinator and aerobics coordinator.

Competencies required for positions in the health promotion category include the ability to develop and deliver customized health promotion and education programs, such as CPR, nutrition, smoking cessation, stress management, and health behavior change. Typical titles are wellness specialist, wellness coordinator, health and fitness specialist, and health promotion coordinator. Health promotion coordinators may have responsibility for fitness programming in addition to the previously mentioned activities. These individuals often serve as consultants and community and worksite organizers.

A health promotion consultant can serve informally as a resource person to provide health education information, data interpretation, or identification of resources. As a formal consultant, the health promoter functions as a technical expert who diagnoses problems, makes recommenda-tions for improving the problem, implements and delivers services, and evaluates outcomes.

A community organizer might work with a non-profit agency such as the American Heart Association. The organizer's role is to promote healthier lifestyle practices within the community through better use, organization, and availability of health resources. A typical activity would be organizing a health fair using a variety of local businesses and hospitals.

One of the most exciting characteristics of the field of health promotion is the opportunity to work with diverse populations in a variety of settings. Depending on your interests, you may choose to work with women, men, children, specific ethnic groups or socioeconomic strata, or people with physical or mental challenges. For example, you could focus on individuals from different socio-economic backgrounds. A health promoter might help to prevent premature births in women from the inner city or work with Hispanic families to incorporate low-fat cooking ideas into their diets.

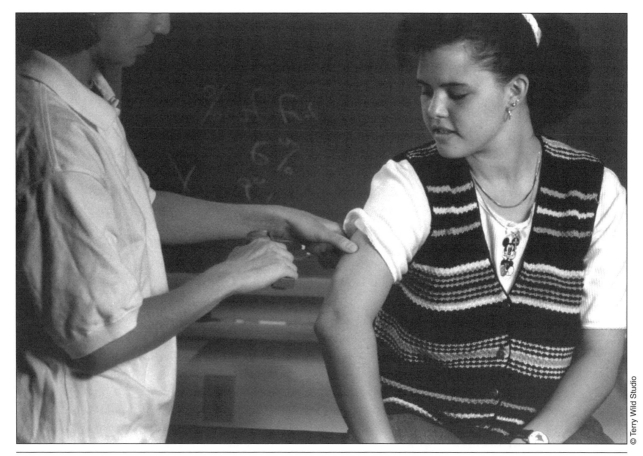

The significant influence of health promotion on disease prevention and health maintenance has led to health promotion programs being started at the workplace and in schools. Here a high school student has the percentage of her body fat measured with a skinfold caliper.

In the first situation, you might work with the city transportation department to provide free bus service to women's health clinics or develop written educational materials appropriate for this population. In the second example, you might contract with dietitians from local hospitals to lead free or low-cost seminars on nutrition or cooking workshops that incorporate many of their traditional dishes.

A major focus of health promotion efforts in the future will be on America's elderly. They are the biggest consumers of health care and require special efforts aimed at preventing and rehabilitating degenerative diseases (Dychtwald, 1986). A growing body of evidence suggests that much of the physical and mental decline among the aging results from lack of disease prevention and health maintenance more than from aging. Consequently, there appear to be many opportunities for health promoters who wish to work with the aging population.

## A Risky Business

Upon your graduation, you are hired by the Sickley Corporation as its Health Promotion Coordinator. The company, located within an industrial park in a major Midwest city, manufactures Widgets for various automobiles. There are four assembly lines that run 24 hours a day. Its 500 assembly-line employees work rotating 12-hour shifts (3 days on, 2 days off). These employees each get 45 minutes for lunch. There is a small cafeteria service available during the day shift, but only vending machines for the night shift. In addition to the line workers, there are 35 office workers, including the plant manager, benefits specialist, safety supervisor, accountant, and clerical support. Office personnel work from 8 A.M. to 5 P.M. Although the office workers have access to computers (e.g., word processing, graphics software, and electronic mail network), line workers do not. There are several bulletin boards posted throughout the plant. There is one conference room that seats approximately 35 people and is equipped with a variety of audiovisual equipment, such as overhead and slide projectors, television (TV) and videocassette recorder (VCR). You recently met with the benefits specialist regarding plant demographics and learned the following about the employees of the Sickley Corporation:

Race: 30% White; 35% African American; 35% Hispanic

Marital status: 40% married; 10% living with partner, not married; 40% divorced; 8% never married; 2% widowed

Gender: 60% male; 40% female

Age: range = 18 to 60 years; average age = 45 years

Average income for office personnel: $45,000

Average income for line workers: $30,000

Average education for office employees: 4-year college degree

Average education for line workers: 10th grade

All employees were invited to participate in a medical screening (blood pressure, cholesterol, blood sugar, height, weight, frame size) and to complete a health-risk appraisal (HRA), which provided information on their relative risks for blood pressure, cholesterol, body weight, physical activity level, nutrition, stress, vehicle safety, smoking status, and alcohol use. Eighty percent of the line workers ($n$ = 400) and one hundred percent of the office employees ($n$ = 35) participated in both the medical screens and HRA. Through the group summary report, you obtained information on the prevalence of various risk factors in the 435 individuals who participated in the medical screens and HRA:

Hyperglycemic (diabetic range) = 22%

Hypertensive (> 140/90 mm Hg) = 23%

High cholesterol (240 or higher) = 33%

More than 20% overweight = 45%

Smoke cigarettes = 42%

Report high stress = 27%

Have poor nutritional habits = 67%

Report high alcohol intake (> 3 drinks/day or > 14/week) = 18%

Use seat belts < 90% of the time = 47%

Sedentary (exercise < 3 times/week) = 65%

## Management

Management positions relate to total project coordination and administration. Individuals in these positions have full responsibility for all aspects of a project, which may entail performing or supervising staff to provide prescriptive exercise and health promotion services and membership development. Fitness managers typically supervise exercise technicians and coordinators in developing, implementing, evaluating, and maintaining prescriptive exercise programs and systems. Health promotion managers and directors often have supervisory responsibilities for more than one site and are ultimately responsible for developing health promotion systems and programs to meet individual client needs. In addition, project and program managers tend to be responsible for developing budgets, allocating funds, hiring and training staff, and recruiting and retaining program members.

## Learning Activity

Invite the health promotion or wellness director from a local hospital or corporation to speak to your class about responsibilities of their position and career opportunities.

## Sales and Marketing

Sales and marketing positions are usually found in management and consulting firms and other organizations that provide services to client organizations. Their primary function is the ongoing identification and development of new client organizations. They may market health-related products, such as computer software, motivational incentives, computerized health assessments (e.g., health-risk appraisal), and health promotion videos and literature. Health-related services that they offer might include providing health screens (e.g., cholesterol, blood pressure, diabetes) and specific health promotion programs (e.g., employee surveys, weight management or smoking cessation lifestyle change courses).

Sales representatives are responsible for meeting sales objectives, developing new business from existing and prospective clients, and representing the organization at industry conferences and vendor fairs. The person in the highest ranking sales and marketing position is usually responsible for directing the entire sales and marketing function within the organization, including market research, forecasting, advertising, and promotion. Other duties include developing sales plans and strategies, and managing and directing the organization's sales force.

Job categories vary by the type of worksite, such as corporate, hospital, and consulting firms.

The AWHP survey (1993) did not investigate job responsibilities or salaries in public health or nonprofit agencies, such as the American Red Cross, American Heart Association, American Cancer Society, and YM or YWCAs. In general, salaries for similar positions within nonprofit organizations tend to be lower than those in corporate, hospital, or consulting settings.

According to the AWHP survey (1993), compensation often depends on the geographical location in which the company is located. For example, staff positions located in the Far West region (Arizona, California, Hawaii, Nevada, and Utah) reported receiving higher pay than other regions for similar positions. The cost of living index for a geographical region is an important consideration, as a $40,000 salary in the Detroit area may be worth relatively more than a $50,000 salary in Los Angeles. Data relative to education, experience, and salaries for various positions in several work settings are presented in table 15.1.

Now that you have an idea of the kinds of jobs available, let's look at a common scenario you might encounter as a worksite health promoter. The Learning Activities that follow represent the responsibilities required if you choose a career in health promotion.

## Recommended Preparation for a Career in Health Promotion

To effectively design, plan, implement, and evaluate the effects of programs, corporate and community health promoters must possess a strong background in a variety of areas. Core competencies of health promotion coordinators and managers include the knowledge and skills to (a) understand the health effects of interactions between individuals and their environment, (b) determine health priorities and identify target audiences, (c) counsel individuals to modify unhealthy behaviors, (d) market and publicize their programs, (e) motivate individuals to participate in their programs, (f) raise funds and budget and allocate them appropriately, (g) identify potential program barriers and how to overcome them, (h) recruit or train instructors, (i) teach health awareness and risk-management programs, and (j) effectively design and evaluate program intervention effects. A list of academic courses and experiences that students will find useful toward their goal of becoming qualified health promoters is presented here.

## Table 15.1
## Types of Careers in Health Promotion and Estimated Salaries
## Based on Education, Experience and Setting

| Category | Average education (degree) | Average experience (years) | Median salaries by worksite (25th percentile to 75th percentile) | | |
|---|---|---|---|---|---|
| | | | Corporate | Hospital | Consulting |
| Technician prescriptive exercise | BS | 1.5 | $23,000 ($21-$31,000) | $21,000 ($19-$25,000) | $21,000 ($19-$23,000) |
| Technician health promotion | BS | 2 | $35,000 ($28-$36,000) | $20,000 ($12-$27,000) | $26,000 ($22-$32,000) |
| Coordinator prescriptive exercise | MS | 2-3 | $31,000 ($29-$41,000) | $27,000 ($26-$31,000) | $28,000 ($26-$30,000) |
| Coordinator health promotion | BS, MS | 5 | $37,000 ($35-$45,000) | $30,000 ($25-$35,000) | $29,000 ($28-$33,000) |
| Management HP manager | MS | 3-5 | $42,000 ($41-$54,000) | $37,000 ($30-$39,000) | $38,000 ($36-$40,000) |
| Management fitness director | MS | 3-5 | $42,000 ($33-$45,000) | $31,000 ($27-$36,000) | $34,000 ($31-$34,000) |
| Management HP director | MS, PhD | 3-10 | $66,000 ($66-$75,000) | $40,000 ($28-$42,000) | $41,000 ($41-$43,000) |
| Sales and marketing rep | BS | 1 | —— | $19,000 ($15-$25,000) | $29,000 ($27-$35,000) |
| Sales and marketing manager | MS | 5-6 | —— | $36,000 ($36-$41,000) | $60,000 ($50-$70,000) |

Data from the Association for Worksite Health Promotion, 1993. *1993 Worksite Health Professionals National Compensation and Benefits Survey.* Delta Consultants.

- General education: anatomy and physiology; behavior modification; communications; computer literacy; cultural diversity; exercise physiology; field experiences; health education; and health psychology
- Specialty areas: counseling techniques; epidemiology; ergonomics; HIV and AIDS; nutrition; public relations; time and stress management; research design and evaluation; statistics; and teaching methodology
- Skills: CPR and first aid; exercise prescription; health-related assessment; laboratory testing and interpretation; risk factor identification; substance abuse; and weight management
- Management: facility planning; marketing; program planning; and program administration

Although these courses are recommended, students will be limited by the curriculum available at their academic institution, as well as by the number of credit hours in their major core and elective courses. For most students, taking all these courses may require more than 4 years and, therefore, may not be logistically or financially realistic. Once students have an idea about the type of career desired, they can better determine which courses would be appropriate for them.

## Professional Associations

There are several professional organizations you can contact for information regarding the field of health promotion. Although the National Wellness Association and the Association for Worksite Health Promotion are highly recommended for health promotion professionals, the associations you choose to join should be based on your interests. There are many benefits to joining these associations, such as receiving journals, newsletters, job placement services, student internship announcements, product information, conference discounts, and networking opportunities. A list of the major associations and organizations that might be of interest to health promoters is presented on page 227.

## Learning Activity

The following activities refer to the case study on page 223. We recommend that you do these learning activities in groups of three to five students. To complete the following activities, you will need to interview health professionals and seek additional information in the library. Refer to the articles cited in this chapter for a place to begin your library search.

1. Based on the information provided, determine your target audience. Why did you select this group? Demographic, lifestyle, socioeconomic, and environmental factors all influence a person's health status. Identify the specific factors you need to consider, and discuss how you think they relate to excess health risk and your proposed program content.

2. Develop a 30-minute health education and awareness seminar on one health need identified in the case study. Write at least two learning objectives and outcomes for employees who will attend your seminar. Objectives must be specific and measurable. For example, "Upon completing the seminar, participants will know how to calculate their target heart rate zone," is better than "Participants will know how hard they should exercise."

3. Based on the health risk you selected, develop a flyer to publicize your program focusing on the unique needs of the selected target population. Your flyer should include the seminar title; a catchy, informative seminar description; and all pertinent information.

4. What methods of communications would you use to publicize the seminar? How would you use these communications? Why did you decide to use these methods?

5. What community or national resources and organizations would you contact for the information to develop your presentation, and which would you contact for program materials and handouts?

6. Write the steps that you think would be required to implement the program, from assessing the needs of the population to the final program evaluation. Estimate the time required for each step and develop a time line for planning and administering the seminar.

7. Incentives are used frequently to increase an individual's motivation to participate in a health promotion program. Describe an incentive you would use and why you selected it.

8. Design an evaluation form to assess the quality and participants' satisfaction with the 30-minute seminar you developed.

## Publications

There are many scholarly and professional journals and newsletters available to health promoters. They may cover a broad spectrum of topics or focus specifically on defined areas within health promotion, such as fitness, program planning, and worksite activities. Publications recommended for health promotion professionals are presented on page 228. Some publications are theoretical or research based, and others focus on general education and programming applications.

## Summary

Health promotion can play a significant role in preventing disease and injury and enhancing health and performance. Its concepts and applications are increasingly used in the fields of medicine, health education, and sports and athletic conditioning. Health promotion has made great strides in the past decade. Increased recognition of the effects of lifestyle practices on health have piqued employer and employee interest in disease prevention and raised the demand for comprehensive programming opportunities in the workplace. With the current trends in national health care restructuring and greater emphasis on health care cost containment, it appears that health promotion professionals may be needed more than ever. It is a profession that can offer students much personal and job-related satisfaction.

We hope this chapter has provided some thought-provoking information that will be useful to the future health promotion professional. The issues, questions, and concerns that we raised were designed to create a new awareness of the role and importance of health promotion. We encourage interested students to contact the professional associations described in this chapter or your local university to assist you in laying the foundation for becoming health promotion professionals.

# For More Information

Following are some of the major health promotion associations and resources.

*American Alliance for Health, Physical Education, Recreation and Dance* (AAHPERD). A nonprofit organization of more than 35,000 professional educators in physical education, health, fitness, sports, athletics, recreation, dance, and related disciplines. The Alliance holds national and state professional meetings, offers various newsletters and journals, provides job listings and professional discounts, and serves as a resource clearinghouse for health education, physical education, recreation, and dance. 1900 Association Drive, Reston, VA 22091-1599, 800-213-2193, FAX 703-476-9527.

*Association for the Advancement of Health Education.* An organization within AAHPERD. The Association offers a professional newsletter and networking opportunities for health educators in various work settings. 1900 Association Drive, Reston, VA 22091-1599, 800-213-2193, FAX 703-476-9527.

*Association for Worksite Health Promotion* (AWHP). Considered by many health promoters to be the preeminent professional society for worksite health professionals, there are approximately 2,500 members internationally. The organization helps set the mission and job standards for worksite health promotion professionals; offers a quarterly newsletter, bimonthly professional journal, and a monthly job bulletin; sponsors international, regional, and state professional meetings.

Regional and local chapters offer networking opportunities. Student memberships are available, and financial assistance can be received for establishing university chapter affiliations. Serves as a resource clearinghouse on worksite health promotion topics. 60 Revere Drive, Suite 500, Northbrook, IL 60062, 708-480-9574, FAX 708-480-9282, http://pages.ripco:8080/~awhp/index.html.

*National Wellness Association.* A nonprofit organization that serves as a clearinghouse for wellness and health promotion developments, resources, programming, research, events, and educational opportunities. It also serves as a source of networking for its members, sponsors national and regional professional meetings, and offers a quarterly newsletter and a monthly job bulletin. Student memberships are available. National Wellness Institute, 1045 Clark Street, Suite 210, P.O. Box 827, Stevens Point, WI 54481-0827, 715-342-2969, FAX 715-342-2979, http://www.wellnessnwi.org/, E-mail: nwa@wellnessnwi.org.

*Wellness Councils of America.* A national nonprofit organization dedicated to promoting healthier lifestyles for all Americans, especially through health promotion activities at the worksite. It has an excellent manual for implementing workplace wellness programs. Its Healthy Workplace Awards provide opportunities for national recognition for organizations meeting various criteria. 7101 Newport Avenue, Suite 311, Omaha, NE 68152-2175, 402-572-3590, FAX 402-572-3594.

# For More Information

Following are some recommended publications for health promotion professionals. They can also be very useful to you.

*American Journal of Health Promotion.* A quarterly journal of research, reviews, editorials, and resources in worksite wellness and public health. P.O. Box 1897, East 10th Street, Lawrence, KS 66044-8897, 800-627-0629, FAX 913-843-1274.

*AWHP's Worksite Health.* The official journal of the Association for Worksite Health Promotion, features original investigations, program and product reviews, comprehensive reviews on current topics in health promotion, and practical tips for health promotion activities at the worksite. Published bimonthly. Free to members. 60 Revere Drive, Suite 500, Northbrook, IL 60062, 847-480-9574, FAX 847-480-9282, http://pages.ripco:8080/~awhp/index.html, E-mail: tsgi@aol.com.

*Journal of Health Education.* A bimonthly journal on topics relevant to health educators in various settings. Offered as an option with AAHPERD membership. 1900 Association Drive, Reston, VA 22091-1599, 800-213-2193, FAX 703-476-9527.

*Total Wellness.* A monthly, eight-page newsletter for the general public covering a variety of health-related topics. Rutherford Publishing, Inc., P.O. Box 8853, Waco, TX 76714, 800-815-2323, E-mail: rpublish@rpublish.com.

*Medicine and Science in Sports and Exercise.* The official journal of the American College of Sports Medicine (ACSM), features original investigations, clinical studies, and comprehensive reviews on current topics in sports medicine. Published monthly. Free to members; annual fee for nonmembers. 351 West Camden Street, Baltimore, MD 21201-2436, 800-638-6423, FAX 410-528-8596, http://www.acsm.org/sportsmed.

*American Journal of Health Behavior, Education, and Promotion.* (Formerly *Health Values*). A bimonthly journal addressing theoretical and applied research related to health educa-tion and health promotion. Provides a 4-hour continuing education activity for Certified Health Education Specialists. PNG Publications, P.O. Box 4593, Star City, WV 26504-4593, 304-293-4699, FAX 304-293-4693.

*Health Education Research.* A quarterly journal addressing theoretical and applied research related to health education and health promotion. Oxford University Press, 2001 Evans Road, Cary, NC 27513.

*Journal of Health Psychology.* SAGE Publications, P.O. Box 5096, Thousand Oaks, CA, 91359, http://www.mdx.ac.uk/www/jhp.

*University of California at Berkeley Wellness Letter.* A monthly, eight-page consumer newsletter covering the latest findings and practical information on achieving a healthier lifestyle. Includes topics such as nutrition, fitness, and stress management. P.O. Box 42018, Palm Coast, FL 32142, 904-445-6414.

*Hope Health Newsletter.* Monthly, four-page publication covering a broad range of health and wellness topics. International Health Awareness Center, Inc., 350 East Michigan Avenue, Suite 301, Kalamazoo, MI 49007-3851, 616-343-0770, FAX 616-343-6260.

*Vitality.* A monthly magazine filled with interesting health and wellness facts, recipes, articles, self-tests, and resources. 8080 North Central, LB 78, Dallas, TX 75206-1818, 800-554-0015.

*Workplace Vitality.* Sixteen-page newsletter published 10 times annually. Published by Vitality, Inc. Interesting and practical articles, self-tests, products, and resources designed specifically for worksite health promotion. 8080 North Central, LB 78, Dallas, TX 75206-1818, 800-554-0015.

*Health Promotion Practitioner.* A monthly, eight-page newsletter designed specifically for health promoters. Includes interesting articles, case studies, and many suggestions for health promotion activities. P.O. Box 1335, Midland, MI 48641-1335, 517-839-0852, FAX 517-839-0025.

# Down the Road

During the next 5 to 10 years, the health promotion field may undergo shifts in emphases and delivery systems. For example, forecasters predict the following.

1. Individualized programs, such as personalized counseling programs and one-on-one lifestyle behavior modification and fitness plans, will become the media through which health promotion is most often delivered.

2. Group programming, such as classes on various health-related topics, may become a less preferred option. Behavior modification programs aimed at altering unhealthy lifestyle practices have not been an effective approach due to the minimal changes reported for the money invested in them. Rather, individualized approaches, such as telephone counseling, will be used more frequently.

3. There will be a greater emphasis on mental wellness, so that more demand will exist for programs that address depression, compulsive behavior, self-esteem, domestic violence, and suicide. Health promotion programs will focus more on work and family issues, including flexible scheduling, maintaining a balanced lifestyle and outlook, drug abuse prevention, and family-related stress, with greater involvement of dependents in activities offered at the worksite (Harris, 1994a).

4. There will be more follow-up case management for high-risk individuals, which will be best addressed by integrated health management teams including health promotion, employee assistance, medical benefits, and disability management (Harris, 1994a).

5. Health promotion generalists, compared to specialists, may be in higher demand. Specialists with skills in only one or two types of wellness programs may find it increasingly difficult to find jobs.

6. Health promotion professionals with a high level of competency, who have excellent communication skills, knowledge of insurance and business practices, and extensive backgrounds in health and fitness will be in greatest demand.

7. Private consultants may be the largest percentage of providers of health promotion services. Hospital-based and in-house corporate programs may slowly be phased out.

# Job Opportunities

## Wellness Coordinator

Energetic, enthusiastic individual needed to coordinate the wellness program at the Sickley Corporation. Must have knowledge and expertise in ergonomics, health promotion and education, safety, and risk-factor reduction. Responsibilities include coordinating, scheduling, evaluating, and presenting health-related programs. Minimum 1 year experience in a manufacturing setting and BA degree required (MS preferred). Excellent salary and benefits.

## Wellness Director

CynDor, Inc. anticipates an opening in their New York office for a wellness director to oversee the development and management of fitness center operations, policies, procedures, and education programs. This position requires a master's degree in health promotion, exercise science, or related field and 3 years experience in successfully delivering wellness and fitness programs to large organizations. We offer competitive salaries and a comprehensive benefits package.

## Wellness Technician and Counselor

Federal Government Services is seeking experienced wellness and fitness specialists to explore opportunities in the western United States. Duties include performing blood pressure and cholesterol screenings, lifestyle counseling, and leading health education seminars and workshops. Salary range $25 to 30K. Minimum 1 year experience and BA in health or fitness related field.

## Manager, YMCA Fitness and Wellness

Community YMCA is seeking a fitness and wellness manager to provide leadership for member and community programs in North Carolina. Excellent opportunity for team-oriented person seeking personal and professional growth. Responsibilities include leadership of fitness programs, corporate wellness, development of collaborative program with hospital. Requirements include skills and experience in fitness assessment, ACSM certification, CPR, and first aid and strong planning, budget, and leadership skills. Three to five years of experience, MS preferred. Competitive salary.

## Health Promotion Specialist

Local hospital is seeking a motivated individual with background and experience in health promotion program planning and evaluation to assist in implementing worksite wellness programs within local businesses. Knowledge of the health care industry and risk identification and management required. BA required (MS preferred). Salary $20,000 to $25,000 depending on experience.

## Health Fitness Instructor

Local HMO is seeking individuals qualified to instruct group exercise and health education classes with 1 to 2 years of college in a related field or comparable experience in a health and fitness environment. Accreditation by ACE, ACSM, or similar nationally recognized body, CPR, and first aid certification required. Must have excellent interpersonal skills; demonstrate knowledge of health risk appraisal techniques and risk factor identification; and be able to recommend safe, effective lifestyle programs. Salary $18 to 22K.

## Community Health Educator

The right candidate will be able to coordinate projects and programs for the community, such as health fairs, and assist with wellness program development for the community and Memorial Hospital employees. Degree in a health-related field required with strong marketing and public relations skills. Candidate should be a self-starter with excellent communications skills. Salary range and benefits are negotiable. Three to five years of experience required.

## Health Promotion Consultant

Wisehealth, a nonprofit organization, is seeking a team player responsible for making our programs come alive for our managed care industry clients. Work with our sales, marketing, and training departments to customize wellness programs. Responsibilities include effective program design and evaluation, budget management, staff supervision, and project coordination. Requirements include travel, knowledge of holistic health practices and teachings, and good people and communication skills. Two to three years experience. Salary range $35,000 to $45,000.

# Chapter 16

# Sport Tourism

**Julie R. Lengfelder and David L. Groves**
Bowling Green State University

---

## Learning Objectives

After studying this chapter, you will be able to

1. identify the interrelationships of sport and tourism;

2. explain the interdisciplinary program of study of sport and tourism;

3. appreciate the historical foundations of tourism and sport;

4. identify careers in sport tourism;

5. name five settings in the sport tourism industry;

6. discuss issues and trends specific to the sport tourism industry;

7. forecast possibilities for the future in sport tourism; and

8. discuss ecotourism.

---

The tourism industry includes those attractions, events, and magnetic experiences that draw **leisure** and business travelers out of their homes or hotels. The sport industry includes business enterprises and other organizations that market the popular pastimes of sport participation and spectator sport activities. When the sport industry merges with the tourism industry, a new industry emerges: sport tourism. Sport is one of the most popular motivators of the tourist (Hawkins & Hudman, 1989), and the sport tourism industry is a progressive concept that focuses on sport attractions, events, and experiences available to tourists.

Sport tourists can be described in two ways. First, as a participant, the sport tourist engages in activities such as tennis, golf, skiing, white water rafting, mountain climbing, pony trekking, hunting, fishing, sailing, scuba and skin diving, boating, as well as many other activities. The wellness and fitness movement has certainly contributed to the popularity of this segment of the travel market. Cruise ships cater to the sport enthusiast, as do resorts and urban hotels. Second, as a spectator, the sport tourist is drawn to events and attractions locally such as community baseball games and horse races. The sport tourist might also travel nationally or internationally to events such as the World Series or the Olympics. Alternatively, sport tourists can sit in their living rooms and channel surf on cable television from one sporting event to the next. The sport tourist participates in the tourism experience for escapism, for a peak experience, for a vicarious thrill, or for the experiential use of the human body.

Many times the sport tourist will contract the services of a travel agent, or specifically a sport travel agent, who arranges a travel package. This package might include golf with a major sport personality along with in-room fitness accommodations at a five-star hotel, or a luxury box at the Super Bowl as the main attraction to the travel experience. In a more innovative way, contemporary technology permits people to transcend these traditional activities and experience sport tourism internationally on the Internet. This virtual reality mode opens whole new vistas to sport enthusiasts to participate and spectate in a variety of sporting events without leaving the comfort of their homes!

The purpose of this chapter is to familiarize you with the sport tourism industry. We will trace the history of tourism as well as the development of the hybrid concept of sport tourism. We will examine industry issues and trends and career opportunities. Finally, we will introduce you to professional preparation, continuing education, and professionalization opportunities.

## Learning Activity

Look at the sports section of a major daily newspaper. How do the articles about sport relate to leisure and tourism?

## Sport Tourism—A New Industry

Sport tourism provides not only a sports adventure but also a social experience for many diverse groups. Travel clubs, agencies, and destinations that cater to people with disabilities and to special interest groups are becoming popular and profitable. There are camps for mommies, gay and lesbian resorts, travel companies for people who are physically or mentally challenged, men's outdoor adventures, cruise programs for the fitness minded—a plethora of special travel opportunities.

## Hallmark Events

Many cities around the world are giving economic focus to developing short-term staged attractions called hallmark events. These events are major, one-time, or recurring events of limited duration, such as the Olympics, the Kentucky Derby, and the Boston Marathon. They are developed primarily to enhance the awareness, appeal, and profitability of a tourism destination in the short or long term. The success of such events relies on the uniqueness, status, or timely significance of the event to create interest and attention.

Hallmark events are major fairs, expositions, and cultural and sporting events of international status, which are held on a regular or one-shot basis. A primary function of the hallmark tourist event is to provide the host community with an opportunity to secure a position of prominence in the tourism market for a short, well-defined time (Hall & Sellwood, 1987). So, although the contest or event is important to many people, the city parents are interested in bidding for such events for economic rather than competitive reasons.

## Learning Activity

Write a mock promotional piece that would attract sport enthusiasts to an international hallmark event.

## Professional Franchises

The existence of professional sport franchises in a city greatly affects the tourism economy, creating both material and perceived image development. The ripple effect of a professional sport organization manifests in developing convention centers, major hotels and restaurants, upscale shopping malls, and many public and private partnerships formed for entrepreneurial purposes (see chapter 5). David Harvey (1989) has labeled this phenomenon the formation of the entrepreneurial city. In addition, the mere existence of the sport franchise has a remarkable public relations impact by enhancing the image of the city. Professional sport event coverage and promotion achieve a similar objective as that of tourism—to create a bonding community of sport enthusiasts who share a love for the sport that spans beyond the boundaries of the entrepreneurial city limits.

© Corbis-Bettmann

President Bill Clinton introduces Muhammed Ali to spectators at the opening ceremony of the 1996 Olympic Games in Atlanta.

## Television

Television also contributes to the development of the sport tourism community. Marketing and promotion help to construct global audiences for big-name sports, giving world-famous entertainment advantages over local entertainers (Whitson & Macintosh, 1993). In fact, famous entertainment events and entertainers have become the most effective (and expensive) carriers for other promotional messages. Now all kinds of products—and cities—gain visibility via their associations with famous entertainers and events rather than through more traditional modes of advertising. "The global reach of information about these events, of course, makes such associations all the more desirable" (Wernick, 1991).

### Learning Activity

From a personal point of view, how did your upbringing, family experience, TV viewing, and other media affect your participation as a sport tourist?

## History of Tourism

One of the earliest recorded examples of tourism was a trip described in the Bible, when the Queen of Sheba went to see King Solomon in Jerusalem (Hawkins & Hudman, 1989). Ancient tourism reached its zenith during the Roman Empire Era (31 B.C. to 476 A.D.) when the Romans established what is now considered the first tourism infrastructure of hotels, taverns, and roads (Hawkins & Hudman, 1989). When the Dark Ages arrived (circa 900 A.D.), people were unable to be tourists due to economic, social, and religious constraints. During this period of feudalism, external sources such as the church made people feel that tourism, leisure, and recreation were evil, a waste of time, and led to immorality. As a result, tourism declined significantly (Schor, 1991). The Renaissance Era (1300-1600) with its emphasis on rebirth of scholarship and the arts, provided a conducive environment for reviving tourism, recreation, and leisure. Tourism, as an acceptable practice, increased during this period but fluctuated thereafter until the advent of the Modern Era (1946 to the present), which is characterized by mass tourism (Hawkins & Hudman, 1989).

During the Modern Era, country after country opened up to the capitalist emphasis on producing goods and accumulating wealth. The influx of dollars left by tourists across the world created many positive short-term effects; yet tourism also resulted in many long-term problems. Two types of tourists existed—**elite tourists** from the wealthy leisure class and **mass tourists**, who arrived with the development of transportation systems. Elite tourists were frequently more welcome in an area than mass tourists, even though mass tourists brought large amounts of money to the host. This was partially due to the negative impact mass tourism can have on the environment, culture, and destination facilities (Plog, 1994).

Some mass tourists carry with them a sense of freedom from the conventional norms of their everyday social structure and do not show respect to their host community. These individuals sometimes engage in actions that have negative impacts on the host environment (Shaw & Williams, 1994). Although the financial contributions tourists make to the host community are welcomed, the attitudes of the local citizens begin to sour as crowds infiltrate the streets that were once serene and quiet. Misuse and abuse of the environment begin to occur, which causes deterioration of natural resources and the physical destruction of the host community (Plog, 1994).

## Growth of the Tourism Industry

The tourism industry includes hotels, airlines, cruise lines, souvenir shops, and any other public or private businesses that are affected by the tourist dollar. The industry has been growing steadily in size and economic importance since the end of World War II (1940s). It now accounts for 12% of the world's gross national product (Hawkins & Hudman, 1989), and few countries in the world are unaffected by the tourist dollar. According to Naisbitt (1994), the World Tourism Organization attributes this dramatic growth to international demographic changes including (a) an increase in financial capabilities of the tourist, (b) an increase in the number of single adults, (c) an increase in paid leave and flex time in the workplace, (d) benefits packages that permit early retirement, and (e) an increase in the number of two-income households. Only recently have individuals, government agencies, and businesses begun to realize the impact of these trends in relation to tourism and its future (Smith, 1989; Naisbitt, 1994).

## Economic Impact of Tourism

The sport tourism industry has few boundaries, although it primarily infiltrates economic, environmental, and cultural domains. Tourism's economic impact is one of the most researched but least understood areas of tourism. According to the World Tourism Organization (1994), the total receipts from international inbound tourism in the United States "grew from nearly $54 million in 1992 to $63.5 billion in 1993" (Hasek, 1994, p. 1). The industry is so expansive that it has caused problems for practitioners and academicians in determining its exact composition. In a survey report published in *The Economist* (March 23, 1991), data from a variety of studies were presented.

> The size of the travel and tourism business is difficult to comprehend, for at least three reasons. First, there is no accepted definition of what constitutes the industry; any definition runs the risk of either overestimating or underestimating economic activity. . . . Second, tourism is a business many of whose activities (like tour guides and souvenir salesmen) and much of whose income (tips) are well suited to practitioners of the underground economy. In countries with foreign exchange controls (which are always evaded), every official figure on expenditure abroad will be wrong. Third, international travel is bedeviled by astounding differences in the data of different countries. (p. 58)

## Symbiotic Relationship Between Tourism and Sport

Sport and tourism share many historical similarities. It has been noted that mass tourism began in the 1940s. This was an era when spectatorship at sporting events also increased in popularity. In the era of mass recreation that followed, it was not surprising that people traveled more to spectate, which was probably due to the advanced transportation systems that were being introduced. In the following period (1958-1974), sport was affected in the same way as tourism, with more free time, high employment, and the availability of credit allowing people to travel farther to either play or watch sports. The economic handicaps of the following decade had a similar dampening impact on sport and tourism. It would be fair to state that the partnership of sport and tourism occurred with such sporting events as the winter and summer Olympics, Wimbledon, Super Bowl, World Cup, European Soccer, organized boxing matches, and vacations where the emphasis is on sport participation.

# Career Opportunities in Sport Tourism

The tourism career field is expected to be the number one employer by the year 2000. It is predicted that 1 out of every 10 workers will be employed directly or indirectly in the tourism industry (Naisbitt, 1994). The sport tourism sector is a significant portion of the tourism industry. Therefore, the career outlook is promising.

The tourism industry has contributed to the industrialization of many nations through its contribution to employment and the resulting alleviation of employment problems. As a labor-intensive industry, it generates a significant amount of employment, both primary (within the tourism industry) and secondary (in other industries serving tourism). Tourism provides jobs to women, people of all ages, unskilled workers, members of minority

## A Global Perspective

As globalization of travel and tourism increases, so do demands on the environment and cultures. The 1990s have seen an increased awareness of the environment through ecotourism. Ecotourism is a three-way, symbiotic relationship among place, visitor, and host community (Johnson, 1994). It gives people an opportunity that was lost in the process of urbanization: the chance to reconnect with nature (Jafari & Ritchie, 1981). According to the Ecotourism Society, ecotourism grossed more than $2 million in 1992 and is the fastest growing form of tourism (Hasek, 1994).

Ecotourism involves low-impact activities, such as backpacking and hiking, that are low in density and take place in natural settings with geographical, cultural, and biological characteristics that attract tourists (Hawkins, 1994). The host region makes a commitment to establish and maintain sites in cooperation with those who market them, live in them, and visit them, while putting the funds obtained back into the area's land management and community development (Ziffer, 1989). Ecotourism is a philosophy, a mind-set, or an attitude imbued in both the tourism guest and host. Running parallel with the ecology movement, ecotourism can be defined as a style of tourism with regard for the environment and fellow human beings. Examples include low-impact camping, cleaning the environment as one travels, or even something as simple as not picking the flowers or not taking photographs of people of indigenous cultures. The main objective of ecotourism is to allow tourists to immerse themselves into a natural setting that demands segregation from their daily, urban existence. Eventually, people acquire a consciousness, thus leading to a deeper interest in conservation issues.

Could there be a move toward ecosport? It could be argued that the answer will be yes as the two industries have followed similar paths. In the coming years, there could conceivably be a rise in the number of organized hiking, climbing, and camping vacations, along with promoting sports and sporting events that do not have negative impacts on the environment. Ecotourism-minded organizations, such as American Youth Hostels (AYH), historically have been concerned with promoting the travel experience with minimal negative impact on the host culture and environment. The goal of ecosport is to provide sport and recreation activities while preserving and enhancing global ecology.

groups, and socially disadvantaged individuals. Tourism also generates employment in non-industrialized areas that have limited sources of employment. Thus, it improves regional balance and helps prevent rural depopulation by providing employment opportunities where other alternatives do not exist. Examples of employment opportunities in sport tourism include

- sport information and promotions specialist;
- special event coordinator;
- sport club manager;
- tour guide;
- resort manager;
- trip manager;
- travel agency manager;
- travel journalist;
- adventure travel coordinator;
- business travel consultant;
- golf course manager;
- guest relations specialist;
- water transportation operator;
- youth activities coordinator;
- ground transportation operator;
- stadium manager;
- sport event promoter;
- tournament planner;
- convention and visitors bureau specialist;
- public relations specialist;
- recreation specialist;
- convention specialist;
- campground manager;
- ski, golf, tennis, and scuba instructor;
- museum interpreter and guide;
- tour broker;
- park manager;
- theme park manager; and
- tennis facility manager.

## Learning Activity

Create a job description listing qualifications for an entry-level position in a sport tourism setting. How would you find a job in a sport tourism setting? What sources would you consult? Develop a portfolio for your job search.

## Professional Preparation

In the past few years, technologies, services, and the economic and social structures of the world have changed dramatically. People are now able to travel to places once off-limits, travel in faster and fancier modes of transportation, while staying in contact with family, work, and friends through computers, cellular phones, faxes, and other technological advancements. The tourism industry has rapidly advanced by these technological improvements, thus creating a complex industry in which specialized education is needed to keep the industry apace with the needs of society (Knowles, 1977).

At the foundation of every task performed and responsibility carried out in the sport tourism industry is a philosophy of service. This service orientation determines success in customer and public relations, the bottom line on the budget, and the smooth operation of facilities. People employed in the sport tourism industry plan and manage events and activities, supervise and evaluate staff, develop budgets, design promotion and publicity campaigns, coordinate and manage ongoing programs, prepare and implement risk-management plans, negotiate and write facility

## From Roller Coasters to Racquets

Susan, a first-year student, recounted her marvelous summer experience working at one of the largest theme parks in the country, Cedar Point, on Lake Erie in Ohio. She talked about the many opportunities in the tourism industry and the course preparation needed to put her on the right path. Determined to follow her dream, she finished her studies at the university, receiving her baccalaureate degree in sport management. While pursuing her degree, Susan had completed an internship working for an internationally known tennis tournament office. During her internship, she made many contacts in the professional tennis business. After graduation, Susan remained in the world of tennis, becoming a public relations director for a major Ohio tournament conducted annually. Little did she know in her days at Cedar Point that she could combine her love of people in the service of tourists with her passion for sport in a career setting. What opportunities do you think might lie ahead for Susan in the next 3 or 4 decades of her career?

contracts, conduct marketing research, and most of all, deal with people of multicultural backgrounds daily.

In the classic model of tourism education, Jafari and Ritchie (1981) developed a 16-discipline concept, which describes career preparation for entry-level positions in tourism (see figure 16.1). The outer circle of the model represents academic disciplines that play a role in the study of tourism. Of course, when this model is applied to sport tourism, a box containing **sport studies** must be added to the outer circle because individuals who are employed in sport tourism should have a thorough understanding of sport as a cultural phenomenon. Discussions of sport as a powerful social institution are in chapters 1 and 3.

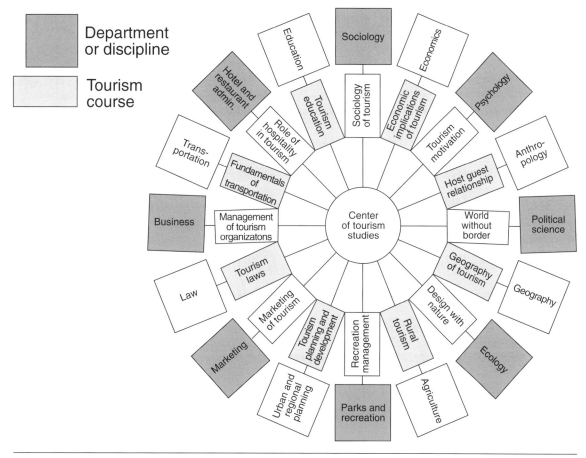

**Figure 16.1**   Jafari and Ritchie 16-discipline concept.
Reprinted, by permission, from J. Jafari and Ritchie, J.R. Brent, 1981, "Toward a framework for Tourism Education," *Annals of Tourism Research* **8**(1): 13-34.

## Down the Road

Incredible and rapid advances in technology and communication will have significant impact on the sport tourism industry. The tourist today can play golf or watch baseball on the Internet. The trip planner can lay out travel itineraries on-line as well as review travelogues of the latest hot spots for vacations. The sport participant can shop for sport products and surf the net for sport museum tours and archives, records, and trivia. Because awareness of sport tourism opportunities will increase, probably *more* people will travel to sporting events in person as opposed to staying home. Education on availability and accessibility will raise the level of spectator participation.

The inner circle of Jafari and Ritchie's model symbolizes the application of the disciplines to the industry through course work specific to tourism. The hub of the spoke and wheel graphic characterizes the integration of disciplines, which is necessary for the interdisciplinary study of tourism.

## Professionalization of the Industry

At the present time, the tourism industry is in the embryonic stages of professional development with no concrete rules determining recruitment of members into the field and mechanisms for monitoring their behavior. As this semiprofession develops, greater efforts will be made to restrict selection of occupational group members through certification, licensure, and accreditation programs. A well-defined, unique body of knowledge will be developed as well as a code of ethics. At present there is no professional organization that has a ubiquitous view and control of the industry. See the For More Information on page 239 for an idea of the number of segments of the tourism industry with professional associations that guide industry progress.

## Learning Activity

Develop a scenario for the 50-year future to use as a television commercial for promoting a sport tourism destination. Take a trip on the Internet: Explore the Grand Canyon, play virtual reality golf in the Carolinas, attend a cricket game in England.

## Summary

Globalization, technology, and multiculturalism have greatly influenced the way we travel. No longer are we limited to local sporting events. The world of sport is available with the press of the TV power button. Entrepreneurial cities are busy developing sport complexes and mega-events that will boost local economies and provide jobs. All these developments bode well for the enterprising student who is considering a career in the sport tourism industry.

The study of sport tourism draws upon the disciplines of sport psychology, sociology, geography, leisure behavior, and others. The tourism and sport industries have grown in parallel with mass participation in the past 5 decades. Although there are many positive aspects of the growth of sport tourism, negative impacts have increased, causing concern to social, physical, and cultural environmentalists. Thus, ecotourism is an emerging movement.

Many job and career opportunities are available in sport tourism. Skills and competencies in areas such as marketing, management, communications, and public relations are required. The sport tourism industry is an emerging profession. As it grows, professional associations will monitor the behavior of its members and upgrade performance standards. The future is bright for this new industry as advanced technology allows tourists greater mobility with increased speed and expanded services and amenities.

# For More Information

Tourism is a wide and varied field. Use these resources to learn more about it.

## Tourism Associations

- Adventure Travel Society (ats@adventuretravel.com.)
- American Camping Association (http://www.aca-camps.org/)
- American Hotel and Motel Association (http://www.d-net.com/csgis/foodasoc.htm)
- American Spa and Health Resort Association
- National Association of Concessionaires
- Caribbean Cruise Association
- Club Managers Association of America (CMAA) http://www.bus.msu.edu/broad/sshb/hsa/cmaa.htm
- Cross Country Ski Area Association (CCSAA) (http://www.xcski.org/ccsaa.html)
- Cruise Lines International Association (http://www.ten-io.com/clia/)
- Dude Ranch Association
- Foodservice Consultants Society International (FCSI)
- Golf Course Association
- Golf Course Superintendents' Association of America
- International Association of Amusement Parks and Attractions (IAAPA) (http://www.iaapa.org/)
- International Association of Convention and Visitor Bureaus (http://www.iacvb.org/)
- International Hotel Association (http://www.ih-ra.com/)
- International Health, Racquet, and Sports-club Association (IHRSA)
- International Sightseeing and Tours Association
- National Swimming Pool Institute (NSPI)
- Outdoor Amusement Business Association (OABA) (http://www.oaba/index.htm)
- Resort and Commercial Recreation Association

- Society for the Advancement of Travel for the Handicapped
- Tourist Attractions and Parks
- Travel and Tourism Research Association (http://www.ttra.com/)

## Tourism Research Journals and Trade Publications

- *Annals of Tourism Research* (http://www.elsevier.nl:80/inca/publications/store/)
- *International Journal of Hospitality Management* (http://www.elsevier.nl:80/inca/publications/store/)
- *International Tourism Quarterly*
- *Journal of Leisure Research* (http://www.gu.edu.au/gwis/hmail/leisurenet/)
- *Journal of Travel Research*
- *Leisure Industry Digest*
- *Leisure Sciences* (http://leeisuresci.fhhs.ac.cowan.edu.au/leisure/)
- *Special Events Report*
- *Tourism ManagementTravel Business ReportTravel Digest* (http://www.canoe.com/Travel/digest.html)
- *Travel Management Daily and Travel Management Newsletter*
- *Travel Weekly* (http://www.traveler.net/two/)
- *Visions in Leisure & Business* (http://ernie.bgsu.edu/~dgroves/vlbo/)

## Additional Web Sites

- Educational and Cultural Exchanges: http://www.usia.gov/usiahome/educatio.html
- National Center for Educational Travel: http://www2.ios.com:80~ncet/
- Hotel Brochures: http://www.travelweb.com
- Speakers: http://speakers.starbolt.com/pub/speakers/webspkr1111.html
- Meetings Industry Mall: http://www.mim.com
- Web Sites: http://www.us.net/~eventweb/

*(continued)*

## For More Information *(continued)*

**Additional Web Sites** *(continued)*

- Meeting Planners: http://speakers.starbolt.com/pub/speakers/web/speakers.html
- Events: http://www.discribe.ca/nbcalendar/>
- Hospitality Newsletter: http://www.u-net.com/hotelnet/hts/
- Table of Moscow Trade Shows: http://www.nar.com/shows.html
- Trade Shows on the Internet: http://www.catch22.com/webexpo
- WWW Bulletin Board: http://www.virtua.com/virtua/bb/
- Expositions and Trade Shows: http://www.expoguide.com/shows/shows.htm
- International Multimedia Entertainment Festival: http://www.futuremedia.com/imef/

- NetGuide's Calendar of Online E-vents: http://techweb.cmp.com/net/calendar/cal.htm
- Media Trade Show Calendars: http://www.catalog.com/buttle/events
- WorldNet Production Int'l: http://www.worldnet.se/
- Trade Shows, Expositions & Conferences: http://www.tradegroup.com/
- Work Now and in the Future: http://www.nwrel.org/edwork/wnf/
- The Worldwide Events Database: http://www.ipworld.com/events/homepage.htm
- Trade Shows Events: http://www.expoguide.com
- Travel Events: http://worldhotel.com/LR/agents/APcalendar.html

# Job Opportunities

## Special Event Coordinator

Individual sought to plan city-wide, year-round special events. Duties include coordination of booking entertainment and attractions, supervising setup crews, publicity and promotion, operation and maintenance of equipment. Must have public relations skills as well as excellent organization abilities. Bachelor's degree in recreation preferred. Salary commensurate with experience.

## Tour Guide

Energetic and enthusiastic person needed to conduct walking tours of the downtown sports, entertainment, and historical attractions. Individual must be bilingual in Spanish and English. Knowledge of city's rich culture and history required. Interested individual should apply to City Parks and Recreation Commission. Flexible hours. Excellent salary per tour.

## Adventure Travel Leader and Coordinator

Adventures Are Yours now accepting applications for travel coordinators and leaders to plan and escort bicycling and hiking trips in the Southwest United States. Trips range from 2 to 4 weeks for various age groups. Experience as a trip leader required as well as a strong desire to work with young people. Bachelor's degree required in sport management, recreation, tourism, or related area. Excellent benefits and salary.

## Convention Specialist

City convention center seeks dynamic professional to promote and sell city as a convention site to trade associations. Certified Meeting Planner (CMP) certification preferred. Individual must feel passionate about the city! Must have excellent planning, organizing, and public relations skills. Bachelor's degree in recreation, hospitality, or related specialization preferred.

## Tournament Planner

Sponsoring corporation seeking individual to assist in the planning, development, and execution of international tennis tournament to be hosted in August. Candidate must have tournament planning experience to supervise committees that oversee a variety of events surrounding the 4-day tournament. Bachelor's degree in sport management, recreation, leisure, tourism, or related area. Salary commensurate with experience.

## Senior Adult Trip Coordinator

Senior Center looking for responsible, energetic person to plan and launch day, weekend, and extended trips for seniors. Applicant must have knowledge of developing trip itineraries and be able to perform trip escort duties. Two years experience working with seniors required. Bachelor's degree necessary. Excellent benefits and salary.

## Youth Activities Trip Leader

YWCA wishes to recruit responsible person to escort urban youth groups on adventure trips to include a variety of activities: skiing, hiking, horseback riding, climbing, and ropes courses. Applicants must have 1 year experience working with behaviorally challenged youth. Bachelor's degree required.

## Guest Relations Specialist

Major hotel corporation seeking energetic, motivated individual to run guest relations operations. Individual must plan activities and programs, escort small groups on the island, and assist in promoting special events hosted by hotel. Individual must have pleasing personality, love working with people, and be active. Bachelor's degree in sport management, hospitality management, recreation management, or tourism management required.

## Chapter 17 Professional Sport

**William A. Sutton and Jay Gladden**
University of Massachusetts at Amherst

---

### Learning Objectives

After studying this chapter, you will be able to

1. define, explain, and discuss the development of professional sport;

2. describe the unique facets of professional sport, including its governance and the labor–management relationship professional team sports depend on;

3. document the significance of the relationship between television and professional sport;

4. describe the major revenue sources for a professional sports team; and

5. identify the types of employment opportunities available in professional sport.

---

Professional sport is any sport activity or skill for which the athlete is compensated for his or her performance. Compensation can be in the form of salary, bonuses, reimbursement for expenses, **personal services contracts**, or any other forms of direct payment. The activity being performed can be a team sport such as basketball, a dual sport such as tennis, an individual sport such as figure skating, or a sport entertainment performance such as the Worldwide Wrestling Federation (WWF). Although these professional sports usually imply the presence of spectators, an audience is not a criterion by which professional sport is defined. For example, some sport organizations such as the Ladies Professional Golf Association (LPGA) and the Professional Golf Association (PGA) have a classification of membership called the **teaching professional**. Although this group of professionals might occasionally compete in tournaments for prize money, they typically earn their livings as teaching pros who instruct others in the skills and strategies of the game. Their skills, therefore, might be directed to a small group of students or perhaps only one individual. Teaching pros also are involved in clinics, lessons, club management, and merchandising ventures, all of which can be lucrative revenue sources. Table 17.1 presents a representative list of North American professional sports.

### Table 17.1
### Representative List of
### North American Professional Sports

| | | |
|---|---|---|
| Auto Racing | Football | Skiing |
| Baseball | Golf | Snowboarding |
| Basketball | Hockey | Soccer |
| Billiards | Horse Racing | Surfing |
| Body Building | Ice Skating | Tennis |
| Bowling | Racquetball | Triathlons |
| Boxing | Rodeo | Volleyball |
| Curling | Roller Hockey | |

*Note*: List was created based on listings provided in G.J. Cylkowski, 1992, *Developing a Lifelong Contract in the Sports Marketplace*, Athletic Achievements, Little Canada, MN, and R.A. Lipsey, ed., 1996, *Sports Market Place*, SportsGuide, Princeton, NJ.

## The Nature of Professional Sport

In the words of David Guterson (1994), professional sport can be viewed:

> as a primary expression of the American character at the end of the twentieth century. Like money, it is something we love, a first waking thought and a chronic passion, as well as a vast sector of the economy, a wellspring for myth and totem, and a media phenomenon of the highest order. Our sports can fend off the brute facts of existence, temporarily arrest the sadness of life, briefly shroud the inevitability of death and provide the happy illusion of meaning through long enchanted afternoons. . . . Sport is a language we all speak. Sport is a mirror. Sport is life. Through sport we might know ourselves. (p. 38)

Guterson's description accurately portrays the powerful role and preoccupation that professional sport occupies in many people's everyday lives. Professional sport exemplifies sport at its highest level of performance, and it generates the majority of coverage attributed to sport through print and electronic media. As packaged events, professional team sports (e.g., football, hockey, soccer, baseball, men's and women's basketball) and professional sports featuring the individual (e.g., golf, tennis, auto racing) provide considerable entertainment and pleasure for spectators. As such, demands on the three principals that form the professional sports industry—labor, management, and governance—are complex, diverse, and ever

changing. **Labor** continues to aggressively protect and procure additional resources for its membership. **Management** is trying to win back some leverage and control lost to labor over the last 2 decades. Finally, **governance** attempts to regulate, but not completely control, both labor and management.

Professional sporting events such as the Super Bowl, World Series, Masters, Indianapolis 500, Wimbledon, Kentucky Derby, and the Stanley Cup now occupy the core of the world sporting mentality. Although we have mentioned both team sports and sports featuring the individual thus far, this chapter will concentrate on professional team sports because of their profound economic impact and the number of job opportunities they provide. Most jobs in professional individual sports are found in sports marketing agencies (see chapter 18). The purpose of this chapter is to provide information and insight about four primary aspects of professional team sport—its historical development, its unique aspects, its revenue sources, and a variety of career opportunities associated with pro sport.

## Overview of the Major American Professional Sports

Professional sport can be traced to ancient Greece where, beginning with the Olympic Games in 776 B.C., a class of professional sportsmen known as "athletai" existed. These athletai were well-paid men recruited from mercenary armies and trained exclusively for brutal competition (Freedman, 1987). In exchange for competing and winning, athletai often received remuneration in the form of prizes and money. Although the notion of amateurism might suggest professional sport did not exist before the late 19th century, an element of professionalism has pervaded sport throughout its development.

Although baseball is often considered America's national pastime, it was not the first sport professionals played. Boxers, jockeys, and runners were paid for their prowess during the early and mid-19th century. Baseball, however, was the first *team* sport to employ professionals. In 1869, the Cincinnati Red Stockings became the first professional baseball team. Their appearance was closely followed in 1871 by the National Association of Professional Base Ball Players, the first professional sports league (Rader, 1983). In 1876, William Hulbert formed the National League, the precursor to Major

League Baseball as we know it today. These early teams were owned by middle-class entrepreneurs and stadia were constructed as a matter of civic enterprise (White, 1996). This is a contrast to the corporate ownership and publicly financed stadia and arenas that exist today.

It was not until after the turn of the 20th century that another sport formed a recognized professional league. In 1917, the National Hockey League emerged after the National Hockey Association of Canada Limited suspended its operations (National Hockey League, 1996). This was closely followed in 1921 with the creation of the National Football League. Interestingly, basketball, the most popular professional sport today, was the last of the four major professional sports to form a league. The National Basketball League (NBL), founded in 1937, was the first professional basketball league. In 1949, the National Basketball Association resulted from a merger between the NBL and the Basketball Association of America (BAA) (Staudohar & Mangan, 1991).

Although professional team sport has been in existence for more than 100 years, it has not been until the last 50 years that professional sport opportunities have existed for many minority segments of the American population. In fact, professional sport opportunities were segregated until 1947, when Jackie Robinson broke baseball's color line with the Brooklyn Dodgers. Before 1947, African American players played in separate, segregated professional leagues. The Negro Baseball League was founded in the late 1800s as an outlet for African American baseball players who were not allowed to play in the all-White Major Leagues. Thus, the league afforded players such as Satchel Paige, Josh Gibson, and even Jackie Robinson an opportunity to play. In addition, most owners, club management, reporters, and umpires in the Negro Leagues were also African American. The demise of the Negro Leagues began with the integration of professional baseball in 1947, ultimately ceasing operations in the late 1950s.

Professional sport outlets for women have also arisen only in the past 50 years. In the 1940s, the first women's professional league, the All-American Girls' Baseball League (AAGBL), was formed. Created in 1943 in response to the decreased player quality in Major League Baseball during World War II and the vast popularity of women's amateur softball, the AAGBL played 11 exciting seasons before folding in 1954 due to poor management (Browne, 1992; Johnson, 1994). Since 1954, there have been several other women's profes-

sional leagues, mainly in the sport of basketball. From 1979 to 1991, there were four attempts to capitalize on the growing participation and interest of women in basketball: the Women's Professional Basketball League (1979-1981), the Women's American Basketball Association (October-December, 1984), the National Women's Basketball Association (October 1986 - February 1987), and the Liberty Basketball Association (February-March 1991). Each league was unsuccessful due to financial difficulty ("A History," 1996).

The 1990s brought a resurgence of interest in women's professional sport. In 1996 two women's professional basketball leagues were formed: the American Basketball League (ABL) and the Women's National Basketball Association (WNBA). In June 1997, the Women's Professional Fastpitch (WPF) softball league was set to begin play. In addition, at the time of this writing, a nine-team women's professional soccer league was in the planning stage (King, 1996).

As professional sport progressed throughout the 20th century, its success was largely tied to the media. The media have served both to promote and to finance professional sport. As early as the 1920s, baseball games were broadcast on the radio. By the mid-1930s, radio networks were paying $100,000 to carry the World Series (Rader, 1983). The popularity of professional sport (mainly baseball) on the radio reached its apex in the 1940s and 1950s. During the 1950s, televised sporting events became commonplace.

In 1961, the Sports Broadcasting Act was passed by Congress, and the relationship between the media and professional sports changed dramatically. Until that time, antitrust law had prohibited leagues from negotiating network television contracts on behalf of their members. However, the leagues felt it was important to the financial viability of their member teams to negotiate a collective (on behalf of all league teams) agreement. This rationale suggested that, as opposed to negotiating contracts with individual teams, the major television networks (ABC, CBS, NBC) would pay significantly larger sums of money if leaguewide rights were offered. As a result, the NFL successfully led a lobbying effort to create an exemption in antitrust law. The Sports Broadcasting Act of 1961 gave sports leagues an exemption from antitrust law, granting them the right to collectively negotiate fees with the networks. This legislation paved the way for the leaguewide, highly lucrative television deals that pervade professional sports today (Gorman & Calhoun, 1994).

# Unique Aspects of Professional Sport

There are four aspects of professional sport that distinguish it from other industries: interdependence, structure and governance, labor-management relations, and the role of television.

## Interdependence

The central premise that differentiates professional team sport from any other business organization is the need of the teams to compete and cooperate simultaneously (Mullin, Hardy, & Sutton, 1993). In other words, the teams depend on each other to stage the games that constitute the product. If some teams fold or go out of business, the entire league is threatened. This is in stark contrast to mainstream business in which a competitor's insolvency would result in an increase in market share and profits for other industry members. For example, the demise of the Athletes' Foot would enhance the business of its major competitor, FootLocker. In contrast, the decline and failure of the Milwaukee Brewers would have no positive economic impact on the other teams in the American League.

In his classic work on the NFL, *The League,* David Harris (1986) describes this unique situation as League Think. According to former Commissioner Pete Rozelle:

> One of the key things that a sports league needs is unity of purpose. It needs harmony. . . . When you have unity and harmony and can move basically as one, you can have a successful sports league. The objective of "League Think" is to reverse the process by which the weak clubs get weaker and the strong clubs get stronger. Favorable results are a product of the degree to which each league can stabilize itself through its own competitive balance and league wide income potential. (pp. 13-14)

When teams function together collectively, some teams sacrifice the potential for higher revenue in the interest of league stability. For example, the Dallas Cowboys sell the majority of NFL licensed merchandise and apparel. However, this money is pooled and shared equally with the other 29 NFL teams. Therefore, the presence of the Dallas Cowboys in the collective bargaining agreement increases the revenue generated for all NFL member teams. Due to their existence in large television markets, the New York Giants and Chicago Bears function in much the same way during television negotiations. The key is that all members make sacrifices and concessions for the long-term benefits and growth of the league. Although each major professional sports league differs in the extent to which they share revenues, each league pools its revenues to some extent. For example, NFL teams all share equally in their national television packages (cable and network), whereas baseball teams share only their national contracts and keep all the revenue from their local agreements. These local agreements can vary significantly in the amount of revenue produced. The New York Yankees local broadcast package is significantly larger than small market teams such as Pittsburgh or Milwaukee.

## Structure and Governance

Each professional sport has its own structure and system of governance. This structure usually involves the following components:

1. League commissioner.
2. Board of governors or committee structure composed of the team owners.
3. A central administrative unit that negotiates contracts and agreements on behalf of the league. The central administrative unit also assumes responsibility for scheduling, licensing, and other functions, such as coordinating publicity and advertising on behalf of the teams as a whole.

For example, at this writing, Major League Baseball is composed of 28 teams (30 with the addition of expansion franchises in Tampa Bay and Phoenix) situated in two leagues (National and American—see table 17.2). Each league consists of three divisions (East, Central, and West). Each league has a president, who reports to a commissioner. It is the responsibility of the commissioner to represent the interests of all parties associated with professional baseball. These parties include owners, players, fans, television networks, corporate sponsors, host cities and venues, and the minor leagues. Contrast this organizational structure to mainstream business. There is no authority over the manufacturers of candy that represents the interests of both Hershey's and M & M Mars as they attempt to make money.

Baseball is unique in its extensive minor league system, which provides an elaborate development system preparing players to participate in the major leagues (see figure 17.1 for an example of a minor league baseball organization). Each major league team has at least four affiliate teams in the minor leagues. These teams are usually involved in a contractual relationship with the major league club, which includes paying the minor league player salaries in exchange for having the contractual rights to those players. In recent years minor league baseball clubs have become excellent profit centers. As a result, it has become more desirable for the parent club to own their minor league affiliates. This is in contrast to the traditional form of team ownership characterized by independent owners who have only a contractual relationship with the major league affiliate.

## Labor-Management Relationship

There are six unique circumstances and conditions related to the labor-management relationship in

Table 17.2
**Organization of Major League Baseball**

| Division | Teams |
|---|---|
| National League East | Atlanta, Florida, Montreal, New York, Philadelphia |
| National League Central | Chicago, Cincinnati, Houston, Pittsburgh, St. Louis |
| National League West | Colorado, Los Angeles, San Diego, San Francisco |
| American League East | Baltimore, Boston, Detroit, New York, Toronto |
| American League Central | Cleveland, Chicago, Kansas City, Milwaukee, Minnesota |
| American League West | California, Oakland, Seattle, Texas |

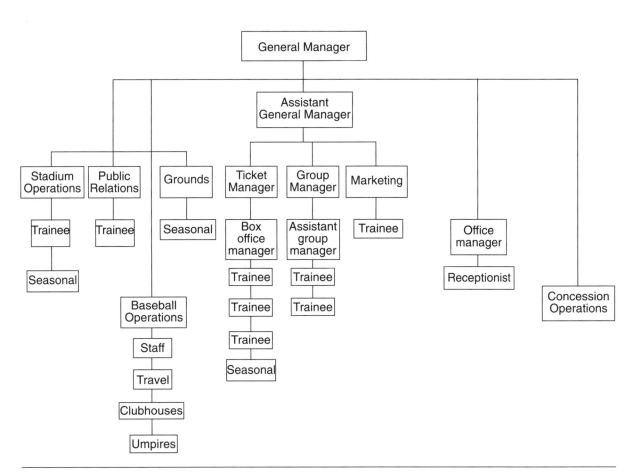

**Figure 17.1**  Richmond Braves organizational chart.

North American professional sport. Some aspects are the opposite of common business practices and philosophies. However, such idiosyncrasies are considered essential by the participating parties to preserve the financial stability of the professional sport product. In the following sections we will examine each element and explain its uniqueness and significance to professional sport.

## Baseball's Antitrust Exemption

Perhaps most unique among the conditions in professional sport is Major League Baseball's exemption from the rules and regulations of the Sherman Antitrust Act. The Sherman Antitrust Act was created to prohibit companies from dominating their respective markets in interstate commercial activity, thus creating a monopoly in which consumers had only one product choice, rather than having several products from which to choose. Normal businesses are prohibited by law from attempting to eliminate all competitors from the marketplace. For example, many recent corporate mergers in the telecommunications industry have been thoroughly questioned and scrutinized by the federal government as attempts to decrease competition.

However, as a result of the United States Supreme Court's ruling in the *Federal Base Ball Club of Baltimore, Inc. v. the National League of Professional Base Ball Clubs* (1922), Major League Baseball was granted an exemption to antitrust law. In its decision, the court deemed that baseball was local in nature and did not involve the **production** of a tangible good and, thus, was not subject to interstate commerce law. In effect, this granted Major League Baseball the right to undertake strategies that would prevent the establishment of competitive leagues. This exemption gives each individual pro team owner significant leverage over the cities in which they operate. Recently, this has led owners to threaten to leave their host cities if new stadia are not built. Although Major League Baseball's exemption from antitrust regulations has been challenged on several occasions, the courts have not overturned the decision.

## Reserve Clause

The reserve clause was a stipulation in the standard Major League Baseball contract that, in effect, made players the property of the team offering the contract for perpetuity. Players were viewed as the exclusive property of the team until such time as the team traded or waived (dismissed) them. Thus, professional athletes had no leverage to improve the terms of their contracts. Players were essentially left with two options: play under the terms offered by the owner or not play at all. Clearly, this practice was in stark contrast to any other business or industry. For example, if a sales representative for Nike were to be offered a better job at Reebok, Nike could not stop their sales representative from leaving. The reserve clause was eliminated in 1975 by arbiter Peter Seitz upon reviewing the cases of baseball players Dave McNally and Andy Messersmith. Subsequent

## A Day in the Life of a Minor League Baseball Intern

Teresa, a 1996 graduate of a sport management graduate program, is completing her internship with the Portland Sea Dogs, a Class AA affiliate of the Florida Marlins. According to Teresa (personal communication, September 3, 1996),

> My primary duties with the Sea Dogs revolve around marketing, sales, and on- and off-field promotions. When I accepted the internship offer I was told that I would also have to help in any area of the organization, including concessions or operations. My first day began at 9:00 A.M. and

didn't end until I returned home shortly before midnight. My first day included cleaning up spills, preparing statistics for the game announcer, welcoming the Colorado Silver Bullets, counting hot dog buns, and conducting the first pitch ceremony. After several weeks, the combination of duties and opportunities appeared to be repetitive, but given human nature, I quickly found out that the simplest, most mundane assignment could become complex and even chaotic. Although the pay was low, I found my experience to be diverse, challenging, and rewarding.

collective bargaining agreements have provided player movement (free agency) after 4 years.

## Collective Bargaining

Workers involved in interstate commerce, which includes all professional team sports (except Major League Baseball because of its antitrust exemption), are covered by the National Labor Relations Act (NLRA). The NLRA provides three basic rights that are the center of labor relations policy in the United States: (a) the right to self-organization, to form, join, or assist labor organizations; (b) the right to bargain collectively through agents of their own choosing; and (c) the right to engage in concerted activities for employee's mutual aid or protection (Staudohar, 1989). In professional team sports, the NLRA provides players the right to join a union, to have a basic player contract (establishing a minimum salary, benefits, and working conditions) negotiated collectively by union representatives, and to strike or conduct other activities that help achieve objectives. The term collective bargaining is used because all active league players are in the bargaining unit and, thus, form a collective unit for negotiating and bargaining with their respective leagues. Teams join together as a league in bargaining with the players' union so that the negotiated contract in each sport applies to all teams uniformly.

Greenberg (1993) suggested common elements of a collective bargaining agreement (the agreed upon settlement by all parties) might include the following:

- specification of contract length,
- compensation (minimum salary), which also includes pensions and other fringe benefits,
- rules for use of labor—in pro sports this would cover the number of games played in a week, starting times related to travel, and, most important, free agency,
- individual job rights—seniority, time served, and possibly morals clauses related to conduct and drug testing,
- rights of union and management in the bargaining relationship—collecting union dues, provisions for union security, and so on,
- methods for enforcing, interpreting, and administering the agreement—details grievance procedures, arbitration, no-strike clauses, and so on,
- rules for agent certification,
- option clauses,
- injury protection and safety issues,
- economic benefits such as severance pay, travel expenses, meal allowances, and so on, and
- discipline—suspensions, fines, dismissal, and so on.

## Free Agency

Free agency is the ability of players, after fulfilling an agreed upon (through a collective bargaining agreement) number of years of service with a team, to sell their services to another team with limited or no compensation to the team losing the players. Thus the terms free agent and free agency have evolved to signify the relative freedom all professional team sport players have to move from one team to another.

However, professional team sport still imposes significant restrictions on its labor. For example, players do not immediately become free agents. Instead, free agency is a negotiated item in the collective bargaining agreement of all professional team sports leagues. The collective bargaining agreement recognizes the investment the team has incurred in developing the player, while also recognizing the fair market value of the player in the open market. Thus, the collective bargaining agreement provides free agency after the player has played an agreed upon (agreed to by labor and management) number of years.

Therefore, rights are granted to the team that initially drafts a player for a specified time. Following that specified period, players are free to seek employment from the highest bidder. Free agents may also be classified according to talent and years of service to a particular team. Based on such classifications, a team signing particular players may or may not be required to provide compensation to the team losing a player. Again, this is different from mainstream business practices, for example, requiring a licensing manager for Champion (sportswear) to work for 3 years before being allowed to take a job with Russell Athletic (another sportswear company).

The implementation of free agency in the mid-1970s had a profound effect on the economics of professional sport. Given the freedom to negotiate with the highest bidder, salaries of professional athletes escalated astronomically. In 1976, at the time of the Messersmith/McNally ruling, the average salary in professional baseball was $46,000. In 1996, the average MLB team payroll was

Alonzo Mourning, drafted by the Charlotte Hornets and now playing for the Miami Heat, has established himself as one of the premier attractions in the NBA.

$31.2 million for a 25-man baseball roster (Atre et al., 1996), for an average annual salary of $1,200,000. Similar salaries exist in the other major professional sport leagues (NHL, NFL, NBA). For example, the average 1995 NFL team payroll (45 to 50 players) was $41.8 million (Atre et al., 1996). The increased power of the players unions and increased salaries of players led to increased labor stoppages in the professional sport leagues. With player salaries continually increasing, owners of professional sport teams are facing revenue-generating challenges. Such concerns have led owners to take an increasingly tough stance during collective bargaining negotiations. As a result of management-labor salary disputes, work stoppages have become a frequent occurrence.

## Salary Caps

Salary caps are agreements in which both labor and management share the revenues generated by the league. Pioneered by the NBA in 1983 and implemented for the 1985-1986 season, the salary cap guaranteed that the NBA players would receive 53% of all gross revenues. Since then, the NFL and Major League Soccer (MLS) have all adopted salary cap structures. These agreements are designed to provide greater **parity** between teams in large cities (markets), such as the New York Knicks and Los Angeles Lakers, and small-market teams, such as the Portland Trailblazers and Milwaukee Bucks. In 1996-1997, NBA players received 59% of all income that the league received. Thus, if league revenues were $1 billion, the players would divide

$590 million. Divided by 29 teams, the salary cap would be $20.34 million per team. The 1996-1997 cap was $24.3 million per team. However, teams are permitted to exceed the cap to retain their players and can pay them any amount—thus, the explanation for Michael Jordan's 1996-1997 salary of $25 million, exceeding the salary cap for the entire Chicago Bulls team (May, 1996).

The reserve clause initially allowed owners to control, and ultimately limit, the earnings of players. However, with the onset of free agency in the '70s, the professional sports industry allowed players to sign with the highest bidder. Therefore, the richest teams could afford the best players. Consequently, the spending on player salaries increased greatly, as already noted. In effect, salary caps also protect owners from each other by setting a ceiling on player payrolls. According to Gary Roberts, editor of *The Sports Lawyer*, the owners in every sport claim that the inherent need for every team to be successful on the field, coupled with the reality that half the teams will always lose, will inevitably fuel an upward escalation of salaries that will make profits impossible for many league members, especially those in smaller markets (Roberts, 1995). As a result, unsuccessful teams in smaller markets would not be able to afford high-salaried players.

Consequently, the competitiveness and profitability of the teams within the league would decline. As a case in point, examine the finalists for the 1996 World Series. Each of the four teams, the Atlanta Braves (4), Baltimore Orioles (2), New York Yankees (1), and St. Louis Cardinals (5), was among the five highest salaried teams in baseball at the time. According to baseball executives, the 1996 season's results provided evidence that the growing disparity in revenue would ruin the competitive balance (Dodd, 1996).

On the other hand, the players believe that the free market should dictate salaries, as it does in almost every industry, and if the owners don't like the results it is their own fault, not that of the players (Roberts, 1995). With these varying opinions, it is easy to understand why the difficulties players and owners had in their negotiations resulted in the baseball and hockey strikes of 1994-1995.

Salary caps are an increasingly popular form of ensuring the financial viability of leagues, particularly in the case of new professional leagues such as the ABL, WNBA, and Major League Soccer (MLS). Implementing modest salary caps in these leagues allows new leagues to minimize their financial losses in their first few years of operations. For example, the ABL used a salary cap to keep its average salary at $70,000 (Horovitz, 1996).

## Player Draft

In accordance with the principles of League Think, the player draft is designed to be an equitable system for distributing new talent among all league members. The draft provides each professional sport league with a mechanism for the teams with poor records to have an advantage over teams with winning records in acquiring the most talented new players. Through the draft, teams voluntarily agree to restrict competition for new talent. As a result, the destination and player salary of a new player is determined solely by the team that drafts the player. Phenomena such as the player draft do not exist in other areas of the labor market. Just imagine a scenario in which top law school graduates were restricted as to whom they could work for and where they could work by an annual draft held by law firms throughout the country!

Recent collective bargaining agreements in basketball and football have sought to limit the number of rounds of the draft. This limiting would result in fewer players being drafted and more players being free agents to sign with anyone offering them a contract. The players union would prefer that this would be the case for all players, but recognizes the need for some type of equal and formal player distribution to maintain competitiveness among the members of the league.

# Role of Television

No single factor has influenced the popularity, escalation in player salaries, free agency, and the growth and increase of corporate involvement in professional sports more than television. Television is also responsible for helping professional sport become more than just competition and athleticism—it has helped professional sport become entertainment. Entering its 27th season in 1996, ABC's *Monday Night Football* was the pioneering effort to package pro sports as entertainment. This prime time extravaganza sought to reach more than just traditional football fans by adding analysis, commentary, special guests, additional camera angles, video replays, graphics, and highlights to enhance the event and broaden its appeal to women and other nontraditional viewing groups (Roberts & Olson, 1995). Based on the success of *Monday Night Football*, the ultimate television sports spectacle, the Super Bowl, was created. Born from the rivalry and merger of the National Football League and the American Football League, the Super Bowl has become one of the most successful televised events of all time, viewed by millions around the world.

As a result of the success in packaging sport for entertainment, hallmark events such as the Super Bowl, along with baseball's World Series, All-Star Games, and the NBA Finals are now shown during prime time (8-10 p.m.). Such hallmark events also can provide an identity as well as a source of tourism revenue for a city or region. Hallmark events impact the perception of a town or region through media coverage of the event, most notably television coverage. Further, hallmark events contribute economically through expenditures relating to lodging, local transportation, and tourism, such as entertainment and shopping (see chapter 16).

On the other side of the coin, professional sports (and in this case football) need television for two reasons. First, as already discussed, the leagues and member teams receive significant revenue outlays from network and cable television agreements. Second, television enhances the enjoyment associated with watching professional sporting events. Consider the following factors in viewing a football game:

- Given the proximity to the action in a large stadium, the action in a football game can be difficult to follow.
- Only a certain number of fans can attend the game in person.
- Football with its numerous formations and free substitution can be confusing. In supporting football, television offers commentary and explanation, many replays, isolations, and other variations of camera angles, all of which allow the viewer to more effec-

## Learning Activity

Justice Oliver Wendell Holmes is responsible for the opinion of the court that granted an antitrust exemption to baseball *(Federal Base Ball Club of Baltimore, Inc. v. National League of Professional Base Ball Clubs, 259 U.S. 200 (1922))*. Find the case in your local law library, read the opinion, and construct an argument for repealing this exemption.

## Learning Activity

In your opinion, is free agency detrimental to baseball clubs operating in smaller markets (Pittsburgh, Milwaukee, Montreal, etc.)? Should free agency be modified to protect the fans living in smaller market cities, and are modifications of any type in violation of the spirit of free trade?

tively understand and follow the game. Lastly, television provides an expansive (and increasingly international) audience, regardless of the weather.

# Revenue Sources for Professional Sports Teams

Pro sport has three primary constituencies: management, labor, and the fans. Each has a unique perspective regarding revenue sources. For example, according to professional team sport owners (management), one out of every five professional teams loses money (Atre et al., 1996). How can this be possible when major professional sports arenas are full and network television fees have been increasing exponentially during the past 10 years? In response, owners will cite the rapid escalation of salaries paid to professional athletes. For example, from 1985 to 1993, the average salary of a Major League Baseball player increased from $330,000 to $1,100,000 (Coakely, 1994).

On the other hand, labor (the players) will suggest that, although salaries have increased, teams have remained profitable and franchise values have increased dramatically (Zimbalist, 1992). In addition, players will cite the fact that owners regularly underestimate their profits in the interest of keeping players' salaries low. From the fans' perspective, both sides are often seen as greedy. Fans frequently suggest that escalating players' salaries have led owners to increase the price of tickets, concessions, and parking. Therefore, from the fans' perspective, they are the only people who are negatively impacted in the labor-management dispute.

Regardless of the point of view, professional teams are under constant pressure to generate revenue. Revenue sources can be separated into five distinct classifications: media contracts, gate receipts, licensing and merchandising sales, sponsorship sales, and public financing of stadia.

## Media Contracts

Media revenues generated through sales of packaged rights to networks and cable operators have increased dramatically during the past 35 years. Currently, with the exception of the National Hockey League (NHL), media revenues comprise one of the most important revenue sources (Howard & Crompton, 1995). Also with the exception of the NHL, national television revenues are distributed equally among member clubs. The National Basketball Association's (NBA) deal with NBC and TNT for $1.15 billion for 4 years (1995-1999) constituted more than 40% of each team's income. Similarly, Major League Baseball's deal with Fox, NBC, ESPN, and Liberty for $1.6 billion during the next 5 years (1996-2000) also constituted more than 40% of each team's income. The National Football League's (NFL) national television package with Fox, NBC, ABC, ESPN, and TNT for $4.4 billion over 4 years (1995-1998) constituted 65% of each team's revenues. Only in the NHL, whose national television deals with Fox and ESPN accounted for $250 million during 7 years (1993-1999), are media revenues not as important ("TV Sports," 1996).

There are several other important distinctions that we must make with respect to media revenues. The NBA, NHL, and MLB allow their member teams to negotiate **local television contracts**. In the case of MLB, this leads to great disparities in the incomes of its member teams (Howard & Crompton, 1995). The NFL, under the notion of League Think, does not allow local television deals, except preseason games. Lastly, the national television revenues for the NHL are not distributed equally—Canadian teams receive a smaller portion due to their lack of influence on American television markets.

In the mid-1990s, media revenues began to plateau after a period of rapid escalation. This was particularly true in baseball where the stability of network television agreements had been in question for several years. After CBS lost millions of dollars with its Major League Baseball contract in the early 1990s, ABC, NBC, and Major League Baseball combined to create the Baseball Network. This joint venture shifted the burden of selling commercial advertising time from the network to Major League Baseball, producing mixed results. Although recently Fox, NBC, and ESPN have settled on a more traditional agreement, revenues still do not match those paid by CBS in the late 1980s. Although the media revenues for the NFL, NBA, and NHL continue to increase, new contracts no longer contain astronomical increases from previous contracts.

## Gate Receipts

As late as 1950, gate receipts and concessions accounted for more than 92% of the typical pro team's revenue (Gorman & Calhoun, 1994). However, with the increasing importance of media revenues, pro teams have become less reliant on gate receipts. Among the four major professional sport leagues, gate receipts account for only 39% of the typical team's revenue (Howard & Crompton, 1995). However, gate receipts remain the major source of revenue for minor league professional sports. In addition, they are the most prevalent source of revenue for start-up professional leagues such as the ABL (Horovitz, 1996). Gate receipts are typically controlled by the home team. In the NBA and NHL, the home team retains all gate receipts. In the NFL, the home team keeps 60% of the gate and the visiting team receives 40%. For American League baseball teams the home teams keep 80%, and the visiting team receives 20%. Home teams in the National League keep 91% of the gate receipts and give the other 9% to the visiting team (Gorman & Calhoun, 1994).

In the future, teams can increase gate receipts by increasing attendance or increasing ticket prices. Increasing attendance may be difficult, however, as each league, except Major League Baseball, currently sells at least 90% of its available tickets (Howard & Crompton, 1995). In addition, given the rapid escalation in ticket prices since the early 1980s, it may not be possible to increase the price of tickets. In 1977, the average ticket for each major professional sports league was less than $10. In 1996, the average ticket price for the NFL, NBA, and NHL all hovered around $25 (Howard & Crompton, 1995). The effect has been to price the common person away from professional sport. Including other costs of attending a sporting event (e.g., concessions, parking, and souvenirs), a family of four often must spend more than $100 to attend a baseball game ("Fan Cost Index," 1994).

Luxury boxes and club seats are innovations created by professional sports teams to increase revenues. Luxury boxes, or special enclosed viewing areas with catered food and beverage service, are becoming a staple in pro sport. The typical new stadium has many luxury boxes leasing for a minimum of $100,000 per year. In addition, luxury box revenues are not shared with the visiting team

(Gorman & Calhoun, 1994). Club seats are individual seats (as opposed to boxes) that offer superior service and amenities for a higher price. First used to help finance the construction of Miami's Joe Robbie Stadium in 1987, such seats are typically in a good location and are characterized by food and beverage service and easily accessible amenities.

## Licensing and Merchandising Revenues

Licensing revenues are generated when leagues and teams grant merchandise and apparel manufacturers the right to use their names and logos. In return for that right, the leagues and teams receive a royalty (i.e., a percentage of the selling price) for each item sold by the manufacturers. These agreements have been an increasingly lucrative source of revenue for pro teams. Between 1980 and 1996, sales of NFL merchandise increased 400%. Sales of MLB merchandise increased from $200 million in 1988 to $2 billion in 1993 (Howard & Crompton, 1995). Licensing programs, administered by the league offices, distribute the revenue equally among teams.

Domestic licensing revenues have begun to plateau as the market for such merchandise has become saturated. In response to this decline, pro sports leagues are looking to overseas markets for increased merchandise sales. Typically employed as one of the first strategies used in entering foreign markets, retail promotions and marketing pro sports apparel has successfully generated additional revenues. MLB international revenues increased from $2 million in 1991 to $200 million in 1995. NBA international revenues increased from $56 million in 1991 to $350 million in 1995 ("Annual Industry Report," 1995).

## Sponsorship

Sponsorship is payment (in the form of cash and product) by corporations to pro sport teams and leagues in exchange for advertising rights, such as signage and promotions related to the team or league. It is estimated that corporate investment in professional sport is five times that of individual investment. In 1993, 133 corporations spent an average of $830,000 on sponsorship deals with major professional sports teams (Howard & Crompton, 1995). One major benefit of a sponsorship deal is visible corporate signage. The demand for signage locations visible to the tele-

vision viewer has led sport marketers to continually seek new and innovative display techniques. **Rotating signage**, stationary signage around the playing area, and electronically transmitted signage during television broadcasts are devices used to increase revenues. In the mid-1990s, a dominant trend was corporate sponsorship of arenas and corporate purchase of the rights to name arenas. For example, in 1996, Pacific Telesis agreed to pay $50 million over 24 years for the naming rights of the new San Francisco baseball park (Pac Bell Ball Park). Atre et al. (1996) have predicted that every professional sporting venue will be named for a corporate sponsor by the year 2000.

## Public Financing of Stadia

While on the topic of revenue sources integral to financing professional sports, it is important to address the increasing involvement of public sector funds. New stadia often provide professional team owners with additional sources of revenue through luxury boxes and club seats. For this reason, many professional sport organizations are attempting to build new stadia. However, many team owners do not posses the wherewithal to finance a stadium and, thus, must turn to cities, counties, and states. In general, there are seven sources of public funding available to professional sports teams building new facilities. Governments can

- offer revenue bonds at a lower interest rate than the private entity could,
- levy or increase taxes and use the additional revenue to help finance a new stadium,
- give the pro sports team an advantageous lease agreement,
- waive property taxes on the land occupied by the stadium,
- provide the team with free land on which to build,
- invest in infrastructure to improve the ease with which spectators arrive at games, and
- provide in-kind services, such as police support, at no cost to the team.

It has become commonplace for an owner to ask a municipality for assistance in funding part or all of such a venture. Public involvement in financing professional sports stadia and arenas first became popular in the 1950s and 1960s (Quirk & Fort,

1992). At least 80% of all professional sports teams now play in publicly funded stadia, and the financial role of city, county, and state governments in the financial viability of a pro sports team continues to increase. For example, in 1996, Hamilton County, Ohio, began generating $540 million for constructing new baseball and football stadia to keep the baseball Reds and football Bengals in Cincinnati (Atre et al., 1996).

Sports teams have been increasingly successful at using their status within a monopoly structure to coerce municipalities into funding new stadia. Sometimes pro team owners threaten to move their franchise to a more lucrative city if the city does not build a new stadium. This strategy is often effective because professional sport leagues limit the number of teams that exist. As a result, demand for professional sports teams is high. Because it appears that cities will continue to aggressively seek professional sports teams, public sector financing will continue to be an important source of revenue.

Community support is central to the continued use of public finances for stadium development. In most cases, the use of public funds for development on behalf of a private sports team requires approval from the community. Such partnerships between cities and teams are funded by cities based on the notion that the team will provide significant benefits to the city. Such benefits often take the form of enhanced economic activity, improved civic image, and the creation of a civic identity (Johnson, 1993). Citizens might believe that losing their pro team to another city will result in significant economic and psychological damage. For example, when the NFL Cleveland Browns moved to Baltimore in 1996, there was an intense backlash from the Cleveland community due to the loss of an integral part of Cleveland's identity. However, as the cost of financing stadia exceeds $100 million per facility, cities have been increasingly suspicious of whether the benefits of a pro team outweigh the costs of retaining one (Johnson, 1993).

## Learning Activity

Which types of revenue are most likely to grow for professional sport franchises in the next 10 years? Why? Which types of revenue are most likely to remain flat? Why?

## Learning Activity

Identify the minor league baseball or hockey franchise nearest to your surrounding area. Attend at least one of their games. Take notes on everything you witness, including stadium operations, ticket sales, concessions sales, stadium design, and the visibility of team personnel. Based on past experiences with major league sports (MLB, NFL, NBA, and NHL), how are the facets of minor league operations different from major league operations? How are they the same?

# Career Opportunities in Professional Sport

Like any business, professional sports organizations constantly attempt to upgrade their efficiency through their personnel. In searching for new employees, management often looks to sport management and administration programs, searches other professional sport organizations, or considers individuals working in the corporate sector who may have skills essential to the sport industry.

The organizational hierarchies of professional sport are far from being uniform. Employment opportunities vary greatly in terms of titles and responsibilities, not only from sport to sport, but also from team to team within the same sport. Some professional sport organizations have a single owner, and others may have several owners. It is also becoming more commonplace that single owners, such as Ted Turner, own teams (Atlanta Braves and Atlanta Hawks) in different sport leagues. Such owners might use some of the same personnel in both organizations. This is the method of operation for the NBA Orlando Magic and the minor league hockey team that it owns, the Orlando Solar Bears. It is also the premise for the Women's NBA, which operates during the summer when the NBA arenas are more available, and the responsibilities of NBA staff are primarily associated with sales. Accordingly, the existing NBA staff will market the WNBA games in each respective city. Lastly, there has been a trend toward fledgling leagues owning the teams within the league. Such is the case with Major League Soccer and the ABL. For an overview of the organizational structure of a league-owned team, see figure 17.2, which presents an organizational chart of the New England Blizzard of the ABL.

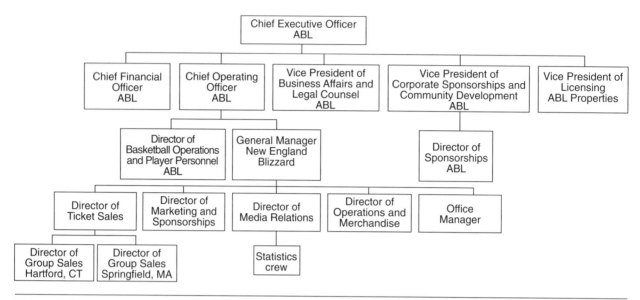

**Figure 17.2** New England Blizzard and American Basketball League organizational chart.

# Common Categories of Work Responsibility

There are a variety of positions within any professional sport organization. The types and existence of positions vary from team to team and sport to sport. For example, Major League Baseball teams employ more people in player personnel than the National Basketball Association or the National Football League because of their extensive minor league systems. In addition, minor league organizations (Minor League Baseball, International Hockey League, East Coast Hockey League) will typically employ fewer people than major league organizations (NFL, NBA, MLB, NHL). Therefore, the following section highlights a variety of positions that may be available within any professional sport organization.

## Administrative or Executive

This grouping normally includes the president, chief executive or operating officer (CEO or COO), chief financial officer (CFO), general counsel, general manager, and executive board members. The main responsibility of this category is to oversee the entire operation of the professional sports team. In many cases, the top executives play the central role in visible actions the team takes. Such actions could include player negotiations, television or radio contract solicitation and negotiation, and lobbying for funds for constructing a new stadium.

## Marketing

This unit is charged with designing the marketing campaign and implementing promotional, advertising, and sales campaigns to achieve the overall marketing objectives (usually stated in terms of revenues generated). Personnel in this capacity may decide to **out-source** (contracting with an outside agency) some functions, such as telemarketing and advertising.

## Public Relations

This department would be involved in assisting and working with the media by providing information necessary for game coverage and publicity. It would also be responsible for all publications, such as media guides, yearbooks, and game programs.

## Community Relations

This department may be part of the public relations or marketing department. The community relations staff is responsible for creating and administering grass roots functions, such as clinics and other charitable events that the team sponsors. They are also responsible for implementing leaguewide programs, such as the NBA's Stay in School Program.

## Player Personnel

This department is involved in identifying, evaluating, and developing potential and current players.

In baseball, this department would also be involved with observing players assigned to the minor leagues. Scouting and trades would be handled by this department.

## Medical, Training, and Team Support

These individuals assume responsibility for the physical (and sometimes mental) preparation and readiness of the players. Responsibilities include medical care, treatment of injuries, rehabilitation, dental care, nutrition, strength training and conditioning, career counseling, and aftercare programs.

## Coaching Staff

This group concentrates on all activities occurring between the lines. In other words, they are primarily concerned with coaching, managing, and training the players on their roster.

## Ticketing

This department may or may not include the sales staff. Ticketing personnel are responsible for managing the ticket inventory. They are responsible for ticket distribution, printing, accounting, game-day box office sales, complimentary tickets, and the financial settlement for the visiting team.

## Equipment and Clubhouse Staff

These personnel maintain, clean, order, repair, distribute, inventory, ship, and pack all uniforms and equipment. They also negotiate with manufacturers and sales personnel for equipment and uniforms. It is their responsibility to determine the suitability of the product and to make appropriate recommendations regarding purchasing. In addition, these personnel have security responsibility for the locker room both at home and on the road.

## Stadium and Facility Staff

This group is responsible for the maintenance, upkeep, and repair of the playing surface. They are also responsible for preparing the team's offices, locker rooms, training facilities, practice facilities, and playing field. They must be familiar with artificial surfaces as well as natural grass playing surfaces. It is their responsibility to ensure that the playing surface is safe and to work in inclement conditions to make the field playable. In terms of playing surfaces and related areas, these individuals are the liaisons between the venue management team and the professional franchise.

## Video Support Staff

Responsibilities of video support staff include producing and editing video, purchasing and

## The Minors Are Not Always Minor

Steve began his career as an intern with the NHL's Pittsburgh Penguins in the summer preceding his senior year of a baccalaureate program in sport management. Steve's internship provided several unique opportunities to distinguish himself, particularly in sales. At the conclusion of the internship, he was offered a full-time position. Steve negotiated his agreement to permit him to work and complete his senior year. Steve became director of telemarketing and was also a sales representative. He worked in this position for 9 years, during which time the Penguins were Stanley Cup Champions twice.

While with the Penguins, Steve was involved in telemarketing projects with other Penguin activities such as Arena Football and Major Indoor Lacrosse. In 1994, Steve perceived that he was at a career crossroads. He needed new responsibilities and experiences to advance in his career, but his options were minimal because of low turnover in the organization. At this time, he was offered an opportunity to become Vice President of Ticket Sales with the Cleveland Lumberjacks of the International Hockey League (IHL). Although the IHL is a minor league, the opportunity to become a vice president and design, implement, and supervise an entire department was an attractive opportunity. Even though it meant leaving his hometown and a prestigious NHL franchise, Steve elected to make the move, not only because of the initial opportunity, but also because of what this experience might do for his professional opportunities in the future.

maintaining video hardware and software products, supervising and coordinating satellite feeds, and coordinating all broadcasting originating at the home facility. The video support staff also is responsible for filming games and maintaining the team's library of game films and player evaluation videos.

### Broadcast Team

The broadcast team includes personalities responsible for play by play and color commentary on both radio and television broadcasts. These individuals may be employed by the team or the flagship radio station.

### Computer Support Staff

The computer support staff is responsible for computer hardware and software used in all operations of the franchise. This department handles all purchasing, network, database, report generation, and so on.

### Hospitality Coordinators

Hospitality coordinators are responsible for the game-related needs of corporate clients, club seat holders, and luxury box owners.

## Securing Employment and Working in Professional Sport

Without question, an internship is essential in securing a position in professional sport. Students should begin to construct an informational file on the teams and organizations with whom they would like to intern and gain employment. This file should contain the names, phone numbers, and addresses of department heads within the organization. Supplement the file with information about the business activities of the franchise. Such information might include newspaper and journal articles, sales brochures, advertising examples, promotional schedules, and so on. It is essential to understand that the business area of the team is most likely where you will be working. Accordingly, you should be prepared to make a difference in that aspect of the organization. Although the box score is often interesting, knowing who hit .300 or the name of the leading rusher won't necessarily help your cause in gaining employment. In addition to knowing the business aspect of sport, prospective employees must understand the social role of sport and the place it occupies as a powerful cultural institution. It is only by understanding both sport business and sport's impact on a culture that one truly comprehends the role and scope of sport.

In addition to developing and maintaining the file, supplement your experience while still in school. Obtaining a worthwhile internship with a solid organization is sometimes as difficult as finding employment. Part-time employment or volunteer experience in sales, game management, or customer service and hospitality are valuable assets on your résumé. You can obtain these experiences while still in school or during the summer. Whenever possible, meet and interview people in your chosen field. To effectively interview for internships and permanent positions, you should comprehend the industry, its leaders, and its issues. You can develop this knowledge through the secondary sources in your file, personal interviews, and attending conferences and other presentations featuring industry leaders.

### Internship

Ideally, the internship should be a mutually beneficial relationship between the student and the host organization. The student should be able to develop a range of employment experience that translates into attractive job skills to a prospective employer. In exchange, the host organization should receive competent and reliable assistance in the performance of assigned tasks. Students should be aware that many pro sport organizations want interns to remain throughout the entire season, not just for a semester. This arrangement is beneficial for both parties. Organizations benefit because they do not have to recruit and train new people in the middle of the year. Interns benefit because they are able to be part of the entire cycle of franchise operations.

## A Word of Advice

Although an internship is critical for employment in pro sport, successful completion of that intern-

---

### Learning Activity

Identify the professional sport franchises, teams, or organizations in your area. Conduct an informational interview with an individual holding a position that would be of interest to you. What are the most attractive aspects of this job? What are the least attractive aspects?

## Learning Activity

Contact three professional sport organizations and solicit information on their internship programs. What are the similarities in these internship opportunities? What are the differences? Determine which internship opportunity would be best for you and explain why.

ship does not guarantee the intern a job with that franchise. Other factors impact the ability of a professional sport franchise to offer part-time, contractual, or full-time employment to a deserving intern. These factors include employee turnover, the economic climate, organizational goals and objectives, and the hiring philosophy and financial stability of team ownership. Even so, interns working in professional sport should strive to be an integral part of the organization and should perform every assigned task to the best of their ability. In addition, it is essential that the intern demonstrates initiative. According to Lisa, a graduate of a master's level sport management program and sponsor services coordinator of the NBA's Cleveland CAVS,

We look for our interns to demonstrate initiative—look and see what needs to be done without being told what to do. After a certain time on the job, we can tell if an intern has the initiative and other qualities we look for in an employee. If interns demonstrate these skills, we consider them for any vacancies that arise. (personal communication, August 18, 1996)

## Summary

Professional sport is a large part of the entertainment, social, political, economic, legal, and cultural fabric of North America. The continued growth of the media and related technology, particularly television, ensures that professional sport is prevalent and highly accessible throughout North America regardless of the demographic characteristics of its audience. Because of this accessibility and prevalence, the importance of the roles that labor, management, and government play often seem out of balance when compared with their role in other forms of business. For the most part, reserve clauses, free agency, League

## From Intern to Employee

Mike, a 1991 graduate with a sport management baccalaureate degree, accepted an internship with the Atlanta Hawks. Mike went to the Hawks with experience in the areas of sales, marketing, and event management he had gained through working at the ShopRite LPGA Classic. Mike's internship responsibilities with the Hawks included formulating sponsorship proposals, game operations, and supervising marketing programs, including NBA All-Star balloting and the Hawks' Dance Team. According to Mike (personal communication, July 10, 1996),

> During my internship I did everything I could to complete my duties professionally, quickly, and to the best of my abilities. When I completed my duties, I looked for other things to do and even asked people in other departments if there was anything that needed to be done. It wasn't long before I had developed a reputation

of being reliable and able to handle and complete several tasks simultaneously and efficiently.

At the conclusion of the season, Mike was promoted to marketing assistant, where his duties expanded to include managing the contractual relationships with sponsors and advertising accounts. After 2 years in that position, Mike was promoted to manager of customer relations, then was promoted to assistant director of sales.

In this case, Mike elected to remain with the Hawks and was able to rise within the organization. This is not always the case. In fact, in most professional sport careers, it is often necessary for individuals to move from one franchise to another, or even from one sport to another to receive promotions or increased responsibility, which are integral to professional growth and job satisfaction.

Think, and antitrust exemptions exist only in the context of professional sport. These concepts are not essential in conducting the traditional activities of mainstream business operations, but appear to be essential to the survival of business as it relates to professional sport. Further, it is these concepts that will be crucial for new professional sports leagues, such as the ABL and WNBA, to understand if they are to be successful. It is by understanding the unique limitations and opportunities of professional sport that one can truly appreciate the career challenges and possibilities in the field.

## Learning Activity

There have been two football leagues, the World Football League (WFL) and the United States Football League (USFL), that have attempted to compete with the NFL in the past 20 years. Why have these leagues failed? In your opinion, could a new professional football league succeed now? Why or why not?

## For More Information

Following are several publications concerning professional sport and its role within the field of sport management.

- *The Sports Sponsor Fact Book* published by Team Marketing Report, Alan Friedman, Editor, Chicago, IL

- *Team Marketing Report* published by Team Marketing Report, Alan Friedman, Editor, Chicago, IL

- *The Sports Business Daily* published by Interzine Productions, Inc., South Norwalk, CT

- *The Sports Market Place* published by R.A. Lipsey, Princeton, NJ

# Job Opportunities

## Assistant Golf Pro

Local country club seeking PGA certified teaching professional to assist club head pro in instructional program, hosting special events and tournaments. Must be willing to work seasonal hours. Bachelor's degree and PGA certification required. Salary commensurate with experience.

## Graphics Specialist

The Pro Logo, Inc. marketing department is seeking a full-time graphics specialist. Primary responsibilities include designing, writing, and creating sports marketing and advertising proposals, executing a corporate newsletter, and providing presentation pieces in support of the marketing department. The successful candidate will be able to fully develop a presentation from conception to completion. Applicants must be proficient with QuarkXpress, Adobe Illustrator, Photoshop, and MSWord, as well as possessing strong writing skills. A 4-year college degree is required and a graphics and or marketing background is preferred.

## Sales Supervisor

The Alabama Avengers are seeking an individual to oversee its sales of suites, group tickets, season tickets, and group hospitality packages. Position reports to the VP of sales and supervises the sales staff and volunteer sales staff. Responsibilities include hiring and training sales staff, recruiting and training volunteer staff, overseeing day-to-day operations of sales department, developing and maintaining database, and coordinating all game-day operations from sales and volunteer perspective. Qualifications include bachelors degree plus 2 years experience in sales management.

## Telemarketing Representative

The SportSales company is seeking several individuals to fill telemarketing positions. The main responsibility of the position is to sell season ticket packages. Leads are provided. Some college experience is necessary and a degree is helpful. Knowledge of pro basketball preferred. Hourly wage plus commission.

## Public Relations

We are seeking an excellent writer to coordinate and create all media releases for a professional football franchise. Also responsible for all game stats, disseminating results to the media, assisting in developing a media plan, working with team services department to coordinate player appearances, and so on. Assist on team publications (media guide, yearbook), serve as media coordinator during training camp, and assist PR director in other duties as needed. College degree plus at least 3 years experience in sports information or public relations at the collegiate or professional level.

## Director of Promotions

The Chattanooga Chargers Baseball Club seeks an individual to become Director of Promotions. The Director of Promotions is responsible for all game promotions, including special events and giveaways. The director of promotions is also responsible for scheduling and coordinating all mascot appearances. This position works with the Director of Marketing to secure sponsors for all promotional events and activities and works with the Director of Sponsor Services to ensure sponsor satisfaction. The Director of Promotions supervises one full-time staff member and recruits and trains interns as needed. College degree and 2 years experience in promotions required. Fluency in Spanish a plus.

## Merchandise Manager

The Massachusetts Diamondbacks stadium store is seeking an experienced merchandise manager to coordinate and manage all retail and catalog merchandise sales. The person selected for this position will be experienced not only in retail sales, but also in buying, inventory control, accounting, and personnel management. This individual will oversee merchandising operations at the stadium, two outside retail outlets, and catalog sales. Seeking an individual with 5 or more years experience, a college degree, who is highly motivated and will motivate others. Salary plus commission and incentives.

# Chapter 18 Sport Management and Marketing Agencies

**William A. Sutton and Mark A. McDonald**
University of Massachusetts at Amherst

## Learning Objectives

After studying this chapter, you will be able to

1. comprehend the role, scope, and impact of sport management and marketing agencies as they relate to the business of sport;

2. differentiate between the types of sport management and marketing agencies to determine which agencies are most appropriate for particular tasks and assignments;

3. understand the evolution and growth of sport management and marketing agencies;

4. define the functions performed by sport management and marketing agencies; and

5. appraise the career opportunities associated with sport management and marketing agencies.

A sport management and marketing agency is a business that acts on behalf of a sport property. This sport property can be a person, a corporation, an event, a team, or even a place. The actions undertaken on behalf of the property may include one or more of the following: representation, negotiation, sales, **licensing**, marketing, or management. Given the scope of activities that encompass the arts, festivals, sport events, resorts, and music, a more appropriate term to describe these agencies is sport and lifestyle management and marketing agencies.

The first sport management and marketing agencies were formed primarily to represent athletes in contract negotiations and to seek endorsements and other revenue streams for these athletes. The International Management Group (IMG), established in 1960 by Mark H. McCormack in Cleveland, Ohio, was the first agency dedicated to representing professional athletes. In their own words, "IMG literally 'invented' sports management and marketing more than three decades ago" (International Management Group, 1995). As time has passed and the marketplace and opportunities have changed, sport marketing agencies have become diverse in their scope and focus. Today, sport marketing agencies are involved not only in contract negotiations but also in myriad other functions.

The purpose of this chapter is to provide an overview of sport management and marketing agencies and to introduce career opportunities within this rapidly growing segment of the sport enterprise. We will shed light on these unique and multifaceted companies through a typology that classifies the many agencies into four categories: full service, general, specialty, and **in-house** agencies. Examples of each type of agency will help delineate the similarities and differences. Finally, this chapter will give basic information about career opportunities and challenges.

## Creating a Sport Management and Marketing Agency Plan

It's a Tuesday morning at First National Bank in First City, USA. At a staff meeting, Ms. Smith, the regional president, states that First National is continuing to lose customers to Second City Federal—a bank that seems to have appeal for younger and more upscale clients. Ms. Smith feels that First National's attempts to communicate with its market through traditional outlets, such as advertising and direct mail, have become too routine and, consequently, the message is not being received. "It is for that reason," said Ms. Smith, "that I have asked Sport Properties Ltd., an international sport marketing agency, to assist us in developing a new communication strategy through sports and special events to help us retain our current customer base and, we hope, attract new customers."

The room begins to buzz and there are many questions. What is a sport marketing agency? What type of sport or special event is best associated with a bank? What services should we promote through the event? What exactly will the agency do?

At the same time, in the regional offices of Sport Properties Ltd., Mr. Brown, regional vice president, is meeting with his staff to discuss their upcoming presentation to First National Bank. "We have an excellent opportunity to use some of our existing properties, such as skiing, kayaking, and in-line skating, to create **grassroots** events that appeal to younger, more upscale individuals in each of First National Bank's primary markets." At that point, Ms. Perez, senior project director, asks about developing a tie-in with participants from each grassroots **venue** competing in a championship or finals at the headquarters of First National in River City. "Excellent concept, Ms. Perez! Perhaps we should also consider finding other sponsors who might want to **co-op** this opportunity with First National. Let's begin preparing our agenda."

## Functions of Sport Management and Marketing Agencies

The scope of functions performed by sport management and marketing agencies is vast. As you read the following list, you can appreciate the degrees of specialization necessary to discharge each duty. Although an agency might perform several or perhaps only one function, some agencies, such as IMG and ProServ, perform *all* of them.

- Client management and representation
- Client marketing and product endorsement
- Event creation and development
- Event management and marketing
- Property representation and licensing
- Television development and production
- Sponsorship solicitation and consulting
- Hospitality services
- Grassroots and participatory programs
- Research and evaluation
- Financial planning and management

### Client Management and Representation

Client management and representation involves representing a client in contract negotiations and making marketing decisions to manage the client's income potential and earnings. The contract negotiations could be between player and team, licensee and licensor, or product and endorser. The management function involves the agency in a strategic planning process for their client that may involve any of the following: financial planning, investment and management, marketing, personal appearances, and other forms of revenue production and management. For example, Michael Jordan's agent, David Falk of Falk Athlete Management Enterprises (FAME), not only negotiates Jordan's contract with the NBA's Chicago Bulls, but also manages and advises Jordan on financial and marketing opportunities (Lombardo, 1994).

Advice may be straightforward, such as which company to endorse, or could be controversial, such as Jordan and Falk's attempts in 1995 to decertify the NBA Players Association.

## Client Marketing and Product Endorsement

Similar to the management function, client marketing involves the agency in the promotion and total marketing of the client. For a professional athlete, this may involve securing endorsement opportunities, product endorsements, personal appearances, books, movies and television films and roles, interview and feature stories, video games, and so on. In the Michael Jordan scenario, it would describe FAME's role in securing Jordan's endorsements for McDonald's and Hanes.

## Event Creation and Development

The growth of sports television in the 1970s, proliferation of sport networks in the 1990s, and the development of new satellite technology such as Direct TV have led to fiscally rewarding opportunities related to creating new sports and events (Crespo, 1995). Sports such as Arena Football and Major Indoor Lacrosse, new events such as the Goodwill Games and the Extreme Games, increased numbers of college football bowl games, and a wider array of collegiate basketball doubleheaders have emerged to capitalize on this opportunity. Some events have been created by television entities such as ESPN and Turner Broadcasting to fill their **inventory**. Others, such as the Quarterback Challenge, which was developed by Buffalo Bill's quarterback, Jim Kelly, through his agency, Jim Kelly Enterprises, were created as primary revenue sources for their originators ("A New Era," 1995). Agencies such as DelWilber and Associates have created the Heartland Classic in St. Louis for the LPGA, which provides additional sponsorship, broadcasting, and licensing opportunities.

## Event Management and Marketing

Given the high cost of personnel (i.e., salaries and benefits), the need for specific expertise, the seasonality of some events, and the geographic scope of the activities, it has become common to hire outside agencies to manage and market events. Event management and marketing agencies are involved in activities such as golf and tennis tournaments, festivals, bowl games, and other sport

and lifestyle special events. This event management may involve any of the following areas: tournament operations, hospitality and entertainment, sponsorship and ticket sales, licensing and merchandising, television production, public relations, and promotion. DelWilber and Associates, for example, which created the Heartland Classic for the LPGA, is also involved in ticket sales for the event, sponsorship sales, public relations, and hospitality activities. As the event manager, DelWilber and Associates can contract with other agencies to provide services outside of DWA's expertise. Hyatt Hotels has a division called Regency Productions, which is an event management company specializing not only in hospitality, but also in event production and setup (Conklin, 1994). Regency Productions is contracted by the National Basketball Association for the NBA Jam Session held during the NBA All-Star Weekend.

## Property Representation and Licensing

Sport management and marketing agencies often represent sport properties in promotional licensing and sponsor **solicitation** and **procurement**. A sport property can be defined as any sport or lifestyle entity that has name or event recognition, desirability, and perceived value and that chooses to offer itself for some type of affiliation. Examples of sport and lifestyle properties include the Rose Bowl, the Rock and Roll Hall of Fame, the Houston Rockets, Camden Yard, the Rolling Stones, the U.S. Tennis Open, The Ohio State University, and the Taste of Cincinnati. The property can be a facility, an event, a team, an athletic program, a band or concert tour, and so on. Property representation can result in the sales of rights fees, promotional licensing opportunities, sponsorship sales, signage and advertising agreements, and endorsements.

For example, IMG represents the Rock and Roll Hall of Fame and tries to secure licensees for it. IMG is currently working to identify exhibit areas that they can market to a variety of potential corporate sponsors and suppliers whose products have a link to the Hall and to the attendees the venue will attract. IMG will create product categories, such as electronics, soft drinks, and fast food, and will solicit prospective clients such as Sony, Coca-Cola, and McDonald's to enter a relationship with the property, the Hall of Fame (Revzin, 1995).

## Television Development and Production

The growth and proliferation of cable, satellite, and pay-per-view have created many opportunities and outlets for developing and producing programming for television. Host Communications, Creative Sports Marketing, and Raycom are agencies that have been involved in packaging rights fees for college football and basketball, and the subsequent sales of these rights to networks such as CBS, NBC, ABC, ESPN, and TBS. The revenue potential of such television programming and the interest of the networks and their sponsors have impacted the traditional conference structure in collegiate sport, resulting in the emergence of 12 team conferences such as the Southeast Conference and the newly formed Big 12 Conference (the Big Eight plus Texas, Texas A & M, Texas Tech, and Baylor), which began play in 1996. For these new conferences, the result has been to produce a lucrative market for a televised conference championship matching the winners of the two six-team divisions.

Traditional sport management and marketing agencies have recognized the opportunities that television presents and have aggressively moved to capitalize on that opportunity. IMG and ProServ have long had their own television production divisions so they could maximize the revenue derived from the properties they represent. A recent development has seen former ProServ president, Jerry Solomon, form a partnership with ProServ to create a new company that specializes in creating made-for-television events. The new company, P.S. Star Games, will feature events starring skater Nancy Kerrigan, volleyball player Karch Kiraly, and other clients represented by ProServ and Solomon (Farhi, 1995).

## Sponsorship Solicitation

The most common functions, regardless of the size or scope of the sport management and marketing agency, are consulting about solicitation and securing corporate sponsorships. Corporations now spend about $3 billion annually—a number that has increased threefold in less than a decade—on sponsorship (Schreiber, 1994). Although many properties (e.g., teams, sport events, festivals) handle these functions in-house, most seek outside assistance in determining value and identifying and obtaining appropriate sponsors. Similarly, corporations and other potential sponsors often employ a sport management and marketing agency to identify properties that may assist them in achieving their corporate goals and objectives. Atlanta-based Bevilaqua International, a specialist in Olympic sport marketing, describes itself as a

marketing consulting firm which specializes in working with corporations and major special events to enhance, protect and **leverage** the marketing investment. We work closely with our clients to develop cost-effective and results-oriented programs directed at corporate objectives such as improving brand sales, elevating awareness and enhancing corporate image. (Bevilaqua International Inc., 1994)

Some corporations, such as Gatorade, Coca-Cola, and Anheuser Busch have in-house sport marketing departments that work directly with properties or through the property's agency to reach an agreement.

## Hospitality Management Services

A frequently overlooked function of a sport and marketing agency is that of creating, arranging, and managing hospitality management services. Hospitality management services include, but are not limited to, transportation and other logistical issues; menu and food service planning and management; corporate sponsor entertainment; special auxiliary event creation and management; housing; and awards, gifts, and recognition programs. As with most events and activities, the type and scope of these services vary greatly according to the event. In the United States, the Super Bowl is, because of geographic location, appeal, and ticket demand, one of the most coveted destinations for hospitality packages in all of sport. Corporations reward their best sales personnel, thank their highest volume customers, and court new clients through invitations to this mega-event. The Super Bowl offers a prestigious opportunity to achieve these objectives. Agencies, such as Party Planners West, arrange transportation; accommodations; meals; auxiliary events such as cruises, golf tournaments, and postevent parties; gifts; and spouse programs (Conrad, 1995).

Clearly, the sport management and marketing agency segment of the sport economy is highly diverse and contains both generalists and specialists. It is also evident that the personnel in a larger sport management and marketing agency are better able to function as specialists, whereas those employed in smaller agencies must have a variety of skills and knowledge to perform their duties effectively. Skills essential to working in sport marketing and management agencies can be classified as people, technical, and organizational.

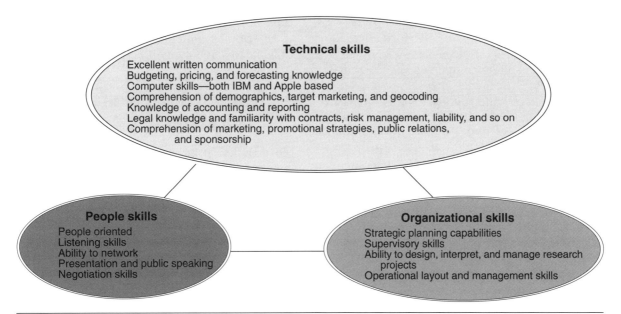

**Figure 18.1** Organizational, technical, and people skills essential for sport management and marketing agency personnel.

Essential skills under each classification are provided in figure 18.1.

## Grassroots Marketing Programs

Grassroots programs are designed to build a following for a product, service, or organization. They may not pay immediate benefits, but are essential to long-term growth by creating an interest among potential consumers. Most grassroots programs are aimed at children and adolescents who may or may not be consumers of the product, service, or organization in question, but possess the qualities, abilities, and potential to become consumers in the future. Grassroots programs are often designed to involve participants in activities and events that are held at local sites, which could be thousands of miles away from the headquarters of the sponsoring organization. These local events and activities are often targeted to certain demographic groups and ethnic markets. For example, Major League Baseball's RBI Program and the NHL's Street Skates programs are grassroots programs targeted to youth in the inner city. According to Dave King, President of Fort Collins, Colorado, based Triple Crown Sports,

> Grassroots marketing is the purest touch in reaching a consumer. The consumer is at a venue for 10-12 hours doing something that they like and enjoy. They are away from the barriers and clutter that usually block mes-

sages and we are able to provide our sponsors and ourselves access to the consumer at an optimum time. (David King, personal communication, June 21, 1995)

## Research and Evaluation

Evaluation and documentation are critical factors in determining the success of the various types of sport management and marketing programs discussed throughout this chapter. **Reengineering**, **downsizing**, **value added**, and measuring the impact are all concepts that stress a high degree of relevance and accountability, both in terms of the sport organization and the agency or program delivering the services. Research, through mail surveys, on-site surveys, personal interviews, pre- and **postevent impact analysis**, focus groups, and other methods, is essential to assist the decision maker in justifying a program's cost, value, and relevance to the company involved with the product or agency.

Most corporations involved in sponsorship or licensing activities perform some type of assessment, either through an in-house department or by contracting with an agency that offers research and evaluation services. It would follow that the research agency selected would not be involved in the sponsorship and licensing sales process because they would have a stake in the findings. Thus, the research agency selected should be a specialist in evaluating sponsorship and licensing programs or perhaps in sport consumer behavior. Joyce Julius and Associates, Performance Research, and Audience Analysts are examples of research or consulting companies specializing in such services.

The services provided by Joyce Julius and Associates are among the most used and reputable in the industry (Cortez, 1992). In fact, through their primary products—*Sponsors Report* and the National Television Impression Value (NTIV) Analysis—Joyce Julius and Associates arguably set an industry standard. *Sponsors Report* is a publication that focuses on the value of the exposure received directly from national television broadcasts. This is done by calculating all clear, in-focus exposure time during the broadcast. Exposure time is the amount of time given to logos, signage, displays, and audio mentions during the broadcast. These exposures are measured and converted to advertising costs per 30 seconds for the actual advertising costs on that specific broadcast. The NTIV Analysis determines the gross impressions from varied exposure sources and values these impressions using a single factor reflecting the comparative cost of national television media purchases (Schreiber, 1994).

The type of research most appropriate and the best agency to employ will vary with the scope and magnitude of the event, whether the event is televised, the types of sponsorship and licensing activities taking place at the event, the budget, and the commitment of the organization to undertake a sound research approach.

# Financial Planning and Management

This is a highly specialized service involving accountants, financial planners and advisors, as well as investment specialists and portfolio managers. There are few sport management and marketing agencies specializing in this type of work. IMG offers this service as part of its client management services and has assisted several of its clients in investing and planning well enough to start their own companies or to enter limited partnerships with IMG creating new ventures. The success of both Arnold Palmer and Jack Nicklaus in creating new companies and ventures is testament to the performance of IMG in discharging their fiscal planning duties. However, except for IMG and a few others, sport management and marketing agencies usually contract these services through

reputable financial planners and accountants whose primary function is not related to sport but to fiscal management and planning.

# Types of Sport Management and Marketing Agencies

More than 700 agencies identify themselves as sport management and marketing agencies (Lipsey, 1995). This figure does not include city or state sport commissions, corporations such as Anheuser Busch and Gatorade, or divisions of leagues such as NBA Properties, Inc. If these quasi-agencies were included, the figure would exceed 3,000.

As we can expect, these agencies vary in size, budgets, type of clientele, and scope of services. Some agencies have been established to perform a variety of services for one client, whereas others work for many clients but perform only one function. For example, ARL Properties represents only pilots of the Unlimited Air Racing Series for licensing and merchandising opportunities. Examining the various types of agencies (full service, general, specialty, and in-house) will illustrate the variety and scope of sport and entertainment management and marketing agencies.

## Full-Service Agencies— The International Management Group

These agencies are exactly what the term implies—the full range of services, including client management, event creation, television development, sponsorship solicitation, hospitality services, research and evaluation, and financial planning are performed by in-house personnel. Attorneys, accountants, sales personnel, public relations personnel, creative personnel, and management information services personnel are all contained in-house. Examining the International Management Group provides an excellent overview of a full-service agency.

IMG, the first completely dedicated sport marketing agency, was initially created to represent the interests of golfer Arnold Palmer. As times changed, and marketing forces such as television increased their impact on the sporting scene, the roles of sport marketing agencies expanded to include not only managing athletes, but other sport properties and events as well. IMG owes much of its early success to being visionary and recognizing the opportunities that the Golden Age of Sport Television (1958-1973) offered.

Arnold Palmer on the links. The International Management Group was founded in 1960 to represent Palmer's marketing interests. Since then IMG has expanded to manage sport properties and events as well as athletes.

The diversity of IMG's endeavors reflects how successful the company has become. IMG represents athletes, performing artists, writers, fashion models, broadcasters, world-class events, corporations, resorts, and cultural institutions. IMG has evolved into the largest sport marketing agency in the world, with 60 offices employing more than 2,000 employees in 26 countries (IMG, 1995). IMG has four core businesses: client management, event management and marketing, television, and corporate marketing (see figure 18.2). Examining each core business is essential in comprehending the entire scope and magnitude of IMG.

## Client Management

IMG's client management activities encompass contract negotiation, personalized strategic planning, endorsement marketing, corporate and re-sort affiliation, personal appearances, broadcasting, publishing, licensing, and merchandising (IMG, 1995). Due to the size and scope of IMG, as well as the many relationships it has constructed during the past 4 decades, IMG may enjoy a major advantage over competitors in attracting clients and providing services. Table 18.1. provides a partial listing of IMG clients.

One key to successful client management is to have satisfied, highly successful, and visible clients involved in a variety of sport and lifestyle activities. The success of the clients ensures successful negotiations and endorsements, while the visibility helps attract new clients who create a cyclical effect. Given the labor unrest in professional sport in 1994-1995, the importance of having a client base that ensures income, stability, and diverse sports or activities can not be overemphasized.

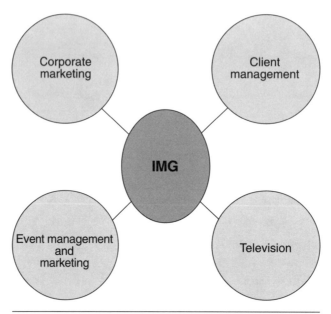

**Figure 18.2**  IMG's four core businesses.
Data from IMG Corporate Report (1995).

### Table 18.1
### Representative Sample of IMG Clients

| Client | Sport or activity |
| --- | --- |
| Arnold Palmer | Golf |
| Wayne Gretzky | Hockey |
| Joe Montana | Football |
| Andre Agassi | Tennis |
| Nancy Lopez | Golf |
| Alberto Tomba | Skiing |
| John Madden | Broadcasting |
| Monica Seles | Tennis |
| Kristi Yamaguchi | Figure skating |
| Bob Costas | Broadcasting |
| Chris Webber | Basketball |
| Lauren Hutton | Acting |
| Itzhak Perlman | Music |
| Jackie Stewart | Auto racing |
| Pat Conroy | Author |
| Niki Taylor | Modeling |

## Event Management and Marketing

IMG is involved in creating, developing, and managing sport and lifestyle activities and events. The company also manages licensing, sponsorship, and broadcast rights for many of the oldest and most distinguished events on the international sport and event calendar. These events include Wimbledon, the America's Cup, the Australian Open, World Championship of Women's Golf, Budweiser Grand Prix of Cleveland, Ringling Brothers and Barnum & Bailey Circus, and the 1994 Winter Olympics. Given the diverse nature and varying levels and demands of these properties, as well as the combination of rights, duties, and obligations associated with these events, the complexity of the event management and marketing industry becomes clear.

## Television

The television appendage of IMG is Trans World International (TWI), the largest independent source and distributor of sports programs in the world. The main function of TWI is to provide programming to major television networks around the world and to represent the entities owning the rights to those events (Parascenzo, 1993). TWI is able to accomplish this in three ways:

1. by serving as an advisor and consultant to rights holders,
2. by negotiating the sale of television rights, or
3. by creating and producing television series and events for sale or distribution.

Overall, TWI packages, produces, and sells more than 300 sports events per year.

## Corporate Marketing

Much the same way that IMG capitalized on the opportunities afforded by television in the 1960s, they also recognized the clutter represented by television advertising in the 1980s and sought an effective strategy for assisting corporations in communicating to their target markets. IMG decided that the most effective way for corporations to communicate was through sport event and lifestyle marketing.

## Sponsorship = Sales & Service

Ann Marie earned a BA degree in economics in 1987. Upon graduation, she worked for more than 2 years as a security analyst in New York, followed by 2 years in the product management department of a major commercial bank in the Boston area. After much reflection, she determined that her ultimate goal was to be involved with a sport-related product, and, thus, she enrolled in a sport management graduate program.

After completing her course work at the master's level, Ann Marie accepted a year-long marketing internship with Boston College. Even though her goal was to obtain a job within the product management department of sport-oriented company, she viewed this internship as an excellent learning opportunity. In this capacity she was involved with several activities with the revenue-producing sports, including corporate sponsorship sales, organization of promotional activities, and collateral production and distribution. Through this internship, she learned that college athletics was not a good fit with her career goals.

Ann Marie's internship coordinator alerted her to another internship possibility with IMG in Boston assisting with two major Boston-area events (a men's professional tennis event and a women's professional golf event). In this capacity, she worked on group ticket sales, print advertising placements, hotel room barters, and gathering ad copy from tournament sponsors. Although not offered full-time employment at the completion of these two tournaments, Ann Marie was given a small stipend to continue with IMG working out of their Chicago office on a women's professional tennis tournament. Fortunately, Ann Marie had access to sufficient financial resources to allow her to accept this position. Finally, after the initial internship with Boston College and an extended internship with IMG in Boston and Chicago, Ann Marie was offered a full-time position in the Boston office of IMG.

With IMG, Ann Marie has been involved with professional tennis, golf, and figure skating. Her typical day has varied dramatically, depending on whether events are 6 to 12 months into the future or 6 to 12 weeks away. Her largest responsibility involves sponsorship sales. When dealing with companies new to sport sponsorship, she has to educate executives on how sport sponsorship can assist an organization in accomplishing goals such as increased visibility, enhanced corporate image, differentiation of products from competition, and client entertainment. According to Ann Marie,

> Selling takes place 365 days a year; however, as an event draws near, other tasks become high priorities. Servicing event sponsors is obviously a top priority. It is crucial that all sponsor needs are addressed and that every sponsorship benefit available to the organization is considered. Tickets, banners, program ads, television and radio spots, logo slicks, on-site promotions, merchandising booths, public address announcements, and on-site parties are all details that must be handled appropriately.

In addition to sponsor relations, Ann Marie is involved with many other event responsibilities, including placement of print advertising, group ticket sales, player and sponsor hotel accommodations, and ordering printed materials (e.g., credentials, parking passes, and scorecards). For golf events, she also serves as the tournament coordinator, which involves many responsibilities such as serving as event liaison between the LPGA, tournament volunteers, pro-am participants, and neighborhood residents. Ann Marie says, "Stating that I wear many hats during the weeks before and during an event is an understatement!"

## General Agencies— DelWilber and Associates

DelWilber and Associates (DWA) is a generalist type of agency located in McLean, Virginia. DWA does not represent athletes or negotiate contracts for athletes nor does it secure endorsements for athletes. DWA has elected not to become involved in representing individual personalities and athletes, but rather to concentrate on sport organizations and events. In examining DWA we find the following business components (DelWilber and Associates, 1994):

DWA Golf provides marketing, tournament management, and public relations for some of the nation's highest quality events, such as the Heartland Classic held annually in St. Louis.

DWA Marketing offers strategic and tactical consulting services tailored to lifestyle-themed programs for corporate clients such as IBM, Mazda, and Frito Lay.

DWA Management provides project management services, including program execution, sponsorship management, site planning and selection, sales promotion, hospitality, and public relations for the IBM Student Pennant Race and Alka Seltzers Plus/Minus Award for the NHL.

DWA Productions develops and implements customized events to address key client objectives in the areas of marketing, public relations, and hospitality for clients such as Seven-Up at the annual business meetings held in association with the Seven-Up Shootout.

DWA Information Services conducts unique market research assignments through its exclusive RAPS (Rapid Audience Profile System) program. Strategic marketing plans are often developed for clients such as the Atlanta Hawks, Detroit Tigers, IBM, Mazda, and Taco Bell as a result of the research.

DWA Properties specializes in sponsorship sales and strategic planning for property clients. It also negotiates broadcast, licensing, and merchandising agreements for such properties as the U.S Baseball Federation, Coors Brewing Company, and the New York Racing Association.

## Specialty Agencies— Bevilaqua and Triple Crown Sports

A specialty agency is an agency that specializes in the types of services it provides or in the scope of its clientele. For example, Bevilaqua International, based in Atlanta, specializes in Olympic marketing. All of its clients engage Bevilaqua International for the purpose of entering into a contractual agreement with the United States Olympic Committee, the International Olympic Committee, or both. The contractual agreement may be endorsement, sponsorship, licensing, and so on, but it will be with an Olympic organizational unit. Thus, although Bevilaqua International performs a wide array of services, they offer these services only in conjunction with the Olympics (Smothers, 1992).

Triple Crown Sports, of Fort Collins, Colorado, is also a specialty agency in that it is solely involved in participatory grassroots programming. Although spectators are part of the overall success of the events, the emphasis is on securing participants. Triple Crown offers event programming in basketball, softball, soccer, in-line skating, bi- and triathlons, and sport festivals featuring two or more of these activities (Wells, 1993). Triple Crown Sports realizes its revenues primarily from participant entry fees and from corporate sponsor involvement at these events.

## In-House Agencies— Professional League Departments

In-house agencies refers to departments of existing companies (Anheuser Busch, Gatorade) that perform many sport marketing functions on behalf of the products and divisions of the parent company. These units are part of the corporation and are housed within that corporation to perform sport and lifestyle management and marketing functions for the corporation. In-house agencies have only one client—themselves—and function as **gatekeepers** in reviewing opportunities presented to them by other entities. In addition to this gatekeeping function, in-house agencies work with other units of the corporation, such as brand or product managers, advertising departments, public relations departments, and community affairs departments to create or implement sport and lifestyle programming useful in achieving corporate objectives.

One example of in-house agencies are professional league departments. Each professional sport league, and most sport organizations, have a department that focuses its marketing and promoting efforts on the entire league or unit. For example, NBA Attractions and Entertainment, a newly formed NBA division, markets and promotes the NBA as a holistic product through special events and activities such as NBA Jam Session, the NBA Draft, and international tours and activities. NBA Attractions and Entertainment personnel work with the marketing departments of individual teams to promote the growth and development of the league itself. In doing that, these personnel must understand the uniqueness and complexities of each team's market and must be prepared to assist teams in maintaining their identity while promoting the image of the whole league.

## Learning Activity

Select a sport event or activity (property). What criteria would you use in selecting an agency to represent your sport property? Construct a marketing inventory of the characteristics of that activity or event that you believe have value and are marketable.

# Careers Within Sport Management and Marketing Agencies

Careers in sport and lifestyle event management and marketing are challenging and varied. Many sport marketing agencies do not hire entry-level personnel. Instead, they bring in experienced people from other industry segments who have a network in place that they can use in generating new clients. A critical consideration in the hiring process, particularly in smaller agencies, is an assessment of a candidate's ability to get along, communicate, and be productive in a working environment with few staff members who must interact daily. In these smaller agencies, interaction involving two or more staff members who function as a team is common, thus, the importance of their compatibility. Sometimes this ability of a team to work together harmoniously is called chemistry.

In terms of educational background, a business degree with a marketing background is preferable. Sport management degrees, with several electives in business, are also desirable. Advanced degrees in business, law, or sport management are an advantage for the applicant. Starting salaries in a

sport and lifestyle marketing and management organization range from the mid to upper $20s to the low $40s, depending on experience and background.

## Learning Activity

Contact a sport management and marketing agency in your area. If there are no sport management and marketing agencies in your area, contact local advertising or public relations firms to determine if they have an appropriate client in the sport and lifestyle marketing area. Arrange an informational interview with someone in the agency who can provide you with an opportunity to learn more about the agency. In conjunction with your faculty advisor, structure a list of questions appropriate to ask during your informational interview. If feasible, attend a grassroots program or event managed or marketed by the agency. Observe signage, promotional activities, and agency employees during the implementation of the activities. Write a critique based on your observations.

## Learning Activity

Using the same scenario outlined in the previous Learning Activity, interview an employee of a sport management and marketing agency to determine the steps in developing their career. What is their educational background? Did they do an internship? What is the scope of their duties on a day-to-day basis? Do they offer internships or part-time employment? What do they look for in an entry-level person?

# Challenges Facing Sport Management and Marketing Agencies

Although the sport management and marketing agency segment of the sport industry is growing in number of firms and job opportunities, agencies still face several difficult challenges in the years ahead. These challenges are similar to those encountered by advertising agencies, public relations firms, and similar enterprises. We can categorize them as follows:

## In-House Versus Out-Sourcing

Simply stated, a sport management and marketing agency can perform at a high level for a client for several years, at which time the client, feeling that she knows the functions that the agency performs, decides to dismiss the agency and bring that function in-house. This is a challenge for the agency because it might mean having to cut personnel and budgets as a result of losing the account. It might also mean losing a key staff member to the client who has hired that individual for his expertise and familiarity with the organization. This practice is becoming more prevalent in professional sports leagues, such as the NBA and NHL, and in collegiate athletic departments because of the need to maximize revenues. By bringing sponsorship, licensing, and broadcasting in-house instead of out-sourcing them to agencies or hiring an outside agency to perform functions on their behalf, the organization feels that it will have more control and generate more income while cutting expenses (agency fees).

## Labor Unrest

The recent labor strife in Major League Baseball, the National Hockey League, and, potentially, the National Basketball Association have created a situation in which sponsors and product manufacturers, two large revenue sources for agencies, are reluctant to commit advertising dollars and resources to support broadcasts, special events, campaigns, and endorsements to sports and players that could be on strike and, thus, out of the public's eye and interest. In this light, agencies must be prepared to develop contingency plans and show that these contingencies would be effective if implemented. Also, agencies might be prepared to help their clients become more diverse in their spending, thus averting dependence on one product or person.

## Legislation and Judicial Review

In 1995, the Clinton Administration worked with various federal agencies to eliminate tobacco and alcohol signage from sport stadia and arenas. This signage was commonplace in most professional athletic facilities throughout the United States, and agencies must determine a new course of action to provide exposure for their clients in these sports. They must also consider alternatives if such restrictions are broadened to include the auto racing industry, where tobacco and alcohol producers constitute a significant portion (if not the majority) of all sponsorship, **entitlement**, and signage at the facilities, on the cars, and on the drivers themselves. Could this situation be extended to beach volleyball and other sports that have significant ties with alcohol and tobacco?

## Summary

A sport management and marketing agency is a business that acts on behalf of a sport property. Although these agencies were initially formed to represent athletes, they have evolved and now serve myriad functions, such as representation, negotiation, sales, licensing, marketing, and management. There are more than 700 companies classified as sport management and marketing agencies. If quasi-agencies such as city and state sport commissions, divisions of leagues, and corporations such as Gatorade are included, the number of marketing and management firms exceeds 3,000. We can classify these agencies into the following four categories:

- Full-service agencies (e.g., the International Management Group)—provide a full range of services performed by in-house personnel.
- General agencies (e.g., DelWilber and Associates)—provide a variety of services to clients, but are not involved in all potential agency functions.
- Specialty agencies (e.g., Bevilaqua International)—specialize in the type of services they provide or in the scope of clientele they serve.
- In-house agencies—departments of existing companies (e.g., Gatorade, NBA Attractions and Entertainment) that perform many sport marketing functions on behalf of the products or divisions of the parent company.

Personnel at larger sport marketing and management agencies tend to function as specialists, whereas those in smaller agencies need to have a greater variety of skills and knowledge. Degrees in business and sport management are preferred, with a background in marketing essential. Careers in sport and lifestyle management and marketing agencies are challenging and varied, drawing starting salaries from the mid to upper $20s to the low $40s, depending on education and experience. Sport management and marketing agencies face several challenges in the coming years—in-house versus out-sourcing, labor unrest, and legislative and judicial review.

# For More Information

The following publications will give you more insight into the world of sport management and marketing agencies.

- *The Sponsor Fact Book* published by Team Marketing Report, Alan Friedman, Editor, Chicago, IL
- *Team Marketing Report* published by Team Marketing Report, Alan Friedman, Editor, Chicago, IL

- *Advertising Age*
- *Amusement Business*
- *The Sponsors Report* published by Joyce Julius and Associates, Joyce Julius, Editor, Ann Arbor, MI
- *Special Events Report* published by the International Events Group, Lesa Ukman, Executive Editor, Chicago, IL

# Job Opportunities

## Event Manager

Agency is looking for a well-qualified and experienced individual to be in charge of operational elements of a major professional golf tournament. Duties include logistics, design and manage all corporate hospitality venues, plan and schedule special events for sponsors and guests, schedule and oversee prevent activities such as the Long Drive competition and the Celebrity Pro-Am tournament.

## Sponsorship Sales

West Coast agency is looking for experienced sales personnel to become members of a dynamic team-oriented sport marketing company. Client list includes several professional sport franchises, NASCAR, and professional golf. Successful candidates will have previous experience in sponsorship or media sales. Experience with Fortune 500 companies a plus.

## Tournament Director

Aggressive East Coast sport marketing company is looking for an enthusiastic, outgoing individual with a strong tennis background to manage premier tennis events in Florida, Puerto Rico, and New York. Responsible for securing players, recruiting and training volunteers, scheduling officials, and working with broadcast and cable networks to ensure player availability. Fluency in Spanish, French, or German essential.

## Agent

ProPlus, a 10-year-old firm specializing in representing and serving the needs of professional athletes, is searching for two new associates to join our team. Successful candidates will have advanced degrees in law, marketing, finance, or a combination thereof. Duties will include a combination of the following: contract negotiations, endorsements, financial management, appearances, and general consulting.

## Product Placement

Large athletic footwear and apparel manufacturing company is seeking an individual to work with its agency of record to secure placement of athletic footwear and apparel products in major motion pictures and television programming. Individual should have a background in marketing or communications. Significant travel involved. Individual should have excellent communication skills and a familiarity with television and motion picture personalities and product use.

## Market Research

Southwest sport marketing agency is looking for an individual with a background in marketing research to provide documentation to clients regarding the impact of sport and special events on product preference and use. Individual should have an advanced degree and training in both qualitative and quantitative research methods.

## Sales Agent

NBA team searching for an individual to become part of an in-house agency to generate auxiliary income not directly related to the NBA franchise, but using the assets of the franchise. Duties may include developing special events such as camps and clinics, and acquiring and marketing minor league franchises. Looking for experienced sales personnel—previous pro sport experience not essential but a plus. Looking for people who can think "outside the box."

# Chapter 19 International Sport

**Ted G. Fay**
Daniel Webster College

## Learning Objectives

After studying this chapter, you will be able to

1. understand the foundations on which the international sport industry has developed with respect to international sport federations, leagues, corporations, and events;

2. demonstrate an understanding of the power structure and processes in which the international sport industry operates, including linkages within the industry;

3. demonstrate an understanding of the import-export exchange process regarding sport products, services, and personnel throughout the world and its potential for expansion;

4. identify the resources available and the knowledge and skills necessary to successfully compete for a job in the international sport marketplace; and

5. discuss trends in this field.

What do the following names have in common: Wimbledon, the World Series, the Super Bowl, the Ryder Cup, the Stanley Cup, the Davis Cup, Nike, Reebok, Adidas, Tiger Woods, Ping, Michael Jordan (23), Wayne Gretzky (99), Baggio, Carl Lewis, Jackie Joyner-Kersee, Graf, Agassi, Schumacher, Tomba, Witt, the Cowboys, the Penguins, the Bulls, and the Dodgers? The answer is that each individual or organization has achieved a high level of worldwide brand name recognition through sport. Each

event, company, team, and sport personality has transcended the isolation and limitations of national borders, tariffs, or mindsets to become the cornerstones in describing what international sport is and what it might become (Barnett & Cavanagh, 1994).

The purpose of this chapter is to delineate the principal structures and organizations that currently shape and define the international sport industry. Due to space limitations, this chapter will not attempt to provide a comprehensive review by sport or by industry type. Rather, it will provide snapshots of individuals, organizations, and events that are part of the international sport scene. This information should foster a better understanding of the ever-changing and expanding dimensions of international sport, presently and as we move into the 21st century. We will emphasize the special skills, experiences, and competencies that will help you gain access to the international sport management career field.

## What Is International Sport?

There are at least two factors that we consider in determining whether a sport is international: (a) the degree or the regularity with which action by an organization is focused on international activity, and (b) the context in which a person or organization operates within the sport enterprise.

For example, is a U.S. college sport team that has one or more foreign players on scholarship or elects to play several international teams during its preseason exhibition schedule involved in international sport? There were nearly 200 foreign male athletes receiving basketball scholarships to play at NCAA Division I colleges and universities in 1995 (Dieffenbach, 1996). In addition to men's and women's basketball, many top-ranked U.S. college ice hockey teams, ski teams, track and field, tennis, softball, and soccer teams regularly use foreign players and play in foreign countries (Hoffer, 1994). Colleges and universities, however, do not have international competition as a primary focus.

The context in which a person or organization operates within the sport enterprise is also an important factor in whether it can be characterized as being international sport. It is a relatively

### Learning Activity

Choose a country and research its most popular sporting activities, sports facilities, and famous athletes to create a profile for a global sport atlas. Describe (if available) the prime sport exports and imports of this country, including the production of goods and services, the existence of prominent sports leagues and events, the development of players and coaches in particular sports, offices of international sport federations (IFs), and so on.

simple task to define the Olympic Games, a world championship in a specific sport, or a multinational corporation such as the International Management Group (IMG) as being among the giants of international sport. It is more difficult, however, to assess whether an organization is engaged in international sport if they operate almost exclusively in one nation or are only occasionally involved with international athletes or clients. We will limit this chapter to discussing individuals, organizations, and events that are involved internationally on a regular basis as a primary function.

## History of International Sport

The past quarter century has witnessed geopolitical and global economic changes that have had a tremendous impact and ripple effect on international sport. Before the mid-1980s, international sport was defined primarily in terms of the quadrennial Olympic Games and soccer's World Cup, with nations and their respective political ideologies clamoring to stake their claims to being the world's best. During this period, we could characterize the United States as primarily an exporter of sport products and services, while being isolationist in its view that its professional team sports were the world's best and most important sporting events.

We could argue that the Summer Olympics of 1972 marked the birth of a new international sports revolution. There were several benchmark events in this special year that have had everlasting effects on the international sport industry and marketplace. The tragic murder of nine Israeli Olympians by terrorists in the Olympic village sent shock waves through the international sports establishment and changed forever the manner in which security would be dealt with in the Olympics and other major international events. Adidas and other sporting goods manufacturers were accused of contributing to the professionalization and commercialization of the 1972 Olympics through under the table payments to track and field athletes, swimmers, and alpine skiers (Guttman, 1994).

The ongoing debate before 1972 over the issue of amateurs versus professionals in the 1972 Olympics was dramatically increased after the Soviet Union's upset victory over the favored U.S. men's basketball team (72-71) in the Olympic basketball finals. The reaction of many to this shocking loss was to accuse the Soviet players of being professionals paid by their government. Many people believe the idea of sending NBA all-stars instead of the best U.S. collegians gained serious momentum as a direct result of this bitterly contested loss.

Fuel was added to this debate when, one month after the Summer Olympics were over, a team of NHL all-stars (professionals) from Canada challenged the Olympic hockey champions (amateurs) from the Soviet Union for the first time. The Canadians emerged victorious in the Series of the Century, which was decided by a single goal after eight games (Terroux, 1972). None of these important sport benchmarks, however, was as significant as U.S. President Nixon's decision to send a table tennis team to China in 1972. This historic event, sometimes called Ping-Pong diplomacy, is often cited as the beginning of the process of normalizing diplomatic and economic relations between the two superpowers.

Subsequent years witnessed the profound impact of three Olympic boycott movements in 1976, 1980, and 1984, causing the International Olympic Committee (IOC) to believe the Olympic movement was in jeopardy (Simson & Jennings, 1992). Faced with a political and potential financial disaster, the IOC reluctantly altered its rules regarding corporate involvement for the 1984 Summer Olympic Games, thus allowing the Los Angeles Olympic Organizing Committee to charge multimillion dollar fees for sponsorship. The financial success of these Games touched off a sport marketing and event management revolution (Stotlar, 1993). In 1985, the International Olympic Committee completed this sport governance revolution when it eliminated all references to the term amateur, thus allowing each respective international sport federation to define its own eligibility rules. This landmark decision, in effect, opened the door to the professionalization of Olympic sports and served to level the playing field between the state-supported athletes of the Soviet bloc and their western counterparts (Wilson, 1994).

## Redefining International Sport

These rule changes, coupled with the aftershocks of the fall of the Berlin Wall in 1989, have had a tremendous impact on redefining the scope of international sport. The collapse of the nation-states of the Soviet Union and East Germany has virtually eliminated some of the most powerful nations from the Olympic Games and helped to add a significant number of new nations to the Olympic family (Powers, 1993). Over the past 25 years, the balance of power in international

sport has dramatically shifted with each breakthrough victory, ranging from Australia's win in the America's Cup in 1983, to the amazing feat of American Greg LeMond in winning three Tour de France titles in 1986, 1989, and 1990, to Chen Liu of China being crowned the 1995 World Ladies Figure Skating Champion. From Swedes, Germans, and Czechs dominating the professional women's and men's tennis tours to Europeans, Africans, and Australians succeeding on the PGA and LPGA tours, single nations are no longer able to dominate a sport (Concannon, 1994).

The 1990s have seen dramatic developments in football (a.k.a. soccer), often referred to as the world's game. In 1994, the United States successfully hosted soccer's World Cup to record crowds of spectators (3.58 million) and television viewers (2.1 billion worldwide). The U.S. men's team, typically unsuccessful in international play before 1994, produced both exciting and tragic results. Unfortunately, the ugly side effects of international sport were witnessed after the Columbian team returned home, having failed to qualify for the second round. A chilling example of nationalistic soccer fever run amuck was the revenge murder of the Colombian defensive player, Andres Escobar, who had inadvertently scored on his own goal in Columbia's 2-1 loss to the United States.

In a more positive direction, soccer continued to grow in popularity with the formation of two new premier professional leagues for men in the '90s. The J-League in Japan and Major League Soccer (MLS) in the United States are attempts to expand soccer's foothold in Asia and North America. The sport's best kept secret, however, might be the ascension of the U.S. women's team to a position of prominence in world soccer. They were the 1993 FIFA World Champions, were runners-up to Norway in 1995, and won the gold medal as soccer made its debut as a medal sport at the 1996 Centennial Olympic Games in Atlanta.

## Assessing the Expanding Market for Sport

A trend in most professional sport leagues in all major international sports has been recruiting and developing top players from nontraditional sources of talent. Examples include Croatians and Africans in basketball (NBA), American and African players in soccer (premier European leagues), and Australians in baseball (MLB) and in women's softball (NCAA). An unexpected star in the

Hideo Nomo of Japan and the Los Angeles Dodgers. A trend in professional sport has been to recruit personnel from nontraditional sources of talent.

aftermath of the 1994 Major League Baseball strike was Hideo Nomo of the Los Angeles Dodgers. Nomo not only became the first Japanese player to play in the major leagues since 1963, but also was named to the 1995 National League All-Star team and the NL Rookie of the Year. These developments have forced major professional leagues in soccer, basketball, baseball, and hockey to form new working agreements with other professional leagues, individual franchises, and international sport federations. This has helped create a new climate of cooperation and more orderly international transfer of players (Dieffenbach, 1996).

The international expansion of sport has also set off a flurry of activity in the sport marketplace. For example, more than 200 million people worldwide participate in basketball (Pitts & Stotlar, 1996). Recognizing the mature market in North America, the NBA launched a global marketing campaign in 1989 to expand the brand awareness of its teams, players, and league-licensed merchandise. This campaign was perfectly positioned to capitalize on the gold medal performance of the 1992 U.S. Olympic basketball team (a.k.a. Dream Team I) led by the NBA's best. It was as much by design as by happenstance, that Michael Jordan and Magic Johnson became international sport icons, eclipsing the fame of even the most famous soccer players of that era.

The end of the Cold War and the dissolution of the Soviet Union also helped spawn sport market economies in the new nation-states of Central and Eastern Europe. A vibrant global marketplace based on new sources and pathways in both the production and distribution of goods and services has stimulated a dynamic export-import exchange process among nations and regions of the world (Klemm, 1994). Sport is a universal product that bridges cultural differences, customs, and belief systems and, thus, is a stable part of the growing international exchange and business. The following story of recent developments in ice hockey clearly illustrates this point.

## Learning Activity

Deliver an oral presentation on current issues and events in international sport. Familiarize yourself with a variety of sources that provide information relevant to international sport. At least half the sources you choose should be from non-USA periodicals or literature. We encourage you to use the Internet and electronic information sources. The presentation should explore critical issues as well as highlight important current events that are international in scope and focus. For ongoing issues and events, add new information in a context based on previous presentations.

# International Sport Industry— The Case of Ice Hockey

What country has the best ice hockey team in the world? Simple, eh? It's Canada, of course, because Canada has the best players. Just look at the Canadian stars who play in the National Hockey League and are on the teams that compete for the Stanley Cup. Plus, Canada's women's ice hockey team won the gold medal at the 1993 and 1995 International Ice Hockey Federation (IIHF) World Championships. Obviously, when it comes to ice hockey, Canada rules.

But nyet! The NHL, the Stanley Cup, and all that is fine, but when was the last time Canada won an Olympic gold medal or a Canadian men's team won an IIHF World Championship? How could anyone deny that 9 Olympic gold medals and 25 IIHF Men's World Championships make Russia (formerly the USSR) the best? Sounds like a typical, everyday difference of opinion among nationalistic sports fans. Or is it that simple?

When a sport is viewed as a national treasure, national pride runs deep, and discussions are held at the highest political levels, as well as sport levels, about who can lay claim to being the best. For many years, the debate over which nation was the best in men's ice hockey was complicated

because top Canadian players were professional athletes who played on NHL teams; thus, they were ineligible to compete in the Winter Olympic Games and the IIHF World Championships. Even when the restrictions on professionals were lifted in 1985, few players were available due to the fact that these two events occurred during the regular NHL season and Stanley Cup playoffs. Availability to national teams was not part of the collective bargaining agreement between the league and the National Hockey League Players Association (NHLPA).

Until 1989, the top Soviet and Czech players were prohibited from competing in the National Hockey League by their own national sport federations and governing bodies. NHL players from Sweden, Finland, and the United States, although free to play in the NHL for many years, also faced conflicts with not being available to their national teams during these important international tournaments. Because there was no single competition that pitted the best players of all countries against each other, there was no standard of comparison to determine who was the world's best.

From 1972 to 1994, the USSR dominated international ice hockey. The lone exception was the Miracle on Ice upset of the USSR by Team USA in 1980. The balance of power shifted in 1994 when Sweden beat Canada 4 to 3 for the gold medal at the XVII Olympic Winter Games. Sweden replicated this gold medal performance by defeating host Norway in the first-ever sledge hockey competition at the VI Paralympic Games held immediately after the Olympic Games in Lillehammer. Two months later, at the 1994 IIHF World Championship, Canada beat Sweden in a similar shoot-out.

## International Hockey and the NHL

The 1994 NHL season proved to be a landmark season, when long suffering New York Ranger fans watched in amazement as their beloved Rangers prevailed over the Vancouver Canucks to win the Stanley Cup for the first time in 50 years. This was not the only story, however, as a number of significant international firsts were recorded. The Most Valuable Player (MVP) of the Stanley Cup playoffs was Brian Leetch of the New York Rangers. Leetch was the first American and non-Canadian to win this prestigious award. His teammates, Alex Kozlov, Sergei Nemchinov, and Sergei Zubov, were the first Russian players ever to play on a Stanley Cup winner, while their Russian compatriot, Sergei Fedorov of the Detroit Red Wings, was the first

Russian and European to win the Hart Trophy as MVP of the National Hockey League (Schoenfeld, 1995).

In 1988, the Soviet Ice Hockey Federation allowed some of their older players to play in the National Hockey League. This action was due in part to the Russians' need to raise hard currency (U.S. dollars) to help defray the federation's expenses (Powers, 1992); therefore, they charged high transfer fees for the release of their players. Since the fall of the Berlin Wall in 1989 and the dissolution of the Soviet Union into sovereign republics, the floodgates have opened for young Russian players leaving to play in professional leagues throughout Europe and North America, including the National Hockey League. This emigration of talent has reached such a critical point that major concerns have surfaced over raiding Russian leagues for young talent by professional leagues in Europe and North America (Gray & Deacon, 1996).

## Who's the World's Best Hockey Team?

So, which nation currently has the best hockey team? Many hockey fans believe this question will finally be answered at the XVIII Winter Olympic Games in 1998 in Nagano, Japan. The world's best men players will be there because the NHL season will be suspended for 16 days to allow professional players to compete for their countries (Ogrean, 1995). Unlike Barcelona in 1992, when Michael Jordan, Larry Bird, and Magic Johnson led Dream Team I to the gold medal for the United States by drubbing all their opponents in basketball, the 1998 Olympic Hockey Tournament promises no fewer than *six* Dream Teams, all viable medal contenders. Moreover, the world's best women hockey players will be there too because, for the first time, women's ice hockey will be a part of the 1998 Winter Olympic Games. Perhaps a clear best team will be crowned or perhaps a new kid on the block will emerge.

## The Effect of Ice Hockey on the International Sport Industry

In spite of the international debate about the best ice hockey team in the world, the argument could be made that the *real* winner in ice hockey is the sport industry itself. For example, the exchange of players from Europe to North America and vice versa has stimulated interest by both the NHL and the International Hockey League (IHL) in estab-

### Learning Activity

Write a press release describing the men's and women's ice hockey competition at the 1998 Winter Olympic Games.

### Learning Activity

Using basic demographic data, create a summary table showing the top Olympic nations through your analysis of per capita income per country, per population, per sport, per medal won in the Olympic Games and the Paralympic Games (Summer and Winter). Who is the best based on the aggregate total available resources (money, population base, etc.) available to it?

lishing European divisions. NHL games are currently distributed on global cable networks and NHL licensed merchandise is exported into the European market. It is not a coincidence that Rupert Murdoch's FOX network has become the network partner of the NHL, thus positioning Murdoch to be able to lock up Europe when the NHL expands to the continent (Dwyer & Engardio, 1994). New licensing agreements between the NHL and the IIHF, the TV contract with Fox, new corporate partners (e.g., Nike, Mastercard, Budweiser), and marquee players from Europe (e.g., Fedorov, Bure, Forsberg, and Selanne) make the establishment of an NHL European division likely within the next decade. Expansion might also include a professional women's league mirroring developments in women's basketball, soccer, and softball.

A worldwide explosion of interest in ice hockey has been stimulated by rule changes (less fighting) and intentional marketing efforts to attract new fans (primarily women), corporate sponsors, and more media exposure. Ice hockey is no longer a sport just for men in the cold regions of the world. National and international federations are beginning to realize that greater diversity in the sport can help change ice hockey from a niche sport into a sport for all. In addition to Olympic and world championships in women's ice hockey, there are Paralympic sledge hockey for competitors with physical disabilities and men's and women's roller hockey on in-line skates.

Corporate sponsorship has received a boost from these developments as Nike has signed an exclusive contract with the International Ice

© Robert Skeoch

The exchange of professional ice hockey players between Europe and North America has sparked interest in both the NHL and the International Hockey League (IHL) in establishing European divisions.

Hockey Federation and 126 national ice hockey federations. This contract gives Nike, which is also a premium sponsor of the NHL, the exclusive right to outfit all national teams in uniforms with the Nike swoosh at all IIHF World Championships, the NHL's World Cup of Ice Hockey, and the Olympic Games from 1996 into the 21st century (Burke, 1995; Ogrean, 1995). This is consistent with Nike's worldwide marketing strategy as evidenced by its 10-year, $100-million sponsorship agreement with the Brazilian National Soccer Team.

Sport business has also benefited from international developments in ice hockey. In 1993, the Pittsburgh Penguins (later joined by Disney Sports Enterprises) purchased the controlling interest in the Central Red Army team (CSKA). CSKA, which has been touted as possibly the greatest hockey franchise in hockey history, is now known as the Russian Penguins. This action was made possible by a breakdown of traditional sport and business barriers between Russia and other countries. The purchase provided a unique marketing opportunity by giving the Penguins and Disney the inside

track to more than 140 million Russian hockey fans.

Ice hockey is only one example of the activity occurring in sport at the global level. In the next few years, you will witness an explosion of interest and expansion in this arena. International sport in the 21st century will be a stimulating and challenging experience!

## Careers in International Sport

The nature and scope of the international sport industry is complex and continues to change so rapidly that you need an up-to-date road map to keep things straight (see figure 19.1). It is essential that a sport manager has a sound working knowledge of the processes of international business and sport and a clear recognition of the key players (organizations). From selling tobacco products, alcohol, Fords, and Hondas in Europe, to sponsoring Formula One car racing, to selling tourism in association with the Olympic Games or a World

Championship, there is a definite relationship between events, products, and talent. Nowhere is there such a direct tie between sport, leisure, recreation, and business than in international sport.

What is essential for you to know as you prepare for your journey into international sport? Pitts and Stotlar (1996) cited the need to understand the basics of finance, manufacturing, distribution, retailing, and human resource management of any U.S. based corporation or sport organization from a global perspective. The first step in your journey, therefore, is developing an understanding of the primary trade treaties and agreements, such as the General Agreement on Tariffs and Trade (GATT), the North American Free Trade Agreement (NAFTA), and the rules and regulations affecting the European Community (EC). This knowledge provides an essential foundation from which you can research other important trade regulations. It is vital for you to know how free or restricted the movement of goods, services, persons, and capital

**Figure 19.1** Where to begin learning how to break into the international sport industry can be confusing. Following these essential guidelines can help you get where you want to go.
Reprinted, by permission, from The Wilkineon Group.

is from nation to nation. Knowing your rights as a foreigner when doing business in another nation is critical. You must have an in-depth awareness of how well you, your employees, and your investments will be protected by a given legal system and what recourse you will have if problems occur.

For example, many professional leagues and teams are concerned about whether trademark and copyright laws of a nation or regional economic group (e.g., the European Community) will protect their trademarks. They also need to know if other countries have laws or regulations that might inhibit the movement of players from one nation to another (e.g., European soccer, Japanese baseball), whether they have a system of binding contracts (e.g., the NBA and the NHL with the European leagues and MLB with their Latin American and Japanese counterparts), and in what currency to base the compensation for a given player (e.g., MLB and the NHL).

## Relocating Manufacturing Companies

Sporting goods manufacturing companies that have relocated most of the production of their footwear to China or Indonesia are faced with financial and ethical concerns. Does the attraction of a large, cheap labor force outweigh concerns over counterfeiting due to weak copyright laws, currency fluctuations and devaluations, and potentially new restrictive export and import laws? What are the ethical considerations when large,

multinational corporations profit from children and women toiling for pennies an hour in sweatshop conditions to produce name brand footwear (Cole & Hribar, 1995; Jones, 1996; Zuckoff, 1994)? Is it exploitation to continuously move footwear production from one third world country to another (e.g., from Korea and the Philippines to China and Indonesia) in search of the cheapest labor supply? What responsibility does a company have to the workers and countries they leave behind? These decisions must be based on ethical value systems as well as on the stability of the political regimes and their respective diplomatic relations with the United States (Katz, 1994).

## International Sport Governance

The second step on your journey is developing an understanding of international sport governance structure (see figure 19.2). Before 1985, it was simple to define international sport by distinguishing amateur sport (IOC, NOC, LOOC, LOCs) from professional sport. International sport governance was focused on amateur sports that were included in the Olympic Games, hemispheric games (e.g., Pan-American Games), and members of international sport federations (IFs) and their related national sport governing bodies (NSFs and NGBs).

As you can see in figure 19.2, however, several new entities have become involved in international sport governance since 1985. The principal additions include professional sport organizations

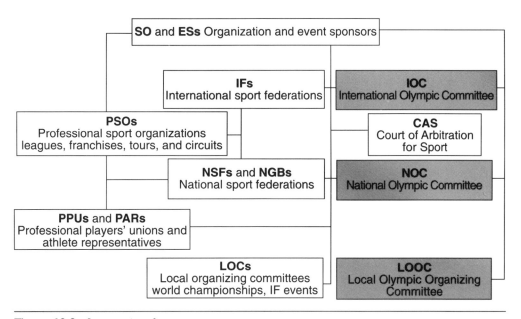

**Figure 19.2** International sport governance.
Data from Fay, 1995.

(PSOs); professional athlete unions and individual athlete representatives (PPUs and PARs); the Court of Arbitration for Sport (CAS); and sport organization and event sponsors (SO and ESs). The following two examples illustrate why these additional groups are included.

## Corporate Sponsorship

In 1992, the U.S. men's basketball team included 11 NBA veterans who had been selected by a committee of NBA coaches and general managers. To obtain approval for each player to participate, the player, his agent, his sponsors, his team, his league, USA Basketball (NGB), and the U.S. Olympic Committee were involved in a series of negotiations to clarify the rules and regulations under which each athlete would be governed. The compensation rules were different, the playing rules were different, the dispute resolution rules were different, and the expectations of behavior and conduct were different from the standard pro contracts.

Reebok was the 1992 official U.S. Olympic outerwear sponsor, providing warm-up jackets to all athletes. The agreements between the athletes and the U.S. Olympic Committee (USOC) were severely tested when some members of the team chose to cover the Reebok name with American flags as they stood on the victory podium to accept their gold medals. This action was initiated by Michael Jordan, who as a Nike sponsored athlete, refused to be seen implicitly endorsing his company's competitor. This incident thrust the USOC, Nike, Reebok, and Jordan into a high stakes public relations battle (Katz, 1993). The USOC has since amended its code of conduct to require athletes to wear the apparel provided by official Olympic sponsors.

## Arbitration

The second illustration involves U.S. Track and Field athlete Butch Reynolds' challenge of Olympic drug testing procedures in 1992. Reynolds failed the drug test and was disqualified from the Games. He subsequently filed suit against the International Amateur Athletic Federation (IAAF), claiming that his urine specimens had been tampered with and that the analysis procedures had been flawed. This controversy highlighted the new, complex entanglements involving an athlete's right to sue an international sport federation over the right to compete in the Olympic Games.

The court held for Reynolds and threatened to freeze IAAF sponsorship money from U.S. based corporations to force the IAAF to fulfill its obligations of a compensatory award (Weiler & Roberts, 1993). The problems caused by this situation and the implications of successful legal action pressured several international sport federations to join with the IOC in supporting the authority of the Court of Arbitration for Sport (CAS) to mediate sport-related disputes that cross national boundaries (Thoma & Chalip, 1996).

## Special Governing Concerns

The International Paralympic Committee (IPC), its corresponding National Paralympic Committee (NPC), and Local Paralympic Organizing Committee (LPOC) are also involved in governance of international sport. The Winter and Summer Paralympic Games involve athletes with physical and sensory disabilities and usually occur 2 weeks after the Olympic Games at the same location and in the same sport facilities. It is worth noting that the U.S. Olympic Committee is the only NOC in the world that also acts as its country's National Paralympic Committee (NPC). This signals a tremendous advance in the movement to integrate athletes with disabilities into the national and international sports mainstream (Landry, 1994; Lindström, 1994).

Other important segments of the international sport industry that are not represented in figure 19.2 include arenas, stadia, sport products, ticketing, security, fitness centers, rehabilitation and sports medicine centers, accommodation, and travel. These elements are crucial to conducting international sport and are the areas in which most growth in the next decade will occur. These sectors will provide the most opportunities for entry-level sport managers.

## Learning Activity

Write a paper about a significant contemporary issue in international sport. Your topic should cut across the sport and international spectrum (e.g., drug use, security, professionalization, commercialization, expansion, governance). This paper should not focus on any particular event per se (e.g., the Olympic Games); however, it could include the Olympics or some other event or league as a focal point. Use the "Point After" column in *Sports Illustrated* as an example for this project.

## Working Environments of International Sport Managers

Essential equipment for someone desiring a career in the international sport industry includes a world atlas, a passport, visas (for some countries), bilingual dictionaries, a pocket guide to currency exchange rates, a credit card with a reasonable credit line, airline tickets (this assumes one is not taking a boat or driving), a laptop computer with modem, and two bags packed full of the most important items necessary to conduct business (Pike & Fay, 1994). You are embarking on an adventure that will test your wits with respect to your personal habits, eating preferences, language skills, cultural understanding, business etiquette, patience, and ability to develop a network of friendships. You will be told that your colleagues from other countries understand English more than they do or that you can obtain the services of an interpreter who, as it turns out, can not or will not convey the nuances of the verbal exchange. In the highly personalized world of international business and sport, even a rudimentary understanding of the language you are engaged in can gain you an invaluable foothold over your competition (Barnett & Cavanagh, 1994; Katz, 1994).

Computer skills and the ability to access the information highway through the Internet are now often assumed as basic skills for entry-level sport management positions. International sport is a phone, fax, and modem culture based on strong oral and written communication skills, complemented by an understanding of electronic etiquette. A sales background and experience as an athlete are not requirements per se, but often are perceived as a bonus in gaining and succeeding at a job. International sport managers must be willing and able to travel, necessitating an adequate level of fitness and health. In addition, there are long flights, long meetings compressed into too short a schedule, and long periods away from home (Katz, 1994). You need to be patient, able to listen, and respectful of existing hierarchies as established by various cultures (Morrison, Conaway, & Borden, 1994).

Individuals involved in or interested in the international aspects of sport management should avail themselves of a wide range of publications, including industry and trade publications, professional journals, newspapers, and magazines in a effort to be up-to-date on international political, business, and sport trends. It is also wise to start a library of books and information that will augment off-the-shelf or library reference material. A daily regimen of reading key periodicals such as the *Wall Street Journal, USA Today,* or similar business and sport business periodicals is vital. This practice will enable you to maintain a knowledge of general business practices in a given culture, what is current in the global economy, and an up-to-date understanding of world events. The Internet and a variety of on-line services provide easy access to key materials and daily periodicals that may not be available in hard copy at a library, bookstore, or newsstand (Bullington, 1995).

A basic knowledge of how an international sport operates, the specific rules of the game, how it is structured, and where the locus of power resides with the sport (politically and on the field of play) can enhance your marketability. Understanding growth and trends in licensing, marketing, promotion, event management, and contracts (player and event) is also helpful (Halbfinger, 1996). Familiarity with the shifting borders within geopolitical regions will prevent any faux pas, such as forgetting that Czechoslovakia is now the separate nations of the Czech Republic and Slovakia (Powers, 1993).

Success in the international sport and business sphere is predicated on personal contact and friendship. Attending meetings of national sport federations, professional associations, and other conferences and symposia help maintain and expand your network of professional contacts. Time availability, relevance to your professional interests, and financial resources are important factors to consider when choosing those associations or annual conferences and trade shows you want to attend. Volunteering at a major international sports

### Learning Activity

In small groups, read and discuss the following books:

Katz, D. (1994). *Just do it.* New York: Random House.

Morrison, T., Conaway, W., & Borden, G. (1994). *Kiss, bow, or shake hands: How to do business in sixty countries.* Holbrook, MA: Bob Adams.

Pendergrast, M. (1993). *For God, country and Coca-Cola: The unauthorized history of the great American soft drink and the company that makes it.* New York: Collier.

Whiting, R. (1990). *You gotta have wa.* New York: Vintage Books.

event, conference, or trade show is an effective way to gain access to the field and to demonstrate your capabilities as a potential employee.

An informational interview of professionals in the field can be valuable in learning more about the realities of working for U.S. sports organizations that do business with other cultures or of the effects of being relocated to a country in which you must speak a different language. There is no one pathway to a career in the expanding and shifting landscape of the international sport marketplace.

# International Sport in the 21st Century

The international sport industry in the 21st century will shift from being perceived as a niche in the sport marketplace to representing the foundation of the sport enterprise (Nichols, 1993). Market share and investment in a given sport product, service, or sport per se will be measured worldwide rather than nationally. References will be made to aspects of the industry in economic terms and scale based on concepts such as the gross global sport product (GGSP). Although there will be attempts to restrict and protect segments of the industry based on national bias and policies, the future portends an almost seamless integration and movement of goods, services, and personnel on a grand global scale (Tuller, 1991). International trade agreements will begin to have a direct impact on the industry, as most sports will be escalating the export and import of international talent at all competitive levels. International exchanges in a broad cross section of sports at youth levels will also be commonplace (Pitts & Stotlar, 1996).

National and international sport federations will challenge professional leagues and franchises for global market share of trademark licensing and merchandise. These federations will also profit from expanding television revenues made possible through worldwide cable deregulation. Name recognition and brand awareness of teams, athletes, and products will become global. These events will bring a host of new challenges to the sport industry, which will be compounded by cultural differences, national laws, and customs (Pitts & Stotlar, 1996).

Concerns about gender equity, diversity, and equal access for athletes with disabilities will become prominent by 2000 (Dodd, 1994). The growth

and expansion of professional team sport leagues for women, particularly in North America, will give rise to expanded marketing and management opportunities. The Paralympic Games and the Special Olympics will achieve major event status through increased television, media, and spectator appeal. These trends will help provide expansion of jobs in the international marketplace in all sport-related areas for women, older people, and individuals with disabilities. Farsighted and socially responsible consumer-oriented companies will stand to gain the most from these developments (Carr-Ruffino, 1996).

A new order of elite decision makers will assume command of the global sport industry based on pragmatic alliances between leagues, international federations, television networks, and corporate sponsors. Corporations will begin to seek brand identification with a particular sport, leading to the formation of corporate and national team alliances (Badenhausen, Nixolov, Alkin, & Ozanian, 1997). New sports like in-line skating, triathlon, snowboarding, and mountain biking will emerge; plus, sports will redefine or expand themselves, such as roller hockey, beach volleyball, and endurance kayaking. All these sports will flourish due to broad, cross-generational participation and to their appeal as televised events that garner the support of lifestyle-oriented corporations. Expanded leisure time for elite and middle classes in South America, Asia, and parts of Africa will continue to fuel expansion of golf, tennis, and other leisure and recreation sports worldwide. Expanded life expectancy will continue to support an international sport and leisure travel industry, necessitating expansion of facilities (Patrick, 1995). These developments will plunge the international sport industry more deeply into debates related to the impact of sport and recreation on the environment (Muench & Armend, 1995). The International Olympic Committee has created a commission and a policy position regarding concerns about the enormity of the impact of the Olympic Games on local and regional environments. No less noteworthy have been the land use conflicts about building large-scale leisure and sport resorts in third world countries, golf courses in sensitive mountain terrain or tropical rain forests, and stadia and arenas in environmentally or economically sensitive areas. A more in-depth discussion of ecotourism is in chapter 16.

There will be expanded career opportunities in areas dealing with jurisdiction and dispute resolution related to international athletes' rights, doping and drug use and abuse, the relocation of franchises from one nation to another, and other policy matters. By 2000, international and national sport federations, professional leagues, sport marketing agencies, cable and network television and radio, arenas and facilities, fitness clubs, and sport product corporations will give hiring preference to individuals with backgrounds oriented to the global marketplace.

So, what should an aspiring sport manager do to get a head start on the future? Those who have the courage to take reasonable risks based on sound research, knowledge, and experience will be rewarded. The road maps outlining the future of the internationalization of the sports industry are rapidly changing and continuously being rewritten. Many clues, however, already exist in the allied fields of international business studies and multicultural management studies. Flexibility, cultural sensitivity, and understanding, coupled with communications and language skills, provide the foundation for entry into the international sport domain.

## Summary

The two factors that determine whether a sport is international are (a) the degree or regularity to which an organization is focused on international activity, and (b) the context in which a person or organization operates within the sport enterprise. Since 1972, several events (e.g., commercialization of the Olympics, Canada's hockey victory over the USSR, Nixon's Ping-Pong diplomacy, and several rules changes) have had a profound effect on sport, and international sport has been redefined. Athletes are now recruited from all over the world by both professional and amateur teams, sport marketing has moved into the international arena, and sport businesses have become part of the global economy. Professional ice hockey is a good example of how the sport industry has benefited from globalization. Hockey might expand to Europe, television networks are waiting for the opportunity to broadcast the games, corporate sponsors are lining up, and a women's ice hockey league is being considered.

Individuals who wish to work in international sport should be familiar with treaties and trade agreements, know the structure of international sport governance, understand the international working environment, and be adept with modern communication technology. Reading relevant literature, attending professional meetings, and conducting informational interviews are wise strategies. The future of international sport promises continued expansion and should bring many opportunities for well-prepared sport managers.

## Learning Activity

The World Championships Are Coming to Your City! Create a student group (4 - 5) and select a sport that is on the Olympic Games, Pan American Games, World University Games, or Paralympic Games program of events. The international sport federation (IF) of your sport has awarded the United States through its NGB the right to host the World Championships in this sport, to be held 3 to 4 years hence. Your group has recently been formed to act as the bid organizing committee from your city to compete for the right to host this event. Your group must prepare a preliminary report and presentation to submit to the executive committee of the NGB of your sport at its annual convention. The executive committee of the NGB will take a vote to determine which city will be awarded this bid. Recently, this World Championships has been integrated to include Paralympic athletes and events in its official program.

# For More Information

Here are some publications for you to look over.

## Publications and Reference Materials

- *World Atlas*
- *The Olympian (USOC)*
- *USOC Fact Book*
- *Olympic Review (IOC)*
- *The Economist*
- *Business Week*
- *Wall Street Journal*
- *Financial World*
- *USA Today*
- *The Sports Market Place*
- *The Sports Business Daily*
- *Journal of Sport Management*
- *The European*

## International Sport Publications

- *Agent & Manager*
- *Sports Business (Canada)*
- *Amusement Business*
- *Sports Industry News*
- *Athletic Business Magazine*
- *Sports Licensing International*
- *CBI or Club Industry*
- *Sportsearch*
- *European Sponsorship Report*
- *European TV Sports*
- *Team Licensing Business*
- *GAISF Calendar of International Competition*
- *Team Marketing Report*
- *IEG Sponsorship Report*
- *Palaestra*

- *IEG Directory of Sponsorship Marketing*
- *International Herald Tribune*
- *The Licensing Book*
- *Sporting Goods Dealer*
- *Sport Marketing Quarterly*
- *International Handbook for the Sporting Goods Industry*

## Professional Associations

- Australian/New Zealand Association for Sport Management
- North American Society for Sport Management
- European Society for Sport Management
- National Sport Federation (sport of your choice)
- People-to-People Sports Committee
- Sport for Understanding
- Sports Facilities, International
- International Association for Sports Information
- International Federation of Timekeepers
- Cultural Exchange and Sports Society
- World Federation of the Sporting Goods Industry
- World Leisure and Recreation Association

## Conference and Trade Shows

- NSF/NGB Annual Conventions
- Olympic Congress
- International Sports Summit
- National Sporting Goods Show
- Super Show
- Athletic Business Conference/IHRSRA Annual Convention

# Job Opportunities

## Positions in International Sports Marketing Training Program

The world's #1 international sports product corporation seeks qualified candidates for positions within the company's new International Marketing & Development Division training program. B.S. in sport management or related field required. Two to four years experience in international marketing and sales with a knowledge of emerging economies a plus. Must be willing to complete a two year training program. Excellent oral and written communication skills are expected.

## Event Site Manager-International Mountain Biking Series

International event management company seeks candidates for this position for the company's new International Mountain Bike Series. B.S. in sport management or related field required, with at least two years experience in event management and international sport preferred. Successful candidate must be able to do extensive traveling and to relocate for periods up to 45-60 days to race sites in the United States, Canada, Japan and Europe during late spring and summer. Prior mountain bike racing experience and a second language required. Salary range is $25,000-$30,000.

## Marketing Fulfillment Associate-FIFA '99 Women's World Cup Soccer

International sport marketing firm seeks applicants for this position to act as account representative to major corporate clients in company's FIFA World Cup Soccer sponsor fulfillment program. B.S. in sport management or related field required, M.B.A. or masters degree preferred. A background of at least two years of sport marketing and sales experience is a must. Candidate must demonstrate excellent oral and written communication skills. Fluency in a second language is a plus. Position requires extensive travel and on-site fulfillment support for clients. Salary range is $28,000-$36,000.

## Delegation Director-2000 Summer Paralympic Games

The United States Olympic Committee invites applications for qualified candidates for the position of Delegation Director for the US Paralympic Team selected to compete in the 2000 Summer Paralympic Games in Sydney, Australia. M.S. in sport management or related field preferred with two to four years experience in event management, international sport and disabled sport preferred. Successful candidate must be able to do extensive traveling and to relocate for 45 day during the conduct of the Games. Prior Olympic/Paralympic experience a plus.

## Regional Sales Manager-Latin America

A leading multi-national sports product manufacturer seeks qualified candidates for this position. B.S. in sport management or related field is required, with M.B.A. or masters degree in international marketing preferred. A background in sport and fitness is a must. Fluency in Spanish, plus three to five years experience in international marketing and sales in developing markets is required. Applicant must be familiar with the cultures and economic structures of Caribbean Rim countries. Must be willing to relocate to corporate divisional office in Mexico City.

## Assistant Director of International Development

The National Hockey League seeks qualified applicants for this position. B.S. in sport management, business or related field required, an M.B.A. in international business/marketing preferred. Fluency in German or Russian and two to four years of work experience in sales and marketing a must. Duties include overseeing and expanding NHL Enterprise merchandising, licensing and television agreements with firms throughout Europe. Prior experience in hockey as a player or at management level is a plus.

# Section IV

# Professional Development in Sport Management

**P**rofessional development includes such elements as striving for a high standard of performance, understanding hierarchies and corporate cultures, working with volunteers, demonstrating professionalism, practicing good business etiquette, and adopting an ethical creed. Equally important are the cultivation of a professional image, values, attitudes, and behaviors. Professional development also encompasses appreciating diversity, being aware of environmental responsibility, developing good communication skills, and maintaining a record of excellent academic achievement.

The process of professional development begins during your college years. You might, in fact, need this information sooner than you think. Within 1 or 2 years, you will probably engage in a field experience in which you will be expected to understand the professional environment and to function appropriately in it. The information in the following two chapters will help you meet that challenge with skill and confidence.

# Chapter 20

# Professional Style

**Beverly R.K. Zanger**
Bowling Green State University

---

## Learning Objectives

After studying this chapter, you will be able to

1. discuss style as an individual perception;

2. explain the role of values, attitudes, and behaviors in professional style;

3. compare the communication problems that exist in "The Three Johns" with those problems present in the Johari Window;

4. describe style progress using the Image Path Model; and

5. estimate your position on the Oral Presentation Inventory.

---

Professional style is an important element for success in an individual's sport management career. By presenting yourself professionally to an interviewer, you can emphasize the positive qualities that you bring to the position. Because human dynamics contribute to the cultural environment of the workplace, the prospective employer is looking for a professional person with a style to complement the company's organizational behavior. It is suggested that individuals bring three selves into the workplace: the real self, the perceived self, and the self they want to be. Now is a good time for you to look into your image mirror for your three selves and (a) identify the real you,

(b) acknowledge the perceived you, and (c) contemplate the person you want to be.

This chapter offers an opportunity to examine individual performance, explore style development, and determine individual style. The content

### Learning Activity

Consider the following statement: "This above all, to thine own self be true." (*Hamlet* Act I, Scene 3—Polonius to his son, Laertes). Name people you know who exemplify this code.

includes descriptions of values, attitudes, and behaviors and an introduction to perceptual awareness, using a historical time line and problem-solving example. The purpose of this material is to encourage you to relate better with those whose frames of reference and subsequent perceptions are different and to revitalize or enlighten your information about human relations and interaction in the workplace. Your point of view may change depending on your specific environment.

The Image Path Model addresses skill, technique, and style, using public speaking as the vehicle to apply the model. You can test your oral presentation skills through the Zanger's Inventory.

## Elements of Professional Style

Style is an individual perception—each of us has our own idea of style. "Now, that's style" is a remark we hear often, and it could refer to clothes, cars, or people. Let's concentrate on people by discussing the perception of an individual's performance and the determination of an individual's style.

## Perception

Perception is the act of interpreting what is happening in a surrounding environment, which can be family, school, friends, jobs, TV, global politics, government actions, and social concerns. Perception is influenced by previous experiences and values, and these are singular to each individual. Values, attitudes, and behaviors can affect how we mentally process, emotionally absorb, and physically accept experiences. Changes in values can occur in extreme situations with a shattering experience. "If something significantly affects us and forces a reassessment of our gut-level values, then we may change. . . . The common denominator of *Significant Emotional Events* (SEEs) is a challenge and a disruption to our present behavior patterns and beliefs" (Massey, 1979, p. 18). Examples of SEEs are the death of a loved one, terminal illness, losing two front teeth, and winning a million dollars.

## Values, Attitudes, and Behaviors

**Values**, **attitudes**, and **behaviors** continually influence professional style, but people's behaviors may or may not coincide with their attitudes. When inconsistency occurs between behavior and attitude, a facade or false front becomes observable, and what we see is not necessarily what exists. The following case study illustrates some discrepancies in values, attitudes, and behavior.

### Seeing Isn't Always Believing

Two supervisors are observing an employee's work. They are complimentary about the speed, accuracy, and quality of the employee's work. They discuss the consistency of performance, including an excellent attendance record. All in all, this worker's evaluation is outstanding. Now, what is the worker thinking at this time? "Oh! I hate this job. I gotta get out of this job. I want to do more with my life."

1. Explain the facade that the worker is using.
2. What is the inconsistency in the worker's actions and attitudes?
3. What beliefs are indicated in this scenario?

Interpretation of an individual's performance by an observer or even by the performer is complex and multidimensional and assumes the individualism of the perceiver. Think of the barrage of perceptions that confronts us each day. No wonder we are misinterpreted, even within ourselves. Refer to chapter 21 for a discussion of the importance of values when choosing a career and chapter 11 for information on "seeing" and "believing."

### Learning Activity

Discuss the perceptual influences of the following statement. "People need to recognize that as they join with others to discuss ethics, the ethical basis from which they are viewing situations needs to be integrated with the others involved, if a single group-ethic basis for actions is to be developed." *Ethics, Yours, Mine, or Ours*? Charles W. White, J. Eugene Kangas, William A. Kennedy (1994).

## Time and Communication Concepts in Job Performance

This viewpoint on perception, values, attitudes, and behavior raises two questions for conceptual-

© Anthony Neste

Interpretation assumes the individualism of the perceiver. That is, a person's interpretation of a performance usually depends on past experiences or what he or she "brings to" the viewing of the performance.

izing an individual's performance. First, what is your relationship to others from a historical time line perspective? Morris Massey (1979) suggests that the events remembered at 10 years of age reflect your values and act as a basis for processing information later in life. For example, you are now in class with many other students, with ages ranging from 18 to 28 years. Some of them are 5 years younger than you and some are 5 years older than you. What a 23-year old remembers at 5 years of age is only the birth date of the 18-year old. Consider the difference between what the 28-year old remembers at 10 years of age when the 18-year old was just born. It is evident your perceptions will differ from a great-grandmother who cooked on a wood-burning stove and certainly didn't have a computer then, but may own one now! Although age is not the only consideration in

the differences in perception and information processing, the historical dateline can clarify and initiate respect for others' perceptions and open communication lines.

Interaction with others presents the second question for conceptualizing individual performance. What is your perceptual reaction when communicating with people? There are many responses when considering this query. Two theories that offer answers come from the mid-1800s in "The Three Johns" by Oliver Wendell Holmes and the mid-1900s with the Johari Window by Joseph Luft and Harry Ingham.

## "The Three Johns"

In 1858 Oliver Wendell Holmes submitted the initial essay, "The Autocrat of the Breakfast Table" for the *Atlantic Monthly.* "The Three Johns" is a segment from this essay and the following excerpt, published in 1891, discusses a conversation.

It is not easy, at the best, for two persons talking together to make the most of each other's thoughts, there are so many of them. . . . When John and Thomas, for instance, are talking together, it is natural enough that among the six there should be more or less confusion and misapprehension . . . that there are at least six personalities distinctly to be recognized as taking part in that dialogue between John and Thomas.

### Three Johns

1. The real John; known only to his Maker.
2. John's ideal John; never the real one, and often very unlike him.
3. Thomas's ideal John; never the real John, nor John's John, but often very unlike either.

### Three Thomases

1. The real Thomas.
2. Thomas' ideal Thomas.
3. John's ideal Thomas.

Only one of the three Johns is taxed; only one can be weighed on a platform balance; but the other two are just as important in the conversation. Let us suppose the real John to be old, dull, and ill-looking. But as the Higher Powers have not conferred on men [sic] the gift of seeing themselves in the true light, John very possibly conceives himself to be youthful, witty, and fascinating, and talks from the point of view of this ideal. Thomas, again believes him to be an artful rogue, we will say; therefore he *is* so far as Thomas's attitude in the conversation is concerned, an artful rogue, though really simple and stupid. The same conditions apply to the three Thomases. It follows that, until a man can be found who knows himself as his Maker knows him, or who sees himself as others see him, there must be at least six persons engaged in every dialogue between two. Of these the least important, philosophically speaking, is the one that we have called the real person. No wonder two disputants often get angry, when there are six of them talking and listening all at the same time. (Holmes, 1891, p. 52-54)

What perceptual questions occur during interpersonal communication? Is there disagreement? What is the basis for not seeing eye to eye? Answers could include respect for others' past experiences and for different points of view. Even when information isn't available, these answers are paramount to conversation between two people or among six individuals as described by Oliver Wendell Holmes. Remember, three of those persons are you!

## Johari Window

About 100 years after Oliver Wendell Holmes expressed his opinions on people's perception during conversation, *Joseph Luft* and *Harry Ingham* developed a graphic model of awareness in interpersonal relations called the Johari Window (see figure 20.1). The title is a combination of the authors' first names, Joe and Harry. Like "The Three Johns" this model also discusses the ambiguities, facades, and voids that exist when communicating in a variety of situations. These settings can be everyday family conversation, a fraternity gathering, a department session, or an annual stockholders meeting.

The following explanation of the Johari Awareness Model is provided by the author, Joseph Luft (1969). The four quadrants represent the total person in relation to other persons. The basis for division into quadrants is awareness of behavior, feelings, and motivation. Sometimes awareness is

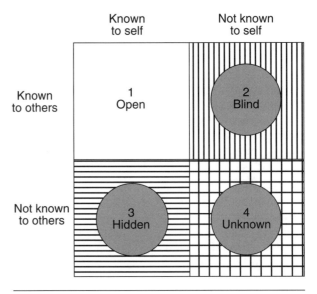

**Figure 20.1** The Johari Awareness Model.
Adapted, by permission, from Jay Hall, 1990, *Models for management: The structure of competencies* (The Woodlands, TX: Woodstead Press), 219.

shared, sometimes not. An act, a feeling, or a motive is assigned to a particular quadrant based on who knows about it. As awareness changes, the quadrant to which the psychological state is assigned changes. . . . Each quadrant is defined:

1. Quadrant 1, the open quadrant, refers to behavior, feelings, and motivation known to self and to others.
2. Quadrant 2, the blind quadrant, refers to behavior, feelings, and motivation known to others but not to self.
3. Quadrant 3, the hidden quadrant, refers to behavior, feelings, and motivation known to self but not to others.
4. Quadrant 4, the unknown quadrant, refers to behavior, feelings, and motivation known neither to self nor to others.

When two strangers meet, windowpane 4 Unknown is a window that doesn't allow the participants to see in or out—the window is a blackout. Remember, the need for respect and understanding of another's frame of reference is essential to open dialogue and to see each other through a window of communication.

When lifelong friends, who might be sisters, companions, or spouses, engage in dialogue, windowpane 1 Open suggests a nonthreatening exchange. The interaction is relaxed because each knows the other's likes, dislikes, biases, dreams, political views, religious views, and much more.

Opening the windows of communication through respect and understanding can be an acumen to individual performance and an identification of individual professional style. Naturally, not everyone will view performance and style in the same manner, because as we discussed earlier, individuals' past experience and frame of reference influence their emotions, logic, and reasoning.

## The Image Path and Professional Style

The following concept offers a process for understanding style (Zanger, 1981). The concept is titled Image Path and is defined by a model that involves style and the two adjunct elements of skill and technique. Definitions of skill, technique, and style are specific to this concept.

The image path concept is critical for mobility in professional fields such as sport management.

### Learning Activity

In small groups, discuss windowpanes 2 and 3. Give examples of a setting in each situation when information is missing from one or the other communicators.

### Learning Activity

Read "The Johari Window: Solving Sport Management Communication Problems" listed in the references at the end of this book (Horine, 1990). Write a paper or have a class discussion about how understanding the concepts in the Johari Window would help you be a more effective sport manager.

How do you perceive professional style? Describing someone as professional is a compliment, implying proper business ethics, good service, and quality products. In addition, professionalism involves a neat appearance, pleasant voice, and fluent but succinct speaking and writing abilities.

## Skill

Skill is the basic learning, the foundation. For example, speaking, writing, counting, running, dribbling, and pivoting are basic skills. Basic skills are present in all areas of learning, and they are stored in our amazing memory banks. Information appears on an invisible disk that we automatically boot up—almost like having a gateway to the Internet operating inside us. Just as you never forget how to ride a bicycle, you have memory bank capabilities for any level of learning.

## Technique

Technique is the development of basic skills into specific approaches and defined ranges of abilities. For example, people who are interested in dance will study with certain masters or dance schools. You go to basketball, hockey, or football camps to study with specific coaches. Writers learn techniques ranging from journalism to fiction, and actors adopt particular methods and have lifetime coaches. Can you give an example in gymnastics or ice skating?

© Daily Illini

Technique is the development of basic skills into specific approaches and defined ranges of abilities.

## Style

Now the coup de grace, style, makes its entrance. After you have developed skill and technique, you add *your* signature to the performance of a skating routine, a football pass, or a reading of an original poem. Style is personal, singular, and one of a kind. We can identify the silhouette of an athlete just by watching the movement. We can identify an author by reading a passage, a speaker just by listening to the voice, or the lead guitarist by listening to a CD. So style is what individuals give of themselves to performances. A performance built on basic skill and technique becomes one of a kind when style is present.

The Image Path Model (see figure 20.2) shows how skills and techniques identify the critical path of individual style and, as shown by the continuous line, the growth pattern for a lifetime. The model is an open concept representing continuous skill practice, changes in technique, and perfection of style. Because it is so essential within the sport management field, public speaking is a viable exercise for testing the Image Path Model and for expounding on the concept.

## Implementing the Image Path With Public Speaking

Public speaking is a nightmare for some people and a pleasure for others. What makes this experience elicit such an individual response? Problems in basic skill, technique, method, or style development could create the schism.

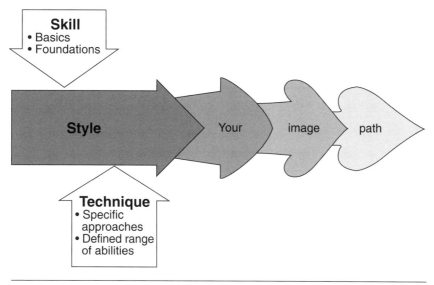

**Figure 20.2**    The Image Path Model.

Using the Image Path Model, mentally assess where you are on the continuum of skill, technique, and style in public speaking. This assessment might help you determine how much skill learning, practice, and technique coaching you need to improve your speaking ability. Zanger's Oral Presentation Inventory, shown in figure 20.3, may help you identify your specific strengths and weaknesses in public speaking.

More important than scores on the inventory, a look at the list of inventory questions in reverse order will give you clues to better speaking. If you concentrate on numbers 9 and 10, prepara-tion and practice, you will lessen problems with 1 through 8.

This inventory could help you identify basic skill problems and correct them. For instance breathing exercises will help solve numbers 1 through 4. You can improve techniques with the assistance of a speech coach or joining a speech club. Style is accumulated, developed, and refined over a lifetime.

When you prepare a speech, do you think about speakers you have heard in the past? Why did you listen? Was the reason the location, the message, the delivery, the performer, or a combination of

---

**Zanger's Oral Presentation Inventory**

|  | No | Seldom | Sometimes | Yes |
|---|---|---|---|---|
| 1. Do you have nervous jitters before a speech? | 1 | 2 | 3 | 4 |
| 2. Do you breathe shallowly before and during your speech? | 1 | 2 | 3 | 4 |
| 3. Does your voice quiver during your speech? | 1 | 2 | 3 | 4 |
| 4. Do your hands and legs shake during your speech? | 1 | 2 | 3 | 4 |
| 5. Do you fail to identify (see) individuals in the audience? | 1 | 2 | 3 | 4 |
| 6. Do you avoid eye contact with the audience? | 1 | 2 | 3 | 4 |
| 7. Do you feel uncomfortable with your appearance? | 1 | 2 | 3 | 4 |
| 8. Do you overuse "verbal fillers" (e.g., *and*, *uh*, *um*, and *ah*)? | 1 | 2 | 3 | 4 |
| 9. Do you fail to research and outline your topic when preparing your speech? | 1 | 2 | 3 | 4 |
| 10. Do you fail to practice your speech aloud several times before delivering the presentation? | 1 | 2 | 3 | 4 |

**Figure 20.3**    Zanger's Oral Presentation Inventory.
*Note.* Scores between 40 and 30 points indicate a need for basic skill courses in oral presentations. Scores between 29 and 20 points indicate a need for technique coaching that will build on established skills. Scores between 19 and 10 indicate a need for continued experimentation with individual style.

the active listening factors that proclaim the speaker's charisma? What do you think are the active listening factors for the following persons?

- Religious speakers
- Teachers
- Humorists
- Special event speakers
- Stand-up comedians
- Political speakers

There are many approaches for stylizing the delivery of a speech. Listed here are four possibilities.

1. Conversational style. "It is so good to see you, talk with you, and have time to enjoy your company." A conversational tone treats the audience as if they were one person.
2. Persuasive style. "The company urges you to accept this offer that is endorsed by your fellow workers. Proof of support is . . . " If you need to convince your audience, debate tactics could be helpful.
3. Entertainment style. A little smile adds a great deal to your face value. Humor is delicate, tasteful, appropriate, and never offensive. A sense of well-timed humor can spark an audience.
4. Dramatic style. "The sun was hidden from this small town by dark and ominous clouds. Warnings had been flashed across the screen, then the television set lost power." The drama of a story line or mental picture could attract the audience.

Be sure the styles that you create are comfortable for you and appropriate for your listeners; your goal is to present content to an actively listening audience.

We have used public speaking as a vehicle for explaining style, but we could have chosen any of the arts, sports, or sciences to illustrate how to formulate your individual style. As Dorothy V. Harris (1990) stated, "Our personal beliefs and expectations about outcomes have a great deal to do with the actual outcomes. As beliefs and thoughts about our performances change, the limits of performances actually do change! Excellence in any pursuit is largely a matter of believing we are capable. At the same time, each of us must commit to maximizing our abilities, working hard, and preparing for the situation" (pp. 171-72).

As you pursue your professional career, review the properties of perceptual awareness, people's behavior, time lines, and interaction with others. Your individual performance can improve as you continue professional growth, and with conscious effort, your individual style has the opportunity to emerge.

Style is unique; it represents you. Take the suggestions in this chapter and mix and match them to fit you as an individual. Skills and techniques can have positive effects on performance but most important is your signature of style.

## Summary

Professional style is an individual perception, which is the act of interpreting what is happening in a surrounding environment. Values are an integral part of our frame of reference, and attitudes are a collection of influences that may or may not be based on fact. Behavior is our observed action, resulting in the perception of us by others. Morris Massey offers a method of understanding the basis of our perception, and Oliver Wendell Holmes, Joseph Luft, Harry Ingham, and Beverly Zanger offer concepts for communicating. These examples address perceptual reactions of all those involved in the communication process and illustrate the variety of each individual's point of view.

Business communities want a professional employee who possesses skills, techniques, and style. Skill is the basic learning, technique is developing basic skills into a specific approach and a defined range of abilities, and style is the individual's signature given to the performance. The Image Path Model presents a method for managing professional style.

Public speaking is a vehicle you can use to relate the Image Path Model to your ultimate stylization. In this chapter we explain a variety of styles for public speaking and provide an inventory to assess oral presentation and test your skill, technique, and style.

## Learning Activity

What does the following statement by Mary Lou Retton mean to you? "As simple as it sounds, we all must try to be the best person we can: by making the best choices, by making the most of the talents we've been given, by treating others as we would like to be treated" (National Girls and Women in Sports Day, 1996)?

**Chapter 21**

# Your Professional Future in Sport Management

**Linda S. Koehler**
University of the Pacific
**Janet B. Parks and JoAnn Kroll**
Bowling Green State University

## Learning Objectives

After studying this chapter, you will be able to

1. discuss the concepts of professional preparation, professional attitude, and professional development as three important elements for success;

2. explain unique aspects of the baccalaureate, master's, and doctoral degrees;

3. discuss three components of the undergraduate sport management curriculum;

4. describe the course work and content areas required by NASPE-NASSM for sport management programs at the undergraduate, master's, and doctoral levels;

5. discuss the major competencies and skills needed for successful careers in sport management in the 21st century;

6. explain the benefits of field experiences for the three sport management constituencies;

7. describe the process for investigating sport management programs at the master's or doctoral level;

8. discuss the components of personal appearance, work transition and adjustment, and manners as each is reflected in your professional attitude;

9. describe the important elements of planning a career; and

10. elaborate on the opportunities in international sport management.

In previous chapters, you learned about the disciplinary foundations of sport management, the history of management theories, critical concepts of organizational behavior, and sport management career fields that hold professional opportunities for you. This, the final chapter, is your springboard to the future, in which you will find information to prepare you for success in the sport industries.

Three elements necessary for success are (a) professional preparation, (b) professional attitude, and (c) professional development.

# Professional Preparation

Over 200 colleges and universities in the United States and Canada offer programs in sport management professional preparation (NASPE-NASSM, 1993). The academic degrees offered at these institutions are the baccalaureate (bachelor's), the master's, and the doctorate. Depending on your career goals, you will need one, two, or all three of these degrees.

## Baccalaureate Degree

Professional preparation at the baccalaureate level is typically called undergraduate education. Baccalaureate programs prepare students for entry-level positions, such as assistant managers, at a variety of sites, including but certainly not limited to health clubs, community recreation programs, professional sport teams, corporate fitness programs, hotels, resorts, marinas, intercollegiate athletics departments, and minor league baseball teams. Most undergraduate sport management professional preparation programs include three components: major courses, field experiences, and general education courses.

### Major Courses in Sport Management

Standards for sport management academic programs have been developed through a joint effort of the National Association for Sport and Physical Education (NASPE) and the North American Society for Sport Management (NASSM). The NASPE-NASSM (1993) program approval standards require undergraduate programs to offer course content directly related to sport in the following 10 areas: the behavioral dimension (e.g., sport sociology, sport psychology, philosophy of sport, sport for individuals with differing abilities), management and organizational skills, ethics, marketing, communication, finance, economics, legal aspects, governance, and field experiences. Programs do not have to dedicate a separate course to each content area, but the content must be covered somewhere within the program.

The course work designated by NASPE-NASSM is focused on sport. It is important to remember, however, that you are not being *trained* for careers in sport management; you are being *educated* for

lives in which you hope to enjoy positions in sport management. Your goal of entering the sport management field, however, might not materialize. Moreover, even if you do begin your career in sport management, you might decide later to pursue some other line of work. In either case, the course content prescribed by NASPE-NASSM is sufficiently broad that you should be prepared to assume positions in a variety of other vocational fields (Parks, 1991; Parks & Parra, 1994).

### Major Competencies in Fitness Management

Curriculum standards are also in place for professional preparation programs in exercise science and fitness management (NASPE, 1995). These standards were established by the Applied Exercise Science Council of NASPE, and they reflect the areas of competency you will need to develop during your undergraduate years. These competencies include scientific foundations (e.g., human anatomy, physiology, biomechanics) and competencies in exercise prescription for typical and special populations. Additional requirements include understanding health promotion, administrative tasks, human relations, and professional development. Practical experiences, such as an internship, are also required. According to the council, these standards will provide you with the entry-level skills and knowledge you will need to perform successfully in a variety of fitness settings.

The curriculum standards for sport management and the competencies required for fitness management are consistent with the broad skills identified by Patterson and Allen (1996) as those needed to succeed in careers of the 21st century: (a) computer literacy in all types of technology; (b) flexibility and adaptability to handle ever-changing roles and management styles; (c) diversity in ability to function and work with people from a broad range of ages, cultures, and learning styles; (d) language skills—especially knowledge of multiple languages for the global marketplace; (e) team players—networking and negotiating skills a must; (f) learning skills and continuous reeducation—we all must be lifelong learners; (g) personal career planning skills (self-assessment, inner worth, current skills); (h) global awareness/orientation—knowledge of a country and region as well as the culture of the people there; (i) oral and written communications skills—become even more valuable as corporations flatten; (j) people must be self-starters; (k) self-comfort—the company no longer defines the worker; (l) strong ethical framework; (m) environmental scanning skills—knowing where your company is going; where the opportunities will be, see which direction to flex forward (p. 61).

## Field Experiences

Field experiences are designed to provide you with first-hand opportunities to learn about the responsibilities and scope of managers while working in a sport or fitness setting. Typically, there are two levels of field experiences: the **practicum** and the internship. After meeting the selection requirements of your university, you can obtain a practicum or internship position at a wide variety of organizations and agencies. Within each organization, you will be given responsibilities commensurate with the objectives of the experience. The following guidelines might help you in selecting a field experience:

- Choose a reputable organization so you will have a good learning experience.

- Be ready to be challenged by the level of responsibility you are given.

- Maintain open communication between you, your on-site supervisor, and your faculty supervisor.

- Keep copies of anything you create (e.g., flyers, press releases, manuals) and include them in your professional portfolio.

- Attempt to arrange your field experience with an agency with which you wish to be employed. If you present yourself well and do quality work, the agency might consider employing you after graduation.

- Include the field experience on your résumé. The experience will have provided you with bona fide managerial experience and will serve you well as part of your professional credentials.

## Benefits of Field Experiences

Field experiences are valuable to three constituencies: you, the student; your university; and the site at which the field experience occurs (Washburn, 1984). These experiences benefit students in a number of ways. First, they help you make the transition from student to professional. Second, they help link theory to practice. Third, the field experience provides opportunities for you to gain practical experience and test the ideas you developed in the classroom. Fourth, field experiences

provide opportunities for you to evaluate yourself while being evaluated by others. Finally, field experiences might serve as a precursor to employment (Cuneen & Sidwell, 1994; Sutton, 1989).

Casella and Brougham (1995) stated "Work experience gained while still in college is being reported as an important factor in career success, particularly in the first year after graduation" (p. 55). As you demonstrate your talents, you might create a niche for yourself in the organization where the field experience is occurring. Casella and Brougham concluded that you benefit from work experiences before graduation by building networks, improving self-organization, establishing a greater sense of responsibility, expanding work skills, learning more about personal strengths and values, and gaining self-confidence.

Field experiences also provide important benefits for the sponsoring university and the cooperating site. The university benefits because of the link to community agencies. As faculty and administrators become in closer touch with the needs of the working world, they can upgrade the curriculum to keep it in step with the world outside of campus (Casella & Brougham, 1995). The sport enterprise (the cooperating site) also benefits from your input into the organization. Practica and internships provide sport enterprises with motivated, career-minded workers at a low cost. These enterprises can reduce their recruiting and training costs by hiring the top interns into career track positions.

## General Education

The general education component of the undergraduate curriculum is vital because university graduates should demonstrate understanding and capabilities beyond those acquired in their major courses. As university graduates, you will be expected to express yourself well, both in writing and in speaking. You should understand and be able to discuss topics such as art, music, language, literature, drama, history, political science, dance, psychology, sociology, anthropology, physical sciences, and human movement. You should be able to deal with a changing society that reflects the cultural diversity of our world. You will be expected to use critical thinking skills to generate original ideas and creative solutions to a broad spectrum of societal and global concerns. Upon graduation, you should be knowledgeable, intellectual, imaginative, socially responsible citizens who will make many positive contributions to society.

**Learning Activity**

Analyze your academic program and programs at other institutions in the context of the NASPE-NASSM standards.

## Master's Degree

As you look toward career advancement and additional responsibilities, you may choose, or be asked by your employer, to pursue a master's degree. The master's degree usually prepares you for more advanced, specialized responsibilities within your employment setting. The NASPE-NASSM (1993) program approval standards mandate that for a master's program to be approved, the following eight content areas must be available in the curriculum: management, leadership and organization in sport; research in sport; legal aspects of sport; marketing in sport; sport business in the social context; financial management in sport; ethics in sport management; and field experience in sport management.

Special features associated with sport management curricula and programs are the location of the program within the university, the industry focus of the program, and the experience and research interests of the faculty. Some sport management programs are located in departments of physical education or sport management, whereas others are housed within schools of business administration, departments of sport administration, or a variety of other units. The location of the program is of particular concern for advanced degree students because its location "unquestionably influences its orientation" (Parkhouse, 1987, p. 109). For example, students interested in the study of sport (e.g., sociology of sport, psychology of sport, or cultural anthropology) as well as the study of sport business will probably find relevant course work in units housed in departments of physical education or sport management and administration rather than in schools of business.

Another concern is the industry focus of the graduate program. Some programs are geared toward athletics administration within the educational structure (e.g., intercollegiate or high school athletics), others focus on sport management in the private sector (e.g., professional sport, fitness and health clubs), and some programs encompass both sectors. As you investigate graduate programs, you will notice that the content and requirements of each program reflect the competencies, skills, and experiences valued by the sector that serves as that unit's focus.

Examining the experience and research interests of the faculty is a critical step in selecting a graduate program. Graduate faculty should be actively involved in some type of scholarship. If you consciously choose a major professor (adviser) whose research and scholarly interests are compatible with yours and who has a record of scholarly productivity, you will increase the probability of gaining valuable research experience at the master's level. This advice is especially important for students who plan to enroll in doctoral studies after earning the master's degree.

Brassie (1989) suggests that once you have contacted a spokesperson from a graduate program, you should ask a series of questions. These questions should address the department's admission, retention, and placement practices; access to physical and human resources; the curriculum; and opportunities for interaction or exchange with other academic areas on campus. Other questions might focus on the number of graduate students admitted annually and the criteria for admission. You might ask about the availability of graduate assistantships and about the management and research experience and interests of the faculty. Finally, inquiries about prerequisites, research methods courses, exit requirements (e.g., thesis, project, or comprehensive examination), internships, and available courses in business or other disciplines will prove useful in screening the different programs (Brassie, 1989).

## Doctorate

During the past several years, because of proliferating sport management curricula in colleges and universities, more sport management professorial positions have become available. For those of you who choose to pursue a career as a professor, academic preparation at the doctoral level is essential. Doctoral study builds on the background gained at the undergraduate and master's levels and is much more specialized in its focus. Course work that should be available in doctoral programs includes foundations of research, sport management theory, specific courses related to your specialization, and an optional advanced internship (NASPE-NASSM, 1993).

In many institutions, sport management professors are expected to conduct and publish research in an effort to build the body of knowledge. Consequently, if you aspire to the professoriate, you should acquire the research skills needed to perform this aspect of your responsibilities (Parks & Bartley, 1996). As you plan your doctoral studies, it will be important to find a major professor who is an established researcher in your area of interest, has experience helping students learn to conduct and publish research, and is interested in assisting prospective professors learn the **pragmatics** of university life.

In a study of the sport management professoriate, Parks and Bartley (1996) discovered information that should be helpful to individuals considering careers in the academy. First, there is an absence of gender and racial diversity among sport management professors, with the vast majority being white males. This finding was replicated in Moore and Parkhouse's (1996) study with the additional finding that individuals with physical differences were also underrepresented in the sport management professoriate. Many faculty and administrators are committed to expanding diversity in the professoriate and would be receptive to applications from qualified candidates who would contribute to that objective.

## NASPE-NASSM Programs

You can obtain a current list of NASPE-NASSM approved sport management programs from the American Alliance for Health, Physical Education, Recreation and Dance, 1900 Association Drive, Reston, VA 22091; (800-213-7193, extension 414).

## Professional Attitude

Planning your future in sport management includes attention to one of the most important elements of your portfolio—your professional attitude. "Cultivating a positive, assertive outlook on life is the most crucial factor that makes the difference between those people who have a successful, satisfying life/career and those who do not" (Sukiennik, Raufman, & Bendat, 1992, p. 28). A professional attitude will enhance your opportunities for employment and advancement. It will also make you a more pleasant person for others to be around. That in itself is a worthy goal!

Attitude is reflected in many ways. Three of these ways are personal appearance, work transition and adjustment (including work habits), and manners. These are the attributes that recruiters evaluate during interviews.

## Personal Appearance

What kind of visual impression do you make? Upon meeting you, other people rely on your physical appearance to make judgments about you. Although this might be unfair, and although initial impressions can change after someone gets to know you, remember that you can make a first impression only once—so why not make it a good one?

The impression you make through your physical presentation is related less to physical beauty than to other factors, all of which are within your control. Some aspects of a professional appearance are listed here.

- Hygiene—Be aware that the aroma of smoke or alcohol on your breath or clothing might give negative impressions to those who come into close contact with you. In some cases, such odors can cause real physical distress to others. It may be difficult to convince an employer that you can be a role model for a healthy and fit lifestyle if tobacco or alcohol are detected during an interview.

- Posture—Your sitting and standing posture give an impression of your attitude. Again, this might be unfair, but it is nonetheless true that people will draw different conclusions about the attitude of a person who is slouching back in a chair with his or her feet on the table than from a person who is sitting erect, feet firmly planted on the floor.

- Self-confidence—You can project a sense of self-confidence by your body language, dress, pride in your accomplishments, your ability to learn from your mistakes, and your ability to accept praise and suggestions from others (Sukiennik et al., 1992). Your comfort level will increase as your confidence increases, and you will be able to focus on others, both socially and professionally.

- Hats—Although baseball caps are a staple of college students' wardrobes, there are certain situations in which caps are inappropriate. Examples of such situations are the classroom, meetings, mealtime, conferences with faculty or administrators, formal presentations (including those you make in your classes), and employment interviews. It has long been customary in North America for men to remove their hats in these situations. Now that women have begun wearing baseball caps, they should adhere to the same etiquette. Aside from being good manners, removing your cap allows others to see your face more clearly and to look into your eyes as they interact with you (figure 21.1).

■ Attire and accessories—You are entitled to choose clothing and jewelry that suit your taste. Remember, however, that employers and customers have their own ideas of what is appropriate, and they might expect you to conform. Although we would defend your right to wear a ring in your ear or in any other part of your body, we would also caution you that some employers will not be lenient in this regard. Only you can decide whether conforming to the norms of a workplace will compromise your values so much that you should look for a job elsewhere.

## Work Transition and Adjustment

Are you ready to face the challenges that will present themselves in the workplace? Are you confident in your abilities and competent in your specific job skills? Are you knowledgeable about the social, political, legislative, technological, and economic trends that have impacted your field? Now is the time to begin practicing for life in the work environment. "Successful employees recognize that the workplace is really a minisociety that sends out a constant stream of information about what is expected of its members and what the rules and limits are" (Carney & Wells, 1995, p. 178). The following tips should help you.

■ Academic preparation—Study hard and acquire the knowledge and understanding that employers expect of a college graduate.

■ Writing—The ability to express yourself in writing is one of the most important competencies a sport manager should possess. Among the many types of writing that will be expected are business correspondence (e.g., memos, cover letters, infor-

mational letters, letters of recommendation, responses to complaints, letters of commendation), reports, and technical manuals. Learn to organize your thoughts logically and to use grammar and punctuation correctly. Investing time and energy in learning to write well will pay huge dividends when you enter the professional world.

■ Development—Commit yourself to lifelong learning, both formal and informal, so you can continue to grow professionally and personally. Participation in business and professional associations increases your knowledge and expands your network of associates. Interaction with colleagues is stimulating and it allows you to grow professionally and contribute to your field.

■ Dependability—Demonstrate your commitment to the organization, supervisors, and colleagues by enthusiastically completing all job assignments within agreed upon deadlines. Your attitude toward work is referred to as your work ethic. Strive to become known as a person with a good work ethic who prepares before meetings, contributes ideas, listens to others, supports colleagues, is team oriented, and follows through on work commitments. Make sure your work is accurate, thorough, and of high quality.

■ Ethics—The mission statements of organizations help you understand their moral perspectives (DeSensi & Rosenberg, 1996); it is advisable, therefore, to become familiar with an organization's mission statement before taking a job and to conduct business in accord with it after becoming an employee.

■ Ask for help—No one expects you to know all the answers. When you start a new job, make sure you understand the duties listed on your job

**Peanuts**

**Figure 21.1**   Hats off!
Reprinted, by permission, from Charles Schultz, 1997, United Feature Syndicate, Inc.

description, what you are expected to do, and how to proceed. Listen carefully to directions, and ask for clarification of any instructions that you did not comprehend fully before beginning an assignment.

■ Teamwork—Work cooperatively with your colleagues and supervisors. Give credit to others when earned and compliment them on their accomplishments. Offer others help freely.

■ Performance appraisals—Appreciate the evaluation process, recognizing that the aim of constructive criticism is to improve your performance. The most important question to ask your supervisor is, "What can I do to be better at my job?"

■ Disagreement—If you disagree with a colleague, a supervisor, or a customer, try to do so without being disagreeable. Carney and Wells (1995) state that workplace differences or conflicts are most likely to occur "when workers are under pressure, when their responsibilities are not clear, or when their personal expectations or needs are violated. . . . Conflict situations offer ideal opportunities for clarifying personal differences and for team building" (p. 179). When viewed in this way, conflict can be healthy.

■ Environment—Understand and respect your work environment. The greatest single adjustment for a new graduate is making the transition from student to employee. Know what types of behaviors are expected in the workplace. These are often found in the organization's policy manual. Pay particular attention to the links in the chain of command. Know where you fit into the hierarchy and where everyone else fits. If you object to hierarchies, you must choose your employment site carefully because most organizations use a hierarchical system. Nevertheless, some companies use team-based systems.

■ Diversity—Appreciate and celebrate diversity of gender, race, religion, sexual orientation, ability, age, and so on. Do not engage in racist, ageist, or sexist behaviors, and let it be known that you do not appreciate such behaviors in others. There are laws to protect people from racial and sexual harassment—but the sensitive and educated person does not need laws to enforce kindness and inclusiveness.

## Manners

People who have good manners know how to make other people feel comfortable. Baldrige (1985) emphasized the importance of good manners in the workplace (1):

> Manners are the very keystone of good human relationships. They govern how people treat each other, whether in the coal mines or in a mahogany-paneled boardroom. When people who work together in either place adhere to the rules of social behavior, their workplace becomes efficient. There is an absence of confusion and wasted time. When people treat each other with consideration, they do not run into each other; there is a minimum of stumbling about feeling awkward, groping for words, or wondering what to do next. (pp. 5-6)

Baldrige continues, "Manners should be part of the curriculum of management. . . . It is a new and most important element of human management training" (p. 7).

As you prepare for a career in management, we encourage you to consider the following reminders:

■ Telephone—Clearly identify yourself and your organization or department every time you answer the telephone. When leaving your phone number on someone's voice mail system, speak distinctly and at a reasonable speed. Refrain from leaving cute or suggestive greetings on your voice mail system. Busy callers do not appreciate cleverness, especially if they are calling long distance.

■ Language—Practice using inclusive language as opposed to gender or racially biased language. The workplace of the 21st century is more likely to contain managers who are women and people of color than at any other time in history, and sensitivity to the nuances of language is one way to create a more pleasant workplace.

■ Electronic mail—Observe established protocols for various listservs and other communications on E-mail. For example, although it might be fun to exchange jokes of questionable taste on humor listservs, the same jokes would be inappropriate on listservs established for professional or scholarly discussions.

■ Thank-you letters—Through these letters, you can express gratitude to someone who provided you with information or with his or her time. A good practice to follow is to send a thank-you letter within 24 hours of a social or business contact or event. You may send thank-you letters within an organization as well as to outsiders.

Making a habit of thanking individuals who help you will go a long way toward establishing your reputation as a true professional.

- Travel—If you use laptop computers or cellular phones on airplanes, be considerate of the people who are sharing the limited space with you. Do not appropriate the middle seat and tray for your papers. Ask your seat mates if they mind your typing or talking, and obey the captain when she or he directs you to put away your electronic devices.

- International experiences—Communicating with and relating to people from other cultures (intercultural relations) require that you learn the protocols, courtesies, customs, and behaviors of other countries. To avoid embarrassment, investigate the customs of foreign countries before traveling there and before entertaining visitors from other cultures. For example, in some countries you will receive gifts and will be expected to give gifts. In Japan, you present your business card with both hands, making sure the type is facing the recipient and is right side up (Axtell, 1990). When receiving a business card, read and digest the information printed on the card; it is considered rude to just pocket it. Never give a Hindu anything made of cowhide or an Indian Muslim anything made of pigskin. This is insulting to their religions.

- Handshake—Use a firm handshake, but do not crush the other person's hand. Grasp the entire hand, not just the fingers. The latter technique is painful, particularly if the person being grasped is wearing rings or has arthritis. Adjust your grip to the state of health and physical strength of the person you are greeting.

- Regardless of your gender, stand when others (e.g., supervisors, customers, guests) enter, especially if they are older than you.

- Refrain from chewing gum and using toothpicks, tobacco, and cigarettes at work, during an interview, or while others are eating.

- Outlook—Look on the positive side of every situation. Optimistic people view problems as opportunities to exercise creativity, resolve difficult situations, and make things happen. The ability to stay calm and composed in stressful situations is a sign of professional maturity. Enthusiasm and a positive self-image are important parts of a professional attitude. A good way to retain a positive attitude and build self-confidence is to reinforce and reward yourself for something you did well each day!

# Professional Development

Many opportunities for professional development are available to you after you obtain your academic degree. Participating in business and professional associations; reading trade and professional journals; and attending seminars, workshops, and conferences sponsored by universities, professional associations, and private companies can help you keep informed and current within your profession. Your professional development is an ongoing process and continues long after you graduate. In addition to continuing education courses or workshops, your professional development will continue as you move into your new position and are faced with the daily challenges of your work.

## Career Planning

Your work choices are more than single exercises in your life. They are based on your total development as an individual and as a growing, changing entity who possesses past life experiences and anticipates the future. As you begin to learn more about yourself and the world of sport management, you will be able to make wise and realistic career choices. Planning for your career is important, and you should begin to think about it now so you can make wise decisions when you graduate.

Some people approach the career decision process with a great deal of apprehension, fearing that they will become trapped into a lifelong commitment that can never change (Michelozzi, 1992). Kroll and Moomaw (1990), however, point out five factors that influence career decisions. First, your academic major does not necessarily predict your career choice. Because careers follow from skills, interests, and values, there is a chance that you will secure a job outside your major field of study. Second, you may not progress in a direct path from college to your ultimate career objective. As you develop new abilities and interests, your career patterns may change, and you may switch career fields three to five times in your lifetime (Sukiennik et al., 1992).

Third, the career planning process is not set in stone. You are continually developing talents and abilities, and the skills that you are acquiring through your course work, leisure activities, volunteer experiences, and summer and part-time jobs may alter your long-range career plans. Fourth, upon graduation, you will have a broad range of skills and talents that will make you marketable in the working world. With a little prompting, you can recognize and learn to appreciate your special abilities.

Finally, although career counselors can not provide instant solutions, they can be extremely helpful in providing guidance and direction in assessing your vocational interests, identifying skills, writing résumés and cover letters, preparing for interviews, developing a professional portfolio, and conducting the job search. Be sure to take advantage of the expert assistance available at your career services office. A sample résumé is presented in figure 21.2 on page 312.

## What Is Important When Choosing a Career?

There are three important factors to consider when choosing your career: values, interests, and skills. Your values are fundamental to career planning and are indicative of what you consider most important in your life. "All the elements of your lifestyle, including family, love and friendship, home and work environments, religious preference, edu-

cation, and recreation—in short, all the choices you make—will reflect your personal values" (Michelozzi, 1992, p. 14). Raths, Harmin, and Simon (1966) developed seven criteria that will help you determine your values. Your actions and decisions truly reflect your values when they are (a) prized and cherished, (b) publicly affirmed, (c) chosen freely, (d) chosen from alternatives, (e) chosen after consideration of consequences, (f) acted upon, and (g) acted upon repeatedly and consistently to form a definite pattern. The choices that you make about your occupational life need to be in harmony with your basic values and belief systems; otherwise you will not find personal satisfaction with your job. Ultimately you will seek an occupation and job that will enhance, strengthen, and support those values that you consider important.

Interests are those activities in which you enthusiastically engage and find most enjoyable. Interests are an integral part of your personality and are related to your values. Throughout your life, your personal experiences shape your interests. These interests often lead to competencies in

© Mary Langenfeld

The choices that you make about your occupational life should be in harmony with your basic values and belief systems.

# Juan C. Rivera

Current address
2000 Main St.
University, OH 43400
419-555-1630
jrivera@email.address.edu

Permanent address
1553 Huron Rd.
Somewherein, NJ 00000
908-555-4488

## Career objective

A program management position with a corporate fitness or community recreational facility where proven leadership skills, academic preparation in sport management, and related experience would contribute to the organization's goals.

## Education

**The State University**   University, OH
*Bachelor of Science in Education*, Sport Management, May 1996
Overall GPA 3.3; Major GPA 3.7

## Experience

**The State University Student Recreation Center**   University, OH
*Weight Room Supervisor*   August 1994 to present
- Conduct weight room clinics to present effective exercise and training techniques to groups of 5 to 12 students.
- Monitor and supervise the use of all exercise equipment in the training areas.
- Perform preventive maintenance on Nautilus, Universal, and other equipment.

**Athletics Department**   University, OH
*Intern Assistant to the Athletic Director*   May 1995 to August 1995
- Completed rotational assignments in various areas of college sport management, including facility operations, purchasing, inventory management, and concession operations.
- Revised the Athletic Department Policy and Procedures Manual, a 50-page manual.
- Gained an excellent understanding of the complexities of athletic administration on a college level.

**The New Age Fitness Center**   Somewherein, NJ
*Assistant Manager and Fitness Instructor*   May 1994 to August 1994
- Acquired more than 50 hours of personal training experience.
- Conducted fitness assessments and instructed members in proper use of exercise equipment.
- Designed and presented seminars on coping with stress, strength building, and healthy lifestyles.
- Wrote a training manual to help orient future employees and interns.

**The State University Intramural Program**   University, OH
*Intramural Official*   August 1993 to May 1994
- Officiated at intramural sporting competitions.
- Completed training program that covered game rules, officiating techniques, and departmental policies.

**Somewherein Parks and Recreation**   Somewherein, NJ
*Children's Sports Instructor*   May 1993 to August 1993
- Taught fundamental techniques of softball, volleyball, basketball, and soccer to children, ages 7 to 15.
- Supervised sport programs. Provided first aid for participants in instances of minor injury.
- Earned certification in Professional CPR and Standard First Aid.

## Activities

- **Sport Management Alliance** (1994 - present), *Vice President of New Member Recruitment and Treasurer*
- **Wood County Special Olympics** (1993 - 1995), *Volunteer*
- **University Activities Organization** (1993 - 1995), *Sport and Recreation Committee and Promotions Committee*

**References** available on request.

**Figure 21.2**   Résumé of a sport management graduate.

the same areas. When your interests are well matched with your occupation, you experience greater job satisfaction. Those of you who have difficulty identifying or articulating your interests might want to seek the assistance of a career counselor at your university career services office. Using interest inventories, career counselors can help you assess your measured interests and match those interests with appropriate occupations.

A skill is the developed aptitude, ability, or personal quality needed to perform a task competently. There are three basic types of skills: job content, functional, and adaptive. Job content skills are the specialized knowledge or abilities needed to fulfill a specific job responsibility. Knowing the rules of basketball is an example of a job content skill for a basketball referee. Functional skills are general abilities that transfer to many jobs or situations. For example, a basketball referee uses functional skills to make quick, accurate decisions and to resolve player conflicts that occur on the court. Adaptive skills are personal attributes or personality traits. In our example, a basketball referee must remain calm and poised under stressful conditions.

To determine your skills, Kroll and Moomaw (1990) suggest following this four-step process:

1. Take an in-depth look at all aspects of your life experiences. Identify several major accomplishments, whether they are related to academics, extracurricular activities, work, or leisure time.

2. From this list of accomplishments, label in your own words the skills used to achieve those accomplishments.

3. Rearrange the skills, clustering them according to patterns that emerge from your list.

4. Rank your skills in a priority order that appeals to you. Ranking will help you identify and define the work tasks and responsibilities you would like to be involved with in your future career. Some examples of management skills that you might uncover are planning, organizing, selling, team building, writing, communicating persuasively, or strengthening interpersonal relations.

A hypothetical example of how you might go through this process is presented in figure 21.3. First, list a few major accomplishments horizontally across the top of the page (e.g., organized a softball tournament, made the most ticket sales, served as president of the athletics association). Then, under each accomplishment, list the skills you used in that endeavor. Third, circle the skills you used most frequently; these are the clusters that create the patterns mentioned in 3 above. Finally, rank these skills 1 to 7 according to your interests. If you construct such a table using your experiences, you will have a revealing graphic description of your skills—you know you possess these skills because you have already demonstrated them!

# Job Search

Three additional factors that affect your career choices in sport management are the sport setting where you wish to be employed, the focus of that sport enterprise, and the specific competencies required by the sport management position you are seeking (Kelley, Beitel, DeSensi, & Blanton, 1990). Considering these factors in conjunction with what you are and what you have to offer will help you find your ideal career situation.

There are many opportunities for you to secure a position in an existing sport management setting. In fact, the position of sports marketing and corporate sales representative appears on a list of occupations that are expected to add a significant number of openings by 2005 (Patterson & Allen, 1996). On the other hand, you could create your own opportunities by becoming an entrepreneur, a concept discussed in chapter 5 (also see Groves, 1990; O'Brien & Overby, 1997). In either event, making solid career decisions requires you to gather extensive information about the occupations you wish to consider. By using a systematic approach, you will be able to compare occupations and make decisions that are compatible with your values, interests, skills, and preferred lifestyle. For each occupation you are considering, gather the following information: the nature of the work, work setting and conditions, personal qualifications required, earnings, employment outlook and competition, methods of entering the occupation, opportunities for advancement, opportunities for exploring the occupation, related occupations, and sources of additional information.

You can learn about the requirements of various jobs through several sources. These include video and print media, computer software, and informational interviews with professionals employed in the field in which you are interested. As shown in For More Information on page 316, there are many publications that you can find in career centers, university libraries, or large public libraries. You can also find occupational information in literature

**Accomplishments**

| Organized softball tournament | Highest in group ticket sales | President of student athletics association |
|---|---|---|
| planned, coordinated | sold | team building |
| cooperated with other teams and individuals | communicated persuasively | leadership |
| attended to details | collected money | motivated others |
| interpersonal communication | established sales goals | delegated tasks |
| composed advertisements | handled complaints | set realistic goals |
| managed budget | followed through | interpersonal communication |
| delegated tasks | listened | conducted meetings |
| followed through | identified target markets | solved problems |
| solved problems | persistence | made decisions |
| analyzed tasks | took risks | listened |
| identified resources | motivated others | organized |
| reserved facilities | | planned |
| worked under a deadline | | gained trust of others |
| made decisions | | managed budget |
| took risks | | |
| motivated others | | |

| Skills clusters | Priority order |
|---|---|
| • planning and organizing projects and events | 4 |
| • interpersonal communication | 2 |
| • managing budgets | 6 |
| • motivating others, leadership | 1 |
| • goal setting | 3 |
| • decision making | 9 |
| • following through on projects | 7 |

**Figure 21.3**   A four-step process to discover your skills.

published by private companies, professional and trade associations, state employment agencies, and national magazines.

Another way of collecting data regarding occupations, educational institutions, and academic programs is through a computerized career information system. Most career services offices have interactive computerized guidance software programs, such as *System for Interactive Guidance and Information Plus (SIGI+)* (Educational Testing Service, 1996), and access to the Internet. Additional sources of information are personal contacts. By attending conferences, workshops, and seminars in sport management, you can gain valuable information and meet interesting individuals as you develop your network of professional acquaintances.

As a college student, you have many avenues for obtaining occupational information through hands-on experience before graduation. In this way, you can test reality by engaging in such opportunities as volunteer experiences, internships, cooperative education assignments, practica, and summer and part-time jobs. Through these experiences, you can gather realistic career information while building skills and gaining confidence that will help you secure full-time employment upon graduation.

Finally, an excellent way to gain additional information about jobs and work environments is to interview and observe employees on site. By conducting an informational interview, you will learn how sport managers feel about their work as well as what skills, qualities, responsibilities, and career paths these individuals have followed. If you call ahead of time to arrange an appointment, prepare a list of questions in advance, and request only a reasonable amount of their time, most professionals are willing to share their knowledge and experience.

# Sport Management From a Global Perspective

Universities and colleges are beginning to develop curricula focused on sport management in the foreign market (Thoma, 1991; Thoma & Chalip,

## Learning Activity

Conduct an informational interview following these six steps:

- Identify and investigate an organization that employs professionals in your targeted career.
- Identify individuals within that organization who work in your targeted career.
- Write or telephone for an appointment.
- Prepare a list of questions for the informational interview in advance.
- Conduct the interview.
- Write and mail a thank-you letter within 3 days of the interview.

1996). Not only will these curricula provide valuable information in the classroom, but you may have the opportunity to engage in an internship or practicum in a foreign country. This could occur through your sport management program or be arranged through the international studies program on your campus. Second, with the vast changes occurring throughout Europe, the role of sport in the European marketplace will take on increased importance. Management philosophy and strategies employed within North American sport settings may prove beneficial to creating a new sport model in Europe.

There is an impressive number of countries that offer sport management programs where you might consider studying. Sport management programs are currently found in the United States, Japan, Australia, New Zealand, China, England, Canada, Germany, France, and South Africa—and the list is growing. Additionally, at the international level, there is an increasing awareness of the role of the media; the development of sports such as golf, soccer, and rugby; women in sport; and the need for a cross-cultural approach to developing sport

(Wilcox, 1994). Many universities sponsor exchange programs with universities in other countries. These programs provide splendid opportunities for you to gain international experience.

As an example, consider the area of international marketing. As teams, professional leagues, and entertainment companies such as EuroDisney expand into foreign markets, there will be a need for sport marketers who can attend to the traditional issues surrounding the political, economic, social, and legal structures of these foreign markets. They must also be able to deal with the new, evolving issues of developing a global perspective, strategic planning, specialized international market analysis, and the impact of culture on business (Grub & Moran, 1995). The chain of events in sport at the international level indicates many opportunities for the sport manager.

## Learning Activity

Investigate opportunities on your campus to participate in international exchange programs.

## Professionalization of Sport Management

As with other professions like law, education, medicine, and physical education, sport management continues to experience the **process of professionalization**. The process of growth and development for a profession includes three distinct stages. The first stage is acquiring the theoretical base of knowledge. This involves a commitment to empirical investigation and scientific inquiry, academic recognition through specialized departments and academic positions, and offering advanced degrees.

The second stage entails developing a distinct subculture. This includes the socialization, or

## A Global Perspective

As you look forward to your career in sport management, be sure to consider opportunities of a global nature. The idea of developing programs and careers geared toward international sport management has been suggested by a number of academics (Koehler, 1992;

MacAloon, 1992; Thoma, 1991). In fact, van der Smissen (1990a) identified globalization as one of the nine strong forces that are reshaping America and will have implications for sport. Globalization will affect you and your career in many ways.

training, of future experts like yourself. It also involves establishing an association representing the profession, a process of professional training and study, developing a code of ethics, and establishing full-time careers within the profession.

The final stage of professionalization refers to community recognition. This addresses the fact that many people outside of the profession, or in the community at large, are aware that the profession exists, and that they should hire you, the experts, within that profession. This stage involves licensing and certifying the future professionals and creating markets within the profession. For example, hospitals create a market for physicians, and schools create a market for educators. Professional sports, community recreation leagues, the military, the media, hotels and resorts, marinas, sport governing bodies, and the retail industry are all examples of creating markets for you, the sport manager.

Sport management is in a challenging and exciting position relative to these stages of professionalization (Koehler & Lupcho, 1990). As an area of study, sport management has witnessed remarkable milestones, particularly regarding the second stage of professionalization. This is reflected, specifically, in the proliferation of academic programs now available to you, the existence of the North American Society of Sport Management (NASSM) as the leading scholarly and professional organization in North America, and that organization's

code of ethics (Zeigler, 1989). However, developing the theoretical base of knowledge for sport management remains a constant challenge, as does perhaps one of the most exciting aspects of your career—educating those around you about the profession of sport management. These are challenging and exciting times for you as a sport manager!

## Summary

Three elements necessary for success in sport management are (a) professional preparation, (b) professional attitude, and (c) professional development. You can find sport management professional preparation programs at the bachelor's, master's, and doctoral levels. The typical undergraduate curriculum consists of general education courses, major courses, and field experiences. Field experiences give you opportunities to apply what you learn in the classroom in sport settings. Master's and doctoral programs will be more specific to your career goals.

Professional attitude is reflected in your personal appearance (e.g., hygiene, posture, self-confidence), your adjustment to the workplace (e.g., academic preparation, writing skills, dependability, ethics, work habits), and your manners (e.g., telephone, E-mail, thank-you letters). Recruiters evaluate professional attitude during interviews.

---

## For More Information

Here are some more sources for you to take advantage of. Good reading and good luck!

### Publications

- Hopke, W.E. (Ed.). (1993). *Encyclopedia of careers and vocational guidance* (9th ed.). Chicago: Ferguson.

- *Occupational Outlook Quarterly*. (1997). Washington, DC: U.S. Government Printing Office.

- United States Department of Labor. (1993). *Dictionary of occupational titles* (5th ed.). Washington, DC: U.S. Government Printing Office.

- Maze, J., & Mayall, D. (1991). *Guide for occupational exploration*. Indianapolis: JIST.

### Information About Careers in Sport

- Cylkowski, G.J. (1992). Developing a life-long contract in the sports marketplace. Little Canada, MN: Athletic Achievements.

- Field, S. (1991). *Career opportunities in the sports industry*. New York: Facts on File.

- Heitzmann, W.R. (1991). *Careers for sports nuts & other athletic types*. Lincolnwood, IL: VGM Career Horizons.

- Karlin, L. (1995). *The guide to careers in sports*. New York: Guild.

- Lipsey, R.A. (1996). *Sports market place*. Princeton, NJ: Sportsguide.

Professional development consists of career planning (determining your values, interests, and skills) and systematically investigating career opportunities. Your academic major does not necessarily predict your career choice. You may not progress in a direct path from college to your ultimate career objective. You are continually developing talents, abilities, and skills through your course work, leisure activities, volunteer experiences, and summer and part-time jobs. Upon graduation, you will have a broad range of skills and talents that will make you marketable in the working world. Career counselors cannot provide instant solutions, but they can provide guidance and direction. In your career planning, you should consider possibilities in international sport management.

## The Life You Would Like

Imagine your life 5 to 7 years from now. You have graduated from college and have the perfect position in an ideal community. Describe your lifestyle and work life in as much detail as you can. Where are you living? What community features do you enjoy most? What leisure activities are available? Who is living with you? Do you live in an apartment, condominium, house? How far is the drive to work each day? Do you work for a large, medium, or small organization? What are your primary job responsibilities? Can you assume new, challenging assignments regularly? How would you describe your work environment or working conditions? Do you work at a desk, travel to customer sites, spend time outdoors? Is there a dress code? How much supervisory direction do you receive? How would you describe your boss's leadership and management style? Who are your coworkers? What are your hours? How are you compensated? In summary, what do you like best about your job and lifestyle?

# Glossary

**Actuality**—the actual voice of the newsmaker used in a broadcast story. If recorded over the phone, the actuality is called a *voicer*. In television, the newsmaker speaking on camera is usually called a *sound bite*. The reporter's voice heard over the video of a television news story is called a *voice over*.

**Agencies**—sites or locations at which sports medicine programs, therapies, and prescriptions are administered and where sports medicine information is disseminated.

**Amateurism**—ideal that characterized sports as pastimes participated in for the love of activity, personal enjoyment, and display of prowess, not for remuneration.

**Americans with Disabilities Act (ADA)**—establishes regulations and standards for existing buildings and new construction to ensure that they are readily accessible to and usable by individuals with disabilities. The act was created to promote equal opportunities for people with disabilities, whether they are employees or consumers.

**Arena**—a flat floor multilevel facility with seating for 8,000 to 25,000 spectators. The sight lines are designed for athletic events such as basketball, hockey, indoor soccer, and ice events as well as concerts.

**Assimilation**—the adaptation of individuals into a new culture.

**Athletic trainer**—professional who treats sports injuries and supervises rehabilitation of athletes.

**Attitudes**—a collection of influences that are not necessarily based on facts.

**Behavior**—the observable action of an individual.

**Biomechanics**—the description and explanation of the laws of physics as applied to exercise and sport.

**Broadcasting**—radio or television signals that can be transmitted over the air without benefit of cable lines into the home, including commercial and public (noncommercial) broadcasting stations. Broadcast stations may be carried by cable systems, but they can be received without wiring or direct satellite systems.

**Cardiac rehabilitation**—procedures and therapies (e.g., exercise) to assist clientele in recovery from cardiac diseases.

**Career wellness** (2)—addresses career goals and paths and finding a balance between life at home and life at work.

**Cartel**—a monopolistic combination of individuals or groups that restrains the actions of others.

**Certification**—refers to the NCAA Certification Program for Division I athletic programs.

**Cock fighting**—contests staged between trained male chickens that have spurs attached to their feet; spectators gamble on which cock will survive the gory fight.

**Communication**—the sharing of meaning among senders and receivers of messages. Information may be exchanged without true communication if there is no shared meaning.

**Concept knowledge**—background information that increases our overall understanding of ideas.

**Co-op**—involvement of many sponsors to share the costs and benefits associated with an event or sporting activity.

**Coronary heart disease**—buildup of fatty plaques on the walls of the coronary arteries; may result in blockage of the artery precipitating a heart attack.

**Cost analysis**—determining how much it would cost to stage an event. Accomplished by estimating revenues from ticket sales and concessions, then, based on these figures, determining if the event will be profitable.

**Country clubs**—exclusive and expensive social and sporting organizations that nurtured the development of elitist sports like golf and tennis.

**Curling**—sport played on ice, somewhat similar to shuffleboard.

**Decoding**—interpreting the meaning behind a message received in the communication process.

**Distance learning**—an educational process in which the student does not sit in a class with the instructor. Classes are carried via various media, including the Internet, direct video feed, telephone, and so on. Correspondence courses also fall under this category.

**Documentation**—filling out and maintaining the proper paperwork to protect facility management in the event of a lawsuit. This includes all forms pertaining to contracts, maintenance schedules, incident reports, safety inspections, and injury reports.

**Downsizing**—becoming a smaller organization through reducing personnel or departments. This may relate to changing the organization's mission or altering direction.

**Duty of care**—the facility must eliminate or adequately identify all known hazards or risks to the patrons.

**Elite tourists**—travelers who have sufficient financial resources to travel in smaller, less impacting groups to destinations that are generally not accessible to the masses.

**Emotional wellness** (2)—addresses personal self. It involves trying to better understand our feelings and emotions.

**Encoding**—creating the meaning behind a message sent in the communication process.

**Entitlement**—associating the name of a sponsor with the name of an event or facility in exchange for cash or other considerations (e.g., the Mobil Cotton Bowl).

**Environmental wellness** (2)—includes the connection between personal wellness and the broader world in which we live. It addresses intercultural awareness, environmental issues, and global unity.

**Eclectic**—composed of information and material gathered from various sources, such as disciplines, doctrines, or systems.

**Entrepreneurs** risk money, time, and effort in business ventures. They are not ordinary business owners; they provide value-added services, features, or utility to existing business concepts.

**Epidemiology**—the science that examines patterns and causes of disease and mortality.

**Ergonomics**—study of the workplace; study of how workers can function safely and efficiently in varied work tasks and environments.

**Exercise specialist**—professional who prescribes exercise testing and prescription for varied populations.

**Exercise program**—organized physical activity intended to accomplish a certain goal (e.g., weight loss, improvement of muscular strength or cardiorespiratory endurance).

**External constituents**—people outside the organization on whose behalf managers act (e.g., customers, fans, vendors, interest groups).

**FCC**—the Federal Communications Commission is a federal agency established by Congress in 1934 to regulate broadcasting. It also has regulatory power over other areas of telecommunication, such as telephones and cable television. There is no parallel regulatory agency for print media. In 1995, Congress proposed sweeping changes in this regulatory power.

**Gatekeeper**—the individual responsible for controlling the flow of proposals or solicitations to the decision maker.

**Gentlemen's agreement**—the description of the unwritten, but staunchly enforced, rule that African Americans would not be allowed to play in the major leagues.

**Giveaways**—items given to people who attend sporting events (e.g., caps, fans, plastic cups); usually emblazoned with the logo of the sponsoring organization.

**Governance**—in professional sport, it is the collection of governing bodies such as the National Basketball Association and the National Football League, which regulate the competition between professional teams.

**Grassroots**—a program targeted to those individuals at the primary level of involvement. These programs are usually targeted to participants rather than spectators.

**Group dynamics**—the study of development and change within a group or groups of individuals.

**Heterosexism**—the societal assumption that heterosexuality is the only acceptable, sanctioned, and normal sexual orientation.

**Hierarchy**—vertical levels of management through which one moves as a manager or administrator; chain of command.

**Home rule**—the term used by the NCAA to describe institutional autonomy in conducting athletic programs.

**Homophobia**—the irrational fear or intolerance of homosexuality, gay men or lesbians, or even behavior that is perceived to be outside the boundaries of traditional gender role expectations.

**Ingress**—flow of vehicular and pedestrian traffic into a facility.

**Imagery**—using all the senses to create or recreate an image in the mind.

**Information society**—the designation of a society that has more of its labor force producing or disseminating information than working in manufacturing or agriculture. The United States has moved from an industrial society to an information society.

**In-house**—managing a function or providing a service within the organization itself.

**Internal constituents**—people in the organization on whose behalf managers act (e.g., subordinates, peers, students).

**Intellectual wellness**—involves a commitment to challenge our minds and investigate our world.

**Interschool**—competition between different schools.

**Internet**—a global network of networks providing access to computers around the world with an ever-expanding menu of services. Surfing the Internet has entered our culture's jargon to describe the use of Internet services and capabilities.

**Inventory**—what a sport property has to sell. This refers not only to quantity but also to characteristics, traits, and other benefits.

**Invasive procedure**—test or method in which the body cavity is entered with a tube, needle, device, or other material.

**Inverted pyramid style**—the standard, traditional format for news stories, which presents the critical information in the opening sentence or lead (who, what, where, when, why, how) and offers the rest of the information in descending order of importance.

**Labor**—in professional sport, labor refers to the on-field talent and performers, the players. Labor refers to the players as individuals and collectively as a labor union.

**Leisure**—a block of discretionary time, a type of activity pursued for pleasure and fun, or an attitude or state of mind.

**Leverage**—to use a licensing agreement to create additional marketing opportunities that may or may not be directly related to the original agreement.

**Licensing**—providing resources of any kind by an organization in direct support of an event or activity to associate the organization's name or product with the event or activity. The licensee uses this relationship to achieve its promotional objectives or to facilitate and support its marketing objectives, which may or may not be profit oriented.

**Licensure**—documentation of professional knowledge through completing a written exam administered by accrediting organizations; typically required for employment in specific professions.

**Litigation**—process one undergoes when involved in a lawsuit, either as the plaintiff or defendant.

**Local television contracts**—agreements made between an individual professional sports team and a local or regional television station or cable outlet. These contracts exist in addition to the leaguewide contracts with national networks.

**Management**—in professional sport, management refers to the entities owning and operating professional sport franchises. It refers to individual teams as well as the collection of teams that act in concert as a league.

**Management movements or schools of thought** provide theories and recommended practices for managers.

**Managers** (administrators)—group of workers in an organization who are responsible for and have the authority to direct the work activities of others.

**Market segmentation**—dividing the total market into designated sections and placing consumers with common characteristics in particular sections.

**March Madness**—the media's label for the popularity of the NCAA Division I Basketball Championship.

**Mass communication**—messages delivered to a large audience by professional communicators, usually simultaneously or quickly over a potentially large geographical area. Mass communication messages are distributed via the mass media, delivery systems with the capacity for transcending the time and space limitations imposed on communication processes like telephone or face-to-face communication.

**Mass tourists**—large groups of travelers who have little income surplus, thus leaving a destination vulnerable to deterioration and negative impacts.

**Media preferences**—information about where consumers can be reached by examining the information sources they use, such as magazines, newspapers, trade journals, TV, or radio.

**Mission**—purpose behind existence that drives programming goals.

**Nontraditional**—anyone who falls outside the traditional 18 to 24 college-age group.

**Natatorium**—facility whose entire philosophy and mission pertains to aquatic activities.

**Out-source**—contracting individuals or organizations outside the professional sports team to perform services that may or may not have been performed previously by a staff member of that franchise. Out-sourcing is viewed as a way of saving money for several reasons: First, because there are no employee benefits to pay, second, the services may not require daily attention, and third, it may be more cost effective to pay for services, such as legal services, as needed rather than to have an attorney on staff.

**Parity**—attempts to prevent one or more teams from dominating the league in terms of on-field performance (winning). Player drafts act to create parity by ensuring that the teams that performed the worst during the past season have first access to the best players emerging from college or other sources of player development.

**Personal services contract**—an agreement between an athlete and ownership or management that guarantees certain benefits and stipulates certain requirements on the part of the player that are usually outside the traditional labor agreement. These contracts are offered only to superstars and, in most cases, guarantee compensation even if the athlete is physically unable to perform or is terminated from the team as a player.

**Philosophic process**—the art and science of wondering about reality, posing questions related to that wonder, and pursuing answers to those questions reflectively.

**Play days**—contests between teams composed of players from several institutions who played sports for fun with an emphasis on socialization.

**Postevent impact analysis**—refers to research conducted (usually by a third party but commissioned by a sponsor or the event itself) after the event has been completed to determine the effects that event had on the sponsor's product (image, awareness, or sales) or on the community in general (economic growth through spending associated with the event).

**Practicum**—a part-time field experience requiring up to 20 hours per week.

**Pragmatics**—behavior rules based on the context of a situation.

**Process of professionalization**—the stages through which professions develop, including establishing a body of knowledge, preparing students, and developing heightened public awareness.

**Procurement**—successful solicitation of financial or other resources on behalf of the sport property.

**Production**—the performance of the professional sport product, playing the game, and all elements that are essential to make the game a spectator event.

**Professionalism**—characterizing those whose actions, such as in sports competitions, occurred for pay.

**Programs**—therapies, prescriptions, or any services rendered by a sports medicine agency.

**Promoter**—an individual who assists in organizing an athletic or entertainment event, usually by means of securing financial support and establishing the terms of the event contract.

**Promotion**—publicity identified and disseminated to increase audience interest or participation in a person or event (e.g., a pro sports team or a recreation facility).

**Psychographics**—information about what consumers want by examining their activities, interests, and opinions.

**Purchasing behavior**—information about what specific brands of products and services consumers buy and use, such as Head tennis racquets, Nike basketball shoes, Pepsi, Snickers, American Express, and Avis.

**Reasonable standard of care**—therapies or professional duties expected or commonly agreed upon by peers in the field that would need to be administered in a specific situation.

**Reengineering**—changing organizational structure or philosophy to capitalize on existing opportunities or changing business environments.

**Rehabilitative program**—standardized exercise program intended to facilitate recovery from an injury or disease.

**Reserve clause**—MLB owners reserved rights to their players, thus preventing them from marketing themselves as free agents to the highest bidders.

**Risk factors for coronary heart disease**—the seven risk factors designated by ACSM that indicate level of coronary heart disease are age, family history of heart disease, current cigarette smoking, hypertension, hypercholesterolemia, diabetes mellitus, and sedentary lifestyle or physical inactivity.

**Rotating signage**—signage that is not stationary, but revolves or rotates to use the same space for multiple sponsors. The ads rotate every 15 to 30 seconds, allowing the organization to sell the same signage space to three or four sponsors that it could only sell to one sponsor using traditional stationary signage.

**Salary cap**—the maximum allowable amount of money that can be paid to all athletes on each team within a league.

**Satellite facilities**—buildings, personnel, and equipment operated by a management team not on site; specialized departments of hospitals that are located throughout a community for easier accessibility.

**Selective attention, perception, and retention**—individuals seek, interpret, and remember information that fits their established interests and preconceived attitudes. Successful communication is more likely if you understand the audience and tailor the message to its members' specific interests and needs.

**Settlement**—process in which representatives of the facility and the promoter determine the expenses associated with the event, such as stagehands, light operators, utilities, or production. They will compare these to the revenue generated from the event to determine the event's cost. Some elements are known as house expenses; these services can not be charged to the event promoter, as they are the responsibility of the facility and are not recoverable cost items.

**Social wellness** (2)—addresses interpersonal relationships and helps us enter into successful and fulfilling relationships with our family, friends, significant others, pets.

**Socialization**—the ways in which a society's dominant values, attitudes, and beliefs are passed down from generation to generation.

**Solicitation**—requesting support or assistance on behalf of a sport property from a potential sponsor.

**Spiritual wellness** (2)—involves finding meaning and purpose in life. This can give us strength to cope with despair and help us feel good about life; may or may not include religion. Some martial arts programming incorporates this wellness concept.

**Sport days**—competitions between teams representing their schools or colleges but with the emphasis on having fun and interacting socially.

**Split**—mutually agreed upon percentage by facility and promoter for dividing such items as ticket, concession, merchandise, and parking revenue.

**Sports agent**—an individual who negotiates playing and endorsement contracts on behalf of an athlete.

**Sports medicine clinics**—agencies in which therapies or exercise programs are delivered.

**Sports medicine team**—a group of professionals who work together to deliver therapies or exercise programs.

**Sport studies**—the study of the disciplinary foundations of sport, such as sport sociology, sport psychology, sport history, and sport and gender.

**Stadium** (pl. **stadia** or **stadiums**)—a single- or multipurpose facility hosting several hundred to many thousands of spectators. Most of these facilities do not have roofs.

**Strength coach**—professional who focuses on improving muscular strength and endurance.

**Subdiscipline**—a portion of a body of knowledge that focuses on a particular topic; may integrate knowledge from several disciplines.

**Systems**—components of facilities that we can group into categories (e.g., lighting, filtration, flooring).

**Target audiences**—grouping consumers according to common characteristics using consumer information (demographics, psychographics, media preferences, purchasing behaviors) to promote, package, and sell the sport product to specific groups of consumers.

**Teaching professional**—a professional athlete that earns his or her living as an instructor of skills and strategies of a sport, usually golf or tennis.

**Underrepresented groups**—people who traditionally have not been hired in sport management positions (e.g., women, people of color, people with physical disabilities).

**Values**—based on a deep-seated and moral nature that propounds beliefs.

**Value added**—the perception, by the consumer, of added or augmented product or service benefits.

**Venue**—a facility or site where a special event or sport activity takes place.

**Victorian**—typical moral standards of conduct associated with the reign of Queen Victoria of England.

**Virtual reality technology**—refers to a whole set of technologies that allow the user to experience rather than watch.

**Work physiology**—study of how the body functionally responds to various occupational tasks.

# References

A History of Past Women's Professional Basketball Leagues (1996). *ABL Courtside*, p. 33. Vol. 1.

Abney, R., & Richey, D.L. (1991). Barriers encountered by black women in sport. *Journal of Physical Education, Recreation and Dance, 62*(6), 19-21.

Abney, R., & Richey, D.L. (1992). Opportunities for minorities. *Journal of Physical Education, Recreation and Dance, 63*(3), 56-59.

Aburdene, P., & Naisbitt, J. (1992). *Megatrends for women.* New York: Villard Books, pp. 35-56.

Acosta, R.V., & Carpenter, L.J. (1988). *Perceived causes of the declining representation of women leaders in intercollegiate athletics: 1988 update.* Unpublished manuscript, Brooklyn College, Department of Physical Education.

Acosta, R.V., & Carpenter, L.J. (1992). *Women in intercollegiate sport—A longitudinal study—Fifteen year update 1977-1992.* Unpublished manuscript, Brooklyn College, Brooklyn, NY.

Acosta, R.V., & Carpenter, L.J. (1996). *Women in intercollegiate sport—A longitudinal study—Nineteen year update 1977-1996.* Unpublished manuscript, Brooklyn College, Brooklyn, NY.

American College of Sports Medicine. (1992). *ACSM's HEALTH/FITNESS Facility Standards and Guidelines.* Champaign, IL: Human Kinetics.

American College of Sports Medicine. (1994). *ACSM Membership Directory.* Indianapolis, IN: Author.

American College of Sports Medicine. (1995). *ACSM's Guidelines for Exercise Testing and Prescription.* Baltimore: Williams and Wilkins.

Ammon, R., Jr. (1993). Risk and game management practices in selected municipal football facilities (Doctoral dissertation, University of Northern Colorado, 1993). *Dissertation Abstracts International, 54*, 3366A.

Ammon, R., Jr. (1995, April-June). Alcohol and event management: Two sides of the same coin. *Crowd Management,* 16-19.

Andersen, M.B., & Williams, J.M. (1988). A model of stress and athletic injury: Prediction and prevention. *Journal of Sport and Exercise, 10,* 294-306.

Annual Industry Report (1995, June). *Team Licensing Business,* pp. 22-37.

Anspaugh, D.J., Hamrick, M.H., & Rosato, R.D. (1994). *Wellness concepts and applications* (2nd ed.). St. Louis: Mosby Year Book, Inc.

Archibald, S. (1996). What price recreation? *Athletic Business, 20*(4), 65-68.

Arnheim, D.D., & Prentice, W.E. (1997). *Principles of athletic training* (9th ed.). St. Louis, MO: Mosby Year Book.

Association for Worksite Health Promotion. (1993). *1993 worksite health professionals national compensation and benefits survey.* Delta Consultants.

Atre, T., Auns, K., Badenhausen, K., McAuliffe, K., Nikolov, C., & Ozanian, M. K. (1996, May 20). The high stakes game of team ownership. *Financial World,* pp. 53-70.

Axtell, R.E. (1990). *The do's and taboos of hosting international visitors.* White Plains, NY: John Wiley.

Baker, W.J. (1982). *Sports in the western world.* Totowa, NJ: Rowman and Littlefield.

Baldo, A. (1993). Secrets of the front office: What America's pro teams are worth. In D.S. Eitzen (Ed.), *Sport in contemporary society* (4th ed.) (pp. 187-195). NY: St. Martin's Press.

Baldrige, L. (1985). *Letitia Baldrige's complete guide to executive manners.* New York: Rawson Associates.

Baldrige, L. (1993). *Letitia Baldrige's new complete guide to executive manners* (Rev. ed.). New York : Rawson Associates.

Barnard, C.I. (1938). *The functions of an executive.* Cambridge, MA: Harvard University Press.

Barnett, R., & Cavanagh, J. (1994). *Global dreams: Imperial corporations and the new world order.* New York: Simon & Schuster.

Beauchamp, T.L. (1991). *Philosophical ethics: An introduction to moral philosophy* (2nd ed.). New York: McGraw-Hill.

Bellingham, R., & Cohen, B. (Eds.). (1987). *The Corporate wellness sourcebook.* Amherst, MA: Human Resource Development Press, Inc.

Berg, R. (1990). The roads less traveled. *Athletic Business, 14*(11), 44-47.

Berger, B.G., & McInman, A. (1993). Exercise and the quality of life. In R.N. Singer, M. Murphey, L.K. Tennant (Eds.), *Handbook of research on sport psychology* (pp. 729-760). New York: Macmillan Publishing.

Berlonghi, A. (1990). *The special event risk management manual.* Dana Point, CA: Author.

Bertalanffy, L. von (1972). The history and status of general systems theory. *Academy of management Journal, 15,* 407-426.

Bertalanffy, L. von (1968). *General system theory: Foundation, development, application.* New York: George Brazeller.

Betts, J.R. (1974). *America's sporting heritage: 1850-1950.* Reading, MA: Addison-Wesley Publishing Company.

Bevilaqua International Inc. (1994). Corporate brochure and sales materials. Atlanta, GA.

Billington, R. (1988). *Living philosophy: An introduction to moral thought.* London: Routledge.

Boucher, R. (1996, June). *Toward achieving a focal point for sport management: A binocular perspective.* Earle F. Zeigler lecture presented at the conference of the North American Society for Sport Management, Fredericton, New Brunswick, Canada.

Boutilier, M.A., & SanGiovanni, L. (1983). *The sporting woman.* Champaign, IL: Human Kinetics.

Boyer, M.L., & Vaccaro, V.A. (1990). The benefits of a physically active workforce: An organizational perspective. *Occupational Medicine: State of the art reviews, 5*(4), 691-706.

Brady, J. (1996, May 26). In step with Hannah Storm. *Parade Magazine,* 26.

Branden, N. (1971). *The psychology of self-esteem.* New York: Bantam.

Branvold, S. (1991). Ethics. In B.L. Parkhouse (Ed.). *The management of sport its foundation and application* (pp. 365-375). St. Louis, MO: Mosby-Yearbook, Inc.

Brassie, P.S. (1989). A student buyer's guide to sport management programs. *Journal of Physical Education, Recreation and Dance, 60*(9), 25-28.

Bressan, E.S., & Pieter, W. (1985). Philosophic processes and the study of human moving. *Quest, 37,* 1-15.

*Broadcasting and Cable Yearbook.* (1995). New Providence, NJ: R.R. Bowker.

Brooks, D.D., & Althouse, R.C. (1993). Racial imbalance in coaching and managerial positions. In D.D. Brooks & R.C. Althouse (Eds.), *Racism in college athletics: The African-American athlete's experience* (pp. 101-142). Morgantown, WV: Fitness Information Technology.

Brooks, C.M. (1994). *Sports marketing: Competitive business strategies for sports.* Englewood Cliffs, NJ: Prentice Hall.

Brown, S.C. (1990). Looking toward 2000. *NIRSA Journal, 14*(2), 32-34.

Browne, L. (1992). *Girls of Summer.* Toronto: Harper Collins.

Brunt, R. (1992). Engaging with the popular audiences for mass culture and what to say about them. In L. Grossberg, C. Nelson, and P. Treichler, *Cultural studies.* New York: Routledge, Chapman, and Hall, Inc., 69-76.

Bullington, T. (1995, June). "Untangling the web: Licensing meets the fax machine of 15 years ago." *Team Licensing Business,* pp. 16-21.

Burke, J. (1995, November). Dream on: Hockey's Olympic dream tournament will premiere in 1998. *American Hockey Magazine,* Minneapolis, MN: The Publishing Group, pp. 22-23.

Carney, C.G., & Wells, C.F. (1995). *Discovering the career within you* (4th ed.). Pacific Grove, CA: Brooks/Cole.

Carpenter, L.J. (1993). Letters home: My life with Title IX. In G.L. Cohen (Ed.), *Women in sport: Issues and controversies* (pp. 79-94). Newbury Park, CA: Sage.

Carr-Ruffino, N. (1996). *Managing diversity: People skills for a multicultural workplace.* Los Angeles: Thomson Executive Press.

Carrell, M.R., Jennings, D.F., & Heavrin, C. (1997). *Fundamentals of organizational behavior.* Upper Saddle River, NJ: Prentice-Hall.

Cart, J. (1992, April 6). Lesbian issue stirs discussion. *Los Angeles Times,* Los Angeles, California, C1; 12.

Cartwright, D. (Ed.). (1951). *Field theory in social science.* New York: Harper.

Case, S. (1995). *Open book management: The coming business revolution.* New York: Harper Business.

Casella, D.A., & Brougham, C.E. (1995). Work works: Student jobs open front doors to careers. *Journal of Career Planning & Employment, 55*(4), 24-27, 54-55.

Cavanaugh, G. (1984) *American business values* (2nd ed.). Englewood Cliffs, New Jersey: Prentice-Hall.

Cetron, M. (1994). An American Renaissance in the year 2000. *Futurist, 28*(2), 1-11.

Chaffee, J. (1991). *Thinking critically.* Boston: Houghton Mifflin.

Chamberlin, A. (1990). Sports information. In J.B. Parks & B.R.K. Zanger (Eds.), *Sport & fitness management: Career strategies and professional content* (pp. 63-72). Champaign, IL: Human Kinetics.

Chelladurai, P. (1986). *Sport management: Macro-perspectives.* London, ON: Sports Dynamics.

Chenoweth, D.H. (1987). *Planning health promotion at the worksite.* Indianapolis, IN: Benchmark Press, Inc.

Clay, B. (February, 1995). 8 great careers in the sports industry. *Black Enterprise, 25*(7), pp. 158-160, 162, 164, 166.

Clement, A. (1990). The future of sport and fitness. In J.B. Parks, & B.R.K. Zanger. (Eds.), *Sport & fitness management: Career strategies and professional content* (pp. 257-265). Champaign, IL.: Human Kinetics.

Coakley, J.J. (1986). *Sport in society: Issues and controversies.* St. Louis, MO: Times Mirror/Mosby College Publishing.

Coakley, J.J. (1990). *Sport in society: Issues and controversies (4th edition).* St. Louis, MO: Times Mirror/Mosby.

Coakley, J.J. (1993). Social dimensions of intensive training and participation in youth sports. In B.R. Cahill & A.J. Pearl (Eds.), *Intensive participation in children's sport* (pp. 77-94). Champaign, IL: Human Kinetics.

Coakley, J.J. (1994). *Sport in society—Issues and controversies (5th ed.).* St. Louis: Mosby.

Cohen, A. (1993, April). Another wonder of the world. *Athletic Business, 17*(4), 49-51.

Cohen, A. (1995). Social service. *Athletic Business, 19*(7), 16-18.

Cole, C.L., & Hribar, A. (1995). Celebrity feminism: Nike Style, Post-Fordism, Transcendence, and Consumer Power. *Sociology of Sport Journal, 12,* 347-369.

Comte, E., & Stogel, C. (1990). Sports: A $63.1 billion industry. *The Sporting News* (January 1), 60-61.

Concannon, J. (1994, August 28). A major shift in balance of power. *Boston Sunday Globe,* p. 88.

Conklin, M. (1994, January 25). Blackhawks' Chelios in spotlight as new ad rep for company. *The Chicago Tribune,* (North Sports Final Edition), p. 7.

Conrad, E. (1995, January 10). "NFL experience: Super Bowl-related bazaar will be running right next to JRS." *The Sun Sentinel* (Fort Lauderdale, Fla.), p. 10.

Cortez, J.P. (1992, June 1). "Julius keeps the score for sports promotions: Leading marketers rely on consultancy's numbers." *Advertising Age, 63*(22), 10.

Cotten, D.J. (1993). Risk management—A tool for reducing exposure to legal liability. *Journal of Physical Education, Recreation and Dance, 64*(2), 58-61.

Covey, S.R. (1989). *The seven habits of highly effective people.* New York: Simon and Schuster.

Crespo, M. (1995, February 14). "You get more eyeballs: Satellite television sports." *Financial World, 164*(4), 94-98.

Crosset, T., Benedict, J., & McDonald, M. (1995). Male student-athletes reported for sexual assault: Survey of campus police departments and judicial affairs. *Journal of Sport and Social Issues, 19,* 126-140.

Cuneen, J. (1992). Graduate-level professional preparation for athletic directors. *Journal of Sport Management, 6,* 15-26.

Cuneen, J., & Sidwell, M.J. (1994). S*port management field experiences.* Morgantown, WV: Fitness Information Technology.

Curry, T. (1991). Fraternal bonding in the locker room: A profeminist analysis of talk about competition and women. *Sociology of Sport Journal, 8,* 119-135.

DelWilber & Associates. (1994). Corporate brochure and sales materials, McLean, VA.

DeSensi, J.T, Kelley, D.R, Blanton, M.D., & Beitel, P.A. (1990). Sport management curricular evaluation and needs assessment: A multifaceted approach. *Journal of Sport Management, 4,* 31-58.

DeSensi, J.T. (1994). Multiculturalism as an issue in sport management. *Journal of Sport Management, 8,* 63-74.

DeSensi, J.T., & Rosenberg, D. (1996). *Ethics in sport management.* Morgantown, WV: Fitness Information Technology.

Dickerson, G.E. (1991). *The cinema of baseball: Images of America.* Westport, CT: Meckler, Inc.

Dieffenbach, D. (1996, February) Bloc party: Immigration, NBA style, has opened the doors for a host of European players. *Sport,* pp. 55-58.

Dimensions of wellness. (1994, Autumn). *Wellness matters.* Cullowhee, NC: Western Carolina University Wellness Program.

Dishman, R.K. (1986). Exercise compliance: A new view for public health. *The Physician and Sportsmedicine, 14*(5):127-142.

Dodd, M. (1995, September 18). Mile high commitment. *USA Today, 13*(258), 3C.

Dodd, M. (1994, November 10). Survey points to disparity in boardrooms: Task forces to focus on ways of reducing gaps for women, minorities. *USA Today,* p. 14C.

Dodd, M. (1996, October 8). Revenue disparity leaves some teams in left field. *USA Today,* pp. 1A-2A.

Donald, J. (Ed.). (1931). *Handbook of business administration* (James O. McKinsey chapters). New York: McGraw-Hill.

Dorman, T. (1988). Addison Club designed to attract residents. *Athletic Business, 12*(4). 40-46.

Drucker, P. (1954). *The practice of management.* New York: Harper and Row.

Drucker, P. (1974). *Management: Tasks, responsibilities, practices.* New York: Harper and Row.

Drucker, P.E. (1986). *Innovation and entrepreneurship.* New York: Harper & Row.

Duncan, M.C., & Hasbrook, C.A. (1988). Denial of power in televised women's sports. *Sociology of Sport Journal, 5,* 1-21.

Duncan, M.C., Messner, M.A., & Jensen, K. (1994). *Gender stereotyping in televised sports: A follow-up to the 1989 study.* Los Angeles: The Amateur Athletic Foundation of Los Angeles.

Dupree, D. (1996, June 18). Reigning Bulls: Re-signing coach and stars is team's priority. *USA Today,* 1C-2C.

Duquin, M.E. (1989). The importance of sport in building women's potential. In D.S. Eitzen (Ed.), *Sport in contemporary society* (3rd ed.) (pp. 357-362). NY: St. Martin's Press.

Dwyer, P., & Engardio, P. (1994, October 17). Murdoch laughs last-again. *Business Week,* p. 68.

Dychtwald, K. (1986). *Wellness and health promotion for the elderly.* Rockville, MD: Aspen Publishers, Inc.

Eddy, J.M., Gold, R.S., & Zimmerli, W.H. (1989). Evaluation of worksite health enhancement programs. *Health Values, 13*(1):3-9.

Educational Testing Service. (1996). *A computer based system of interactive guidance and information* [Computer Program]. Princeton, NJ: Author.

Everly, G.S., Jr., & Feldman, R.H.L. (1985). *Occupational health promotion.* U.S.: John Wiley and Sons.

Fact file: Projections of college enrollment, degrees, and high-school graduates, 1994 to 2005, (1995, February 17). *Chronicle of Higher Education, 41*(23), p. A38.

Fail, H. (1949). *General and industrial management.* (Constance Starrs, Trans.). London: Pitman.

Falla, J. (1981). *NCAA: The voice of college sports—A diamond anniversary history 1906-1981.* Mission, KS: National Collegiate Athletic Association.

Fan cost index (1994, April). *Team Marketing Report,* p. 6.

Farhi, P. (1995, March 31). "ProServ president to head new firm: Fiancee Nancy Kerrigan to move with him to sports talent agency." *The Washington Post, 118,* F3.

Farmer, P., Mulrooney, A., & Ammon, R., Jr. (1996). *Sport facility planning and management.* Morgantown, WV: Fitness Information Technology, Inc.

Federal Base Ball Club of Baltimore, Inc. v. National League of Professional Base Ball Clubs, 259 U.S. 200 (1922).

Feltz, D.L. (1988). Self-confidence and sports performance. In K.B. Pandolf (Ed.), *Exercise and sport sciences reviews* (pp. 423-457). New York: MacMillan.

Fiedler, F.E., & Chemers, M. (1984). *Improving leadership effectiveness: The leader match concept* (2nd ed.). New York: John Wiley & Sons, Inc.

Fiedler, F.E., Chemers, M., & Maher, L.M. (1977). *The leader match concept.* Rev Ed. New York: Wiley.

Fiske, J. (1992). Cultural studies and the culture of everyday life. In L. Grossberg, C. Nelson, and P. Trechler, *Cultural studies.* New York: Routledge, Chapman, and Hall, Inc., 154-164.

Fitzgerald, M.P., Sagaria, M.A.D., & Nelson, B. (1994). Career patterns of athletic directors: Challenging the conventional wisdom. *Journal of Sport Management, 8,* 14-26.

Flint, W.C., & Eitzen, S. (1987). Professional sports team ownership and entrepreneurial capitalism. *Sociology of Sport Journal, 4,* 17-27.

Frank, R. (1984). Olympic myths and realities. *Arete: The Journal of Sport Literature, 1*(2), 155-161.

Franks, R. (1995-96). National directory of college athletics. Amarillo, TX: Ray Franks Publishing Ranch.

Freedman, W. (1987). *Professional sports and antitrust.* Quorum Books. NY.

Gantt, H.L. (1910). *Work, wages, and profits.* New York: Engineering Magazine.

Garfield, B. (1993, March). A's get major league hit from goodby campaign. *Advertising Age, 64,* 50.

Gerber, M.E. (1986). *The E myth.* New York: Harper Business.

Gerdes, R.S. (1996, January 17-23). CBS golf analyst booted. *Focus Point, 1*(3).

Gerson, R. (June/July, 1987). Starting up, keeping up. *Dance Exercise Today,* 47.

Gilbreth, F.B. (1917). *Applied motion study.* New York: Sturgis & Walton.

Gilbreth, L.M. (1914). *The psychology of management.* New York: Sturgis & Walton.

Glueck, W.F. (1980). *Management* (2nd edition). Hinsdale, IL: The Dryden Press.

Gordon, V. (1992). *Handbook of academic advising.* Westport, CT: Greenwood Press.

Gorman, J., & Calhoun, K. (1994). *The name of the game: The business of sports.* New York: John Wiley and Sons.

Gorman, J., & Calhoun, K. (1994). *The name of the game: The business of sports.* New York: Wiley.

Gray, D.P. (1996). Sport marketing: A strategic approach. In B.L. Parkhouse (Ed.), *The management of sport: Its foundation and application*, (pp. 249-289), St. Louis, MO: Mosby.

Gray, M., & Deacon, J. (1996, January 22). Russia's brawn drain: The NHL continues to lure the best of the east. *McLean's*, p. 54.

Greenberg, M.J. (1992). *Sports law practice.* Charlottesville VA: Michie.

Greendorfer, S. (1993). Gender role stereotypes and early childhood socialization. In G.L. Cohen (Ed.), *Women in sport: Issues and controversies* (pp. 3-14). Newbury Park, CA: Sage Publications.

Griffin, P. (1993). Homophobia in women's sports: The fear that divides us. In G.L. Cohen (Ed.), *Women in sport: Issues and controversies* (pp. 211-221). Newbury Park, CA: Sage.

Griffin, P., & Genasci, J. (1990). Addressing homophobia in physical education: Responsibilities for teachers and researchers. In M.A. Messner & D.F. Sabo (Eds.), *Sport, men and the gender order* (pp. 211-221). Champaign, IL: Human Kinetics.

Groves, D.L. (1990). Consulting and entrepreneurship. In J.B. Parks & B.R.K. Zanger (Eds.), *Sport & fitness management: Career strategies and professional content* (pp. 129-136). Champaign, IL: Human Kinetics.

Groves, D.L., & Zanger, B.R.K. (1995). A study of the holistic and affective elements that influence the cultural expression of sport. *Visions in Leisure and Business, 14*(1), 4-18.

Grub, P.D., & Moran, R.T. (Eds.). (1995). *Global business: Strategies for the year 2000.* Washington, DC: Beacham Publishing, Inc.

Grunig, J.E., & White, R. (1992). Communication, public relations and effective organizations. In J.E. Grunig (Ed.). *Excellence in public relations and communications management.* Hillsdale, NJ: Erlbaum.

Gulick, L., & Urwick, L. (Eds.). (1937). *Papers on the science of administration.* New York: Institute of Public Administration.

Gusser, J. (1993, October 12). Phillies fit well in Philly. *Toledo Blade, 19*, 22.

Guterson, D. (1994, September). Moneyball: On the relentless promotion of pro sports. *Harpers Magazine*, p. 38.

Guttman, A. (1994). *The Olympics: A history of the modern games.* Chicago: University of Illinois Press.

Guttmann, A. (1991). *Women's sports—A history.* New York: Columbia University Press.

Halbfinger, D.M. (1996, January 14). Agent entrepreneur: Solomon pursues payoff in blending sports and entertainment in multimedia projects. *Boston Globe*, pp. 45, 51.

Hall, C., & Merrill, D. (1996, April 24). Sporting Goods Manufacturers Association. *USA Today*, 1c.

Hall, C.M., & Sellwood, H.J. (1987). Cup gained, paradise lost? A case study of the 1987 America's Cup as a hallmark event. In LeHeron, R., Roche, M., & Shepherd, M. (Eds.), *Geography and society in a global context* (pp. 267-274). Palmerston North, NZ: Massey University, Dept. of Geography.

Hampton, D.R. (1981). *Contemporary management* (2nd ed.). New York: McGraw-Hill.

Harris, D. (1986). *The League: The rise and decline of the NFL.* New York: Bantam Books, pp. 13-14.

Harris, D.V. (1990). Avoiding self-sabotage. In J.B. Parks and B.R.K. Zanger (Eds.), *Sport and fitness management: Career strategies and professional content.* (pp. 165-173). Champaign, IL: Human Kinetics.

Harris, D.V., & Harris, B.L. (1984). *The athlete's guide to sport psychology: Mental skills for physical people.* Champaign, IL: Leisure Press.

Harris, J.S. (1994a). The future of health promotion. In M.P. O'Donnell & J.S. Harris (Eds.), *Health promotion in the workplace* (2nd ed., pp. 525-543). Albany, NY: Delmar Publishers, Inc.

Harris, J.S. (1994b). The health benefits of health promotion. In M.P.O Donnell. & J.S. Harris (Eds.), *Health promotion in the workplace* (2nd ed., pp. 3-40). Albany, NY: Delmar Publishers, Inc.

Harvey, D. (1989). *The Condition of Post-Modernity.* Oxford: Blackwell.

Hasbrook, C.A., Hart, B.A., Mathes, S.A., & True, S. (1990). Sex bias and the validity of believed differences between male and female interscholastic athletic coaches. *Research Quarterly for Exercise and Sport, 63*, 259-267.

Hasek, G. (1994). Inbound travel spending soars. *Hotel & Hotel Management, 209*(2), 1.

Hatfield, B.D., & Landers, D.M. (1983). Psychophysiology: A new direction for sport psychology. *Journal of Sport psychology, 5*, 243-259.

Hawkins, D.E. (1994). Ecotourism: Opportunities for developing countries. In W.G. Theobald (Ed.), *Global tourism: The next decade* (pp. 261-273). Oxford, London: Butterworth-Heinemann.

Hawkins, D.E., & Hudman, L.E. (1989). *Tourism in Contemporary Society: An Introductory Text.* Englewood Cliffs, NJ: Prentice-Hall.

Heil, J. (1993). *Psychology of sport injury.* Champaign, IL: Human Kinetics.

Hemphill, D. (1983). *The social responsibility of a professional sport franchise to a community.* Unpublished manuscript.

Henderson, A.M., & Parsons, T. (Trans.). (1947). *The theory of social and economic organization.* (Max Weber Chapters). Glencoe, IL: The Free Press.

Hendricks, T.E. (1990). New challenges for government managers. *The Bureaucrat, 19*(1), 17-20.

Hersey, P., & Blanchard, K.H. (1982). *Management of organizational behavior* (4th ed.). Englewood Cliffs, NJ: Prentice-Hall.

Herwig, C. (1994, January 25). Equality of salary, exception, not rule. *USA Today*, 8C.

Herzberg, F. (1966). *Work and the nature of man.* Cleveland, OH: World Publishing.

Hoffer, R. (1994, June 6). Foreign legions. *Sports Illustrated*, pp. 46-49.

Holmes, O.W. (1891). *Autocrat of the breakfast table: Every man his own Boswell* (4th. ed.). New York: The Riverside Press Cambridge, Houghton Mifflin Co.

Horine, L. (1990).The Johari Window: Solving sport management communication problems. *Journal of Physical Education, Recreation and Dance, 61*(6), 49-51.

Horovitz, B. (1996, October 18). A basketball league of their own: Women athletes leap through hoops to live their dreams. *USA Today*, p. 1B.

Howard, D.R., & Crompton, J.L. (1995). *Financing sport.* Morgantown, WV: Fitness Information Technology.

Hunsacker, P.L., & Cook, C.W. (1986). *Management organizational behavior.* Reading, MA: Addison-Wesley.

International Health, Racquet & Sportsclub Association. (1995). *The 1995 IHRSA Report on the State of the Health Club Industry.* Boston, MA: Author.

International Management Group. (1995). Corporate Report, Cleveland, OH.

Ivancevich, J.M., & Matteson, M.T. (1990). *Organizational behavior and management* (2nd ed.). Homewood, IL: BPI Irwin.

Jafari, J., & Ritchie, J.R. (1981). Toward a framework for tourism education: Problems and prospects. *Annals of Tourism Research, 8,* 13-34.

Johnson, A.T. (1993). Rethinking the sport-city relationship: In search of partnership. *Journal of Sport Management, 7,* 61-70.

Johnson, B.D., & Johnson, N.R. (1995). Stacking and "stoppers": A test of the outcome control hypothesis. *Sociology of Sport Journal, 12,* 105-112.

Johnson, D.P. (1994). General session: Editor's roundtable. In R.G. Porter (Chair), *Prospering from change: A consumer perspective.* Synopsis conducted at the 1994 Travel Industry National Conference and 9195 Travel Outlook Forum, Alexandria, VA.

Johnson, S.E. (1994). *When women played hardball.* Seattle: Seal Press.

Johnson, W.B., & Packer, A.E. (1987). *Workforce 2000: Work and workers for the 21st century.* Indianapolis, IN: Hudson Institute.

Jones, D. (1996, June 6). Critics tie sweatshop sneakers to 'Air' Jordan. *USA Today,* p. 1B.

Jones, J. (1994). *The student companion.* Redwood City, CA: The Benjamin/Cummings Publishing Co.

Jowdy, D.P., & Harris, D.V. (1990). Muscular responses during mental imagery as a function of motor skill level. *Journal of Sport and Exercise Psychology, 12,* 191-201.

Kane, M.J. (1990). Psychology of sport and exercise. In J.B. Parks & B.R.K. Zanger (Eds.), *Sport and fitness management* (pp. 197-211). Champaign, IL: Human Kinetics.

Kane, M.J. (1996). Media coverage of the post Title IX female athlete: A feminist analysis of sport, gender, and power. *Duke Journal of Gender Law & Policy, 3*(1), 95-127.

Kane, M.J., & Disch, L.J. (1993). Sexual violence and the reproduction of male power in the locker room: The "Lisa Olson incident." *Sociology of Sport Journal, 10,* 331-352.

Kane, M.J., & Greendorfer, S. (1994). The media's role in accommodating and resisting stereotyped images of women in sport. In P. Creedon (Ed.), *Women, media and sport: Challenging gender values* (pp. 28-44). Thousand Oaks, CA: Sage Publications.

Kane, M.J., & Parks, J.B. (1992). The social construction of gender difference and hierarchy in sport journalism—Few new twists on very old themes. *Women in Sport and Physical Activity Journal, 1,* 49-83.

Karlin, L. (1995). *The guide to careers in sports.* New York: E.M. Guild.

Katen, T.E. (1973). *Doing philosophy.* Englewood Cliffs, NJ: Prentice-Hall.

Katz, D. (1993). Triumph of the Swoosh. *Sports Illustrated,* August, 54-73.

Katz, D. (1994). *Just do it.* New York: Random House.

Katz, D., & Kahn, R.L. (1978). *The social psychology of organizations* (2nd ed.). New York: John Wiley & Sons, Inc.

Katz, R.L. (1974). Skills of an effective administrator. *Harvard Business Review, 52*(5), 90-101.

Kelley, D.R., Beitel, P.A., DeSensi, J.T., & Blanton, M.D. (1990). Career considerations. In B.L. Parkhouse (Ed.), *The management of sport: Its foundations and application* (pp. 12-26). St. Louis, MO: Mosby.

Kernaghan, S.G., & Giloth, B.E. (1988). *Tracking the impact of health promotion on organizations.* Chicago: American Hospital Publishing, Inc.

Kerr, S., Hill, K.D., & Broedling, L. (1986). The first line supervisor: Phasing out or here to stay. *Academy of Management Review, 11*(1), 103-114.

Kinder, T.M. (1993). *Organizational management administration for athletic programs* (3rd ed.). Dubuque, IA: Eddie Bowers.

King, P. (1996, August 4). Ms. Popularity: Victorious U.S. women's teams made friends and influenced people. *Sports Illustrated,* p. 34.

Klemm, A. (1994, August). The export game. *Team Licensing Business,* 18-25.

Knight Foundation Commission on Intercollegiate Athletics (1991, March). *Keeping faith with the student-athlete: A new model for intercollegiate athletics.* Charlotte, NC: Author.

Knowles, A.S. (1977). *The International Encyclopedia of Higher Education.* San Francisco: Jossey Bass.

Koehler, L.S. (1992). International sport and fitness management. *The Chronicle of Physical Education in Higher Education, 3*(2), 10.

Koehler, L.S., & Lupcho, P. (1990, June). *Sport management and the process of professionalization.* Paper presented at the Fifth Annual Conference for the North American Society for Sport Management, Louisville, KY.

Kofman, F., & Senge, P.M. (1993). Communities of commitment: The heart of learning organization. *Pre-Publication Draft Organizational Dynamics,* 9.

Koppett, L. (1994). *Sports illusion, sports reality: A reporter's view of sports, journalism, and society.* Urbana: University of Illinois Press.

Krane, V. (1995 September). *Anxiety and stress: Reflections of the past and visions for the future.* Dorothy Harris Young Scholar-Practitioner Lecture at the meeting of the Association for the Advancement of Applied Sport Psychology, New Orleans, Louisiana.

Krane, V. (1996, August). *A conceptual approach to understanding lesbians in sport.* Presentation at the meeting of the American Psychological Association, Toronto, Ontario.

Kremer, J.M.D., & Scully, D.M. (1994). *Psychology in sport.* Bristol, PA: Taylor & Francis.

Kretchmar, R.S. (1994). *Practical philosophy of sport.* Champaign, IL: Human Kinetics.

Kroll, J., & Moomaw, R. (1990). Career planning. In J.B. Parks, & B.R.K. Zanger (Eds.), *Sport & fitness management: Career strategies and professional content* (pp. 139-154). Champaign, IL: Human Kinetics.

Laczniak, G., & Murphy, P. (1985). *Marketing ethics.* Lexington, Massachusetts: D.C. Heath and Co.

Lamb, D.R. (1984). The sports medicine umbrella. *Sports Medicine Bulletin, 19,* 4, 8-9.

Landry, F. (1994). "Olympism = Paralympism." In R.D. Steadward, E.R. Nelson, & G.D. Wheeler (Eds.), *VISTA '93 -The Outlook* (pp. 488-499), Edmonton, AB: Rick Hansen Centre.

Lapchick, R., & Benedict, J. (1993, Summer). 1993 racial report card. *Center for the Study of Sport in Society Digest.* Boston, MA: Northeastern University, 1, 4-9.

Leith, L.M. (1983). The underlying processes of athletic administration. *The Physical Educator, 40*(4), 211-217.

Lenskyj, H. (1992). Unsafe at home base: Women's experiences of sexual harassment in university sport and physical education. *Women in Sport and Physical Activity Journal, 1,* 19-33.

Lessig, W.J., & Alsop, W.L. (1990). Intercollegiate athletics and professional sport. In J.B. Parks & B.R.K. Zanger (Eds.), *Sport & fitness management: Career strategies and professional content* (pp. 17-33). Champaign, IL: Human Kinetics.

Levin, G. (1993, April). Baseball's opening pitch: Winning over new fans. *Advertising Age, 64,* 1, 42.

Levine, P. (1985). *A.G. Spaulding and the rise of baseball: The promise of American sport.* New York: Oxford University Press.

Lewin K. (1951). *Field theory in social sciences.* New York: Harper & Row.

Lewin, G.W., & Allport, G.W. (Eds.). (1948). *Resolving social conflicts.* New York: Harper.

Lewis, J. (1992, June). Crowd control at concerts: Hazards of festival seating. *Trial,* pp. 71-72, 74-75.

Likert, R. (1961). *New patterns in management.* New York: McGraw-Hill.

Lindström, H. (1994). Integration in sports for persons with disabilities: An overview. In R.D. Steadward, E.R. Nelson, & G.D. Wheeler (Eds.), *VISTA '93-The Outlook* (pp. 333-344), Edmonton, AB: Rick Hansen Centre.

Lipsey, R.A. (Ed.). (1995). *Sports Market Place.* Princeton, NJ: Sportsguide.

Lombardo, J. (1994, January 28). David Falk. *Washington Business Journal, 12*(37), 18-20.

Lopiano, D. (1994). Foreword. In M.A. Messner & D.F. Sabo (1994). *Sex, violence, and power in sports* (p. 1), Freedom, CA: The Crossing Press.

Loy, J.W. (1968). The nature of sport: A definitional effort. *Quest, 10,* 1-15.

Lucas, J.A., & Smith, R.A. (1978). *Saga of American sport.* Philadelphia, PA: Lea & Febiger.

Luft, J. (1969). *Of human interaction.* Palo Alto, CA: National Press Books.

MacAloon, J.J. (1992, April). *International sport management: Intercultural relations theory.* Paper presented at the Sport Management Theory Conference, New Orleans.

Mahoney, T.A., Jerdee, T.H., & Carroll, S.G. (1965). The job(s) of management. *Industrial Relations, 4*(2), 97-110.

Mangus, B.C., & Ingersoll, C.D. (1990, Winter). Approaches to ethical decision making in athletic training. *Athletic Training, 25,* 340-343.

Martens, R. (1986). Science, knowledge, and sport and exercise psychology. *The Sport Psychologist, 1,* 29-55.

Maslow, A. (1965). *Eupsychian management.* Homewood, IL: Irwin-Dorsey.

Maslow, A. (1962). *Toward a psychology of being.* Princeton, NJ: D. Van Nostrand.

Mason, J.G., Higgins, C.R., & Wilkinson, O.J. (1981). Sports administration education 15 years later. *Athletic Purchasing and Facilities, 5*(1), 44-45.

Massey, M. (1979). *The people puzzle: Understanding yourself and others.* Reston, VA: Reston Publishing Co., Inc., A Prentice-Hall Company.

May, P. (1996, July 21). LA has star, no supporting cast. *The Boston Globe,* p. F8

McAuley, E. (1992). Understanding exercise behavior: A self-efficacy perspective. In G.C.Roberts (Ed.), *Motivation in Sport and Exercise* (pp. 107-128). Champaign, IL: Human Kinetics.

McCarville, R.E., & Copeland, R.P. (1994). Understanding sponsorship through exchange theory. *Journal of Sport Management, 8,* 102-114.

McClelland, D.C., Atkinson, J.W., Clark, R.A., & Lowell, E.L. (1976). *The achievement motive.* New York: Appleton-Century Crofts.

McCleneghan, J.S. (Summer, 1995). The sports information director—No attention, no respect, and a PR practitioner in trouble. *Public Relations Quarterly, 40*(2), 28-32.

McGregor D. (1966). *Leadership and motivation.* Cambridge, MA: The MIT Press.

McGregor, D. (1960). *The human side of enterprise.* New York: McGraw-Hill.

McGregor, M.C. (1994, Fall). Organizing your sport clubs program. *NIRSA Journal, 19*(1), 46, 48.

McLuhan, M. (1966). *Understanding media: The extensions of man.* New York: McGraw-Hill.

McPherson, B.D., Curtis, J.E., & Loy, J.W. (1989). *The social significance of sport: An introduction to the sociology of sport.* Champaign, IL: Human Kinetics.

Means, L.E. (1973). *Intramurals: Their organization and administration* (2nd ed.). Englewood Cliffs, NJ: Prentice-Hall.

Meier, K.V. (1989). The ignoble sports fans. *Journal of Sports and Social Issues, 13*(2), 111-119.

Melnick, M. (1992). Male athletes and sexual assault. *Journal of Physical Education, Recreation and Dance, 63*(5), 32-35.

Meltzer, M.F. (1967). *The information center: Management's hidden asset.* New York: American Management Association.

Mescon, T.S., & D.J. Tilson. (1987). Corporate philanthropy: A strategic approach to the bottom line. *California Management Review, 29*(2), 49-61.

Messner, M.A., & Sabo, D.F. (1994). *Sex, violence and power in sports: Rethinking masculinity.* Freedom, CA: The Crossing Press.

Metcalf, H.C., & Urwick, L. (Eds.). (1941). *Dynamic administration: The collected papers of Mary Parker Follett.* London: Pittman.

Michelozzi, B.N. (1992). *Coming alive from nine to five: The career search handbook* (4th ed.). Mountain View, CA: Mayfield.

Mill, J.S. (1969). *Utilitarianism.* In E.M. Albert, T.C. Denise, & S.P. Peterfreund (Eds.), *Great traditions in ethics: An introduction* (2nd ed.) (pp. 227-252). New York: D. Van Nostrand. (Original work published 1861).

Miller, L.K. (1993). Crowd control. *Journal of Physical Education, Recreation and Dance, 64*(2), 31-32, 64-65.

Mintzberg, H. (1973). *The nature of managerial work.* New York: Harper & Row.

Mintzberg, H. (1990). The manager's job: Folklore and fact. *Harvard Business Review, 90*(2), 163-176.

Montville, L. (1995, June 12). Ringer from down under. *Sports Illustrated, 82,* 76.

Moore, M.E., & Parkhouse, B.L. (1996, May). *An examination of diversity in sport management professional preparation programs for women, minorities, and individuals with disabilities.* Paper presented at the conference of the North American Society for Sport Management, Fredericton, New Brunswick, Canada.

Morrison, L.L. (1993). The AIAW: Governance by women for women. In G. Cohen (Ed.), *Women in sport: Issues and controversies* (pp. 59-78). Newbury Park: Sage.

Morrison, T., Conaway, W., & Borden, G. (1994). *Kiss, bow and shake hands: How to do business in sixty countries.* Holbrook, MA: Bob Adams.

Moss, A. (Ed.). (1995). *The sport summit sports business directory.* Bethesda, MD: E.J. Krause & Associates.

Moss, C.L., & Parks, J.B. (1991). Athletic training in an undergraduate sport management curriculum. *Athletic Training, 26,* 178, 180-183.

Mueller, P., & Reznik, J.W. (1979). *Intramural-recreational sports: Programming and administration* (5th ed.). New York: John Wiley & Sons.

Muench, H., & Amend, P. (1995, January). International: Japan. *CBI, 16*(1), pp. 20-23.

Mull, R.F., Bayless, K.G., & Ross, C.M. (1987). *Recreational sports programming: Sports for all* (2nd ed.). North Palm Beach, FL: The Athletic Institute.

Mullin, B.J. (1980). Sport management: The nature and utility of the concept. *Arena Review, 4*(3), 1-11.

Mullin, B.J., Hardy, S., & Sutton, W.A. (1993). *Sport marketing.* Champaign, IL: Human Kinetics Publishers.

Naisbitt, J. (1994). *Global paradox: The bigger the world economy, the more powerful its smallest players.* New York: William Morrow and Co.

NASPE. (1995). *Basic standards for the professional preparation in exercise science.* Reston, VA: Author.

NASPE-NASSM Joint Task Force. (1993). Standards for curriculum and voluntary accreditation of sport management education programs. *Journal of Sport Management, 7,* 159-170.

NATA Board of Certification. (1995). *Role delineation study* (3rd ed.). Philadelphia: F.A. Davis.

National Hockey League: Official guide and record book, 1995-1996 (1996). New York: Author.

National Intramural-Recreational Sports Association (1996, Spring). *NIRSA Newsletter.* Corvallis, OR: Author.

National Intramural-Recreational Sports Association. (1992). *Recreational sports: A curriculum guide.* Corvallis, OR: Author.

NCAA Committee on Athletics Certification. (1993). *1993-94 Division I Athletics Certification Handbook.* (Available from The National Collegiate Athletic Association, 6201 College Blvd., Overland Park, KS 66211-2422).

NCAA Education Services. (1996). *Senior woman administrator* [Brochure]. Overland Park, KS: Author.

Nelson, M.B. (1994). *The stronger women get, the more men love football: Sexism and the American culture of sports.* New York: Harcourt Brace.

*New York Times* (1993, April 15). "Do beer and Olympics mix?" Vol. 142, B12.

Newell, K.M. (1990). Kinesiology: The label for the study of physical activity in higher education. *Quest, 42,* 269-278.

Newman, M., & Dao, J. (1992, December 27). A year after nine deaths, the scars endure at City College. *The New York Times,* p. 14.

Nichols, M. (1993, August). International licensing: The next frontier. *Team Licensing Business,* pp. 20-26.

Nielsen, W.V. (1994, Winter). Ethics in coaching: It's time to do the right thing. *Olympic Coach, 4,* 2-5.

Nieman, D.C. (1995). *Fitness and sports medicine: A health-related approach.* Palo Alto, CA: Bull Publishing.

Nixon, H.L., & Frey, J.H. (1996). *A sociology of sport.* Belmont, CA: Wadsworth Publishing Company.

O'Brien, D.B, & Overby, J.O. (1997). *Legal aspects of sport entrepreneurship.* Morgantown, WV: Fitness Information Technology.

O'Donnell, M.P. (1992). *Design of workplace health promotion programs* (3rd ed.). Rochester Hills, MI: American Journal of Health Promotion.

O'Donnell, M.P., & Harris, J.S. (Eds.). (1994). *Health promotion in the workplace* (2nd ed.) Albany, NY: Delmar Publishers Inc.

Ogrean, D. (1995, November). From the executive director. *American Hockey Magazine.* Minneapolis: The Publishing Group, p. 44.

O'Keefe, M. (1985, May/June). Whatever happened to the crash of '80 '81 '82 '83 '84 '85? *Change,* pp. 37-41.

Opatz, J.P. (Ed.). (1987). *Health promotion evaluation: Measuring the organizational impact.* Stevens Point, WI: National Wellness Institute.

Oxendine, J.B. (1988). *American Indian sport heritage.* Champaign, IL: Human Kinetics.

Ozanian, M.K. (Feb. 14, 1995). Following the money: FW's first annual report on the economics of sports. *Financial World, 164,* pp. 26-27, 30-31.

Parascenzo, M. (1993, May 3). Prime time. *Business Week,* pp. 100-103.

Parkhouse, B.L. (1987). Sport management curricula: Current status and design implications for future development. *Journal of Sport Management, 1,* 93-115.

Parkinson, R.S., & Associates. (1982). *Managing health promotion in the workplace: Guidelines for implementation and evaluation.* Palo Alto, CA: Mayfield Publishing Company.

Parks, J.B. (1991). Employment status of alumni of an undergraduate sport management program. *Journal of Sport Management, 5,* 100-110.

Parks, J.B., & Bartley, M.E. (1996). Sport management scholarship: A professoriate in transition? *Journal of Sport Management, 10,* 119-130.

Parks, J.B., & Olafson, G.A. (1987). Sport management and a new journal. *Journal of Sport Management, 1*(1), 1-3.

Parks, J.B., & Parra, L.F. (1994). Job satisfaction of sport management alumnae/i. *Journal of Sport Management, 8,* 49-56.

Parks, J.B., Chopra, P.S., Quain, R.J., & Alguindigue, I.E. (1988). *ExSport 1*: An expert system for sport management career counseling. *Journal of Research on Computing in Education, 21*(2), 196-209.

Parks, J.B., Russell, R.L., & Wood, P.H. (1991). [Demographic characteristics of 608 NCAA Division I-A athletics administrators who had been in their current positions for an average of 7.7 years]. Unpublished raw data.

Parks, J.B., Russell, R.L., & Wood, P.H. (1993). Marital and other primary dyadic relationships of intercollegiate athletics administrators. *Journal of Sport Management, 7,* 151-158.

Parks, J.B., Russell, R.L., Wood, P.H., Roberton, M.A., & Shewokis, P. (1995). The paradox of the contented working woman in athletics administration. *Research Quarterly for Exercise and Sport, 66,* 73-79.

Parks, J.B., & Zanger, B.R.K. (1990). *Sport & fitness management: Career strategies and professional content.* Champaign, IL: Human Kinetics.

Patterson, V., & Allen, C. (1996). Occupational outlook overview: Where will the jobs be in 2005? *Journal of Career Planning and Employment, 56*(3) 32-35, 61-64.

Patton, R.W., Corry, J.M., Gettman, L.R., & Graf, J.S. (1986). *Implementing health/fitness programs.* Champaign, IL: Human Kinetics.

Pavett, C.M., & Lau, A.W. (1983). Hierarchical level and functional specialty. *Academy of Management Journal, 26*(1), 170-171.

Pearce, P.L. (1994). Tourist-resident impacts: Examples, explanations, and emerging solutions. In W.F. Theobald (Ed.), *Global tourism: The next decade,* 103-123. London: Butterworth-Heinemann.

Peters, T. (1987). *Thriving on chaos: Handbook for a management revolution.* New York: Harper & Row.

Peters, T., & Waterman, R. (1982). *In search of excellence.* New York: Harper & Row.

Peterson, M.W. (Ed.). (1986). *ASHE reader on organization and governance in higher education* (3rd ed.). Lexington, MA: Ginn Press.

Petit, T.A. (1975). *Fundamentals of management coordination: Supervisors, middle managers and executives.* New York: John Wiley and Sons.

Phillips, J. (1991). The integration of central positions in baseball: The black shortstop. *Sociology of Sport Journal, 8,* 161-167.

Pike, L.L., & Fay, T.G. (1994). Cross-cultural studies: Implications on professional preparation and management training in global sport (pp. 53-72). In R. Wilcox (Ed.), *Sport in the Global Village.* Morgantown, WV: Fitness Information Technology.

Pinchot III, Gifford. (1985). *Intrapreneuring.* New York: Harper & Row.

Pitts, B.G., Fielding, L.W., & Miller, L.K. (1994). Industry segmentation theory and the sport industry: Developing a sport industry segmentation model. *Sport Marketing Quarterly, 3*(1), 15-24.

Pitts, B.G., & Stotlar, D.K. (1996). *Fundamentals of sport marketing.* Morgantown, WV: Fitness Information Technology.

Plog, S.C. (1994). Leisure travel: An extraordinary industry faces super ordinary problems. In W.F. Theobald (Ed.), *Global tourism: The next decade* (pp. 40-54). London: Butterworth-Heinemann.

Powers, J. (1992, September 20). Vodka economics. *Boston Globe Magazine,* pp. 8-9.

Powers, J. (1993, February 21). New world borders. *Boston Globe Magazine,* pp. 16-22, 29-31.

Powers, S.K., & Howley, E.T. (1994). *Physiology of exercise: Theory and application to fitness and performance.* Madison, WI: Brown & Benchmark.

Pronger, B. (1990). Gay jocks: A phenomenology of gay men in athletics. In M.A. Messner & D.F. Sabo (Eds.), *Sport, men & the gender order* (pp. 141-152). Champaign, IL: Human Kinetics.

Quarterman, J. (1992). Characteristics of athletic directors of historically black colleges and universities. *Journal of Sport Management, 6,* 52-63.

Quarterman, J. (1994). Managerial role profiles of intercollegiate athletic conference commissioners. *Journal of Sport Management, 8,* 129-139.

Quirk, J., & Fort, R.D. (1992). *Paydirt: The business of professional team sports.* Princeton, NJ: Princeton University Press.

Rader, B.G. (1983). *American sports: From the age of folk games to the age of televised sports.* Englewood Cliffs, NJ: Prentice Hall.

Rader, B.G. (1984). *In its own image: How television has transformed sports.* New York: Free Press.

Rainey, J., & Lindsay, G. (1994). 101 questions for community health promotion program planning. *Journal of Health Education, 25*(5):309-312.

Randall, E.D. (1994, January 3). Pop culture lights fire under top performers. *USA Today,* 3B.

*Random House unabridged dictionary.* (2nd. ed.). (1993). New York: Random House.

Raths, L.E., Harmin, M., & Simon, S. (1966). Values and teaching: working with values in the classroom. Columbus, OH: C.E. Merrill Books.

Rawls, J. (1971). *A theory of justice.* Cambridge, MA: Harvard University Press.

Redding, W.C., & Sanborn, G.A. (1964). *Business and industrial communication: A source book.* New York: Harper and Row.

Rejeski, W.J., & Brawley, L.R. (1988). Defining the boundaries of sport psychology. *The Sport Psychologist, 2,* 231-242.

Revzin, P. (1995, June 19). "IMG's star-studded, money-making machine rolls on: McCormack offers top-quality representation, but the price is high." *The Wall Street Journal, 13*(95), 12.

Rintala, J. (1995). Sport and technology: Human questions in a world of machines. *Journal of Sport and Social Issues, 19,* 62-75.

Robbins, S.P. (1976). *The administrative process: Integrating theory and practice.* Englewood Cliffs, NJ: Prentice-Hall.

Robbins, S.P. (1988). *Management: Concepts and applications.* Englewood Cliffs, NJ: Prentice-Hall.

Robbins, S.P. (1991). *Management* (3rd ed.). Englewood Cliffs, NJ: Prentice Hall.

Roberts, R. (1995, Spring). *The salary cap in professional sports. The sports lawyer,* p. 1.

Roberts, R., & Olson, J. (1995). *Winning is the only thing: Sports in America since 1945.* Baltimore: Johns Hopkins University Press.

Robinowitz, J., & Youman, R. (Eds.). (1990, August 11). Special report: TV, sports and money. *TV Guide 38*(32).

Roethlisberger, F.J. (1939). *Management and the worker.* Cambridge, MA: Harvard University Press.

Rosner, D. (1989, January 2). The world plays catch-up: Sport in the 90s. *Sports Inc., 2,* 6-9.

Ross, W.D. (1930). *The right and the good.* Oxford: Clarendon Press.

Rowe, A.J., Mason, R.O., & Dickel, K.E. (1986). *Strategic management: A methodological approach.* New York: Addison Wesley.

Ryan, A.J. (1989). Sports medicine in the world today. In A.J. Ryan and F.L. Allman, Jr. (Eds.), *Sports Medicine.* (pp. 3-21). San Diego, CA: Academic Press.

Sara Lee Corporate Annual Report, 1995, p. 20.

Sauer, M.F. (1993, Summer). Going private. *Panstadia International*, 23.

Schaaf, P. (1995). *Sports marketing: It's not just a game anymore*. Amherst, NY: Prometheus Books.

Schoenfeld, B. (1995, April 17). Star search? *The Sporting News*, pp. 50-52.

Schor, J. (1991). *The overworked American*. New York: Basic.

Schramm, W., & Porter, W. (1982). *Men, women, messages, and media: Understanding human communication* (2nd ed.). New York: Harper & Row.

Schreiber, Alfred L. (1994). *Lifestyle & event marketing*. NY: McGraw Hill.

Sharp, L.A. (1990). *Sport law*. National Organization on Legal Problems of Education (Whole No. 40).

Shaw, G., & Williams, A.M. (1994). *Critical issues in tourism: A geographical perspective*. Cambridge: Blackwell.

Siedentop, D. (1990). *Introduction to physical education, fitness and sport*. Mountain View, CA: Mayfield.

Simson, V., & Jennings, A. (1992). *Dishonored Games: Corruption, money & greed at the Olympics*. New York: SPI Books.

Skinner, S.J., & Ivancevich, J.M. (1992). *Business*. Homewood, IL: Irwin.

Smith, R.A. (1988). *Sports and freedom—The rise of big-time college athletics*. New York: Oxford University Press.

Smith, S.L. (1989). *Tourism analysis: A handbook*. New York: John Wiley & Sons.

Smothers, R. (1992, July 27). Barcelona Games start, and Atlanta is starting. *The New York Times*, p. A13.

Snyder, E. (1990). Sociology of sport. In J.B. Parks & B.R.K. Zanger (Eds.), *Sport and fitness management* (pp. 213-222). Champaign, IL: Human Kinetics.

Snyder, E.E., & Spreitzer, E.A. (1989). *Social aspects of sport*. Englewood Cliffs, NJ: Prentice-Hall.

Spears, B., & Swanson, R. (1995). *History of sport and physical education in the United States (4th ed.)*. Dubuque, IA: Wm C. Brown Publishers.

*Sport Magazine*. (1995). A new era in the NFL: Expansion '95. Volume 86, No. 9, p. 61.

Sport Management Art and Science Society. (1982, Winter). *SMARTS Membership Newsletter, 2*(1).

*Standard Rate and Data Service*. (1996). Des Plaines, IL: B & B Service Corporation.

Stangl, J.M., & Kane, M.J. (1991). Structural variables that offer explanatory power for the underrepresentation of women coaches since Title IX: The case of homologous reproduction. *Sociology of Sport Journal, 8,* 47-60.

Staudohar, P.D. (1989). *The sports industry and collective bargaining*. Cornell, NY: ILR Press.

Staudohar, P.D., & Mangan, J.A. (1991). *The business of professional sports*. Urbana, IL: University of Illinois Press.

Steiner, A. (1991, April 9). Park plan targets girls' self image. *The Minnesota Women's Press, 1,* 6-7.

Steiner, G.A. (1972, Winter). Social policies for business. *California Management Review,* 17-24.

Steinhardt, M.A., & Carrier, K.M. (1989). Early and continued participation in a work-site health and fitness program. *Research Quarterly for Exercise and Sport, 60*(2):117-126.

Stotlar, D. (1990). Facility management. In J.B. Parks & B.R.K. Zanger (Eds.), *Sport and fitness management: Career strategies and professional content* (pp. 35-43). Champaign, IL: Human Kinetics.

Stotlar, D.K. (1993). *Successful sport marketing*. Brown & Benchmark, Dubuque, IA.

Straub, W.F., & Williams, J.M. (1984). Cognitive sport psychology: Historical, contemporary, and future perspectives. In W.F. Straub & J.M. Williams (Eds.), *Cognitive sport psychology* (pp. 3-10). Lansing, New York: Sport Science Associates.

Straub, W.F., & Williams, J.M. (1993). Sport psychology: Past, present, future. In J.M. Williams (Ed.), *Applied sport psychology: Personal growth to peak performance* (pp. 1-10). Mountain View, CA: Mayfield Publishing.

Sukiennik, D., Raufman, L., & Bendat, W. (1992). *The career fitness program: Exercising your options* (3rd ed.). Scottsdale, AZ: Gorsuch Scarisbrick.

Sutton, W.A. (1989). The role of internships in sport management curricula: A model for development. *Journal of Physical Education, Recreation and Dance, 60*(7), 20-24.

Tailor, F.W. (1947). *Scientific management: The principles of scientific management*. New York: Harper & Bros.

Tannenbaum, R., & Schmidt, W. (1958). How to choose a leadership pattern. *Harvard Business Review, 36* (2), 95-101.

Terroux, G. (1972). *Face-off of the century: The new era Canada, USSR*. Montreal: Collier-Macmillan.

Thoma, J. (1991, June). *International sport management education*. Paper presented at the Sixth Annual Conference for the North American Society for Sport Management, Ottawa, Ontario.

Thoma, J.E., & Chalip, L. (1996). *Sport governance in the global community*. Morgantown, WV: Fitness Information Technology.

Thurston, B. (1995, June 14). Night shift at the high school: Some students attend regular class after dark. *USA Today*, p. 6D.

Tillman, K.G., Voltmer, E.F., Esslinger, A.A., & McCue, B.F. (1996). *The administration of physical education, sport, and leisure programs* (Rev. ed.). Boston: Allyn and Bacon.

Title IX of the Education Amendments of 1972, Publ. L. No. 92-328, 86 stat. 235, codified at 20 U.S.C. 1681-1688 (1973).

Tuller, L.W. (1991). *Going global*. Homewood, IL: Business One Irwin.

TV sports: The $3.5 billion addiction (1996, May 13). *Broadcasting and Cable*, pp. 34-40.

U.S. Bureau of Labor Statistics. (1994-95). *Occupational Outlook Handbook*. Washington, DC: Author.

U.S. Department of Health, Education and Welfare. (1979). *Healthy people: The Surgeon General's report on health promotion and disease prevention*. Washington, DC: U.S. Government Printing Office.

Van Dalen, D.B., & Bennett, B.L. (1971). *A world history of physical education (2nd. ed.)*. Englewood Cliffs, NJ: Prentice Hall, Inc.

van der Smissen, B. (1987). Sport management: Its potential and some developmental concerns. In J.D. Massengale (Ed.), *Trends toward the future in physical education* (pp. 95-120). Champaign, IL: Human Kinetics.

van der Smissen, B. (1990a). Future directions. In B.L. Parkhouse (Ed.), *The management of sport: Its foundation and application* (pp. 381-404). St. Louis, MO: Mosby.

van der Smissen, B. (1990b). *Legal liability and risk management for public and private entities.* Cincinnati: Anderson Publishing Co.

VanderZwaag, H.J. (1988). *Policy development in sport management.* Indianapolis, IN: Benchmark Press.

Vealey, R.S., & Walter, S.M. (1993). Imagery training for performance enhancement and personal development. In J.M. Williams (Ed.), *Applied sport psychology: Personal growth to peak performance* (pp. 200-224). Mountain View, CA: Mayfield Publishing.

Visani, D.H. (1995). Frontline design. *Athletic Business, 19*(12), 67-69, 72.

Voltmer, E.F., & Esslinger, A.A. (1949). *The organization and administration of physical education* (3rd ed.). New York: Appleton-Century-Crofts.

Vroom, V. (1964). *Work and motivation.* New York: John Wiley & Sons.

Vroom, V. (1973, Spring). A new look in managerial decision-making. *Organizational Dynamics,* Spring, 66-80.

Vroom, V.H., & Yetton, P.N. (1973). *Leadership and decision-making.* Pittsburgh: University of Pittsburgh Press.

Wann, D.L., & Branscombe, N.L. (1993). Sports fans: Measuring degree of identification with their team. *International Journal of Sport Psychology, 24*(1), 1-17.

Washburn, J.R. (1984). What does academe need from business/ agencies? Supervision: A participatory activity. In B.K. Zanger & J.B. Parks (Eds.), *Sport management curricula: The business and education nexus* (pp. 79-83). Bowling Green, OH: Bowling Green State University.

*Webster's Dictionary.* (1987). Larchmont, NY: Book Essentials Publications.

Weiler, P.C., & Roberts, G.R. (1993). *Sports and the law: Cases, materials, and problems.* St. Paul, MN: West Publishing, pp. 699-705.

Weinberg, R.S., & Gould, D. (1995). *Foundations of sport and exercise psychology.* Champaign, IL: Human Kinetics.

Weisman, L. (1993, November 29). Tagliabue likes to see big picture. *USA Today,* 1C-2C.

Wells, G. (1993, May 7). "Ex-player raising roundball ruckus: Dan Cramer, president of Triple Crown Sports, Inc." *Denver Business Journal, 44*(34), 1-2.

Wernick, A. (1991). *Promotional culture.* Newbury Park, CA: Sage.

White, C.W., Kangas, J.E., and Kennedy, W.A. (1994). *Ethics: Yours, mine, or ours?* Paper presented at the annual meeting of the Midwest Business Administration Association, Chicago, IL.

White, G.E. (1996). *Creating the national pastime: Baseball transforms itself.* Princeton, NJ: Princeton University Press.

White, J. (1993). Minority patients: Clinical strategies to promote exercise. *The Physician and Sportsmedicine, 21*(5):136-144.

White, T.I. (1988). *Right and wrong: A brief guide to understanding ethics.* Englewood Cliffs, NJ: Prentice-Hall.

Whitson, D., & Macintosh, D. (1993). Becoming a world-class city: Hallmark events and sport franchises in the growth stages of western Canadian cities. *Sociology of Sport Journal, 10,* 221-240.

Widmeyer, W.N., Brawley, L.R., & Carron, A.V. (1992). In T. Horn (Ed.), *Advances in sport psychology* (pp. 161-180). Champaign, IL: Human Kinetics.

Wilcox, R.C. (Ed.). (1994). *Sport in the global village.* Morgantown, WV: Fitness Information Technology.

Willis, J.D., & Campbell, L.F. (1992). *Exercise psychology.* Champaign, IL: Human Kinetics.

Wilson Sporting Goods and Women's Sport Foundation. (1988, June). "The Wilson Report: Moms, Dads, Daughters and Sports."

Wilson, J. (1994). *Sport, society, and the state: Playing by the rules.* Detroit: Wayne State University Press.

Wilson, P.K. (1988). Cardiac rehabilitation: Then and now. *The Physician and Sportsmedicine, 16,* 75-80.

Wong, G.M. (1988). *Essentials of amateur sports law.* Dover, MA: Auburn House.

Wong, G.M., & Barr, C.A. (1993). Equal payback. *Athletic Business, 17*(9), 13-14.

Wong, G.M., & Barr, C.A. (1994). Equally divided. *Athletic Business, 18*(9), 12.

Zanger, B.K. (1984). Sport management curriculum model. In B.K. Zanger & J.B. Parks (Eds.), *Sport management curricula: The business and education nexus* (pp. 97-109). Bowling Green, OH: Bowling Green State University, School of Health, Physical Education, and Recreation.

Zanger, B.R.K. (1981). *Style in athletics: The triad of techniques, strategy and style with comparative patterns in education and business.* Paper presented at the annual meeting of the American Society of Cybernetics, George Washington University, Washington, D.C.

Zanger, B.R.K., & Groves, D.L. (1994a). Industrialization of sport. *Visions in Leisure and Business, 13*(3), 46-52.

Zanger, B.R.K., & Groves, D.L. (1994b). A framework for the analysis of theories of sport and leisure management. *Social Behavior and Personality, 22*(1), 57-68.

Zeigler, E.F. (1989). Proposed creed and code of professional ethics for the North American Society for Sport Management. *Journal of Sport Management, 3,* 2-4.

Ziffer, K.A. (1989). *Ecotourism the uneasy alliance.* Washington: Conservation International and Ernst & Young.

Zimbalist, A. (1992). *Baseball and billions.* New York: Basic Books.

Zuckoff, M. (1994, July 10). Taking a profit, and inflicting a cost. *Boston Sunday Globe,* pp. 1, 18.

# ■ Index

# ■ About the Editors

Jerome Quarterman, Beverly R.K. Zanger, and Janet B. Parks

**Janet B. Parks**, DA, is a professor, graduate studies coordinator, and former sport management division chair for the school of human movement, sport, and leisure studies at Bowling Green State University (BGSU) in Ohio. She was a founding executive council member of the North American Society for Sport Management (NASSM) and a member of the National Association for Sport and Physical Education (NASPE) Task Force on Sport Management Curriculum Accreditation.

Dr. Parks was an Honorary Fellow of the Women's Studies Research Center at the University of Wisconsin-Madison and has received NASSM's Earle F. Zeigler Award. Her published works include textbooks, book chapters, journal articles, and research reports. The editor-in-chief of the Sport Management Library and one of the original co-editors of the *Journal of Sport Management,* Dr. Parks makes frequent presentations to professional societies and serves as a consultant to several university sport management programs.

Dr. Parks received a doctor of arts degree from Middle Tennessee State University in 1977. A member of NASSM, the North American Society for the Sociology of Sport, and the American Alliance for Health, Physical Education, Recreation and Dance (AAHPERD), she lives in Bowling Green, where she enjoys biking and working out.

**Beverly R.K. Zanger**, MEd, a retired assistant professor emerita from BGSU's school of health, physical education, and recreation, helped initiate and design BGSU's sport management program. She served as conference chair for the National Sport Management Curriculum Symposium at BGSU in 1983, and she presented at the First International Conference on Sport and Recreation Management in Johannesburg, South Africa.

Beverly Zanger has developed courses in designing and directing fitness and sports programs, as well as professional resources in sports and activities. She was a founding NASSM executive council member, and she has over 40 years' teaching and 25 years' coaching experience. She now lives in Waikoloa on the Big Island of Hawaii. Her diverse interests include swimming, dancing, and fencing.

**Jerome Quarterman**, PhD, is an associate professor of sport management at BGSU, where he teaches undergraduate and graduate classes in sport administration. His research interests include leadership and managerial behaviors, skills, and roles of first-line managers in various segments of the sport industry. He has published articles in journals ranging from the *Journal of Sport Management* to the *International Journal of Sport Psychology* and *The Coaching Clinic.*

Prior to his service at BGSU, he was an assistant football coach, women's basketball coach, and track coach at the collegiate level. He also served as an academic chair of physical education and as an intercollegiate athletics director.

Dr. Quarterman received a PhD from The Ohio State University in 1978. He lives in Maumee, Ohio. His leisure activities include fast-pace walking, tennis, basketball ("horse"), and softball.

# ■ About the Contributors

**Robertha Abney**, PhD, is an Associate Professor and Associate Athletic Director at Slippery Rock University. She is an authority in the areas of women and minorities in leadership roles in sport. Dr. Abney has served as President of the National Association for Girls and Women in Sport (NAGWS) and currently serves on the National Collegiate Athletic Association (NCAA) Division II Nominating Committee. Internationally, she has represented the International Council for Health, Physical Education, Recreation, Dance, and Sport in Beijing, China. Dr. Abney continues to publish and be very active professionally and holds numerous professional memberships.

**Rob Ammon, Jr.**, EdD, is an Associate Professor at Slippery Rock University, where he is the coordinator of the undergraduate Sport Management program and Graduate Coordinator for the Physical Education Department. Dr. Ammon teaches undergraduate and graduate courses in sport law, facility and event management, and management of sport. His areas of research include legal liability for teachers, coaches, and athletic trainers; risk management in sport and athletics; and management and special events marketing. Dr. Ammon has written a number of articles and book chapters and is a co-author of *Sport Facility Planning and Management.*

**F. Wayne Blann** earned an EdD degree from Boston University and is a Professor of Sport Sciences and Coordinator of Sport Management at Ithaca College. Dr. Blann pioneered research on American collegiate and professional athletes' and coaches' career transitions. He has served as consultant to the NBA, the NFL, the NHL Players' Association, and Major League Baseball's Players' Association. Since 1996, the Professional Athletes Career Transition Program (PACTP) developed by Dr. Blann has served as the model for athlete career education programs. He has given a number of presentations at national and international conferences and has published articles in sport management, applied sport psychology, sport sociology, and applied research in coaching and athletics journals and newsletters. As a former collegiate athlete, coach, and athletics director, Dr. Blann is an honorary member of the Johnson State College (Vermont) Sports Hall of Fame.

**Kathy D. Browder**, PhD, is an Assistant Professor and Director of the Biomechanics Laboratory in the Department of Health and Kinesiology at Georgia Southern University. She received a PhD in Biomechanics from Texas Women's University and an M.S. in Physical Education from The University of Tennessee at Knoxville. Dr. Browder's research focuses on the interrelated contributions of mechanics, psychology, and physiology to energy production and utilization in gait. She has published her work in numerous professional journals. Her professional affiliations include the International Society of Biomechanics, the American Society of Biomechanics, the American College of Sports Medicine,

and the American Alliance of Health, Physical Education, Recreation and Dance.

**Susan C. Brown** received a PhD in sport management from The Ohio State University in 1988. She is an Associate Professor and program coordinator for sport management at Western Carolina University, where she has been a member of the faculty since 1988. She is editor of Managing Campus Recreation  Facilities, a 1998 publication of the National Intramural-Recreational Sports Association. Dr. Brown has over 15 publications in campus recreation and legal issues in sports and over 20 presentations at state, regional, and national conferences.

**Lynn A. Darby**, PhD, is an Assistant Professor in the School of Human Movement, Leisure, and Sport Studies at Bowling Green State University. She received her PhD in Exercise Physiology from The Ohio State University and completed a two-year post-doctoral research fellowship in the Physiology Depart-  ment of the School of Medicine at St. Louis University. Her research focus is on the study of physiological factors that affect the energy cost and measurement of physical activities such as running, walking, and aerobic dance. In addition, Dr. Darby's work focuses on making scientific information applicable and usable for a variety of practitioners. Her work has been published in a number of professional journals. Dr. Darby's professional affiliations include the American College of Sports Medicine, the American Alliance of Health, Physical Education, Recreation, and Dance, and Sigma Xi.

**Joy T. DeSensi** is a Professor and Unit Leader of Cultural Studies in Education at The University of Tennessee at Knoxville. She received an EdD from The University of North Carolina at Greensboro. Her primary research interests are the sociocultural foundations of sport, including multiculturalism, gender, race, and ethnicity in sport, and ethics, and leadership in sport management.

In addition to being a member of the Founding Executive Council of NASSM, Dr. DeSensi has served as editor of the Journal of Sport Management and president of the Philosophic Society for the Study of Sport. She has made numerous national and international presentations and is the author and co-author of a number of book chapters and articles. Dr. DeSensi is co-author of *Ethics in Sport Management,* which received the Most Outstanding Book Published Award in 1996 from the European Association for Sport Management.

**Ted Fay**, PhD, is an Assistant Professor of Business and Director of the Sport Management Program at Daniel Webster College in Nashua, New Hampshire. He taught courses in international sport management and event management during his doctoral studies at The University of Massachusetts-Amherst.  His research interests include international sport management, the Paralympic and Olympic movements, and comparative policy studies examining equity in management with respect to race, gender, and disability. Dr. Fay has worked in administrative positions with a variety of national sport governing bodies and remains actively involved in the International Paralympic Movement. He was a member of the 1988 Winter Olympic Team as a cross-country ski coach.

**James M. Gladden** is an Assistant Professor of Sport Management at The University of Massachusetts-Amherst, where he received a PhD in 1997. Dr. Gladden's research interests are in sport marketing, event management, and sport management. He has published research examining the develop-

ment of brand equity for professional collegiate sport teams. Dr. Gladden has served as a Project Manager for DelWilber & Associates, where he conducted market research and wrote strategic marketing plans for a variety of sport and special event clients, including the Los Angeles Dodgers, Iowa State University, Anheuser-Busch, and the Ladies Professional Golf Association (LPGA).

**David Groves**, EdD, is a Professor in the School of Human Movement, Sport, and Leisure Studies at Bowling Green State University. His primary expertise is in environmental relationships in leisure and sport systems. Dr. Groves has published more than 250 refereed articles in respected leisure parent  science journals. He also has over 25 years of consulting and entrepreneurial experience.

**Steve Horowitz**, PhD, has more than 25 years experience in the field of health and fitness. He is an Assistant Professor of Health Promotion in the Department of Family and Consumer Sciences at Bowling Green State University and faculty advisor to the student chapter of the Association for Worksite Health  Promotion. Dr. Horowitz was formerly the Manager of Corporate Wellness at Owens-Corning, where he designed and implemented a multisite award-winning wellness program. He received a PhD in Exercise Science, with a specialization in Health Promotion, from The University of Michigan. Dr. Horowitz has published several articles on worksite wellness intervention, serves as a private consultant to industry, and is a Fellow in the Association for Worksite Health Promotion.

**Mary Jo Kane**, PhD, is an Associate Professor in the College of Education and Human Development and the Director of the Tucker Center for Research on Girls and Women in Sport at The University of Minnesota. In 1996, Dr. Kane was awarded The Dorothy Tucker Distinguished Chair for Women in Sport and Exercise Science, the first

 Distinguished Professorship related to women in sport and physical activity. Dr. Kane is an internationally recognized scholar on issues related to sport and gender. She is particularly interested in the media's treatment of female athletes, as well as the decline of women in leadership positions in women's athletics.

**Linda S. Koehler**, PhD, is an Associate Professor and the Director of the sport management program at The University of the Pacific in Stockton, California. Her professional contributions include service as past president of the North American Society for Sport Management, former member of the  editorial board for the Journal of Sport Management, and current member of the NASPE/NASSM Sport Management Program Review Council. Dr. Koehler's particular areas of interest are curriculum development, international sport management, and gender issues in management.

**Vikki Krane**, PhD, is an Associate Professor with the School of Human Movement, Sport, and Leisure Studies at Bowling Green State University. She completed her PhD in Exercise and Sport Science at The University of North Carolina at Greensboro. Dr. Krane's main research interests con-  cern the relationship between competitive anxiety and athletic performance and feminist and diversity issues in sport. Dr. Krane has numerous publications in sport psychology journals, and she is active as a sport psychology consultant with elite youth sport, high school, and college athletes.

**JoAnn Kroll** is Director of Career Services at Bowling Green State University. She received an MEd in Higher Education Administration from Kent State University. In 1997, the National Association of Colleges and employers honored her department with its Award of Excellence for Educational Program-

ming. She was also the first recipient of the College Placement Council Award for Excellence for Educational Programming in Career Planning and Placement in 1987. She has also done consulting work in Russian to help establish the first Career Service Center and a national network of Career Services professionals. She has authored several book chapters and is a frequent speaker at professional conferences.

**Julie R. Lengfelder**, PhD, is an Associate Professor in the School of Human Movement, Sport, and Leisure Studies at Bowling Green State University. Her research focus is on tourism curriculum planning and design. Dr. Lengfelder teaches in the recreation and tour-

ism program, with an emphasis on management in the tourism industry. Both her professional and personal interests revolve around international travel and global issues related to tourism education.

**Ming Li**, EdD, received a PhD in Sport Management from The University of Kansas and is an Assistant Professor in the Department of Recreation and Sport Management at Georgia Southern University. He is coordinator of the undergraduate Sport Management program and teaches courses in

Sport Management at both undergraduate and graduate levels. Dr. Li's major interests are the financial and economic aspects of sport and comparative sport management. He has published more than 18 articles in refereed journals and several book chapters.

**Angela Lumpkin** is Dean of the College of Education at The State University of West Georgia. She holds a PhD from The Ohio State University. Dr. Lumpkin is the author of seven books including *Physical Education and Sport: A Contemporary Introduction* and *Sport Ethics: Applications for Fair Play.*

She has published articles in professional journals and delivered numerous presentations about the history of sport. Dr. Lumpkin has received honor awards from the North Carolina Alliance for Health, Physical Education, Recreation and Dance, the College and University Administrators Council, and the American Association for Active Lifestyles and Fitness. She has also won the Mabel Lee Award from the American Alliance for Health, Physical Education, Recreation and Dance.

**Mark McDonald** is an Assistant Professor of Sport Management at The University of Massachusetts-Amherst, where he received a PhD in 1996. Dr. McDonald has published articles numerous professional journals and has given more than 25 presentations in the United States and abroad. Dr. McDonald

has consulted with numerous sport organizations including the NBA, the NHL, the Orlando Magic, the Cleveland Cavaliers, and Hoop-It-Up. He worked with the International Health, Racquet, and Sportsclub Association to produce an industry report titled "Profiles of Success."

**Mary Kennedy Minter**, EdD, has been a college faculty member for over 20 years, having taught organizational behavior, communications, and management. She received a PhD in higher education administration from The University of Michigan. Dr. Minter has taught at several post-